EXPLORE YOUR WORLD
Discovery
CHANNEL

prehensively revised and updated by **Robin Shepherd** and **Zuzana Karabinosova**, under the direction of managing editor **Clare Griffiths**.

Shepherd worked as a journalist for Reuters in both the Czech and Slovak Republics for much of the 1990s and is author of *Czechoslovakia: The Velvet Revolution and Beyond*. For this edition, he wrote new chapters on food and drink and Czech cinema.

Karabinosova was born in South Moravia to a Czech mother and Slovak father. She moved from Bratislava, where she worked on a daily newspaper, to London in 2000 to study English.

This new edition of the book builds on the work of editor **Alfred**

Horn, who also wrote the chapters on the Prague and the spa towns of Western Bohemia, and **Jan Jelínek**, who acted as adviser to the project. **Boris Docekal** wrote the revealing article on rural life while **Josef Tucek**'s chapter highlights the tense relationship between ecology and economy in the two countries. **Jan Plachetka** supplied the articles on theatre, literature and music.

Much of the Places section of the book is the work of its original authors. The original chapter on Central Bohemia and destinations within easy reach of Prague were written by **Bronislav Pavlík**. **Jan Cech** wrote about Western Bohemia, Northern Bohemia is described by **Hana Vojtová**, while **Irena Jirku** outlines a tour of Eastern Bohemia.

Joroslav Haid wrote the original chapter on Southern Moravia, **Petr Zizka** wrote Northern Moravia. The feature article on Czechs and Slovaks was written by **Ondrej Neff**. **Rudolf Procházka** wrote about the outstanding natural beauty of the Slovak Republic.

A number of German authors were also assigned to assist with the project. They included **Werner Jakobsmeier**, **Wieland Giebel**, **Annette Tohak**, **Chris Pommery** and **Peter Cargin**.

This book features the superb photography of **Werner Neumeister**, **Mirek Frank** and **Oldrich Karásek**. New photographs were supplied by **Glyn Genin** and **Phil Wood** for Apa. This edition was expertly proofread by **Bronwen Barber** and indexed by **Penny Phenix**. **Sylvia George** gave the book a final editorial polish.

Map Legend

⊖	Border Crossing
—	International Boundary
---	Province Boundary
— •	National Park/Reserve
- - -	Ferry Route
Ⓜ	Metro
✈ ✈	Airport: International/Regional
🚌	Bus Station
ⓘ	Tourist Information
✉	Post Office
†	Church/Ruins
†	Monastery
☾	Mosque
✡	Synagogue
🏰	Castle/Ruins
⌂	Mansion/Stately home
∴	Archaeological Site
∩	Cave
⚑	Statue/Monument
★	Place of Interest

The main places of interest in the Places section are coordinated by number with a full-colour map (e.g. ❶), and a symbol at the top of every right-hand page tells you where to find the map.

CONTENTS

Insight Guide
CZECH & SLOVAK REPUBLICS

Maps

Inside front cover:
Czech Republic
Inside back cover:
Slovakia.

Rural scene
in Central
Slovakia

Travel Tips

Places

A SPECIAL RELATIONSHIP

*As soon as the Russians left, the Czechs and Slovaks went
their own ways. Can they be brought together again?*

As the Czech and Slovak Republics make their final approach to membership of the European Union (EU), this sometimes quarrelsome old couple seem certain to join hands again. They will never be as close as they once were but as new boys in an expanded EU they will have many of the same battles to fight and lessons to learn. Their 75-year-old marriage was brought to an amicable end in 1993, as the former Czechoslovakia failed to accommodate Czech desires for rapid economic reform and Slovak demands for greater moderation and devolution of political power. Despite a fair amount of bickering, the split was a pretty mild affair and contrasted sharply with the bloodshed and recrimination which accompanied the demise of the other former communist east European federation in Yugoslavia.

Pivotal to Europe, the Czechs and the Slovaks have certainly experienced their fair share of violent conflict. But, crucially, they have never been especially violent towards each other and the atmosphere between them is not charged with ancient hatreds or shocking betrayals. They have in fact been joined once before, more than 1,000 years ago, in a kingdom called Great Moravia and so, despite their cultural and linguistic differences, the Czechs and Slovaks have common links that go back a long way.

Perhaps the most obvious difference between them was the relative prominence of the Czech lands to the outside world and the corresponding obscurity of Slovakia. Historically, Bohemia played a central role in the Holy Roman Empire and, under Charles IV, Prague became one of the greatest capitals of Europe. Today Prague is a highly popular tourist destination but as far as the rest of the country is concerned, however, large-scale exposure is still to come.

Slovakia has also yet to be discovered by mainstream tourism. Until 1918 the country's destiny was always more closely bound up with events in Hungary than with the course of developments further west. During the long reign of the Austro-Hungarian emperors, when the Czech lands of Bohemia and Moravia were politically and economically powerful, Slovakia became an impoverished neighbour. Despite subsequent industrialisation, Slovakia remains essentially rural in character and proud of its cultural traditions and folklore. In addition to this it also possesses some splendid scenery, including the High Tatras, which are among the most spectacular mountains in Europe. ❏

PRECEDING PAGES: the Old Mill, Prague; a rape field in Eastern Bohemia; the first snows in the High Tatras; wintertime in the Krkonoše.
LEFT: couple dancing at a traditional festival.

Decisive Dates

THE FIRST SLAVS

AD 500–600 The ancestors of the people who become known as Czechs and Slovaks arrive in the region around the 6th century.

8th century Cyril and Methodius arrive. They invent the Glagolitic alphabet (based on the Slavonic dialect used in the area surrounding their native town, Salonika) which is the foundation for the Old Slavonic language. From this time onwards the empire of Great Moravia grows in the areas now occupied by Moravia and western Slovakia.

THE CZECHS ESTABLISH THEMSELVES

1198 Otakar is crowned first king of the Czechs. The title is recognised by Pope Innocent III in 1204.

1316 Charles IV is born in Prague. In 1347 he becomes king of Bohemia. In 1355 he travels to Rome and is crowned Holy Roman Emperor. Charles elevates Prague to the capital of the Holy Roman Empire, summoning the finest architects to build several of the great constructions which adorn the city to this day. He also sets up the first university in central Europe and enlarges the city by establishing the New Town.

1415 Czech religious reformer Jan Hus is burned at the stake on 6 July after castigating the sale of indulgences in the Catholic church. He becomes a national hero and sparks off the Hussite rebellions.

1458 George of Poděbrady, the last Czech king, comes to the throne. After his death in 1471 the Polish Jagiellon dynasty takes power.

1526 After the death of the Jagiellon King Ludwig the throne of Bohemia and Hungary goes to Ferdinand von Habsburg. His accession marks the start of nearly four centuries of Habsburg rule over the present day Czech and Slovak Republics.

DEFEAT AT THE BATTLE OF WHITE MOUNTAIN

1620 The Catholic League and the Habsburg emperor are incensed by the assertiveness of the protestant Bohemian estates who choose a new king. The Battle of White Mountain at the gates of Prague spells disaster for the Czech nation and unleashes a wave of persecution. Catholics establish domination. The Habsburgs take undisputed control of the region.

1743 Empress Maria Theresa is crowned Queen of Bohemia in Prague. In the wars over the throne, Prague is attacked several times.

1848–49 Czechs and Slovaks make nationalist demands against their imperial rulers. Hungary proves particularly hostile to Slovak assertiveness.

1850 Tomáš Garrigue Masaryk, the future leader of the first independent Czechoslovak state, is born in South Moravia.

1867 The dual monarchy of Austria-Hungary is formed – unfortunate for the Slovaks whose country is subjected to a ruthless policy of Magyarisation.

1914–1918 Czechs abroad led by Masaryk use the war years to cajole Western leaders into accepting the need for a Czechoslovak state. They succeed.

CZECHOSLOVAKIA IS BORN

1918 Czechoslovakia is established as an independent state after the collapse of the Austro-Hungarian empire at the end of World War I. The state is democratic in character but fails to satisfy the demands of the large ethnic German minority or the Slovaks.

1938 The Munich agreements deprive Czechoslovakia of territory in a major triumph for the German minority and Hitler's Germany alike. Western powers are accused of selling out.

1939 The protectorate of Bohemia and Moravia is established by the Nazis. Slovakia is given semi-independent statehood under the auspices of Hitler's Germany. Highly authoritarian regimes are established with particularly dire consequences for hundreds of thousands of Jews who are sent to death camps in neighbouring Poland. Some 30,000

Czechs and Slovaks lose their life in German prisons or as resistance fighters.

1945 The Americans and Russians liberate the former Czechoslovakia but the country is designated as falling within the Soviet sphere of influence. Communists gradually assert themselves. The three million strong German minority is expelled en masse in a policy of popular and state-sponsored retribution for alleged collaboration with the Nazis.

COMMUNIST RULE ESTABLISHED

1948 The communists seize power. Democracy comes to an end. Industry is nationalised. Political opponents are arrested; they face imprisonment, execution and torture. As the terror gathers force, high-ranking communists are arrested and subjected to show trials. Many are hanged.

1968 Alexander Dubček launches his programme of socialism with a human face. The Prague Spring brings new hope of democracy. Soviet tanks invade in August. Dubček is kidnapped at gunpoint and taken to Moscow. By 1969, Dubček has been replaced by Gustáv Husák, a fellow Slovak but a loyal stooge of Moscow.

1977 Václav Havel and others establish the Charter 77 dissident movement. The charter asks the Czechoslovak government to respect international human rights agreements which it has signed up to. The dissidents and their families face constant harassment, secret police surveillance and imprisonment.

1989 In November, hundreds of thousands of Czechs demonstrate on the streets of Prague, demanding an end to communist rule. The Communist Party hesitates but in the absence of Soviet support and as communist regimes topple across Europe it faces reality and gives in. On 28 December, Alexander Dubček is made chairman of the federal assembly. A day later he leads Václav Havel out to become president.

BEYOND THE VELVET REVOLUTION

1990 The first free elections. Democratic umbrella parties in the Czech and Slovak Republics and their allies score decisive victories over the communists.

1993 Czechoslovakia splits up in a "velvet divorce" brokered by political leaders from both the Czech and Slovak Republics. In the absence of a referendum some say a vague but popular desire to maintain some form of common state has been

PRECEDING PAGES: an engraving of Karlsbad.
LEFT: Albrecht von Wallenstein.
RIGHT: Václav Havel.

ignored. Czechs push on with privatisation and economic reform while Slovakia falls under the shadow of authoritarian prime minister Vladimír Mečiar.

1995 Czechs become the first former communist country to join the Organisation for Economic Co-operation and Development (OECD).

1997 Czech prime minister Václav Klaus's government collapses as the economy threatens to slide into deep recession and financial scandals rock the political establishment.

1998 Slovakia's Vladimír Mečiar is ousted at general elections. The new pro-Western government pledges to re-democratise society. Talks open on European Union (EU) accession by the Czech

Republic and, later in the year, Slovakia.

1998 Czechs win the gold in the ice hockey tournament at the Nagano Winter Olympics, crowning five years of sporting success including three ice hockey world championships and the runners-up medal in the 1996 European soccer championships in Britain. Sporting success helps bring the new Czech Republic a stronger sense of national identity.

1999 The Czech Republic joins the North Atlantic Treaty Organisation (NATO) along with Poland and Hungary. Slovakia remains on the sidelines.

2000 Prague hosts the IMF/World Bank conference. Demonstrators receive a hostile reception from most locals in a country that relies heavily on direct foreign investment by multinational companies. ❏

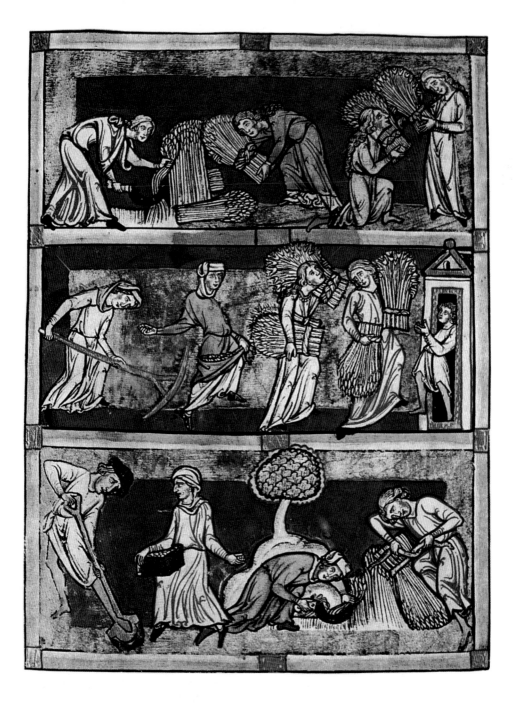

SLAVIC SETTLEMENT AND PREMYSLID RULE

The first Slavs arrived in the 6th century and it took many centuries
of battles and betrayals before Czechoslovakia was finally born in 1918

The frontiers of the Czech lands and Slovakia did not assume their present boundaries until this century, and yet the region can claim a long history as one of the focal points of Central European civilisation and as a bridge – or sometimes a watershed – between the cultures of eastern and western Europe. Furthermore, the Czech lands of Bohemia and Moravia lay at the crossroads of the traditional trade routes from the Atlantic coast to the Black Sea and from the Mediterranean to the Baltic. This valuable strategic position gave the entire continent a vested interest in the region's history.

Archaeological excavations have produced fine examples of pottery, testifying to the fact that Moravia and Slovakia were the homes of settled communities as long as 25,000 years ago. During the 5th millennium BC the members of the Danube civilisation practised extensive agriculture. The potter's wheel was discovered in about 3,000 BC; by 2,000–1,500 BC the members of the Únětice culture living near Prague had discovered how to smelt bronze and hence how to produce tools and weapons. This technology also allowed them to make religious cult figures and intricate jewellery.

The first Slavs – the earliest ancestors of the present-day Czechs and Slovaks – settled in the region from the 6th century AD onwards. Their migration route across Europe from the east brought them through the Carpathian Pass, the Moravian Gate and the Tisa valley, until they reached the area which was subsequently to become their new home. Here they encountered the Celts, who had been in the area for many years, as well as groups of Germanii who had also gained a foothold in the region. The gradual assimilation of the original inhabitants marked the beginning of the political history of

the Western Slavs. To protect themselves against the warlike incursions of the nomadic Avars they first formed a tribal association. They chose as their leader the Frankish merchant Samo, who had built up a powerful private army to

protect his trading caravans. But no sooner had they beaten off the Avars, than they were attacked on their western flank by the king of the Franks, in 637. In the subsequent Battle of the Vogastisburg, the Slavic army won the day, and the Western Slavs proceeded to establish an extensive kingdom, though this quickly disintegrated after the death of Samo.

The spread of Christianity

More clearly defined and better organised was the state of Great Moravia, which grew up after 833 in the regions of modern Moravia and Western Slovakia and expanded to include all of Bohemia, the southern part of modern

LEFT: a depiction of harvest around AD 1000.
RIGHT: a figure from the Libuše legend of the founding of Prague at Vyšehard.

Poland and the western part of modern Hungary. Thanks to his good relations with Byzantium, Prince Rastislav was able to arrange for Christian missionaries to be sent by the rulers of the Byzantine Empire. The arrival in 863 of two learned brothers, Cyril and Methodius, the apostles of the Slavs, was a key event in the subsequent political, religious and cultural development of the region. They not only converted large numbers of the population to the new state religion, but also developed the Slavonic Glagolitic

BROTHERLY LOVE

Prince Wenceslas was murdered in 935 by his brother, Boleslav. He was about to attend morning Mass when the assassin struck.

crushing defeat at their hands near Bratislava in the year 907. The princes of Bohemia had already asserted their independence. Under their rule, the Czech Přemyslid dynasty emerged as the supreme power in the whole of Bohemia. Although the first of the Přemyslid leaders, Prince Wenceslas (Václav), was able to become sole ruler over Bohemia, he was forced to swear allegiance to the German emperor Henry I in 929.

This subordination, together with an alliance with Saxony, lost him the support of the

script. Once the Pope had given his official blessing to their accomplishments, permission was granted for sermons to be given in Slavic after the lesson had been read in Latin. This concession was crucial to the rapid spread of Christianity. But Prince Svatopluk, the most notable ruler of this early state, was soon forced to recognise the superior strength of his neighbours, the Franks, and to grant additional rights to the western Church.

A Swabian bishop was installed in his capital, Nitra, and the followers of the Slavic apostles were expelled. At the turn of the 10th century the state came under increasing threat from the Magyars, and finally collapsed following a

Bohemian ruling classes. Their resistance became more determined when Henry I enslaved Slavs east of the frontier with Saxony.

The prince's brother, Boleslav, led the conspiracy against him and was personally responsible for Wenceslas's murder in 935. Boleslav then created one of the most powerful states in Central Europe. He ruled over Bohemia, Moravia and parts of Slovakia as well as Silesia and Southern Poland while defending his kingdom against attacks by the Holy Roman Emperor, Otto I. After the death of Boleslav I (*circa* 967) and with the support of the Pope, Boleslav II succeeded in establishing the kingdom. He founded the bishopric of Prague in

973. Boleslav's successor, Břetislav (1035–55), tried to defend the borders and even to extend his realm. His principal achievement was the permanent union of Moravia and Bohemia.

But for the German emperor, Henry, the united kingdom represented an unacceptable threat; in 1041 he forced Břetislav to recognise Bohemia's dependence on the German rulers who endeavoured to maintain the Czechs' position as vassals in a state of subordination to the empire. In this they were assisted by local noblemen. Even the Přemyslids asked them for support in quarrels concerning the throne. This provided the German rulers with an excuse to play an active role in Czech affairs. However, the Přemyslids maintained their autonomy and turned the problems of the Germans to their advantage by offering their services as allies.

The 13th century saw a fundamental change in the status quo. In 1198 Otakar was crowned the first king of the Czechs; in 1204 Pope Innocent III also recognised the title. A further milestone was reached in 1212, when Emperor Frederick II ratified the Sicilian Golden Bull. This confirmed all the privileges which the Přemyslids had achieved to date and emphasised the unity of the land inhabited by the Czechs, which meant that the nation was finally granted official recognition at international level, and became a power to be reckoned with.

Pushing out the frontiers

The second half of the 13th century was dominated by the political and military successes of King Přemysl Otakar II (1253–78). His power, based on the wealth of the silver mines of Bohemia, rose until he reached a position of hegemony in Central Europe.

After the battle of Kressenbrunn in 1260 he succeeded in advancing into Hungary, occupying Bratislava and pushing the frontiers of Bohemia to the Adriatic. The compliant attitudes of both the pope and the emperor show the extent of Otakar II's authority; the chroniclers of the period call him the Golden King. He died in 1278 at the Battle of Durnkrut, fighting against Rudolf of Habsburg.

His death unleashed a crisis concerning the succession, but the situation became more stable when the claims of King Wenceslas

(Václav) II to the Polish throne were recognised. His young son Wenceslas III tried to continue the expansionist policies, but he was assassinated during his Polish campaign in 1306 and the Přemyslid dynasty ended with his death. The following years saw bitter fighting for the throne of Bohemia, which had become the most lucrative sinecure in Europe. Forming an alliance with the Czech aristocracy, Duke John of Luxembourg was in a position to swing the balance of power in his favour.

His marriage to the heiress of Bohemia, Elizabeth, the younger daughter of Wenceslas II, added a note of legitimacy to his claims; when

he stood with his armies before the walls of Prague on 3 December 1310, the citizens offered no resistance. He was crowned king of Bohemia the following year. John was a soldier who devoted more energy to waging war than to ruling his kingdom. This resulted in a drain on national finances, but also weakened his position within Bohemia, where the aristocracy was becoming discontented.

The loss of confidence in the crown and the internal crisis within the Czech provinces soon reached major proportions. The hopes of the aristocracy and bourgeoisie alike were focused on the crown prince Charles, John's son. They were not to be disappointed. ❏

LEFT: replica of St Wenceslas's crown.

RIGHT: Sts Cyril and Methodius, by Slovak artist Fulla.

CHARLES IV

*This 14th-century ruler, probably the most influential figure in Czech history,
built many of the most beautiful monuments in present-day Prague*

Charles IV was born in Prague in 1316 and spent much of his early childhood playing on the banks of the Vltava. As a small boy he was sent to Paris to the court of his uncle, the king of France. His tutor during these years was the future Pope Clement VI. Although he was christened Wenceslas, Charles

abandoned his baptismal name and adopted that of his role model, Charlemagne. He studied at the university of Paris and travelled extensively in Europe, learning at first hand the languages and cultures of the different nations. His first wife, Blanche of Valois, was an equally worldly and influential partner.

Charles's early years were marked by a tempestuous relationship with his father. At one point he even took refuge in Italy, entering the service of the Doge of Venice as the leader of an army of mercenaries. Following a reconciliation, his father proclaimed him governor of Bohemia and Moravia. Although he was only 17 at the time, Charles already had consider-

able experience of life. From now on he dedicated himself to the task of bringing new prosperity to the country.

Charles's first real success was the elevation of the bishopric of Prague to the rank of archbishopric in 1344. The support of the pope was instrumental in this, and in securing his nomination as king of Germany in place of the excommunicated Louis IV, in 1346. His father, now suffering from blindness, died in the saddle at Crécy only six weeks later, and Charles became king of Bohemia in 1347.

The Golden Bull

It was now understood that the German imperial crown was based on the crown of Bohemia, and in 1355 Charles travelled to Rome, where he was duly crowned emperor. Although throughout his reign he was mainly concerned with his native Bohemian lands, as these provided his greatest source of strength, Charles did not neglect his imperial duties. In 1356 he proclaimed the Golden Bull, a kind of imperial constitution. It confirmed the right of the seven electors to choose the German king; in return, the emperor acknowledged their absolute jurisdiction within their own territories, and decreed that the rule of primogeniture was henceforth to govern the laws of inheritance and succession. These statutes eliminated a potential source of strife for the emperor and ensured the loyalty of his most powerful vassals.

Whilst the rest of Europe seemed in danger of sinking into chaos, with England and France engaged in the mutually destructive Hundred Years' War and Italy shattered by petty intrigues and civil wars between its minor princes and city states, Charles cleared the way for making his native country the hub of his newly acquired empire. The conquest and purchase of further territories and his four marriages (each of which brought him increased power and additional land), as well as the skilful negotiation of the marriage of his son, Sigismund, to the daughter of the King of Poland and Hungary, strengthened his sphere of influence and gradually shifted the centre of political power within his empire in an easterly direction. Charles encouraged the growth of the cult of St Wenceslas, the national patron saint. The "Lands of the Crown of St Wenceslas", which apart from Bohemia and Moravia also included Silesia, Lusatia and for a short while even Brandenburg, acquired increasing relevance.

THE GOLDEN AGE

During Charles IV's reign Bohemia and Moravia flourished. The era was described, even at the time, as the Golden Age.

Czech and, despite large numbers of German immigrants, he managed to prevent the outbreak of ethnic and nationalist conflict.

Charles raised Prague to the position of capital of the Holy Roman Empire, gradually transforming the city where he had been born into a thriving European metropolis. He summoned the best architects of the time to his capital on the banks of the Vltava for the construction of the Cathedral of St Vitus.

In 1348 he founded in Prague the first university in Central Europe, the Carolinum, and

Trade flourishes

Bohemia was located on the crossroads of the trading routes between Venice and the Baltic

countries as well as those between Flanders and Kiev and the Byzantine Empire. Under Charles the standard of the existing roads was greatly improved. The Vltava and the Labe (Elbe) provided access to the North Sea and the additional markets of the Free Imperial Cities and the towns of the Hanseatic League.

Settlers were persuaded to make their homes in the country in order to encourage the renewed use of agricultural land that had been left fallow, and to increase manufacturing potential. Charles spoke German as well as

enlarged the city's area by the establishment of the New Town. The king was generous in his support of the church. No fewer than 35 new monasteries were established throughout Bohemia and Moravia, and many old churches were rebuilt.

This feverish activity was not without its disadvantages, however; the underdeveloped taxation system placed a disproportionate burden on the poorer classes, heightening the social tensions between the masses on the one hand and the aristocracy and the Church on the other. This growing problem was to lead ultimately to the Hussite rebellion during the 15th century. ❏

LEFT: statue of Emperor Charles IV.
ABOVE: the emperor with imperial insignia.

Papz zpowieda Septissky rde numurzky

Alz ge biskupen se nazwali aod wozme w giniti Swaty Ambroz
O pane geziss nwoz pasterzi zuwaks sus v wlk Marzz wbin
ge kmeze w swodze spelati wpilati gisk osimkne S. Bernath

THE HUSSITES

Jan Hus was burned at the stake for his opposition to corruption in the Church, beginning a long tradition of Czech dissidence and creating a national hero

Charles was succeeded as German emperor and king of Bohemia by his eldest son, Wenceslas IV (1378–1419). The latter unfortunately lacked his father's talent and energy. He allowed Germany to slide into anarchy and was ultimately deposed as emperor by the electors in 1400. In Bohemia, his main problem was the Church, which during the reign of his father had still been a reliable pillar of support for the ruling house. The English reformer, John Wyclif, had already openly challenged the authority of the Church as a secular power. By virtue of the marriage of Wenceslas's sister Anne to King Richard II of England and the ensuing close contact between the two countries, Wyclif's revolutionary theories spread rapidly throughout Bohemia.

The blatant self-enrichment and extravagance of the senior clergy, the bigoted attitude of the priests and the prevailing situation in the abbeys and convents, where monastic rules were openly defied, now called for decisive action on the part of the monarch. But Wenceslas IV was not a decisive man and entrenched himself in a diehard conservative position.

In Prague, the centre for critical theologians was not the university but the Bethlehem Chapel in the Old Town, erected in 1391 to accommodate up to 3,000 of the faithful. The sermons were often held in Czech – an almost unprecedented act of boldness for the time, but one which greatly increased their appeal to the ordinary people. A new generation of Czech and German-speaking preachers arose, among whom Jan Hus was to become the most famous. Hus's death at the stake in 1415 *(see panel on Jan Hus, page 28)* gave rise to a storm of indignation and protest throughout the whole of Bohemia. In Prague, a defensive league of aristocratic supporters of the Hussites from Bohemia, Moravia and Silesia was quickly formed. Together they asserted their belief in the freedom of the word of God.

LEFT: the Pope as depicted by the Hussites.
RIGHT: Jan Žižka, commander of the Hussite army.

Their petition, addressed to the council, was eventually signed by 450 noblemen. The Hussite Movement also found widespread support among the working classes, both within the towns and in rural areas. What had initially started out as an internal reform movement within the Church rapidly developed into a

broad-based protest movement pitted against the power of the monarchy, the Catholic Church and German supremacy in Bohemia.

First Defenestration of Prague

The violent overture to what was to turn into 20 years of conflict took place even before the death of Wenceslas. At the end of July 1419, the citizens of Prague, led by Jan Želivský, threw several councillors from the window of the new town hall when they refused to release a number of Hussite prisoners. Unrest spread: the Hussites occupied the town hall and elected their own councillors. Wenceslas confirmed the appointments, but when he died soon after-

Jan Hus

Master Jan Hus, the preacher and philosopher whose teachings formed the foundation of the revolutionary Hussite Movement, is one of the legendary characters of Czech history. More than any other national hero, he was an inspiration to the common people and he crops up in folk songs, plays and in recent years films. The anniversary of his death, 6 July 1415, is celebrated as a national festival of remembrance.

Jan Hus was born in 1371 in the village of Husinec in Southern Bohemia. He graduated from

Charles University in 1396 and was then appointed as an ordinarius professor. In 1400 he was ordained priest and became the first Czech rector of the Charles University in 1409.

During his youth he devoted his attention to the written works of the English theologian and reformer John Wyclif, who attacked the secularisation of the Church and demanded a return to the doctrine and practices of the early Christian communities. Wyclif considered that the only real sign of membership of the Church was an exemplary lifestyle; he acknowledged the Bible as the one true foundation of faith. Hus developed Wyclif's thesis further, emphasising the social aspects. The unadorned Bethlehem Chapel in Prague, to which Hus was summoned as preacher in 1402, proved an ideal forum for disseminating his message to the widest possible audience. In order to get his points across, Hus, who was a brilliant rhetorical speaker, developed his own, often unconventional methods. He delivered most of his sermons and commentaries in Czech, even going so far as to write a number of texts on the walls of the chapel. He translated hymns and religious songs, thereby enabling a wide spectrum of churchgoers to take an active part in the service.

One by-product of this approach was that Hus modernised spoken Czech, elevating it to the level of the written language. Hus found widespread support amongst many German-speaking theologians of the time; they even endorsed his demands for equal rights for the Czechs in Bohemia, seeing it as a justifiable pastoral and social affair.

But what had begun as brotherly criticism of the Catholic Church soon developed into a vitriolic attack upon the institution as he saw it. Hus's demands for a return to the traditional poverty of the clergy and a general improvement in the moral standards of public life aroused the enmity of the upper echelons of the priesthood as well as causing animosity on the part of those members of the aristocracy who saw their privileged lifestyle about to disappear.

The conflict came to a head in 1411, when Hus castigated the sale of indulgences as amoral charlatanism. There were public demonstrations for and against his theories; the Church excommunicated Hus and forbade him to exercise his priestly office, although he continued to preach at the Bethlehem Chapel and to teach at the university. But when he lost the support of King Wenceslas IV, who shared in the proceeds of the sale of indulgences, Hus left Prague and began to preach in rural areas; here he found time to examine his doctrines in greater depth and to publish them under the title *De ecclesia* in 1413.

During the spring of 1414 Sigismund, the King of the Germans, challenged Hus to declare his position before the Council of Constance. He was promised a safe passage and so, against the advice of many of his friends, Hus set out to attend. His hearing before the council developed into a fierce theological dispute; in the end, the conservatives won the day and Hus was found guilty of heresy. When he refused to recant his beliefs he was burned at the stake. ❑

LEFT: a portrait of the great reformer.

wards the Bohemian throne was claimed by his half brother Sigismund, the German king responsible for Hus's death. For Sigismund the Hussites' actions were sufficient justification to start a crusade against the heretics. During the following year, at the head of an army, he laid siege to the city. By employing guerilla tactics, however, the Hussite "soldiers of God", under the command of their heroic leader Jan Žižka, were able to put the attackers to flight. Žižka, whose military experience included fighting for the English at Agincourt in 1415, had been chosen leader of the popular party in 1419.

> **THE HUSSITES**
>
> The religious and social revolution represented by the Hussites was the first reform movement to have a wide political impact on Europe and Bohemia's neighbours.

Having conquered Emperor Sigismund's army and captured Prague after the Battle of Vítkov Hill in 1421, he proceeded to erect a fortress at Tábor, which became the centre of the Hussites' utopian religious state. The Hussites overran and plundered not only Bohemia, Moravia and Slovakia, but also Austria, Bavaria, Saxony and Brandenburg. The imperial army was defeated by Žižka and his forces in a succession of battles.

The Council of Basle finally took up negotiations with the Hussite leaders, at which point a schism developed within the movement. The moderate Utraquists, supported by the nobles, agreed to a compromise in the Four Articles of Prague in 1433, which contained acceptance of their principal requirement: the administration of the communion to the laity in both kinds (i.e. both bread and wine). The radical Taborites, on the other hand, fought on under their general Andrew Procop until, in 1434, they were defeated in a battle at Lipany by the combined forces of the Catholics and the Utraquists.

The Hussite legacy

And so, after almost 20 years of Hussite wars, the moderate Czech Utraquists were the clear victors. For the next 200 years the power of the Catholic Church was to remain at a low ebb, despite the fact that the majority of the population was Catholic – or at least professed to be. The Germans, who had hitherto enjoyed political and economic superiority, lost both power and possessions; furthermore, they were forced to settle in the frontier regions of the country.

RIGHT: the Bethlehem Chapel in Prague.

Their dominant position was taken over by the Czech nobility and upper middle classes; the poorer people still had no say in the government of the country. The devastation of war drove farmers and peasants even deeper into debt and subservience. And yet, the success of the Hussite Movement was one of the key episodes in Czech history, in particular because it was the first time that there was widespread support for the foundation of a separate Czech state – even though it was unsuccessful.

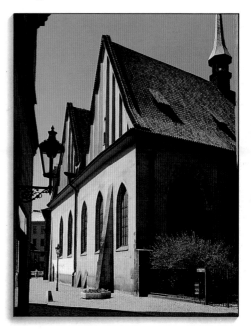

The new order arising from the end of war was personified by George of Poděbrady and Kunštát who, as leader of the aristocratic Utraquists, was to rule from 1439 as imperial administrator, and from 1458–71 as king. But George did not bring lasting peace or prosperity to Bohemia. After his death the Bohemian Estates elected Prince Vladislav, of the Polish Jagiellon dynasty, king. In 1491, in the Testament of Bratislava, the succession to the throne of Bohemia and Moravia was granted to the House of Habsburg. When the king's childless son, Ludwig, died fighting against the Turks in 1526, the country passed to the Habsburgs. Together with Austria, it was to remain under their rule until 1918. ❏

nic̓ Bohu̓ Synoc̓ swu̓oy gest dokonal.

THE HABSBURGS

*The Habsburgs took over in the 16th century and their descendants dominated
the cultural and political life of the Czech lands until the end of World War I*

After the Hussite wars Bohemia's frontiers remained inviolate, but within the country itself unrest continued to ferment. An uneasy peace ensued when George of Poděbrady, the leader of the Utraquist aristocracy, came to the throne in 1458. He earned a place in the annals of European history with his proposals for a general treaty of non-aggression involving all the countries of Europe including Turkey. The plan was never realised because of the rivalries between the various rulers, but it was the first attempt of its kind and served as a model for future alliances.

George of Poděbrady was the last Czech king. Between 1471 and 1526 he was succeeded by the Jagiellon dynasty from Poland. Under their rule the power of the upper aristocracy resumed its former strength. With the coronation of Vladislav II Jagiello as king of Hungary in 1490, Slovakia, which had been part of the Hungarian kingdom ever since the destruction of Great Moravia in the 11th century, was once more included in the union with Bohemia and Moravia. In 1526, following the death of the young Jagiellon King Ludwig while fighting the Turks in the Battle of Mohacs in southern Hungary, the throne of Bohemia and Hungary passed to Ferdinand von Habsburg.

This transition marked the start of almost four centuries of Habsburg rule over Bohemia, Moravia and Slovakia. The Habsburgs concentrated political power in the hands of the king, supported by the Catholic Church and a handful of powerful magnates.

Ferdinand, who was also crowned Holy Roman Emperor in 1556 following the abdication of his elder brother Charles V, attempted to strike a balance throughout his vast empire between Catholics and Protestants. At the same time, however, he actively supported the Counter-Reformation in the lands of the Bohemian crown by summoning the Jesuits to

LEFT: George of Poděbrady, the last
Bohemian king (1458–71).
RIGHT: Rudolf II of Habsburg.

Prague. The Jesuit Collegium Clementinum, founded by the king, gave the Bohemian capital a Catholic university, and its reputation was soon to outstrip that of the Carolinum.

Rudolf II

Even this could not prevent the Catholics

sinking progressively into a minority within the lands of the Bohemian crown; by the end of the 16th century at least 80 percent of the population claimed to be Protestant. Ferdinand's son, Maximilian II, found himself beset by almost insurmountable problems in the face of increasingly violent religious quarrels within his fragile kingdom.

His successor, Rudolf II (1576–1611), was more interested in the arts than in affairs of state – his collection of the visual arts included masterpieces and curiosities from all over the world. Born in Vienna, he moved his official residence to Prague Castle in 1583, initiating unexpected prosperity in Prague. In 1593 the

Turks attacked again following a long period of truce and the Habsburgs had difficulty keeping them at bay. Matthias, Rudolf's younger brother, eventually took over command of the army and managed to conclude a new peace with the Turks in 1606.

The emperor, who was now mentally deranged, died in 1612, one year after he had been forced to abdicate the Bohemian throne in favour of his power-hungry brother.

The Bohemian Estates could only make tem-

RUDOLF'S CURIOSITIES

Rudolf II's huge collection of curiosities and art undoubtedly made Prague into the "artistic treasure house of Europe"; sadly much was later lost during the Thirty Years' War.

window of the chancellery in Prague Castle. This second Defenestration of Prague unleashed the Bohemian War, which was to develop into the Thirty Years' War involving all of Europe.

Occupying the throne of Bohemia at the time was Ferdinand II, who became king of Hungary in 1618 and Holy Roman Emperor a year later. This fact no longer interested the self-confident Protestant Bohemian Estates; they declared Bohemia an electoral monarchy, deposed Ferdinand and in

porary capital out of the family quarrel; in 1609 Rudolf had granted them complete freedom of religion and various other privileges in a *Letter of Majesty* – advantages which they had to defend against Matthias. The conflict intensified as both sides attempted to secure their positions by means of alliances: the Catholic princes formed the League, the Protestants the Union.

Prague's second Defenestration

The religious time-bomb finally exploded on 23 May 1618. In accordance with an old Bohemian custom, the rebellious representatives of the Bohemian Estates threw two of the emperor's men and their secretary from the

August 1619 chose Friedrich of the Palatinate as their new king. The insult hit deep, for with the election of the leader of the Union it seemed as if the empire would not only lose Bohemia itself, one of the central countries of Europe, but also that the balance of power on the continent would be tipped in favour of the Protestants. The emperor and the Catholic League reacted immediately by sending in a powerful army under General Tilly.

The Thirty Years' War

The Battle of the White Mountain, before the gates of Prague, took place on 8 November 1620. It was decided within the space of a few hours.

Friedrich, the "Winter King" – so called because his reign had lasted for less than one year – was forced to flee, losing all his electoral privileges within the empire. The enemy troops had little difficulty overcoming the hastily erected barricades; for weeks they plundered and destroyed everything they could lay their hands on. Hundreds of people were indiscriminately condemned to death or driven into exile, from ringleaders to people who had not even been involved.

Ferdinand tore up Rudolf's *Letter of Majesty* with his own hands, expelling all non-Catholic priests from the city and forcing the aristocracy and citizens alike to return to the fold of the Catholic Church. During the following years the Catholic Church soared to new heights of power, achieving an authority it had failed to enjoy since the Hussite revolution. Protestant intellectuals, such as the famous philosopher and teacher Jan Amos Comenius (1592–1670), the bishop of the Bohemian Brethren, were forced to leave their native land.

Even after this fearful blood-letting there was no peace within the country. Merciless persecution and local uprisings continued to shatter Bohemia and Moravia and, following the intervention of Sweden, the war entered a second violent phase. This was the hour of Albrecht von Wallenstein, also known as Waldstein, a Bohemian nobleman who had converted from Protestantism to Catholicism in 1606 and had earned his military spurs as an officer under General Tilly.

Having been awarded supreme power over all imperial armies, Wallenstein reached the zenith of his power when his opponent, Gustav Adolf, was killed in the battle of Lützen, near Leipzig, in 1632. But wary of his ambitions for power, his enemies soon closed rank and persuaded the emperor to denounce him; Wallenstein was ultimately assassinated in 1634 in Cheb. Even without him, the imperial army won a decisive victory over the Swedish forces near Nördlingen; with the Treaty of Westphalia of 30 May 1635, the stifling peace of the Habsburgs descended on this part of Europe.

LEFT: the Defenestration of 1618.
RIGHT: Vladislav Hall in Hradčany at the time of Rudolf II, from a 1607 engraving by Aegidius Sadeler.

Under the Habsburg yoke

The failure of the rebellion had catastrophic consequences. The Habsburgs could now expand their absolute power without fearing any resistance; they moved the centre of political power once and for all to Vienna. Although nominally retaining their independence, the lands of the Bohemian crown became a provincial backwater, a situation which had disastrous effects on what had once been a buoyant, independent culture. This was most obvious in the field of literature;

CATHOLIC BAROQUE

One of the effects of the Catholic and Habsburg ascendancy was the restoration of churches and the building of new ones in the baroque style in Prague.

Czech came to be regarded as the language of urban working people and rural peasants while German came to dominate lawyers' offices and literary salons alike. From 1763, university lectures were mostly held in German; it was not until 1791 that a chair of Czech language and literature was established at Prague University.

The economy, also largely controlled by the Germans, suffered badly from the devastation of towns that had prospered on their flourishing trade and skilled craftsmen. The tightening of serfdom in the country slowed down productivity and prevented a rapid revival. Peasants whose farmsteads had survived the war were now faced with the burden of paying feudal dues and socage (service) to the nobility so exorbitant that their very existence was threatened. The personal freedom of the individual was severely restricted: not only every marriage, but also the practice of a trade or the attendance at a place of further education had to be given the official seal of approval.

An era of tolerance

The status quo remained unchanged until the reign of the Empress Maria Theresa, who was crowned Queen of Bohemia in 1743 in Prague. Her son, Joseph II, who from 1765 ruled Bohemia jointly with his mother, was respon-

within the Habsburg empire. The manufacture of textiles provided the basis for an accelerated exploitation of industrial resources. Before the turn of the century an English spinning machine was inaugurated in Northern Bohemia. A few years later, steam-driven machinery was widely used in Brno and Prague. The glass-blowing and porcelain industries conquered the European market; heavy industry followed in 1821 with the first iron blast furnace.

The rapid economic expansion failed, however, to remove social and national tensions. Above all, the language dispute continued to seethe, for Czechs and Slovaks alike demanded

sible for a new tolerance which permitted the existence of faiths other than Catholicism and allowed Jews to leave the ghettos.

Of more far-reaching importance for the subsequent development of the country was the edict proclaiming the abolition of serfdom in 1781, a move which paved the way for a liberalisation of the economy and society as a whole. The release of workers to satisfy the rapidly growing requirements of firms and businesses was as much a prerequisite for the industrial revolution as the improvement and expansion of educational opportunities.

Bohemia and Moravia rapidly expanded to become the most profitable economic region

official recognition for their languages, and parity with German. The dispute provided a continual source of strife: for example, when the Czech aristocracy was gathered in Prague for the coronation of King Leopold II, they refused to speak anything but Czech in protest at the language policy of the Habsburgs. The resulting discord shattered the hopes for harmony of the new monarch, who had travelled to Prague specially for the occasion.

In spite of a number of concessions the Czechs and Slovaks were unable to reach agreement; indeed, they believed that the discrimination against their language was a symptom of the lack of respect for their nationality and an attempt to wipe out once and for all their cultural identity. Nationalism became the dominant theme of the revolutionary years 1848–49. But although all the movements were directed against absolutism and centralism, there was a conflict of national interests and goals.

The revolutionary years

It was the main goal of the German Nationalist Movement that it should create a united Germany. Even those Germans who lived in Czechoslovakia aspired to this goal. They automatically assumed that Czech territories should be part of a united Germany. This idea

Slavic Congress in June 1848 in Prague. He demanded the transformation of the Austrian monarchy into a national federation, in which the united Slavs were to have decisive influence. But the Slavic rulers were uncoordinated. When unrest broke out in Prague and barricades were erected in Vienna, the imperial troops were soon able to regain the upper hand.

During the spring of 1848, Slovakian society supported the results of the Hungarian revolution. Their representatives voted for Slovakia to assume an autonomous position within the framework of a federal Hungarian state. Although encouraged by the Habsburgs' centralised

met with violent opposition on the part of the Czechs themselves, who in their turn sought allies amongst the other oppressed Slavic peoples and who – like the Czech delegation from Bohemia – turned down the invitation to attend the German National Assembly in St Paul's Church in Frankfurt on the grounds that they were not Germans. This attitude found expression in the doctrine of so-called Austroslavism.

The historian František Palacký had himself elected speaker of the movement at the First

administration, these Slovakian nationalist demands met with opposition on the part of the Hungarian revolutionary government, which instead used all its influence to assert a Hungarian nationalist policy. After the creation of the dual monarchy of Austro-Hungary in 1867, the Hungarian government resumed control over Slovakia, and with its policy of Magyarisation many Slovaks to emigrate, mostly to the United States. Slovakia remained a province of Upper Hungary until 1918.

A president from Moravia

After 1848 Czech political representatives supported the federalisation of the monarchy.

LEFT: the Jewish quarter around 1900.
ABOVE: a Czech farmer and his wife.

When Austria rejected such demands out of hand, more radical suggestions gradually gained support. Towards the end of the 19th century a generation of self-confident professional politicians emerged and the various sections of Czech society, increasingly aware of their group and class interests, formed independent political organisations.

By the turn of the century, German national groups began to demand unification with the German empire of areas settled predominantly by Germans; the radical Young Czechs, on the other hand, demanded a Czech state within a federation with Hungary and Austria as well as unity with the Slovaks. The new trend was known as Political Realism; its most famous representative was Tomáš Garrigue Masaryk, who was to become the first Czech president.

World War I and independence

Masaryk had already established a reputation as a moderate politician devoted to a humanistic ideal of statehood. When war broke out, he emigrated in turn to Rome, Geneva and Paris, convinced that he had to fight for an independent Czechoslovakia from abroad. Together with Eduard Beneš, he founded a Czechoslovak National Council, from which a provisional government was created in 1918. In 1917 he had organised the Czech Legion, which earned a fine reputation among the Allies for their assistance during the anti-Soviet intervention.

Whilst the Allies initially saw Masaryk as no more than a useful instrument in their anti-Habsburg propaganda machine, Masaryk gradually succeeded in convincing the leaders of the Entente powers – the United Kingdom, France and the United States – of the viability of a united Czech and Slovak state, which he saw as the best antidote to Habsburg arrogance and German lust for power.

It was Masaryk's greatest accomplishment that he brought to the conference table the scattered Czechs and Slovaks, an achievement which culminated in the Pittsburgh Convention of May 1918 containing the joint statement of the Czech and Slovak leaders in support of the foundation of a common federal state. At the eleventh hour, Emperor Charles I of Austria attempted to save what was beyond repair: on 16 October he announced the transformation of his empire into an alliance of sovereign nations.

On 28 October the Czechoslovak Republic was proclaimed in Prague; on 14 November, three days after the emperor's abdication, the National Assembly elected Masaryk as the president of the new nation. Over 14 million people – 5.5 million Czechs and 3.1 million Germans, 3.5 million Slovaks and 750,000 Hungarians, 460,000 Carpathian Ukrainians and 70,000 Poles in areas without clearly defined boundaries, not to mention 200,000 Jews and other minority groups – unexpectedly found themselves part of a new country. ❏

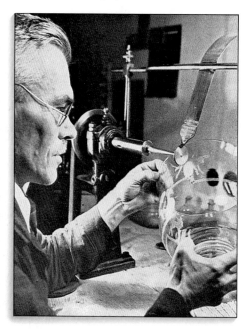

TOMAS GARRIGUE MASARYK

The first president of the democratic Republic of Czechoslovakia was a philosophy professor. Born in Moravia, Masaryk (1850–1937) planned to become a blacksmith. But his intelligence enabled him to attain a doctorate in philosophy from the University of Vienna. During World War I, Masaryk went into exile, gaining foreign support for a state of Czechoslovakia, and in 1918, he became president. During his office Czechoslovakia flourished as a centre of culture, industry and freedom. He did not live to see his country crushed by the Nazis, but his legacy lives on in the ideals of an ethnically diverse society based on democracy.

LEFT: Bohemia became famous for its fine cut glass.
RIGHT: a tram in Prague (1913).

FROM REPUBLIC TO PROTECTORATE

*Czechoslovakia was born at the behest of World War I's victors and then betrayed
by many of the same countries in 1938, setting the scene for World War II*

The section of society which set the tone in the new independent state of Czechoslovakia was the Czech bourgeoisie. During those first years, it devoted its energies to transforming Prague into the capital of a modern European industrial country.

But it soon became evident that the country had inherited a number of basic structural problems stemming from the centuries of non-autonomous development: whilst the well-developed consumer goods industry found its market reduced in the first instance from the vast area occupied by the former Habsburg Empire to the much smaller internal market of Czechoslovakia, the country's heavy industry suffered from the lack of previous development and proved inadequate to supply the demands of the internal market.

Economic collapse

Even during the boom years of the 1920s the planners were unable to make any fundamental changes to this imbalance; after the advent of the Great Depression, there was neither the time nor the money for far-reaching reform. Agricultural development suffered a similar fate. The potential of the comparatively intensive farming industry was squandered by inadequate attempts at land reform; the victims of the spreading crisis were above all small and medium-sized farmers, especially those living in the ethnically mixed border regions.

The period of the Great Depression exacerbated the ethnic conflicts, which had remained a perpetual problem within the new republic. On the one hand, Czechoslovakia was a state with a democratic constitution, offering religious and ethnic minorities a high degree of protection and therefore providing asylum to growing numbers of political refugees from the increasingly authoritarian countries whose borders it shared: Germany, Poland and Hungary. On the other

hand, the ruling Czech elite was not prepared to keep the rash promises it had made to other minority groups within the country.

The Slovaks and the Carpatho-Ukrainians, who had been bold enough to join in the common adventure of Czechoslovakia in 1918, felt they had been cheated of their promised

autonomy. And instead of cultural autonomy the German-speaking population found itself faced with wide-ranging discrimination in public life, culminating in the closure of the German university in Prague in 1934. There were already signs that a storm was brewing within the country when the new republic came face to face with dramatically deteriorating conditions on the international scene.

German rule

From the beginning the state's founders and first two presidents, Tomáš G. Masaryk from 1918 to 1935, and Eduard Beneš from 1935 to 1938, had seen the hegemony of France's

LEFT: Tomáš G. Masaryk, a leading Slavic nationalist.
RIGHT: the emblem of the Austro-Hungarian monarchy was thrown out of Prague Castle in 1918.

position within the continent of Europe and the cooperation with the victorious Entente powers as a guarantee of Czechoslovakia's survival. But the Treaties of Versailles, St Germain and Trianon (1918, 1919, 1920), which determined Czechoslovakia's international frontiers, soon proved to be a very shaky barrier in the face of new territorial demands on the part of neighbouring countries. The Little Entente, the alliance formed in 1922 by the Czech foreign minister, Eduard Beneš, with Yugoslavia and Romania, both equally threatened by Hungary's quest for land, provided some temporary stability on the southeast flank. Nonetheless, sations in Czechoslovakia. In the 1935 elections, as the leader of the Sudeten German Party, he won 68 percent of all German votes, thereby becoming the head of the strongest group within the parliament in Prague. Henlein now demanded autonomy for the regions inhabited by German settlers in Bohemia and Moravia. After discussions with Adolf Hitler, he clarified and increased his demands in the Karlsbad Programme of 24 April 1938. The basic tenets were self-administration, equal rights and reparation; during the local authority elections in May of that year the party won 92 percent of all German votes. When, under pres-

everyone was aware that the biggest danger threatening Czechoslovakia lay to the west and north, where not only the Germans but also the Poles were demanding more land. Furthermore, both countries were able to exert considerable pressure on account of the minority groups actually living on Czech territory.

As early as November 1918, the German-speaking areas of Bohemia and Moravia declared themselves part of "German-Austria", upon which Czech troops had used force to break up the local and provincial government apparatus. In 1933 Konrad Henlein founded the Sudeten German Home Front as an umbrella organisation for all German nationalist organi-

sure from the Western powers, the Prague government intervened, Henlein demanded the Anschluss with the German Reich.

The Munich Agreement

Late in the summer, Britain's special envoy, Viscount Runciman, tried to act as arbitrator in Prague. He recommended the relinquishment of the German-speaking areas. During subsequent discussions with British premier Neville Chamberlain, Hitler agreed to making 1 October 1938 the date for the transfer. Under the chairmanship of Italy's dictator, Benito Mussolini, the Munich Agreement was signed by France, the United Kingdom and the German Reich on 29 September 1938. Chamberlain and the French premier, Edouard Daladier, announced that they had thus ensured peace within Europe; the Soviet Union criticised the treaty but was neither able nor willing to risk war.

Czechoslovakia was not consulted, and was forced to look on passively when, on 1 October, German troops in official support of "human rights" marched into the so-called Sudeten German Gau, to the jubilant cheers of the German populace. Poland and Hungary also took advantage of the favourable conditions to annex border areas.

The Little Entente collapsed. On 5 October Eduard Beneš resigned and fled into exile in the United Kingdom.

Bohemia and Moravia

Not content with this triumph, Hitler was anxious to "deal with the rest of Czechoslovakia", as a secret order of 21 October 1938 reveals. He encouraged the continued territorial demands of Poland and Hungary, and incited the Slovaks to proclaim their own independence. In Berlin on 15 March, by means of undisguised military threats, he forced the national president of Czechoslovakia, Emil Hácha, to sign an agreement confirming the creation of the National Protectorate of Bohemia and Moravia. Just a few hours later on, German troops marched into Prague.

Formally speaking, the Protectorate remained a state under the protection of the German Reich; it had, however, no independent policies in the realms of foreign affairs, economics and defence. It retained its own head of state and a puppet government for home affairs, justice and culture. This secured the cooperation of some of the 7.3 million inhabitants.

The true power lay in the hands of the German protector, whose seat of administration was in Prague. The governing body not only organised the arrest and deportation of Jews but also devoted considerable efforts to silencing the Czech intelligentsia. The closure of schools and universities, institutes of culture

THE HOLOCAUST

Immediately after the occupation of Bohemia and Moravia by Hitler's army, Czech Jews were deprived of their citizenship and were eventually deported to the gas chambers of Auschwitz.

and newspapers, the ban placed upon the choice of some professions and the enforced deportations took a heavy toll amongst teachers, academics, artists and journalists. The world-famous Barrandov Studios were forced to devote themselves to making propaganda films, such as the shallow comedies about the passionate Matjuschka and her handsome young lieutenant, designed to keep the troops at the front entertained and happy.

The Nazis employed the same thorough

approach in their efforts to turn the Protectorate into an impregnable centre of armaments production and industry. Weapons would continue to be manufactured here right up to the end of the war, owing to the limited range of the Allied bombers.

Massacre at Lidice

The workforce was lulled into submission by high wages and comparatively favourable working conditions. Since repression within Czechoslovakia was almost complete, resistance efforts had to be steered from abroad. The assassination of the deputy Reichsprotector Reinhard "The Hangman" Heydrich on 27 May

LEFT: Tomáš G Masaryk promulgated the independent Czechoslovak Republic in Philadelphia, USA, on 18 October 1918. RIGHT: a Prague public library, where Jews were not allowed to borrow books.

The Ghetto of Terezín

The little town of Terezín (Theresienstadt) nestles idyllically in the valley of the Labe (Elbe) at the foot of fertile volcanic hills. The pretty surroundings are deceptive, however; today, for most citizens of the Czech Republic, Terezín is a symbol of man's inhumanity to man.

The *malá pevnost*, the little fortress overlooking the town, was built by Emperor Joseph II at the end of the 18th century as part of the line of defences protecting Austria against Prussian aggression. Because of the alleged military urgency

of the project, the entire complex was completed within only 10 years. Paradoxically, however, it never proved necessary for the castle to serve its true purpose. During World War I it was used as a prison; when the Nazis invaded Bohemia, they used it for the same purpose – but this time for the imprisonment of Jews.

During World War II the German occupying forces created in Theresienstadt a notorious walled ghetto for Jews. Shipment of Jewish captives into Theresienstadt began in November 1941. Accordingly, the entire non-Jewish population of the town, numbering some 3,700, was hurriedly resettled elsewhere in order to make room for the new arrivals. The Nazis claimed that the camp they were build-

ing here was a Jewish settlement with its own administration. When the International Red Cross insisted on visiting a concentration camp, the delegation was sent to Theresienstadt where it was treated to a week of cultural entertainment.

It was, of course, a propaganda lie designed to deceive the rest of the world; for a long time, however, many Jews also believed in it and failed to flee to safety.

Theresienstadt occupied a special position in Hitler's plans for the extermination of the Jewish race. It served as a distribution centre for the transport of Jews (its location at the heart of Europe prevented the construction of a proper extermination camp of the kind to be found in the remotest corners of Eastern Poland). The Gestapo sent prisoners not only from Prague but also from the entire Protectorate of Bohemia and Moravia.

Deportation trains from other countries also deposited their human cargo here. Through the gate surmounted by the cynical motto *'Arbeit macht Frei'* (Work Liberates) passed thousands of Jewish prisoners from Poland, Austria, Belgium, the Netherlands, Italy, Russia, Latvia, Lithuania, Greece, Spain, Yugoslavia and France. Towards the end of the war, as the battle front closed in on Germany and camps such as Treblinka had to be dissolved in order to hide the traces of the brutal mass murders, internees of other concentration camps were brought to Theresienstadt.

During the five years of its existence some 140,000 prisoners passed through the camp; over 30,000 died in the dense overcrowding of the ghetto itself and 88,000 were shipped on to the extermination camps, especially Auschwitz.

Transport convoys bringing new inhabitants arrived continuously in the camp. No fewer than 500 trains – in other words, an average of one every three days – came to a halt here between November 1941 and April 1945. Amongst the largest contingents were the 40,000 Jews brought from Prague, 9,000 from Brno, 13,500 from Berlin, and 4,000 from Frankfurt.

When liberation finally came in May 1945, the Allies encountered thousands of emaciated, terrified prisoners. This statement of bald facts cannot convey the agonies they endured in their perpetual state of uncertainty and fear that the following day they, too, might be taken away. Today, their most poignant memorial lies not in words but in the national place of remembrance. ❑

LEFT: a tour of the concentration camp in Terezín.

1942 was the work of a group of émigrés. Upon instructions from the government in exile in London, they parachuted into Prague and threw a bomb at Heydrich's car. They were finally shot in their hiding place in the Church of Sts Cyril and Methodius. Not content with a wave of executions and arrests in Prague, in retribution the Gestapo shot all adult male inhabitants of the mining village of Lidice on 10 June 1942 and sent the women and children to concentration camps. On 5 May 1945 the citizens of Prague rose in united rebellion against the German occupying forces. Three days before the end of the war they directed their pent-up anger against the Sudeten Germans too; most of the latter were forced to leave their homes; of a total of some 3 million, only 200,000 stayed. When the victorious Red Army came, it was rapturously greeted by the populace, who believed the moment of freedom had come.

REBELLION

On 5 May 1945 the people of Prague rose up against the Germans. When the Red Army entered the city they were greeted as liberators and brother Slavs.

The Protectorate of Slovakia

The majority of Slovaks, deeply disappointed at the policy of the Prague government in the nationalities question, had watched more or less passively the threatened dismemberment of Czechoslovakia. The strongest voice was the fiercely nationalist Slovakian People's Party under the leadership of the Catholic priest Jozef Tiso. Slovakian politicians who spoke out in favour of cooperation with the Czechs quickly lost the support of the people.

On 6 October 1938, as a consequence of the Munich Agreement, Slovakia proclaimed itself an autonomous unit within the federal Czecho-Slovak state. Tiso was appointed prime minister. Early in the following year, however, he demanded complete sovereignty for Slovakia. Hitler announced his support for this move on 13 March 1939 in Berlin; the following day Tiso declared the state to be fully independent.

Hitler made the Slovaks pay dearly for this favour; on 23 March 1939 the state was forced to place itself under the protection of the German Reich, relinquishing all claims to independent foreign, economic and defence policies. Further humiliations followed in the

form of the construction of German defences in Western Slovakia, complete cultural autonomy for the German minority population and territorial concessions to Hungary, which had an alliance with Germany. The most tragic chapter in the story of the German-Slovakian alliance was the active cooperation of the Slovakian government in the persecution and extermination of the Jews. Some 110,000 Slovakian Jews were mercilessly handed over to the Germans and sent to concentration camps. Only when

the Vatican's protests became unequivocal did Tiso abandon the practice. In 1944 the approaching Red Army incited the populace to resist the Fascist regime; in August, even Čatloš, the Minister of War, defected to the resistance with some sections of the army. But assisted by German troops, the regime was able to remain in power for some months longer. On 4 April 1945 the Red Army entered Bratislava; in the 5 April Košice Programme the resistance leaders under communist leadership proclaimed the fraternal unity of the Czech and Slovak peoples and demanded the nationalisation of key industries and financial institutions. Tiso was executed on 18 April 1947 in Bratislava. ❏

RIGHT: to the indignation of the populace, German troops marched into Prague on 15 March 1939.

THE SOCIALIST REPUBLIC

The Yalta Conference in 1945 set the stage for a communist takeover three years later, inaugurating more than 40 years of totalitarian rule

In the autumn of 1939, from his London exile, Eduard Beneš had established a Czechoslovak National Council which was recognised by the Allies as a provisional government. Despite their support from Moscow, even the Czech communists under the leadership of Klement Gottwald recognised the legit-

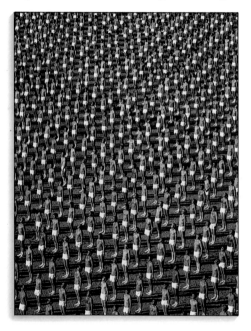

imacy of this government in exile; in 1943 the Soviet Union concluded a treaty of friendship and assistance. They agreed on the rejection of the Munich Agreement and the expulsion of the Sudeten Germans.

The role of the Soviet Union was in any case crucial as the Western Allies agreed at the Yalta Conference in 1945 that the rearrangement of political relationships within Czechoslovakia should take place under the aegis of Josef Stalin, and that the country should therefore be liberated by the Red Army. Accordingly, the American troops who had liberated Plzeň and Western Bohemia retreated once more in the face of the advancing Russian forces.

The national president, Eduard Beneš, and the prime minister, Zdeněk Fierlinger, who had taken up office in Prague in May 1945, saw no reason for alarm. During the turmoil and tragedy of the previous years the Soviet Union had shown itself to be a loyal ally, and in any case the Russians were Slavs. The population demonstrated their confidence in the communists by awarding them almost 38 percent of the votes during the last free elections in 1946. Klement Gottwald was appointed leader of a coalition government. President Beneš defined the role of the new Czechoslovakia as a bridge between east and west.

The peace was deceptive: in February 1948 the communists seized power by means of an arranged putsch with staged demonstrations and strikes. The move was non-violent but highly effective. The non-communist ministers resigned from the government; Beneš also stepped down. Jan Masaryk, the son of the founder of the Czech state, had been foreign minister since 1945. On 10 March 1948 his body was found beneath the open window of the foreign ministry in Prague, and it was assumed he had killed himself in protest at the Stalinisation of his homeland.

Collapse of a utopia

During each year of its existence (from 9 May 1948 as a People's Democratic Republic, and from 1960 as the Socialist Republic), the inevitable failure of the utopian vision became increasingly evident. The country, once one of Central Europe's most prosperous bastions of tolerance, was transformed into a prison. The political climate was dominated by elaborate show trials. All Western influence was designated as evil by the communist ideologists. The Soviet Union was upheld as the only logical model for development; Marxist-Leninist doctrines were glorified as the all-embracing ultimate philosophy.

The country became the victim of intransigent socialist policies. Whilst thousands of citizens, especially the intellectuals, fled from the country once more – leading to an acute shortage of qualified doctors, teachers and scientists – the government embarked upon the enforced collectivisation of agriculture and the development of heavy industry without any proper regard for mankind or the environment.

The economy was subject to long-term planning policies, known as the Five-Year Plans, and was under the direct guidance of the Central Committee. External trade became increasingly dependent upon the Soviet Union. In 1949 Czechoslovakia became a member of the Council for Mutual Economic Aid (COMECON); in 1955 it joined the Warsaw Pact.

Even after Stalin's death and the Twentieth Communist Party Conference in 1956, the situation within Czechoslovakia was little changed. The reign of terror inflicted by the leaders in Hradčany Castle was surpassed only on occasion by that of the rulers of the German Democratic Republic.

The Prague Spring

From the early 1960s it was public knowledge that the system was bankrupt; even within the party, voices of criticism could be heard, supported by writers, film makers and journalists, who ventured out of hiding despite threats of banishment and their repeated arrest. The Fourth Congress of the Czechoslovakian Writers' Union in June 1967 marked a milestone along the road to the Prague Spring of 1968; for the first time a number of young writers dared to speak out openly in vehement protest. The lecture given by the dramatist Václav Havel, who was only 31 at the time, was greeted with wild enthusiasm.

In January 1968 the reform movement asserted itself. Alexander Dubček became the party leader and announced the new era of "socialism with a human face", respect for civic rights, protection for minorities and the urgently needed settlement of the Slovak problem. Oldřich Černík, a respected economist, began a comprehensive reform of the economy. The Prague Spring was seen by millions of Czechs as well as by citizens of other countries within eastern and western Europe as the last chance to put into political practice the true ideals of socialism.

LEFT: falling into line at the Spartacus Games.
RIGHT: Alexander Dubček, pioneer of the Prague Spring.

The Kremlin leaders and their puppets in eastern Europe were alarmed; they feared the collapse of the Soviet national system and the loss of their own power. The Supreme Soviet's president, Leonid Brezhnev, insisted that the Soviet path was the only path to real socialism, and this doctrine justified the invasion of Czechoslovakia by Warsaw Pact troops on 20 August 1968. The citizens struggled desperately; pictures of old women and young students attempting to hold back the tanks with banners and slogans on Wenceslas Square were wired around the world.

All to no avail – the hopes of a generation

were crushed. Dubček was forced to retract his reform doctrines but, even so, he was replaced by the political hard-liner Gustav Husák. The agony of Czech society was to continue for two more decades. In spite of widespread resignation, many refused to give up; however, they now no longer demanded a reform of socialism, but a complete and unconditional democratisation of their country. With no organised support from the people, Czech civic rights campaigners such as Jiří Hájek, Jan Potočka and Václav Havel formed the Charter 77 in 1977, demonstrating that, even under a system which denied basic human rights, it was still possible to hold up one's head. ❏

LIFE AFTER REVOLUTION

Czechoslovakia was confronted with a "triple transition" from communism entailing radical reform of politics, economics and, fatefully, the federation itself

The collapse of the Soviet Union's empire in eastern Europe in 1989 shook a continent and sent shock waves around the world. It was one of the great moments of the 20th century. For some it marked the end of history. For others it marked the rebirth of a history which had been held in suspended animation since the end of World War II. Perhaps the most extraordinary aspect of that great year of revolutions was that it came as a surprise to almost everybody.

It is easy to be wise with hindsight. Mikhail Gorbachev's assumption of power heralded the arrival of a new generation of leaders in the Soviet Union. Against the background of a declining economy they were more realistic about the limits of their influence and were clearly unwilling to use force to defend their empire in the manner which had brought such tragedy to Czechoslovakia in 1968. Discontent, which had surfaced most explosively in Poland, was also bubbling under in most of the countries of the region.

Poland was, in fact, the first to take advantage; in Hungary, too, the democratic process advanced at a rapid pace, and in East Germany the citizens rose in protest until the Berlin Wall – the most tangible symbol of the Iron Curtain – finally fell in November 1989.

The communist leaders of Czechoslovakia saw the disintegration happen before their very eyes, but they observed the tempestuous changes with apparent indifference, as if paralysed. The team was, broadly speaking, the same one which had been carried to power by Brezhnev's tanks.

A peaceful demonstration began on 15 January 1989 on Wenceslas Square in memory of the self-immolation of the student Jan Palach in 1969. Police and army troops brutally separated the crowd. They returned at double and triple strength, and the demonstration continued until 19 January. Blows and arrests no longer frightened the citizens. In June a petition entitled "A Few Sentences" was put into circulation, and thousands clamoured to add their names. Even now, however, the communists were not prepared to enter into discussions with the opposition, but preferred to maintain their approach in an attitude of unreal invinci-

bility. The rejection of the last offer of talks was, it transpired, the final and crucial mistake of the ruling committee.

The Velvet Revolution

The peaceful student demonstration on 17 November 1989, in memory of the student Jan Opletal, who had been shot by the Nazis 50 years previously, triggered the course of events. Some 50,000 people took part; it was the largest mass demonstration since 1969. The police tried to prevent it by parking lorries across the route and by driving cars in a threatening manner. The hated Red Beret units attacked the demonstrators with batons. After this first

---

LEFT: catching up with old friends.
RIGHT: memorial to the victims of the 1968 riots.

example of brutality against the younger generation, events got out of hand more rapidly than in any other eastern European country. The opposition took matters seriously. Two days later it founded the Civic Forum Movement (Občanské Fórum – *OF*), demanding the resignation of all members of the inner circle of the Central Committee of the Communist Party who had been involved in the intervention of 1968, and calling simultaneously for the immediate release of all political prisoners as well as a general strike. One day later the movement Public Against Violence (Verejnost' proti násiliu – *VPN*) was founded in Bratislava.

chambers of the Federal Parliament passed a series of radical changes to the constitution. The lifting of the party dictate – which had originally been officially passed by the highest legal authority – was greeted with delight within the country and with respect abroad. It was a decisive moment for the continued progress of the peaceful revolution, because it paved the way for the necessary dialogue which was subsequently to develop over the following days and weeks in a new climate of free speech and increasing openness.

On 10 December Prime Minister Marián Čalfa, a Slovakian communist, formed a new

Non-aggression wins through

In spite of much provocation, the democratic opposition honoured the rule of non-aggression. The resistance during those November days in 1989 went down in history as the "velvet revolution". For a whole week, 20–27 November, hundreds of thousands of citizens demonstrated in Wenceslas Square, demanding the resignation of the government. The Secretary General of the Central Committee, Miloš Jakeš, was forced to resign on 24 November. Nonetheless a general strike throughout the country began on 27 November. Students were joined by actors, writers, artists and musicians. On 29 November the general assembly of both

VÁCLAV HAVEL

Havel, a playwright and poet, had been a prominent participant in the Prague Spring of 1968. Following the Soviet clampdown, his works were banned and his passport confiscated. During the 1970s and '80s he was repeatedly arrested and served four years in prison for his human rights activities. In between imprisonment, he was obliged, like many other intellectuals, to earn his living doing manual work. Havel remains president, but his health is uncertain. His second wife, a former actress with a talent for tactless remarks, has also lost him some popularity. But he will always be associated with "saving" the country from communism.

"Government of National Understanding". Gustáv Husák resigned from his post as president and on 28 December the Federal Assembly elected Alexander Dubček as his successor. It was an office he had already filled during the Prague Spring, and for which he possessed not only the necessary moral authority but also the best qualifications as a representative of Slovakia, in accordance with the conditions of the federal constitution.

On 29 December the parliament met in an historic session in Hradčany Castle. After 41 years of communist rule, Václav Havel, until then a persecuted playwright and dissident, was

the common enemy disappeared. The differences of opinion surfaced during debates on lustration, the barring of high office to those who had held senior positions in the Communist Party or who had close connections with the secret police. It was meant not only to be an atonement by a handful for the rest of society, but also a practical measure to prevent tainted officials from holding any kind of public office for a period of five years.

Goodbye Czechoslovakia

The key question was how to achieve the economic reform that would lead to a free market.

elected by a predominantly communist parliament as the new representative of a democratically reformed Czechoslovakia. Havel was an immensely popular figure, and in June 1990 he led Czechoslovakia into the first truly free elections since 1946. The Civic Forum and the movement Public Against Violence in Slovakia received the endorsement of most of the electorate. But its leaders gradually drifted apart as

LEFT: a two-hour strike called on 27 November 1989 resulted in radical changes to the constitution.
ABOVE: prisoners cast their vote in the first free elections of 1990.
RIGHT: Václav Klaus, champion of the free market.

Throughout 1990 and early 1991, the great hope was foreign investment. When this failed to materialise on the scale required, an ambitious coupon scheme was introduced, giving every adult the chance to buy shares in the state firms being privatised. The enormous, early success of the scheme boosted support for Václav Klaus, the country's finance minister and champion of the free market.

The 1992 elections produced a clearer result than expected. Around 34 percent voted for Klaus's right-wing ODS (Civic Democratic Party) and Vladimír Mečiar's HZDS (Movement for Democratic Slovakia). The electorate had chosen two strong leaders with conflicting views about the pace and scope of economic reform, with Klaus opting for fast-track privatisation. More importantly, in supporting Mečiar's HZDS, the people of Slovakia had signalled, unwittingly or not, their approval for national independence. President Havel proposed a referendum but when this solution was rejected, he resigned, refusing to preside over the inevitable split.

At the beginning of December 1992, parliament passed the law providing for the dissolution of the country and from 1 January 1993 the state of Czechoslovakia ceased to exist. In the early years, the new Czech Republic was

After the "velvet divorce"

The consumer boom of the early 1990s created a huge demand for Western goods and services at the expense of domestic suppliers, leading to a ballooning trade deficit. Many economists began to argue that low unemployment had been bought at the price of merely superficial industrial restructuring.

During the first half of 1996, as inflation showed signs of rising, ordinary Czech savers were hit by a spectacular wave of banking collapses, amid allegations of fraud and corruption. Unfortunately for the government, these worrying trends coincided with elections

showered with praise for the apparent speed of its shift to a Western-style market economy. Inflation remained low. Unemployment barely topped 5 percent as late as 1995. Growth began to kick in and Klaus openly suggested that the transformation phase had now come to an end.

The highpoint was reached towards the end of 1995 when the Czech Republic became the first post-communist state to join the Organisation for Economic Cooperation and Development (OECD), an important step on the road to the government's long-term goal of full membership of the EU. However, to those who were prepared to look below the surface, there were already signs of trouble ahead.

in which the Social Democrats, the main rivals to Klaus's ODS, quadrupled their number of seats. A year later, Klaus's government was forced into a series of desperate economic rescue packages, the currency collapsed in the wake of a worldwide emerging market crisis, the economy began to move into deep recession and, finally, the fragile centre-right coalition fell apart amid bitter recrimination. Since then, things have picked up again.

Prime minister Miloš Zeman's Social Democrats, kept in power by an extraordinary deal with Klaus, moved to sort out some of the economy's most deep-seated problems. Major banks were finally privatised. Attempts have been made to sweep corruption out of the financial markets and growth has finally recovered. Despite all the problems, the Czech Republic has made great strides in its efforts to reintegrate with the West.

In March 1994 the Czechs signed up to the "Partnership for Peace", a programme of military cooperation with the NATO countries. This was only a year after they had signed a Treaty of Friendship and Cooperation with Russia, which had already made its strong opposition to NATO expansion clear. Despite similar opposition voiced by Slovakia's premier, Mečiar, later dismissed as "paranoid" by Václav Havel, it became clear that the Czech Republic was a likely candidate for inclusion in the first wave of new members. The Czechs, together with Poland and Hungary, were officially invited to join the club in June 1997.

The Slovak Republic

If the Czechs had a difficult time in the first decade after the break up of Czechoslovakia, Slovakia almost suffered disaster. Mečiar's partnership with far right and far left parties made for an unenviable cocktail of populist nationalism. Corruption became endemic with allies in the business world being granted huge swathes of Slovak industry for knock-down prices. Political opposition, while never entirely smothered, was viewed with disdain. Journalists faced harassment. One dissident MP from Mečiar's party was simply ejected from parliament. A month later a bomb exploded outside his home. The son of the country's president – one of the few anti-Mečiar figures in the establishment – was kidnapped by the security forces, beaten up and dumped outside a police station in neighbouring Austria. A referendum on establishing a directly elected presidency was scuppered. State television became nothing more than a propaganda platform for Mečiar's supporters.

At the same time, economic growth, respectable by regional standards, was undermined by large budget deficits and hugely inefficient infrastructure projects. Unemployment remained well above 10 percent. Perhaps the most sinister development was the emergence of an increasingly confident Mafia

which controlled large parts of the economy and appeared to have the police force in its pocket. Not surprisingly, the West was unimpressed. After a series of diplomatic protests, Slovakia was excluded from the first wave of European Union applicant countries and was left out of the NATO expansion process.

By 1998, the country was heading for deep crisis. But the elections of that year were accompanied by a huge drive from the country's youth, determined to oust Mečiar and bring their country back into the European mainstream. They succeeded in spectacular fashion. The 11-party coalition which suc-

ceeded Mečiar wasted no time in garnering the support of the international community. Serious efforts have been made since then to redemocratise society, stamp out corruption and bring to trial those suspected of the most brazen abuses of the Mečiar era.

It has not been easy. Tensions within the government have led to bickering. Unemployment crossed the 20 percent threshold. But the rewards have been real as well. The foundations for future prosperity have been laid. In 1998, Slovakia looked as though it had slipped out of sight. If it can keep the momentum going it will not be far behind its northern neighbour when the gates to the EU finally open. ❑

LEFT: schoolchildren in Prague.
RIGHT: the business centre in Bratislava.

CZECHS AND SLOVAKS

Czechs and Slovaks are now well used to living apart
but they may come together again as members of the European Union

After the best part of a decade of living separately, Czechs and Slovaks still have mixed feelings about the break-up of their common state in January 1993. Although reunification is completely off the agenda in both countries, many feel a certain nostalgia for the Czechoslovak state. Such feelings sometimes become tinged with anger when it is recalled that the citizens were denied a referendum on the split which was brokered above their heads by the leading Czech and Slovak political parties.

Of course, the split itself was entirely peaceful and contrasted sharply with the bloodshed and recrimination which accompanied the disintegration of Yugoslavia just a few hundred miles to the south. Also, to those who recognised that neither Czechs nor Slovaks had even considered living together in one state until the end of World War I, the failure to develop a common national identity despite common goals and common achievements came as no surprise. In any case, membership of the European Union is so central to policy-making in both countries that controversy over the split has been eclipsed by more important matters.

Historical differences

From the start, Czechoslovakia suffered from the fact that it was an artificial political unit welded together from fragments of the disintegrated Habsburg Empire. The last attempt of Czechs and Slovaks at forming a common state had been with the Kingdom of Great Moravia more than 1,000 years ago. After its collapse, the Czech lands and Slovakia essentially went their own separate ways, and their paths did not meet again until 1918. During all that time, the destiny of Slovakia was controlled by the Hungarians; even under the Habsburgs, Slovakia

---

PRECEDING PAGES: church congregation in the High Tatras in Slovakia.
LEFT: jazz music became a symbol of Western capitalism under the communist government.
RIGHT: market stall holder.

was considered part of Hungary. The industrial backbone of the Habsburg monarchy was formed by the twin Czech lands of Bohemia and Moravia; Slovakia was the poor neighbour.

The founding of the new nation in 1918 was a rushed affair; its leading lights – Masaryk, Beneš and General Štefánik – were all academ-

ics. Their political approach has been described, not unjustly, as the Professors' Revolution; something of this legacy no doubt played a role in the country's "velvet revolution" in 1989.

National tongues

At the Writers' Congress in 1967, Milan Kundera asserted the responsibilities of the Czech intellectuals when he claimed that "Czech writers bear the burden of being for the entire nation" – a responsibility that Václav Havel accepted quite literally. Even the national revival during the 19th century was in the first instance a purely Czech, academic affair. The national tongue, Czech, had to be transformed from a despised rural dialect into a written language capable of doing justice to literary aspirations. Slovakia, however, had been subjected to Hungarianisation for so long that by the beginning of the 18th century the Slovak language had almost ceased to exist at all. It was only under the influence of the Czech national revival that the Slovaks rediscovered their language; the awareness of an independent written culture started some 50 years later than in Bohemia and Moravia. František Palacký, Czech historian and "Father

LANGUAGE LINKS

Although the Czech and Slovak languages are different – even in their basic nouns – the two are mostly mutually comprehensible.

Czech people, who also paid for it to be rebuilt two years later after it was destroyed by fire. In contrast, until 1920 only German and Hungarian artists appeared in the National Theatre in Bratislava.

Reluctant partners

Disparities continued during and after the formation of Czechoslovakia. The Czechoslovak National Council was formed in 1916 by Czech and Slovak exiles in the US, but not until the Habsburg monarchy was collapsing did the Slovaks in the US accept the ideas of

of the Fatherland", began his lengthy account of the country's history in 1836. The first volumes appeared under the title *The History of Bohemia*, and were written in German. The Czech edition followed in 1848, by which time the title had become *The History of the Czech People in Bohemia and Moravia*. Palacký exerted a considerable influence over the development of the Czech people during the 19th century, but he did not pay any attention to the Slovaks. To date, a Slovak version of Palacký has yet to appear. A further example of Slovakia lagging behind can be seen in the National Theatre. The theatre in Prague was constructed between 1868 and 1881 with funds raised by the

Masaryk, and join in signing the Pittsburgh Convention on 31 May 1918. In the future republic of Czechoslovakia, Czechs and Slovaks were to have equal individual rights.

After 1918, the Prague government tried to reinforce the Slovak education system and help the Slovaks develop their own intelligentsia. There were Czechs working in Slovak schools and colleges, in administration, in the judicial system and in other departments. Of course, this led to misunderstandings – the Slovaks felt first patronised and then oppressed by the Czechs. However, the Czechs also contributed to this misunderstanding. The Pittsburgh Convention stated that the Slovak people were to be equal partners in the new republic, but this was soon forgotten in Prague, and many Czechs came to look upon Slovakia as their colony.

Discontent in Slovakia found its expression in the Slovak separatists, the Slovak Populist Party. In March 1939, when the rest of Czechoslovakia was occupied by Hitler, the separatists felt that their moment in history had come. Under Monsignor Jozef Tiso, they split off from the republic and, under Hitler's "protection", formed a supposedly independent fascist Slovak state, allied to Nazi Germany. After the communists came to power in February 1948, Slovakia was subjected to a strictly centralised, Czech-dominated government. The constitution promulgated in July 1960 theoretically gave Slovakia equal rights with the Czech lands, and after 1969 the Slovak Socialist Republic had equal representation with Czech counterparts in the Federal Assembly.

Spirit of free enterprise

It is easy to understand ordinary Czech and Slovak citizens who may have felt rather bemused by all the dramatic changes that took place in their name. Despite the intrinsic differences between the two countries, many people, particularly Slovaks, failed to see any advantage to be gained from splitting up, in a Europe that is supposed to be edging closer together.

Many looked back to the days of the First Republic, when Czechoslovakia possessed one of the most flourishing economies in Europe, with a well-qualified workforce, a solid foundation of medium-sized companies and highly developed industrial production in a variety of fields. One need only think of the Bat'a (pronounced Batya) shoe manufacturing company. During the long years of state control, the name remained for Czechs and Slovaks alike a living memory of the golden years of free enterprise.

Upholding traditions

Although the first empire founded within their borders was much older than, for example, the Holy Roman Empire of German Nations, the periods when Czechs and Slovaks lived under the rule of a king of their own are negligible compared with the many centuries of foreign domination. It was correspondingly difficult for the

young republic to build up an awareness of its own historic traditions. The memories of the Hussite tradition had to be resuscitated during the 19th century. But this identification was only partly successful, for despite massive criticism of the Church of Rome, Catholicism has remained a determining factor, particularly in Slovakia.

The socialist government became aware of a national vacuum and tried to fill it with patriotic traditions and folklore. National costumes suddenly reappeared in towns and rural areas where they had long since been forgotten. In his novel *The Joke,* Milan Kundera describes the ideological intentions behind this "revival":

"Nobody had ever done more for folklore than the communist government. It made vast sums of money available for the foundation of new ensembles. Violin and dulcimer were to be heard every day on the radio. Moravian and Slovakian folk songs flooded the colleges, May Day parades, youth rallies and open-air concerts. Not only did jazz disappear completely from the country; it came to be seen as a symbol of Western capitalism and decadence. Young people no longer danced the tango or the boogie-woogie at parties; instead, they grasped each other by the shoulder and circled the floor in a round dance. The Communist Party was at pains to create a new lifestyle. It

LEFT: traditional Easter custom in central Slovakia.
RIGHT: worker from Slovakia.

took as its credo Stalin's definition of the New Art: socialist doctrine in national form. Only folklore was able to give this national form to our music, our dancing and our poetry."

The folkloric tradition was employed to serve the interests of socialism. Folklore festivals mushroomed, open-air museums were opened and new life was breathed into ancient village traditions. Writers laboured under the collective duty of creating a folk literature. An endless succession of folk song competitions was announced. Much of what was written during this period was later condemned as kitsch, but some of it had a lasting value.

Slovakia is another area where the traditional folk culture has been retained. In July Slovakian ensembles gather with their traditional instruments – the bagpipes *(gajdy)*, the native fiddle and the dulcimer, pipe *(píšťala)* and the powerful shepherd's shawm *(fujara)*. Dance groups regularly perform old dances such as the *Chorodový*, a communal dance for women, the *Kolo, Hajdúch, Verbunk* and *Čardáš*, the polka and the *Odzemok*, the traditional shepherds' dance. A highlight of the festival is performance of the Jánošík songs, which relate the exploits of the eponymous robber and folk hero from the time of the Turkish invasions.

Many artists who were later critical of the regime nevertheless found their first arena in the folklore movement. Under the guise of a folk song or fairy tale it was possible to give expression to many opinions which ran counter to the idealised views of the communist world. During the times when public lies were on every tongue, this critical strain within the folklore movement became one of the pillars of national identity and protest. These artists have lost none of their popularity. The cultivation of national customs survived even without socialist subsidies. Eastern Moravia, with its big folk festival in Strážnice, is one important centre in this respect; the region around Východná in

By, in and on the water

Despite – or perhaps because of – the fact that they live so far from the sea, both Czechs and Slovaks have always had a special affiliation with water. Smetana's best-loved composition was dedicated to the River Vltava, and in summer the Republics' rivers and lakes are abuzz with amateur sailors. The relatively unpolluted tributaries of the Vltava, Lužnice and Sázava rivers become the domain of canoeists and families in rubber dinghies, who coast along from landing stage to landing stage, gathering as dusk falls by the obligatory camp fire to toast *špekáček* (the traditional sausages). Touring by boat is still one of the least expensive kinds of holiday, particularly recommended for those who prefer the countryside to visiting historical and architectural sites. More ambitious canoeists will find that since the opening up of former military areas (for example in the Bohemian Forest), a number of more challenging watercourses have become available.

Although the major watercourses swell beyond the national borders into mighty rivers, within the Czech and Slovak Republics they retain more modest proportions. Over the years the inhabitants have devoted considerable energy to the art of keeping their water within the country for as long as possible. For this reason,

once stood sentinel on a rock – hence the name, which means "eagle's eyrie" – is now a moated castle. The foundations were reinforced with a thick layer of concrete against the waters. Another reservoir on the Vltava, the picturesque Slapy Reservoir to the south of Prague, has become a popular recreation area. Moored along its banks are houseboats, sailing yachts and simple rowing boats for fishing. Any visitor who has witnessed the bustling activity here on a hot summer weekend will immediately realise why the city centre seems populated only by tourists. By the water, in the water, on the water – Czechs and Slovaks alike are in their

artificial lakes account for a large proportion of the water surface area. They serve a variety of purposes: some are used for fish farming, whilst others are reservoirs designed for flood protection or power generation.

The construction of reservoirs and dams for industrial purposes began during the First Republic. After World War II, increased energy demands led to the building of many more. The most important are the Lipno Dam on the upper reaches of the Vltava, the Orava Reservoir and the dam below Orlík Castle. The latter, which

LEFT: Slovakian zither players.
ABOVE: Northern Bohemian miners at the coalface.

CARP LAKES

The Czech and Slovak Republics have many artificial lakes. Most impressive are the carp lakes of Southern Bohemia; these were excavated during the Middle Ages by engineers whose fame spread far and wide throughout Europe. Other important carp lakes are found in the lowlands of the Labe (Elbe) and in Southern Moravia. In late autumn they are fished with heavy-duty nets to provide the carp for the national Christmas dish. As Christmas Day approaches you will often see long queues of people buying carp from barrels. For many people, Christmas Eve would be unthinkable without a fried carp (smaženkapr).

element. That may at least partially explain why the joint Slovakian-Hungarian section of the vast Danube canalisation scheme, the controversial Gabčíkovo-Nagymaros project, has met with far less opposition here than in Hungary or Austria.

Acid rain

The Czech national anthem waxes lyrical about the forests, which "tumble across the rocks". But despite the fact that one-third of the land is covered with woodland, any talk of the harmony between man and nature in this part of the world must be hedged with reservations

(see Environmental Concerns, pages 124–125). Acid rain, partly blown in from abroad and partly caused by the high sulphur levels in the brown coal reserves, has been responsible for appalling environmental damage, especially in Northern Bohemia. On many days of the year there is a smog warning in Teplice – once one of the most famous spas in Bohemia, where Goethe, Beethoven and Wagner took the waters. To the east of Chomutov the vast brown coal excavators have eradicated more than 100 villages. The historic town of Most, where coal

ABOVE: country women on a sightseeing tour.
RIGHT: picking cauliflowers.

mining began in 1613, was simply moved and rebuilt on another site: the venerable deaconry church had to be moved half a mile.

Refuge in the forests

Entering the Czech Republic via the Bohemian Forest or Slovakia via the High Tatra, you can wander through immaculate woodland which casts into doubt the accuracy of a UN study claiming that over 70 percent of the total forested regions of the Czech and Slovak Republics is severely damaged. You will encounter areas of untouched primeval forest – the best-known is the Boubín in the Bohemian Forest – in which time seems to have made little progress since the Middle Ages. The nearer you are to the cities, the busier the forests seem. For city dwellers they provide a refuge from the stresses of everyday life. The desire to seek solace in nature is not just a modern phenomenon.

The straitjacket of socialism and the steadily increasing housing shortage have only exacerbated a trend which started between the wars. In those days young anarchists, or so they called themselves, disenchanted with conventional living formed groups and, equipped with little more than guitars and rucksacks, set off to pursue an alternative lifestyle in the countryside. They saw themselves as the pioneers of a new, anti-bourgeois lifestyle, and their ideals, based on a return to nature and brotherly love, were popularised in songs, many of which are still sung today.

You will, however, find few traces of this attitude to life in the weekend colonies of today. In the years immediately following World War II, the houses of the expelled Germans were appropriated; soon after that, the flight from the cities became a mass exodus, with the result that the government found itself obliged to intervene in the development of the *chalupy* (farmhouses) and *chaty* (cottages).

For many Czechs and Slovaks, their weekend *chata* forms the real centre of family life. Many families have transformed their simple cottages into comfortable dwellings or retirement homes. Mushrooms and blackberries grow in profusion in the nearby woods, meat and potatoes are brought from town, and beer is fetched in large jugs from the village tavern. Many houses have a large wooden barrel in which the owners collect the fruit to make their *slivovice* (Slivovitz), a plum brandy, which is drunk during the winter and at times of celebration. ❑

MINORITIES

*The former Czechoslovakia was a genuinely multinational state
whose population included Czechs, Slovaks, gypsies and Hungarians*

The "minorities problem" in eastern Europe is a favourite topic of discussion among scholars of the region and considering the veritable mosaic of national groups present in the former Czechoslovakia alone it is easy to see why. But from the late 1990s onwards the importance of the national question was seen and felt outside the ivory towers of academia. Asylum seekers, particularly gypsies, or Roma, from the Czech Republic and Slovakia have sought refuge in the countries of the west claiming that everyday persecution has made life impossible for them back home. In its turn, the asylum issue has risen to the top of the political agenda in countries such as Britain where some locals have expressed concern at the numbers of refugees coming into their communities.

Historical background

Following the collapse of the Habsburg Empire in 1918, the Treaty of Versailles allotted generous territories to the newly formed state of Czechoslovakia. It seemed as if the Czech and Slovak patriots' dream of independent nationhood had finally been fulfilled. But the very existence of the multinational state was threatened from the outset by the tensions between the politically dominant Czech majority and the sizeable ethnic minority groups.

Out of a total population of 13.6 million, barely half were actually Czech; in addition there were over 2 million Slovaks, 750,000 Hungarians living in Slovakia, some 100,000 Poles in the region bordering on Silesia and 500,000 Ukrainians and Carpatho-Ukrainians. The largest minority group comprised 3.2 million Germans living in Western and Northern Bohemia, Southern Moravia and the Carpathian mountains. To complicate matters still further, the racial melting pot was enriched by the presence of more than 100,000 Jews who had been living in the region for centuries.

LEFT: German costume from Vyškov in Moravia.
RIGHT: a portrait of S.J. Rapport, the Prague chief rabbi and scholar, by Antonín Machek.

The Czechs took advantage of their numerical superiority, whilst the minority groups, especially the so-called Sudeten Germans, made increasingly aggressive demands, which resulted in the collapse of the First Republic and the subsequent German invasion. Later, under the communists, the red flag of international broth-

erhood fluttering in the breeze served only to distract attention from the conflicts. In the 1990s both the Czech and Slovak Republics are facing yet another crisis riddled with ethnic tensions and deep-rooted prejudice.

The Germans

Germans began settling in the region as long ago as the Middle Ages. České Budějovice (Budweis) became world famous as a result of the Budvar beer produced by the Municipal Brewery founded in 1794. The chequerboard layout of the Old Town displays the typical characteristics of a German town of the time. Bruntál was founded by settlers from Bavaria and Franconia; they came as farmers, summoned by the kings of Bohemia to improve the fertility of the barren soil. The free cities of Engelsberg, Herlitz and Wurbenthal developed from German mining communities.

Traditionally, the Bavarian-Bohemian border region was an area of cultural interaction rather than division. For example, the Bavarian-born master builders, the Dientzenhofer brothers, were apprenticed in Bohemia (Christoph and his son Kilian Ignaz were to become the masters of Prague baroque). During the 17th century, important South German baroque buildings were designed along the lines of the

for the Czechoslovak government had denied them any right of self-determination.

Following the Munich Agreement of September 1938, Czechoslovakia lost a considerable proportion of its industry and defensive power. Only six months later, Prague was occupied by the German army. Within the German Protectorate of Bohemia and Moravia, the former status of the ethnic groups was reversed. In line with the doctrines of the National Socialists, the Czech working class was to be Germanised, whilst the intelligentsia was to be repressed. From 1939 until the end of the war, all Czech universities, places of higher education and

Jesuit church of St Ignatius in Prague. Today, many Czechs work in Franconia, and German shops have engaged Czech-speaking staff to cope with the influx of customers from the other side of the border.

But when it comes to a darker period in 20th-century history the Sudeten Germans are understandably reluctant to enter into discussion. and instead, they prefer to idealise the "good old days". It is therefore essential to consider the events which preceded their exile. During the 1930s the Sudeten Germans fixed their hopes firmly upon the German Reich; they spread the message of the "breakthrough to nationhood" and saw National Socialism as their salvation,

THE HUNGARIANS

The 600,000 strong Hungarian minority in Slovakia (11 percent of population) has fought hard, but peacefully, for its rights. Following the break-up of Czechoslovakia the Hungarians worried that resurgent Slovak nationalism would rekindle old hostilities. For a while after 1993, there was even talk of transferring the Hungarian minority south to the motherland. But since the election of a reformist coalition government in 1998 things have improved. Nevertheless, there is still a degree of mistrust between the two communities which occasionally spills out into the public domain. Violence has, thankfully, never threatened to emerge.

teacher training colleges were closed. As early as March 1939, over 5,000 individuals suspected of opposition were arrested.

The expulsion of 3 million Sudeten Germans began in 1945, shortly after the war ended. Overnight they were driven from their houses with only a minimum of personal possessions. According to some estimates, over 200,000 died as a result of massacre, hunger, exhaustion or suicide. The numbers are hotly disputed but no one denies that many died, or that many Czechs suffered as a result of the Sudeten German collaboration. After the revolution, attempts to heal the wounds of the past were made on several

and Zittau in Upper Lusatia in Germany have formed a close bond. They signed twinning agreements and organised an international conference on the Three-Country European Project. The will to cooperate is in evidence on a human, practical and political level.

The gypsies

But at least the Hungarians, as well as the ethnic Ukrainians and Poles, can rely on the support of their respective mother countries. Not so the gypsies. They are a people without a state; for better or for worse their fortunes are totally dependent on the prevailing attitudes in the

occasions. In February 1997, the Czech lower house of parliament finally approved a reconciliation agreement with Germany. The Czechs expressed regret for the expulsions while conspicuously refusing to apologise. The Germans expressed sorrow for the initial occupation. It was a diplomatic compromise.

Within the three-country triangle where the frontiers of Poland, the Czech Republic and Germany meet, the three towns of Jelenia Gora on the northern Polish side of the Krkonoše, Liberec (Reichenberg) in Northern Bohemia,

country in which they live. Since the revolution in 1989, life has arguably become less tolerable for the approximately 1 million gypsies living within the boundaries of former Czechoslovakia. With the new freedoms they have certainly acquired the right to speak up about their plight and freedom of movement has added a new dimension to the problem.

It all started in the late 1990s when rumours began to spread among the Czech gypsy community that some of their fellows had emigrated to Canada and were prospering. After several hundred attempted to follow suit, the Canadian government imposed visa requirements to stem the influx. The gypsies then turned their atten-

LEFT: Salzmanns Beer Hall, Liberec, pre-World War II.
ABOVE: a gypsy girl plays the violin.

tion to Britain and other Western countries. It was clear evidence of a deep seated problem.

In their settlement areas in eastern Slovakia, as well as in Ostrava in Moravia, the northern Bohemian towns of Teplice and Most, and even in the Prague suburb of Žižkov, the *cikáni*, as they are derogatorily referred to, are daily confronted with hate. After the creation of the First Republic, President Masaryk encouraged many gypsies to move from eastern Slovakia and settle in the industrial centres that were emerging at that time.

Following the expulsion of the Sudeten Germans in 1945, a similar migration of gypsies

unveiling, Marián Čalfa, the local prime minister, had it removed because he was concerned about its effect on the reputation of Slovakia abroad. The plaque was in memory of the Slovakian Fascist Jozef Tiso, who in 1939 declared the independence of Slovakia as a "Protectorate" of the German Reich.

Tiso had been involved in the extermination of the Jews, and by the autumn of 1942 had sent 58,000 Slovakian Jews to certain death. Of an original total of 135,000 Jews living in Slovakia, only one-third survived. The removal of the memorial plaque in Bánovce and Bebravou was not the end of the story, however. Nationalistic

occurred into that area, where labour was in great demand. Large communities of gypsies still live there today. Life is hard; many have no work and are forced to live in very basic conditions. Both Czechs and Slovaks claim that in areas inhabited by gypsies the crime rate is much higher than in the rest of the country. The authorities are attempting to counter this racial discrimination, although there is little evidence that any practical measures are being taken.

The Jews

A modest plaque in the little village of Bánovce in Slovakia was the cause of a minor uproar during the autumn of 1990. Two weeks after its

PRAGUE'S JEWISH MUSEUM

With almost unbelievable cynicism, the Nazi authorities planned to establish in Prague a museum of the extinct Jewish race. Valuable items were brought to Prague from synagogues nationwide, making it the most extensive collection of Jewish sacred items in the world. The historians who were entrusted with the work of cataloguing the items were executed before the end of the war and the collection was dispersed. Under the auspices of the Jewish Museum the remains of the collection found a home in Josefov, Prague's Jewish Quarter. The museum was founded in 1906 and is the third oldest Jewish Museum in Central Europe.

attitudes to life and anti-Semitism are both deep-seated. During March 1991, 7,000 supporters of Tiso demonstrated for an independent Slovakia. Not only did they voice their demands for independence; in the presence of President Havel and Slovakian leaders, a crowd of thousands also chanted "We want no Jews!"

Gangs of nationalist skinheads still keep the ugly flame of anti-Semitism burning although today their hatred is mainly directed towards the gypsies. For the few Jews, such groups revive fearful memories, for, apart from brief periods of harmony, they can look back on over 1,000 years of persecution. They have been forced repeatedly to be on the defensive against both rulers and mob. In 1096, crusaders en route for the Holy Land massacred large numbers of Jews living in Prague and plundered their property.

During the 11th century they were deprived of their civil rights and forced to earn their living as money-lenders. This represented a loss of social status for all of them, although for some it meant an improvement in their economic position. The city's oldest synagogue was burned down on the first occasion in 1142, and the Jews were permitted to make their homes only on the right bank of the Vltava.

Things eased under King Otakar II, who used his royal privileges to encourage Jews from Germany to settle in Prague. Nonetheless the position remained unstable for many centuries. Depending on the policies of the various kings – or, more precisely, upon their financial position – the Jews were the victims of stick-and-carrot tactics. In 1648 they were praised for their distinguished service in the defence of the country against Sweden; a few years later, under Maria Theresa, they were exiled from Prague and subjected to unfair taxes. Emperor Joseph II, on the other hand, needed money and passed a decree of religious tolerance, allowing the Jews to build secular schools and requiring them to do military service.

Equality before the law was not achieved until after 1848. This finally led to closer links on a cultural level, and to the widespread adoption by Jews of the German language, traditions and way of life. Until the mid-20th

LEFT: a cemetery in the Jewish Quarter.
RIGHT: memorial to victims of a Jewish concentration camp.

century Jews formed the heart of the capital's liberal élite: writers, musicians and many of those connected with the theatre. A unique spirit of peaceful assimilation between the two cultures finally evolved.

Annihilation

When the German army invaded in March 1939, 56,000 Jews were living in the city. Adolf "The Butcher" Eichmann took over the direction of the Central Office for Jewish Emigration. By the end of 1939, a total of 19,000 Jews had succeeded in escaping to Palestine, but the rest, some 40,000 from Prague alone, were

transported to the concentration camp at Terezín (see page 42), and from there sent to the extermination camps. Inscriptions around the interior walls of the Pinkas Synagogue in Prague record the murder of 77,812 Jews within the space of half a decade.

During the short interval before the communists assumed power in 1948, the Jewish population increased rapidly. In Prague alone there were 11,000 Jews. But during the two decades which followed, half of them emigrated; anti-Semitism, actively encouraged by the authorities, continued. Now it is to be hoped that the Jews can resume their role in society without fear of discrimination. ❏

RURAL LIFE

The rural beauty of the Czech and Slovak Republics should not be missed, especially the mountainous region of eastern Slovakia

The break-up of Czechoslovakia around a decade ago has had little effect on the destinations most commonly chosen by tourists. Slovakia still remains a largely undiscovered country while, in the Czech Republic, most visitors concentrate their attentions on Prague and the towns, villages and castles which surround it. But the Czech and Slovak countryside is well worth a visit, whether for walkers looking for magnificent scenery or for those hoping to lap up a taste of the slower pace of life in the villages. The adventurous will be rewarded. The country folk themselves have remained friendly and hospitable, despite the vicissitudes of history. And facilities have been updated in all but the remotest areas.

The old way of life

Up until 1950, rural life was based on the traditional pattern, whereby local affairs were run by three people: the chairman of the parish council, the parish priest and the head teacher of the local school. The communists soon put an end to all that. Small communities came under the control of a central village. The bulk of investment was concentrated here, leaving the established structures of the outlying communities to decay. The top posts in the local authorities were no longer occupied by respected local citizens, but by unknown officials with good party connections.

Only in a few regions were priests able to maintain their influence on the population; notably in Slovakia and southern Moravia. Religious education was, in any case, banned everywhere. Evidence of the declining influence of the church in rural areas can be found in the depressing state of repair of so many of the country's magnificent religious buildings, and the fact that one seldom sees young people in the congregations.

The influence of the village school teacher has also disappeared. Under the communists

LEFT: prize vegetables from southern Slovakia.
RIGHT: a Slovakian farmer makes hay.

school timetables were completely changed and acquired a new bias towards teaching the skills appropriate for the technical professions. Hundreds of small schools were closed, with the result that many children in rural areas have long journeys each day to the central community school in the larger villages or towns.

Communist agriculture

Under the communists, Czechoslovak agriculture was amongst the most advanced in Eastern Europe, with better than average yields. But the environmental costs of this achievement have been immense. Forty years ago the countryside of Czechoslovakia resembled a multi-coloured patchwork quilt. Narrow strips of tilled land were sown with golden corn, potatoes, hops, flax or yellow flowering mustard. There were grassy hedgerows and meadows of wild flowers.

Today, little remains of this agricultural pattern; valleys and hills are often characterised by a dreary monoculture. In the First Republic the estates owned by the aristocracy and big landowners were redistributed in accordance with the new land reforms; the communists, however, combined existing parcels of land to form large fields, ploughing up the hedgerows as they went along.

Unlike in Poland, virtually all agriculture in Czechoslovakia was collectivised. One-third of the available land was farmed by national collectives; the rest was handed over to the agricultural production cooperatives. The communists realised that it was essential to

RETURNING HOME

After the 1989 revolution, much of the property that had been taken over by the state was returned to its pre-1948 owners, although generally in very poor condition.

case, they have good cause to fear the dissolution of the cooperatives: the soil, exhausted by 40 years of irresponsible farming, is no longer capable of yielding a satisfactory harvest.

Environment-friendly farming is still in its infancy, and despite a concerted effort it will be many years before the land becomes fully fertile once again. But new technology is gradually being introduced and the heavy tractors and combine harvesters from the former Soviet Union and East Germany are being phased out.

destroy all inherited ties with the land if they were to put an end to the dominant conservative ethic in rural areas. In accordance with Soviet practice, medium and large-sized farmers were designated as *kulaks* and evicted by force. The minority of small farmers who resisted this brutal expropriation were quickly made to see reason by officials.

Although land was then supposed to be restored to the individuals from whom it was confiscated, many members of the various cooperatives showed little interest in recovering their former farms. They receive a fixed wage and are able to supplement their incomes handsomely by means of their smallholdings. In any

In search of a rural idyll

The rural regions, with their pretty villages linked by tree-lined avenues, still enchant travellers. The country scenes recall paintings by old masters: ducks waddle across the road, dogs stretch out contentedly on warm cobblestones and hens scratch around in the ditches. To find the unspoilt backwaters you need to turn off the main road. But the smaller country lanes have, in many cases, now been recovered.

Unfortunately many of the facades of the once splendid houses have decayed and the addition of ugly new houses does sometimes spoil the idyll. But here again, Czechs are beginning to see the benefits to the value of their properties by renovation and are usually faithful to the original designs.

Traditional country houses are now built only in the foothills of the mountains, above all in Slovakia. In the less well-developed regions such as southern Bohemia, famous for its baroque buildings, an individual style of rural architecture has developed. Paradoxically, the owners of weekend homes were the first to recognise the value of preserving the fine carpentry of many cottages and farmhouses; the villagers themselves have demolished many of the finest examples of domestic architecture, or ruined them with inappropriate extensions.

Travellers who want to discover the joys of country life, to explore myriad nooks and crannies, have an easier time of it these days. Many old style restaurants serving nothing more than pickled sausages and watery goulash still exist. But the rural economy has come a long way in recent years with newly refurbished hotels and especially private boarding houses springing up almost everywhere.

Villages and culture

The folklore of Bohemia, Moravia and Slovakia is equally fascinating, although not as prevalent as it used to be. From the 1950s folklore, "the people's culture", was unscrupulously used by the socialist state *(see page 57)* as a bulwark against the decadence of Western society. During the annual May Day processions, the villagers – dressed in traditional costumes – cheered the Red Flag and the local bigwigs to the sound of dulcimer and brass bands.

This cynical exploitation of local culture is the principal reason for the younger generation's rejection of their traditions. In some regions folklore is almost extinct, upheld only by semi-professional ensembles – not least because membership of these ensembles used to be one of the few ways of securing a trip to the West.

In the wine-growing areas of Moravia, in the Bohemian Forest, in the Tatra Mountains and along the Danube, an independent tradition has survived the embrace of Soviet-style socialism;

HIKING TRAILS

Hiking is a very popular pastime with people of all ages and there is a good network of trails throughout the countryside that can be used all year round.

and in some other regions a renaissance of old traditions is gaining impetus. Here and there you will see the masques traditionally worn by villagers as they celebrate with due ceremony the arrival of spring or the beginning of the grape harvest.

One of the populist solutions of the communists was to turn many villages into towns. Many a village thus acquired an ostentatious "House of Culture". During winter these became the venue for balls, dances and cultural evenings in which "famous musicians

from Prague" occasionally performed. It is hardly surprising that today district finance officers tear out their hair in despair at the high running costs of these sterile barracks; for some years now the rural population has tended to prefer an evening at home in front of the television to a dose of culture.

Family life

Just as was always the case, the kitchen incorporates the heart and soul of everyday life in the home. However, it has changed considerably in recent years. The old dressers have been replaced by fitted kitchens and the porcelain-tiled stoves have been abandoned in favour of

LEFT: a Sunday stroll at the foot of the High Tatras.
RIGHT: a farmer's wife weighs apples.

gas cookers; the most important item of equipment is a large deep-freezer. Every summer it is filled with fruit, poultry, rabbits and pork.

Only in the evening does the family migrate to the living room, where a three-piece suite, built-in shelving, a few pictures and sometimes a crucifix or a portrait of the Virgin Mary dominate the scene. Pride of place is occupied by the embodiment of prosperity, a colour television set.

Once upon a time, several generations would live together in the farmhouse; today, this is the exception rather than the rule. Young couples invariably try to escape as quickly as possible

WEEKEND COUNTRY-STYLE

If you would like to see a house that is still furnished as it would have been in times gone by, you should try to see the inside of a cottage whose owners are town-dwellers. They are the ones who cherish and repair the old porcelain-tiled stoves, rescue hand-painted chests and cupboards, and spend good money on old cups, jugs, pots, butter churns and spinning wheels. Their yard is likely to be lovingly adorned with old cartwheels and even hand-made replicas of pre-war ploughs. It's all a bit contrived – a weekend refuge from the stress of everyday urban life and an attempt to recover an idealised golden past.

from the strict control of their parents by building their own house or moving into the nearby town. Once the children have left the house a whole storey often stands completely empty, and only when they and other relatives descend for holidays and family celebrations will the former family home recover its old vitality, radiating warmth and comfort in spite of the characterless furnishings.

Town and country

Many children who grew up in villages moved to the city as soon as they were independent. A few of them joined the professional classes, becoming teachers, doctors and engineers. The majority, however, ended up in factories. Even today, the town exerts a magnetic pull on many country-dwellers, though most like to maintain some contact with their rural roots. Country life has its advantages: relatives supply them with fresh eggs, meat, vegetables and fruit, and the money thus saved can be spent on furnishings for the flat, cars or holidays. In many cases the parental home is regarded as a comfortable weekend *chata*.

Many who now live in the city have also remembered the art of mushroom picking. Many a weekend is spent scouring the forest and you will see men and women on the Prague underground holding baskets full of mushrooms to be used for the evening meal or to be pickled for later use.

The town-dwellers have quickly adapted to urban conditions. Most of the young people who have migrated to the city argue that nothing ever happened at home in the country, and that the town has more to offer.

In recent years, however, the trend has been reversed. Increasing numbers of people are discovering the attractions of living in countryside within commuting distance of a town. They cite the clear air, the forests, the peace and quiet and the close-knit community as their reasons for preferring the country. Of course, the reality of country life isn't always so perfect, but anyone visiting the rural Czech and Slovak Republics can be sure that the old adage still holds true: "Every guest brings blessings upon the house". ❏

LEFT: the belfry in Hrousek.
RIGHT: throughout the Czech Republic, pork is commonly served with cabbage and dumplings.

THE RELIGIOUS SPECTRUM

*Religious figures have played a big part in Czech and Slovak history
but the two countries are becoming increasingly secular*

Pravda vítězí! – "Truth prevails!" In 1918, at the request of Czechoslovakia's founder president, Tomáš Masaryk, this old Hussite motto was incorporated into the emblem of the new republic. During the Prague Spring of 1968, it was written in bold on the banners hanging from the windows, demanding the end of Stalinism. Václav Havel had the same words emblazoned on his presidential standard, and while in prison as an opponent of the regime had even written a piece entitled: "Try to live in truth". Things may not have turned out quite as he hoped, but the search for the truth goes on.

Five hundred and seventy-five years after Jan Hus was burned at the stake as a heretic in Constance, the head of the Catholic Church visited the native country of the Bohemian religious reformer. On 21 April 1990 in Prague, Pope John Paul II celebrated Mass before a congregation of more than half a million. Since then he has been twice more and after President Havel's trip to Rome in December 1999 the Polish pontiff went as far as to express regret for the burning of Hus at the stake in 1415.

The Catholics

As in the case of Poland, an appreciable proportion of the opposition to the communist regime was to be found concentrated in the ranks of the Catholic Church and its elderly but imperturbable representative, the then Archbishop of Prague, Cardinal Tomášek. But the Catholic Church sees itself faced with almost as many problems now as it did in the former socialist republic. The consequences of policies towards religion during the socialist era are still much in evidence. The socialist state dissolved religious orders (with a few exceptions), sentencing large numbers of clergy to imprisonment in a series of mock trials. Access to theological colleges was strictly controlled;

national salaries for priests were restricted to the bare minimum. Since the Church of today is faced with a new range of important social tasks, the shortage of newly qualified young priests is especially problematic.

From 1977, an "underground church" developed alongside the official religious bodies.

Lying outside the sphere of influence of the State and maintaining close contact with the activists of the opposition Charter 77 group, it developed a range of spiritual and social welfare activities.

Its members formed a congregation around a secretly ordained priest, it celebrated Mass during "mountain walks" and similar events; illegal publications were distributed and theological courses organised. Just after the revolution, the number of illegal priests was estimated at 260. The priests are considered to have been officially ordained, even though many of them are married. Their position within the Church has not yet been fully resolved. A further problem

LEFT: Levoča (Leutschau) in the High Tatras is the destination of a Holy Virgin pilgrimage.
RIGHT: a mountainside shrine.

is the return of confiscated church property, which is proving more difficult to realise than originally expected. Many of the monastery buildings are not only in a desolate state of repair, but also house public facilities such as libraries and archives. Only a part of the ancient Czech Premonstratensian monastery of Želiv, for example, could be handed back: converted into a prison during the 1950s, the main abbey now houses a psychiatric clinic.

At least until it became clear that Czechoslovakia was going to split into two separate countries, the Church was also confronted with the problems posed by the attitude of the Catholic clergy in Slovakia.

While the Catholic bishops of Bohemia and Moravia – together with the Ecumenical Council of the Churches of Czechoslovakia – warned of the impending disintegration of the state, the Slovakian Bishops' Conference considered that the Slovaks had a perfectly legitimate right to self-determination.

In contrast to Bohemia and Moravia, the proportion of practising Catholics in Slovakia is very high. Broadly speaking, the biggest problem faced by the Catholic Church in the Czech

> **CZECH FAITH**
>
> Less than half of all Czechs describe themselves as atheists, while about 40 percent are Roman Catholic. Among minority Christian faiths the Hussite Church is the largest.

Republic is the same one faced elsewhere in Europe – young people are generally uninterested and priests face the prospect of an ageing congregation which is not being replaced as it gradually dies out.

The Hussites in history

Following the death of Jan Hus, revolution broke out in 1419 in Bohemia. The armies of Hussite zealots penetrated deep into the neighbouring countries, shattering the faith of the Christian Middle Ages. Their theological negotiators attained a

degree of religious recognition during the Council of Basle in 1433, in that they were granted what was called the lay chalice – in other words, the right to receive the Eucharist in the forms of both bread and wine.

They acquired their name Utraquists from the Latin *utraque*, meaning "each of two". But the Hussites failed to gain any political advantages from their military superiority. The moderate Utraquists, who had maintained amicable relations with the Roman Catholic Church, ultimately joined forces with the Czech Catholics and defeated the radical Taborites at the Battle of Lipany in 1434. For almost a century their modified form of

Catholicism was to form the basis of an independent Bohemian Church. Under the influence of the German Reformation movement, the majority of Utraquists subsequently allied themselves with the Protestants. Following the defeat of the Protestant forces in the Battle of the White Mountain in 1620, the Utraquists were outlawed in Bohemia and Catholicism became the only established state religion for almost two centuries.

The present-day Czech and Slovakian Hussite

DEVOUT SLOVAKS

Slovaks are more religious than their Czech neighbours. Sunday services are a time of family worship and weekday services are also well attended by workers on their way home.

and is consequently still seeking its own identity today. On the occasion of his assuming office, the Hussites' new patriarch, Vratislav Štěpánek, spoke of the "many sins" of the past and stated that the primary task for the future was the search for common ground with the Catholic Church. The most important theological elements of the Hussite Church remain the Eucharist in both forms and the apostolic succession, as well as the right of priests to marry and the ordination of women.

Church has only indirect links with the old Hussite tradition, in that it claims to have created the idea of an independent national church. It was formed in 1920 as the natural result of the movement seeking independence from Rome under Masaryk's inspiration.

During the First Republic it claimed some 750,000 members. Under the socialist regime it conformed largely to the orthodox party line

LEFT: St Vitus is flanked by Charles IV and Wenceslas IV on the Old Town Bridge Tower in Prague.
ABOVE: Tábor, the town of the Hussites, named after the New Testament mountain of Christ's Transfiguration in a painting by Julius Marak.

The Bohemian Brethren

The Unity of the Bohemian-Moravian Brethren (Unitas Fratrum) was founded in 1457 by Waldensians and a handful of Taborites. They aspired to a religious community based on the stories of the apostles; its pacifist and escapist tendencies originated from the writings of Petr Chelčický (1380–1460).

Until the expulsion of their last bishop, the educationalist Jan Amos Comenius (1592–1670) in 1628, the Unitas Fratum was subject to repeated persecution by the Catholic authorities. Some respite was gained by the establishment of links with the German Reformation; Lutherans, Calvinists and Brethren agreed on a common doctrine, the "Bohemian Confession" of 1557. This formed the basis for the Letter of Majesty of 1609, in which Rudolf II granted freedom of religious practice to non-Catholic sects within Bohemian territory. But after the Catholics' victory in 1620, dissidents were faced with a choice between emigration or conversion to the state religion. Many paid only lip service to Catholicism and secretly remained faithful to their old beliefs. At the beginning of the 18th century, a small number of Brethren moved to nearby

> **VISITING CHURCHES**
>
> Most small churches in the Czech Republic are only open when services are held. The best time to visit is 7–8am or 6–7pm.

day. In general, members of the Lutheran Church tend to be Slovakians whilst Reformists are mostly Hungarian. During the communist era all attempts to forge links between Czech and Slovak Protestants were forbidden; today, however, the two communities emphasise their common historical links, particularly in the doctrines of Hus, Comenius and Luther. Nowadays the Evangelical Church of the Bohemian Brethren is a popular church with a Presbyterian constitution. Men and women have equal rights and privileges.

Lusatia, where they founded a new community in Herrnhut and embarked upon missionary campaigns throughout the world. Joseph II's Edict of Tolerance in 1781 granted both Lutherans and Calvinists certain freedoms within Habsburg territory. The Unitas Fratrum, however, remained excluded from the new conditions. Freedom of worship was not granted to all sects until 1918, the year in which the Czechoslovak Republic was founded. In this year the Lutheran and Reformed communities in Bohemia and Moravia were amalgamated to form the (unified) Evangelical Church of the Bohemian Brethren. In Slovakia the two denominations have remained separate to this

The highest authority within the church is the General Synod. In the first democratic government after the fall of the communist regime the Chief Elder of the synod of the time, Josef Hromádka, was appointed the first minister of Religion as well as deputy prime minister of Czechoslovakia.

The Orthodox Church

For as long as anyone can remember a dispute has raged in eastern Slovakia concerning church ownership. The protagonists are the Orthodox Church and the Greek Catholic Church (also known as the Uniate Church, since it was a product of the union with Rome in 1646). After World War II, the Orthodox and the Uniate Churches were forced to amalgamate here as in the Soviet Union and in Romania. Although it was considerably more extensive, in 1952 the entire property of the Uniate Church fell to the Orthodox community. In the aftermath of the Prague Spring the Greek Catholic doctrines were permitted once more, but it was not until 1990 that the Uniate Church was finally able to enjoy full reinstatement of its original privileges. These historical developments have resulted in the Orthodox Church losing much of its original importance in Slovakia. The church, whose doctrines are based on the teachings of the Slavic apostles Cyril and Methodius, suffers in particular from its failure to build its own churches and colleges.

Today they are faced with the loss not only of their bishoprics but also their seminaries. In country areas, services are not infrequently held in the open air because church buildings were appropriated by the Uniates.

Religion in everyday life

As already indicated, there is a marked religious watershed separating the east from the west. In the Czech Republic religious or church-oriented social patterns are adopted by only a minority. In 1980, only 4 percent of couples in this region were married in church. Church baptisms represented only 13 percent and burials only 30 percent of the respective totals. In eastern Slovakia, during the same period, 86 percent of all babies were baptised, 84 percent of all couples were married in church and 92 percent of those who died were buried according to the rites of the church. Today only 10 percent of the population of Bohemia claims membership of the Catholic Church; in Moravia the figure is 35 percent and in Slovakia over 50 percent.

One can only speculate as to the role which the Church – or rather, the various churches – will play in future. Religious communities, like all other sections of society, must rearrange their priorities. It is one thing to overturn a system which has lost its credibility; it is another to develop a new, robust system which finds a consensus in society.

LEFT: Cardinal Tomášek on his way to Mass in St Vitus's Cathedral, 1989.
RIGHT: Broumov Monastery.

Mild atheism

Bearing in mind the wide media coverage of the Catholic Church during the first weeks following the Velvet Revolution, a number of voices were raised in warning against a new clericalism. As far as Bohemia is concerned, such fears have proved unfounded. The citizens may well have a religious faith, but they are by no means zealots. You will find none of the arch-conservative Catholicism typical of Poland or even some areas of Slovakia.

Bohemia is traditionally secular; perhaps it is here that the true legacy of the Hussites is found – in the sceptical approach to all doctri-

nal philosophies. On every street corner you will hear opinions such as "Anybody who supports a system as authoritarian as that of the Catholic Church cannot be a good democrat." One Prague theologian just after the revolution spoke of a mood of "mild" atheism which has replaced the totalitarianism of the past years.

Demonstrating a deep understanding of popular feelings, Cardinal Vlk was noticeably mild in his demands for the return of confiscated church property, for example church buildings being used as schools. In a region which has always presented pastoral difficulties for its clergy, a mood of premature rejoicing on the part of the Church was the last thing required. ❏

FOOD AND DRINK

A traditional Czech meal consists of heavy goulash and dumplings washed down with beer, but modern cuisine is somewhat more refined

Traditional Czech food is heavy. You could certainly sell thick goulash and dumplings (*guláš* a *knedlíky*) as the perfect base for a night's drinking. You could tempt a hungry traveller with a plate of pork steak, sauerkraut and dumplings (*Vepro knedlo zelo*). And the absolutely ravenous could easily fill themselves up on a three pound joint of pork knee (*Veprové koleno*). But you could never describe any of these typical Czech meals as refined. Tasty and filling certainly. But health food it is not.

For various reasons the Czechs have been described as the Germans of the Slavic world. After a brief glance down a typical menu it is easy to see why. The traveller coming in from Munich or Vienna will encounter much that is familiar. Apart from the recipes mentioned above, sausage (*klobása*) with mustard is on almost every pub menu as is pork schnitzel (*smaený veprový rízek*) with a slice of lemon, a range of heavy and smelly cheeses (*Olomoucké syrecky* are the most pungent) and strudel (spelt the same way).

It is much more appetising than it sounds, especially if you bear in mind that the most common venue for eating it is the pub (*Hospoda* or *Hostinec*). Czech food is designed to support the beer you will consume before, during and after you have eaten it. And after you have tasted the beer, you will understand why (see below).

Having spent more than 40 years in virtual isolation from western influences, it is perhaps unsurprising that culinary traditions have remained strong. And they still dominate. But the first decade after the end of communism has witnessed a flowering of restaurants offering dishes from around the world. Chinese restaurants were among the first to make an impression, although many Westerners still find it extraordinary that prices, for what in their countries counts as good

value food, are relatively high. Italian restaurants and pizza places, many of excellent quality, are now almost as common as in the major cities back home. French, Indian and Lebanese food have all made an entrance.

For vegetarians the situation has improved dramatically, although almost any change from

the early days would count as dramatic. It is still possible to find menus offering fried cheese (*smažený sýr*) with ham in the middle under the section headed "vegetarian" (*bezmasé jídla* or *vegetariánské*). But salad bars, though few in number, are making their presence felt.

Home cooking

Barely has the guest's coat been hung by the door, shoes kicked off to be replaced by slippers, as is the custom, than the host will have a plate of home-baked cakes (*zákusky, koláce* and *buchty*) on the living room table. Hospitality comes naturally and is offered freely. Since most Czechs have a country retreat, which may

Prague's Coffee Houses

Praguers these days don't seem to have the time in their fast-moving lives to while away their days in the city's venerable cafes, that great institution of the interwar First Republic. At one time Prague cafe society was equal to that of Paris and Vienna. Many of the most storied cafes frequented by their forebears have faded into history – gone, for example, are the National and the Arco, the meeting place of the "Arconauts",

who included Franz Kafka, Max Brod, Franz Werfel and others. But some of Prague's other illustrious cafes are still humming with a vibrant mix that includes students, entrepreneurs with their mobile phones, ladies of a certain age, and the inevitable tourists from all over the world.

Several of the city's time-honoured coffee houses (kavárny) have been given a facelift in recent years, and cafe society seems to be making a gradual comeback.

The Malostranská kavárna underwent renovation in 1997, and the famed Café Slavia re-opened with much fanfare in November the same year. Once filled in its heyday with poets, painters and actors from the National Theatre across the street,

the Slavia today still gets an occasional visit from one-time habitué and the current Czech president, Václav Havel.

Prague's coffee houses are excellent places for people-watching, and an afternoon can be pleasantly spent observing the comings and goings from a windowside table while sipping a cup of espresso or glass of herbaceous Becherovka, the national liqueur.

Coffee is usually drunk black, although a Viennese variation, topped with whipped cream, is also popular and tourists have brought with them the cappuccino. In these cafes the staff won't mind if you spend half the afternoon nursing a single cup of coffee while you write in your journal or glance through the newspapers or magazines made available to customers. You can also nibble a pastry as an accompaniment or indulge in a light meal, or occasionally something more substantial, at most of these venues.

Most of the best cafes are ideally situated on lively pedestrian thoroughfares, and are a great place to escape from the bustle and just sit back and unwind. They often feature sumptuous interiors that can quickly sweep you back to an earlier era when cafes were the nexus of Prague social life. A good place to start might be at the cafe in Obecní dům, whose art nouveau splendour was lovingly restored to great acclaim in the late 1990s. Or try the cafe in the Hotel Evropa on Wenceslas Square, with its still sumptuous, though slightly faded art nouveau interior.

In cafes such as the Slavia or the Café Louvre on Národní třída you are likely to find waiters and waitresses who take great pride in their profession, dressed smartly in bow-ties and crisp white aprons. Another good bet for its elegant setting is the Café Savoy, set back from Vitězná near the Legions' Bridge, an airy and genteel space decorated with restored murals.

A few of Prague's cafes are attempting to resurrect the traditional connection between coffee houses and literature. The Literární kavárna G + G in the Vinohrady neighbourhood, which is connected with a publisher of the same name, hosts regular poetry readings in Czech and English for the clientele, as well as music recitals. And the expat-owned Globe Bookstore and Coffeehouse occasionally organises readings by some of the big names among Czech and English-language writers passing through Prague. ❏

LEFT: cafés were once the nexus of Prague social life.

double as the home of the grandparents, the real treats will come if you get an invitation to stay for the weekend. But broadly speaking, the fare offered on the pub menu is typical of the kind of food Czechs eat at home. Simple and often heavy it may be, but it will also often be home grown or, in the case of mushrooms, picked from a neighbouring forest.

Czech eating habits are informal. There is none of the stuffiness that marks many a middle-class English or American dinner party. Bottles of beer will litter the table. The young son or daughter may have gone down to a local pub to fill up a household jug with draught beer. Garlic soup *(cesneková polévka)* is a common and delicious starter. A main course – pork, beef, chicken but rarely lamb – will often be served up with a variety of the ubiquitous dumplings, normally based on either bread or potatoes. And cakes will almost always be offered for dessert.

One particularly surprising aspect of Czech cuisine is the Christmas dinner, fried breaded carp pieces with potato salad. The carp may not be to everyone's liking, but the home-made potato salad – often cubes of boiled potato mixed with eggs, cucumber and a generous helping of mayonnaise – is a treat in itself.

Bring on the beers

If you don't know before you arrive why the Czechs are the world's biggest per capita beer consumers, it will take you little time to find out when you are there. There are some hidden treasures, but broadly speaking the best Czech beers are the most famous – Pilsner and Budvar. Nevertheless, the Czechs take a real pride in their beer and there is a vast difference between the quality of draught beer served up in the local pub and the imported, bottled variations available in the supermarkets of the West.

Czech beer is brought directly to your table by the waiter. Going up to the bar will normally be greeted with incomprehension or, alternatively, an angry stare indicating that you are getting in the way of the very serious business of serving up the locals with their favourite brew. In many lower class establishments the waiter will already be hovering. Sign language – usually a raised thumb – will sometimes be

enough to make your intentions clear. Normally, the waiter will come to your table. The word for beer is *pivo* (the same word is used in all Slavic-speaking countries) but the English word will almost always be understood. When you get your beer the waiter will mark the quantity ordered with pen strokes – one for each beer – on a white strip of paper. When it is time to pay up, the lines will be totted up and a sum will be written at the bottom. It is usual to leave a small tip, often rounding up to the nearest five or 10 crowns but more (10 percent) if you have eaten or you are in a higher-class establishment.

RIGHT: catching carp for a traditional Christmas meal on Wenceslas Square in Prague.

Czechs take beer seriously (there is even a prayer devoted to it) and there is a simple ritual which should be followed if you intend to respect national traditions. The first point to note is that Czechs always say cheers *(na zdravi)* and clink their glasses before starting a new pint. It is also considered a mark of sincerity to make eye contact in the process. The worst thing you can do is to pour the remainder of a nearly finished beer into a fresh one, something like the equivalent of eating off a stranger's plate in Czech eyes.

FRIENDLY FOG

The anti-smoking brigade that has captured most of the Western world has not reached the Czech and Slovak Republics yet. Be warned: pubs are thick with cigarette and cigar smoke.

Further guidance on beer is not really necessary because it is almost impossible to travel anywhere in the Czech Republic without encountering the possibility of drinking it. Beer is not the only libation on offer of course. South Moravia supplies the country with vast quantities of cheap and often quite drinkable red and white wines. The whites are the best bets, particularly the Riesling and Tramín varieties which are available in most restaurants. South Moravia is also famed for its plum brandy *(slivovice)*. But before you leave you must sample a glass of the country's national liqueur, Becherovka. This yellow green spirit is a joy to behold. Hailing from the spa town of Karlovy Vary, Becherovka is made from a secret recipe rumoured to comprise dozens of herbs and almost certainly made from local spring water.

Slovak food

If you make the trip down to Slovakia, and it is well worth it, you will find many of the same traditions as in the Czech lands. Dumplings are a little less common, hot peppers are a little more prevalent. Until 1918, the Slovaks endured almost a thousand years of Hungarian domination.

The legacy is evident in the food. Menus will often include Halászlé, superb Hungarian freshwater fish soup and meat stuffed paprika *(plnená paprika)*. Home cooking is similar to the Czechs and the Slovaks are, if anything, even more hospitable. The Slovak national dish, especially common in the mountains, is called *Halušky*. It is a gooey, hot, porridge-like mush made up of flour, potatoes and water often covered with a sprinkling of bacon. It is far better than it sounds but don't expect to lose weight if you eat lots of it.

Wine, slivovice and vodka

Unlike the Czech Republic, Slovak drinking culture is not dominated by beer. The climate affords greater opportunities for wine growers and the Tokaj, which comes from the Slovak-Hungarian villages of the east, is truly world-class. But the Slovaks are famed for the hard liqueurs, especially the home-made versions, which, though strong, will often be of higher quality than those available in the shops. Slivovice is the most widely drunk. Borovicka, a kind of aromatic gin, is a treat which may well be thrust upon you whether you like it or not.

Vodka is drunk, too, and most bars serve rum, whisky and the other most widely drunk international spirits. The selection of foreign food outlets is far more limited than in Prague although Greek, Italian, French and Chinese restaurants have all sprung up in recent years. Part of the reason for the lack of international variety is, simply, that Slovakia remains a largely undiscovered country by tourists. That, however, is a big part of its charm. ❑

LEFT: Czechs are big beer drinkers.
RIGHT: enjoying the sunshine at a street café.

MUSIC

The Czechs have a fine tradition of classical music which can be sampled at the many public recitals in Prague

Smetana, Dvořák, Janáček: whenever anyone mentions Czech music, the names of the Big Three are uttered in a single breath. Smetana gave the world the most frequently performed Czech opera, *The Bartered Bride*, as well as celebrating the countryside and history of his native land in his music cycle *Má Vlast (My Fatherland)*. Dvořák, on the other hand, was a master of the symphony, chamber music and oratorio; his compositions were rapturously received at home and abroad. Janáček took up the aims of Smetana and Dvořák and developed his own theory of the "speech melody", according to which the melodic form followed the tone patterns of speech. Janáček elevated this stylisation of speech melodies to one of the fundamentals of composition in his operas.

Early Czech music

Compared with that of its neighbours, music in the Czech lands developed relatively late, although the beginnings of an independent musical tradition reach back to the Middle Ages. During the period of the Greater Moravian Kingdom, mass was celebrated in Slavic, not in Latin, and the Hussite Chorale influenced considerably the hymns of the German Reformation. During the baroque era the attempts at national assertion were nipped in the bud, and many musicians found themselves with no alternative but to leave and settle in another country. Among them was Johann Wenzel Stamitz, who composed at the court of the Elector Karl Theodor in Mannheim. He is regarded as one of the leading exponents of musical classicism, especially the sonata.

Vienna, a city long favoured by the muses, attracted numerous Czech composers. The virtuoso violinist and conductor Pavel Vranický came to live here – he was to be chosen by

Beethoven to conduct the premiere of his First Symphony – as did Jan Leopold Koželuh who, for many years enjoyed a popularity equal to that of Mozart; and Jan Václav Hugo Voříček, the leading representative of Czech musical classicism in Vienna.

While Vienna was welcoming Czech com-

posers, Prague was enthusing over Mozart's *The Marriage of Figaro* and extending an invitation to its composer to visit their city. There he was commissioned to write an opera for the Nostitz Theatre (now the Estates Theatre). *Don Giovanni* premiered there in 1787 and Mozart became, and remained, Prague's most honoured adopted son.

Musical life in Bohemia was so rich that on his journey through the country in the late-18th century the English traveller Charles Burney christened it the "Conservatoire of Europe". This wealth of musical talent was largely due to the many minor musicians, mostly church cantors, who found inspiration in the simple folk

LEFT: music school for children with impaired sight in Prague.
RIGHT: Mozart loved Prague; here is his bust in the Villa Betramka.

songs of their land as well as in the virtuoso compositions of the Italian masters. The most important among them was Jan Jakub Ryba whose popular pastorale *Hej mistře! (The Bohemian Christmas)* is one of the most frequently performed compositions during the festive season.

Bedřich Smetana

Bedřich Smetana (1824–84) is the favourite composer of the Czech nation, although the works of his somewhat younger contemporary Dvořák are more frequently performed in inter-

PRAGUE FESTIVAL

The International Musical Festival, held in Prague between 12 May and 3 June, is a tradition that goes back more than 50 years.

national identity was being forged. While the Czech old guard imagined it would be a potpourri of traditional melodies, the avant-garde Smetana demanded a fully developed dramatic style which would do musical justice to the newly discovered melodic patterns of the Czech language. He was accordingly scorned by his opponents as a "Wagnerian" or a "Germaniser", almost the equivalent of being charged with high treason. And yet, Smetana was also granted a few happy hours in his musical life. In 1868, as the representa-

national concert halls. The careers of the two men were strangely linked.

When Dvořák first arrived in Prague, Smetana left the city to try his luck in Gothenburg for five years. By the time he returned, Dvořák had already completed his first compositions. And when Dvořák returned to the Bohemian capital at the peak of his popularity after a triumphant visit to England, Smetana had just been committed to the city's mental asylum, where he died shortly afterwards.

One of Smetana's biggest preoccupations was the development of an independent Czech popular opera, a matter which aroused great interest and debate, at a time when a sense of

tive of all Czech artists, he laid the foundation stone of the National Theatre. The same year he conducted the premiere of his dramatic opera *Dalibor*. Though initially well received, the new work was performed only a few times and was not rediscovered until after the composer's death.

When the National Theatre finally opened in 1883, Smetana's opera *Libuše* was the first work to be performed there. Based on the legend of Princess Libuše, who inspired the foundation of Prague, it was a suitably stirring subject. After a catastrophic first performance in 1866, Smetana's opera *The Bartered Bride* soon won the hearts of the Czech populace. It did not achieve an international breakthrough until after the composer's death, following a brilliant guest performance by the newly-formed Czech National Theatre in Vienna in 1892. Smetana had a far higher opinion of *Dalibor* than of his infinitely more successful comic opera. On the 100th performance of *The Bartered Bride* in May 1882, he said: "*The Bartered Bride* is really only a piece of nonsense which I allowed myself at the time. I composed it not out of ambition but in a spirit of contrariness, because after my *Brandenburgs* they all accused me of being a Wagnerian incapable of composing anything in the lighter national idiom."

about the premiere of Dvořák's opera *Rusalka*, the ardent Smetana fan Zdeněk Nejedlý said: "Since we allow no other form of lyrical drama than musical drama, we must judge *Rusalka* to be flawed in its very inception, a failure." Nejedlý later became Minister of Culture and was largely responsible for the reaction against Dvořák's work in the 1950s.

Dvořák's success abroad was all the more controversial. He attracted musical fame beyond the boundaries of his native land, something Smetana was denied throughout his life. Dvořák's first triumph was in London, where his *Stabat Mater* was rapturously received, fol-

Antonín Dvořák

Antonín Dvořák (1841–1904), the butcher's apprentice and self-styled "simple Czech musician", initially played second viola in.Smetana's orchestra in Prague. He revered the older composer; the latter in his turn tried to support Dvořák's work as a composer. All the more incomprehensible to outsiders, therefore, was the conflict between the supporters of Smetana and Dvořák, which reached its climax in 1912 and left traces which are still evident today. Writing

LEFT: a brass band in Mariánské Lázně (Marienbad).
ABOVE: an open-air concert in the Old Town Square in Prague.

lowed by New York, Berlin, Vienna and Budapest. He was helped in this by his older friend and patron Johannes Brahms, who not only invited Dvořák and his entire family to Vienna at his own expense, but also established his first contact with the Leipzig publisher Simrock and added a number of necessary corrections to the scores.

It was Dvořák's international reputation that brought him in 1891 the offer of directorship of the New York Conservatory. The three years which he spent in America resulted in his most popular orchestral score, *Symphony No. 9, From the New World*, the one most widely played on a worldwide basis. Its premiere in the Carnegie Hall in New York in 1893 was a runaway success. Dvořák wrote home: "The success of my symphony on 15 and 16 December was magnificent: the newspapers maintain that no other composer had ever enjoyed such a moment of triumph."

Critics emphasised the "American accent" of the themes. In this new work the Czech composer set an important trend for the development of an independent American national musical tradition. At the same time he helped the new music of his own country achieve world recognition. Like Smetana, Dvořák rejected a direct transcription of folk melodies.

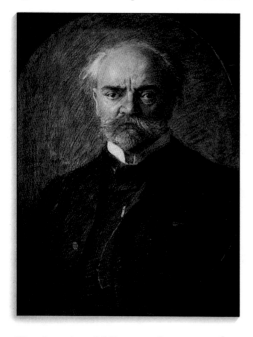

His adaptation of folk songs always resulted in a completely new setting of the works. His cycle *Music from Moravia* (1875), which paved the way for his international recognition, demonstrates a sensitivity bordering on genius in his interpretation of Moravian folklore. The piano accompaniment is simple but often contains surprisingly sophisticated harmonic progressions which provide a perfect translation of the poetic lyrics.

Unlike the city-dweller Smetana, who was only driven to the country by the poverty of old age, Dvořák was a country-dweller who never felt quite at home in the city. While working in New York he remained, like his peasant fore-

bears, an early riser. He did not go out after 6pm and spent his evenings playing cards with the family. During an entire year he visited the Metropolitan Opera only twice. Dvořák was always happiest at Vysoká, his country estate.

Dvořák left for posterity an impressive collection of compositions: 31 works of chamber music, 14 string quartets, 50 orchestral works and nine symphonies, including such works as the *Slavonic Dances*, whose wealth of catchy melodies has caused them to be condemned as merely light music by some composers, rather like Smetana's *Vltava (The Moldau)*.

Modern music

The distinguished musical tradition of Czechoslovakia did not end with the dawn of the 20th century. Leos Janácek (1854–1928) proved a worthy successor to Smetana and Dvořák. He composed, amongst other works, the world-famous operas *Jenůfa, The Cunning Little Vixen*, and *Katja Kabanová*. Janáček was searching for new forms of expression, for a personal musical language, but he also intended his music to relay a message of common humanity, a proclamation of his humanistic ideal. Janáček founded the College of Music in Brno, and the annual autumn festival of classical and contemporary music focuses on his work.

Bohuslav Martinů, who lived in the US from 1940, also has a place in the country's modern musical history. Artistically speaking Martinů was an all-round genius who understood Impressionism as well as jazz. He was one of the first composers to incorporate elements of the latter in his works. His 400-plus compositions covered a remarkable range, comparable only with that of Mozart. He had a talent for mixing classical elements with avant-garde features to produce a completely new synthesis of sound. Two of his highly imaginative works, the ballet *Špalíček* and the opera *Juliette,* are still performed regularly today.

Music continues to play an important role in the lives of Czech and Slovak people and there is a lively tradition of street music. In Prague there are performances at the State Opera House, concerts in the Rudolfinum, open-air summer concerts and the internationally famous Prague Spring Music Festival. ❏

LEFT: Antonín Dvořák was inspired by America to compose his ninth symphony, *From the New World.*

Smetana's Moldau

From the Smetana Promenade on the right bank of the Vltava (Moldau), Prague presents itself to the visitor from its most attractive angle: the graceful masonry of the Charles Bridge spans the gleaming silver ribbon of water in front of the picturesque panorama of the churches and palaces of the Lesser Quarter, above which tower the massive bulk of the Castle and the Cathedral of St Vitus.

Today the Smetana Museum is housed in what used to be the municipal waterworks, near the former mills of the Old Town, a building complex which extends into the river itself. It is maintained by the Smetana Society, founded in Prague in 1931, and contains the composer's manuscripts and sponsors the publication and performance of his works. Smetana loved to walk along the banks of the Vltava. He repeatedly found new ideas and inspiration for his compositions.

A friend of his, Josef Srb-Debrnov, remembered: "Most of the enchantingly emotional melodies in *The Bartered Bride* owe their creation to the evening moods on the Moldau Promenade opposite Hradčany Castle and the Lesser Quarter. The maestro would take a walk by the river here at dusk virtually every day, reading as he did the text sent to him piece by piece by Sabina, his librettist. The melodies flowed through his brain like a torrent. Returning to his apartment in the Palais Lazansky, he would sit down at his desk and make rough notes on manuscript paper of the ideas he had already worked out in his mind."

By the time he started to compose a grandiose musical monument to his beloved Vltava, Smetana was no longer able to enjoy his nightly walks along its banks. A rapidly worsening affliction of the hearing tract prevented him from listening to the river's song. Impoverished and derided by resentful critics, he was ultimately forced to seek refuge in the country, in the hunting lodge of his son-in-law.

When *The Moldau* was given its concert premiere on 4 April 1875, the audience was ecstatic, but the composer himself was unable to hear a single tone. He had become completely deaf whilst working on the score. *The Moldau* is the best-known and most frequently performed movement of the orchestral cycle *Má Vlast (My Fatherland)*, in which Smetana's love of his Bohemian homeland

and its people finds its most eloquent expression.

The inspiration for the entire cycle, which Smetana wrote between 1874 and 1879, grew gradually over a period of many years. It is maintained that Smetana's earliest ideas about the subject started to crystalise some 20 years before the work was first performed. The programme of the six cycles was sketched by Smetana himself: *Vyšehrad* tells of the heroic fights of the knights of old; in *The Moldau* the listener follows the river along its course from its source to the Vyšehrad Castle in Prague (the main theme is played by two oboes, symbolising the mountain springs, and repeated in rondo form in ever-changing variations

before ending in a hymn-like E major passage). *Šárka* conjures up a Bohemian myth with an Amazonian love story dominated by a stormy orchestral symphonic section; *From Bohemia's Meadows and Forests* is a succession of folkloric portraits, with peasants dancing the polka and airs played on the horn, recalling traditional melodies.

Tábor recalls the tragic-heroic fate of the Hussites, whilst *Blaník* provides an optimistic final note to the entire cycle, echoing the hope that the warriors of the Lord will return victorious when the people's need is greatest. Non-Czechs sometimes have difficulties with the patriotic symbolism of the two last cycles, but few will fail to feel to the powerful emotions aroused by *The Moldau*. ❑

RIGHT: Bedřich Smetana is considered to be the Czech national composer.

LITERATURE

The Czech literary tradition is rich and internationally respected,
boasting writers such as Franz Kafka and Milan Kundera

When anyone mentions Czech literature, most people tend to think in the first instance of *The Good Soldier Schweik*, the eponymous hero of the world-famous novel by Jaroslav Hašek who is often thought to represent the Czech national character. Václav Havel is well-known as a politician, but how many people can say they have read his dramas and diaries?

The origins of the literary tradition in the lands of the Bohemian crown stretch back as far as the 9th century. Seeing his kingdom of Greater Moravia threatened by the Franks, and as a kind of cultural offensive against the growing influence from the West, Prince Ratislav summoned the Slavic apostles from Byzantium.

The learned brothers Cyril and Methodius who arrived in 863 invented the Glagolitic alphabet, based on the Slavonic dialect used in the area surrounding their native town, Salonika, and which was the foundation of the Old Slavonic language. The first book to be written in Old Slavonic was probably the Bible, but other Old Slavonic texts that can be assigned to this era are the 10th-century *Legends* about St Wenceslas (the Bohemian Prince Václav). The Old Slavonic language ceased to be used when Latin was introduced as the liturgical language of the country at the end of the 11th century. Cyril is also credited with inventing the Cyrillic alphabet, although this may have been the work of his followers.

The historic foundations of Czech literature lie in the *Bohemian Chronicles*, the work of the Deacon Cosmas (died 1125). The Latin chronicle recounts the history of the land from the legendary times of the founding father, Čech, until the beginning of the 12th century. In the courts of the Přemyslid kings, encouragement was given to German literature, and the earliest preserved texts in Czech were only written in

the latter part of the 13th century. During the reign of Charles IV (1347–78) learning and literature flourished in both German and Czech.

In the 15th century, the social and moral questions addressed by the Hussite Movement gave rise to a great deal of writing in the vernacular, in the form of treatises and hymns.

Hus's own importance for Czech literature lay not only in his vernacular sermons and his letters; he also set about the reform of Czech orthography, which he laid out in the treatise *De orthographia Bohemica*.

One of the outstanding personalities in Czech literary history was the humanist Jan Amos Komenský (1592–1670), generally known by his Latin name Comenius. He was a teacher, writer and theologian whose influence spread across many countries. The son of Protestant parents, he studied in Heidelberg and became a preacher in the Community of Bohemian Brethren in 1616. He endeavoured to improve the lot of man (in preparation for the kingdom

LEFT: Jan Amos Komenský (Comenius; 1592–1670) was one of the most important scholars of his time.
RIGHT: Jan Neruda, the famous Prague storyteller of the 19th century.

of heaven) through his reform of the educational system. Piety, virtue and learning were the cornerstones of his philosophy. His most famous work, *Orbis Sensualium Pictus* (*The World in Pictures*, 1654), was for many years the most widely used textbook in Germany.

The reforms of Emperor Joseph II, in particular the abolition of serfdom, prompted a period of national revival which marked the beginning of a new phase in Czech literature. The philologist and historian Josef Dobrovský, together with Josef Jungmann, produced philological works documenting the history of the language as well as a two-volume German–Czech dictionary. *May*

tures of Old Prague, a collection of short stories and imaginative pieces, transport the reader to late 19th-century Prague. The famous Chilean writer Pablo Neruda, the Nobel Laureate of 1971, adopted the surname as a mark of admiration and respect.

At the turn of the 20th century the classics of international literature dominated the literary scene. Numerous translations of literary works from other parts of the world, not least the German classics, helped to raise the general level of education to a higher rung and simultaneously paved the way for the integration of Czech into the broader European literary con-

(1836), the epic poem by the Romantic poet Karel Hynek Mácha, is regarded as one of the milestones in modern Czech poetry. Outstanding men of letters of this period, which reached its zenith in 1848, included the prose writer Božena Němcová, publicist and poet Karel Havlíček and dramatists Josef Kajetán Tyl and Václav Kliment Klicpera.

The transition from romanticism to realism was marked by Božena Němcová's novel *The Grandmother*, published in 1855. The Prague writer Jan Neruda (1834–91) achieved fame as the author of the *Tales of the Lesser Quarter* (1878), a collection of novellas and humorous, reflective sketches from the Malá Strana. *Pic-*

text. In those days a knowledge of German was *sine qua non* in Bohemia, so many readers were able to claim first-hand knowledge of the works in question.

Prague as a literary centre

The Golden City on the Vltava was a centre of literary talent at many points in its history. At the beginning of this century, German and Czech enjoyed equal status as literary languages. A bohemian society similar to that of Paris established itself in the capital, gathering in coffee houses such as the legendary *Café Arco*.

The Bohemian capital, moreover, had traditionally enjoyed a special position in European culture. Apart from the resident Czechs and Germans, a significant Jewish community had evolved, which also made an important contribution to literary history. It is possible that some natives of Prague, such as Max Brod (who published the work of Franz Kafka against the latter's will), or Franz Werfel, are still underestimated today. But even during his lifetime and despite his own uncertainties, there were a few who recognised Franz Kafka as a great writer. Kafka (1883–1924) was almost an exact contemporary of the perennially

THE GOOD SOLDIER

Humourist and satirist Jaroslav Hašek's main work, *The Good Soldier* is still the best known work in the Czech langauge.

"scribblings" after hours as his "only desire". His prose has turned Prague into a major literary landmark. Although Kafka's diaries and letters fill over 3,000 pages, for many years little was known about his life. This had less to do with his own desire for privacy than with the political upheavals and repression – first the German occupation, then the communist regime – which prevented his work from being made public. In 1931, the Gestapo confiscated a large number of Kafka's manuscripts and these must be regarded as lost.

popular humourist and satirist Jaroslav Hašek (1883–1923), whose main work, *The Good Soldier Schweik*, is still the best-known book in the Czech language.

Franz Kafka, a German-speaking Jew, was born on 3 July 1883 in Prague. He seldom left his native city and at the end of his short life was buried there, in the Straschnitz Cemetery. For 14 years Kafka worked as a legal clerk at the Workers' Accident Insurance Institution of the Kingdom of Bohemia, but he regarded his

FAR LEFT: Franz Kafka and his fiancée, Felice Bauer.
LEFT: Franz Kafka memorial in Prague.
ABOVE: President Masaryk meeting Karel Čapek.

The first Czech translations of his writings did not appear until 1957. Most of the Prague houses Kafka lived in are still standing, including two which have since become small museums: one in the Old Town Square, beside St Nicholas' Church, and his sister's house in Golden Lane.

In contrast to some of Prague's other German-speaking writers, Kafka actively sought contact with the Czech population and demonstrated openly his sympathy for the socialist cause; in later years he supported the idea of a socially-oriented Zionism. Kafka's work remains controversial and the interpretations of his message are legion. In his posthumously

Jaroslav Hašek

Like his contemporary Franz Kafka, Jaroslav Hašek, who was born on 30 April 1883, lived to be just 40 years old. Hašek worked as a bank clerk, but by the age of 17 he had begun to write his first satirical articles for local newspapers. By the time he was 21, he had become the editor of a number of anarchist publications. Drafted into the Austro-Hungarian Army, Hašek allowed himself to be captured by the Russians during World War I. While in Russia he joined the Czech liberation army, but then fell into the ranks

of the Bolsheviks, for whom he wrote communist propaganda. Returning to Prague, he devoted himself to writing. His world-famous novel *The Good Soldier Schweik*, a masterful and wonderfully humorous satire on military life, was published in 1921. Brought to the attention of the international public by the Austrian writer Max Brod, it first appeared in English in 1930.

Hašek was a compulsive and accomplished hoaxer and practical joker who hated pomposity and authority. In many ways, the story of Schweik, a scrounger, liar and undisciplined drunkard, largely reflects Hašek's own eventful life, which ended in a haze of alcoholic apathy (he often only wrote in order to pay his drinking debts). Hašek drew a great deal of inspiration from the world of Prague taverns, where he noted down many a beery truism for use in his works.

Particularly famous is the scene in *The Good Soldier Schweik* where Schweik says to his fellow soldiers: "When the war is over you'll see me in my cups in the Chalice again." It guaranteed immortality for the tavern U Kalicha (The Chalice) and provided Prague with a meeting place for locals and visitors hoping to find wit and literary conversation. The venerable Chalice ("with blackened oak panelling and brass hinges on the bar") also formed the central stage in Berthold Brecht's comedy *Schweik in World War II*.

Readers the world over have laughed at the sly dog trader who took advantage of World War I to gain personal freedom "through idiotic senselessness and a clown's mask". Literary critics never tire of pointing out that the hero is not a prototype, to be found anywhere at any time. Schweik is the product of a highly specific milieu and a particular period – that of the Austria of the last century. That is why he has become living history.

F. E. Weiskopf, who lived in Prague at the same time as Hašek, insists that Schweik is an "historical" rather than a fictional character: "He could only arise in that period of narrow-mindedness, carelessness, good-natured treachery, anachronistic absolutism and national suppression which characterised the Danube monarchy of those days. He could only become the laughable, foolishly artful hero he was in wartime, in this era in which the rotten carcass of state lay in its death throes. And ultimately it was the mischievous, fatalistic sabotage of a Schweik which destroyed the state itself."

The combination in Schweik's character of genuine and feigned denseness, of the apathy and submissiveness of the little man, with artful cunning, slyness and cynicism, was rejected by Czech intellectuals as being damaging to the national idea of what it meant to be Czech.

Brecht, on the other hand, maintains that it is not the little man himself who is to blame, but the circumstances in which he lived. In his play, the chorus insists that:

The times are changing.
The grandiose plans of the powerful
are coming at last to a halt.
And they will walk on like bloody fighting cocks.
The times are changing.
And no force can alter the fact. ❑

LEFT: a depiction of *The Good Soldier Schweik*.

published novels *The Trial* and *The Castle* he expresses the fears and alienation of 20th-century man by means of his dream-like visions. Of paramount importance in his imagination was a life-long struggle with the dominant figure of his father as well as the perpetual conflict inherent in his relationship with women, in particular Felice Bauer and Julie Wohryzek, both of whom were at one stage engaged to be married to him, as well as Milena Jesenská and Dora Dymant, with whom he spent the last year of his life in Berlin.

Norbert Fried, a German Jew, commented on the themes that preoccupied the authors of Prague: "The German-speaking authors of Prague often took as subject matter the dark events of the time, bringing to life the split personalities. Whether they were Jews or not, they turned their attention to the Golem and other legends and to the teachings of Rabbi Löw, or they wrote about the mysterious cabinet of curiosities of Rudolf II. During the 1920s the Jews probably sensed the dreadful fate which would befall them in 1938, whilst the non-Jews had a premonition of what they would face in 1945. Those who wrote in Czech, on the other hand, saw Prague only as the Golden City or the Matička ('Little Mother')." But Franz Kafka remarked that "The little mother has claws…!"

The independence years

The foundation of the independent Czechoslovak Republic in 1918 opened up new perspectives for the country's writers. Some of the greatest achievements of Czech literature date from the 1920s. Among them are the satirical plays of Karel Čapek, the son of a country doctor, who was a friend of the new republic's first president, T.G. Masaryk. Čapek's best works describe the problems of a centrally organised machine age. His play *RUR*, first performed in 1921, invented the word "robot", which has passed into international usage. The plot deals with the construction of a mechanical man which eventually overthrew its masters.

Also writing at this time was Jaroslav Seifert, who many years later, in 1984, was to become the first Czech writer to be awarded the Nobel Prize for Literature. Seifert was also a journalist and had been publishing poems since 1920. Until 1929 he was a supporter of the commu-

nists, but later became an ardent opponent of Stalinism. Egon Erwin Kisch, a contemporary of Kafka, and like him a native of Prague, was the author of works of social criticism. He has gone down in literary history as the roving reporter, the title of his most famous work. Kisch travelled widely, fighting for the Republicans in the Spanish Civil War and writing about China, Australia and Mexico. He returned to Prague in 1945 and died in 1948.

The German occupation interrupted the history of Czech literature, although the works of Václav Řezáč did break new ground in the genre of the psychological novel. After the

communist takeover in February 1948, Řezáč, like many of his contemporaries, declared his support for "socialist realism".

Until the beginning of the 1960s no works of any great significance were produced. Then political control relaxed slightly, and literature blossomed with the novels of Josef Škvorecký, Milan Kundera and Ludvík Vaculík, the short stories of Ivan Klíma, Bohumil Hrabal and Arnošt Lustig and the plays of Václav Havel. Klíma's collection of short stories, *My Merry Mornings,* is a wonderful evocation of life in Prague. Many of these works are now available in several languages. For 20 years after the repression of the Prague Spring in 1968, three

RIGHT: Egon Erwin Kisch, the "roving reporter".

distinct literary traditions existed side by side: the "official" authors who were allowed to publish their works with the approval of the state and the party; the literature of Czech exiles, which had difficulty finding a new international audience; and the native *Samizdat*, the works of writers who continued to live in Czechoslovakia but whose writings were banned. Only small numbers of their books were printed and these relied on hand to hand distribution.

Perhaps the most successful of the exiled Czech authors was the prose writer Milan Kundera. Born in 1929, Kundera worked at the Prague Institute for Cinematographic Studies

until the Soviet invasion of 1968. He subsequently lost his job, and his biting satirical novel on Stalinism, *The Joke,* was banned. He now lives in Paris, where he wrote his most famous work, *The Unbearable Lightness of Being.*

Pavel Kohout also played an active role in the reform movement of 1968. In company with many others he was forced to take cover during the next decade; after signing the Charter 77 demanding basic human rights he was driven into exile. His *Diary of a Counter-Revolutionary* describes clearly the determination of many artists not to give way in the face of wrong. Josef Škvorecký is another exiled writer who deserves mention. He went to Can-

ada where he distinguished himself by founding 68 Publishers, which published the works of exiled authors, and wrote, among many other novels, *The Engineer of Human Souls,* which satirises the police state.

The most famous of all the writers banned after the failed Prague Spring of 1968 was the dramatist Václav Havel – also one of the first signatories of the Charter 77. Like many of his contemporaries, Havel was imprisoned on occasions, and censorship forced him to do manual work to earn a living, but he continued to write. Until his death in February 1997, Bohumil Hrabal was widely regarded as the greatest Czech writer of his generation. His best known work, *Closely Observed Trains,* was made into an Oscar-winning film in 1967.

Slovak literature

The literature of Slovakia was closely interwoven with that of the Czechs until an independent language developed from the Slovakian dialects. After the disintegration of the kingdom of Greater Moravia, Slovakia became part of Hungary for a thousand years. As a result, its literature has strong Latin and Hungarian influences.

The most important names in Slovak literature before the creation of the Czechoslovak Republic in 1918 were the national revolutionary, writer and politician Ľudovít Štúr (1815–56), who is credited with creating the literary Slovak language; and the poet Pavol Orságh Hviezdoslav (1849–1921), who also gained fame as a skilled translator. After 1918, conditions for the development of an independent Slovakian literature improved dramatically, and the newly acquired freedom was put to good use by a variety of literary trends, ranging from poetic symbolism to decidedly proletarian literature, and categorised by the all-enveloping term "Slovak Modern".

The most important group of writers advocating social revolution, including the influential Laco Novomeský, established itself around the newspaper *Dav* (Mass) whose socialist realism after 1948 became the official doctrine. It remains to be seen how Slovak literature will develop, but those interested in international contemporary writing will watch with interest. ❏

LEFT: paperback cover for Milan Kundera's novel *The Unbearable Lightness of Being.*
RIGHT: plaque commemorating Jan Neruda in Prague.

JAN
NERUDA

ZDE ŽIL
A SVOJI
LITERÁRNÍ
ČINNOST
ZAPOČAL.

* 1834 ✝ 1891

—————

PÉČÍ SPOLKŮ
MENŠÍHO MĚSTA
PRAŽSKÉHO.

R. 1895.

THEATRE

Theatre is taken seriously in the Czech Republic. They even elected
a celebrated playwright, Václav Havel, as president

As long ago as the Middle Ages the Czechs could boast the beginnings of a national theatre in their native language, but its true roots lie in the period of national revival which began in the late 18th century. The first dramatic performance in Czech took place in Prague in 1771 – although the actors were German, and unable to pronounce the hitherto despised language properly. In a way it was the Theatre of the Absurd, long before the latter actually made its entrance in theatrical history.

At the end of the 18th century, the first major national play was the dramatisation of *Oldřich and Božena*, an 11th-century legend. Almost 200 years later, in 1967, the same plot was presented once more, brought up to date by František Hrubín. In 1781 Count Anton Nostitz, one of the city's leading figures, founded the Nostitz Theatre, a lovely, neo-classical building which is now called the Estates Theatre. It opened with *Emilia Galotti*, one of the best known works of Gotthold Lessing, a German dramatist who died that same year. The play, written some nine years earlier, is a tragedy with a strong social theme, which delighted the German-speaking upper classes.

Real stage history was written, however, with the first performance of Mozart's *Don Giovanni* (1787), which went on from here to conquer the opera houses of the world. Not always appreciated in his native Austria, Mozart had been received with open arms by the people of Prague, and is still regarded as a favoured adopted son, although he spent relatively short periods in the city.

Czech players briefly won permission to stage plays in their own language in the Nostitz Theatre, but soon were forced to move out to a little wooden theatre, called The Bouda, in the Horse Market (now Wenceslas Square). For the time being, the Nostitz was to remain the preserve of the wealthy, German-speaking citizens of Prague, although it was later to play a part in

the history of Czech nationalism. It was here, in 1834, that a musical comedy by Josef Kajetán Tyl (1801–56), entitled *Fidlovačka*, introduced the song "Where is my native land?" which became the Czech national anthem.

Two hundred years ago, ordinary people flocked in droves to the theatre and formed an

enthusiastic audience – thankful to be able to see a play written in their own language, even if it was in the humble little Bouda.

National theatre

This enthusiasm was the beginning of the Czech national passion for all things theatrical, which reached its architectural climax in the construction of the National Theatre, funded by public subscriptions. Opened in 1881, the building almost immediately burned down, and was promptly rebuilt, also with money raised from the willing public, so keen were the people of Prague to have a theatre to call their own. The magnificent building was designed by

---

LEFT: Milan Sládek performs *The Whale*.
RIGHT: theatre ticket touts in Prague.

Josef Zítek, and the rebuilding was largely the work of Josek Schulz, who also designed the National Museum.

The theatre was a symbol of nationalist aspirations and opened, appropriately, with a performance of Smetana's opera *Libuše,* based on the legend of the princess who married a humble farm-hand and inspired him to found the city of Prague and the Přemyslid dynasty.

The foundation of the first Czechoslovak Republic in 1918 saw a second upturn in the fortunes of the Czech and Slovak theatre. (The Slovakian National Theatre was founded in 1919: until then, only German and Hungarian

works had been performed in Bratislava's main theatre.) The most important dramatist of the time was undoubtedly Karel Čapek. His brother Josef, an outstanding caricaturist who is remembered for a series of drawings entitled *The Dictator's Boots,* which he created at the time when Hitler was in the ascendant, was also a prose writer, and was mostly responsible for the production of Karel's plays. Some of the most successful examples of their work are *The Insect Play, The White Illness* and *The Mother.* In his futuristic play *RUR,* which stands for Rossum's Universal Robots, Čapek first uses the word *robot* – one of the few Czech words to have entered the international vocabulary. The

robots in his play acquire human emotions and then rebel against their overbearing masters – a theme which would not have been popular under the Soviet regime several decades later.

The communist years

In the 1930s, it was the D-34 Ensemble, founded by Emil Frantisek Burian, and the aptly named Liberated Theatre (Osvobozené divadlo) which rejuvenated the Czech theatrical scene with their satirical and musical productions. The war years, under the German occupation, were a naturally dark time for the Czech theatre. Hopes of a bright new dawn when the war ended were soon dashed, as the communist regime favoured socialist realism above genuine artistic expression. During these years, however, a number of small theatres opened up in the capital, breathing fresh life into the musty atmosphere which prevailed.

Most important among them were the Divadlo Na zábradlí (Theatre by the Railings), Semafor, Rokoko, the Činoherní klub (The Actors' Club), and the Divadlo za branou (Theatre behind the Gate). They engendered a new spirit of optimism and excitement, but this was to be harshly crushed by the Soviet intervention during the Prague Spring of 1968.

The absurdity of the situation in which Czech theatre found itself during the past two decades was the fact that its most significant writers – Václav Havel and Pavel Kohout – were only able to arrange performances of their works abroad. When, in 1975, an amateur group in České Budějovice (Budweis) attempted to present one of Havel's plays, all the tickets were bought up by the local security police. The only people able to enjoy an evening of subversive drama were the local functionaries of the Communist Party.

Václav Havel

Havel began his theatrical career as an assistant stage manager at the ABC Theatre, before moving as a dramatist to what was to become his home base, the Theatre by the Railings. It had been founded in 1958 as the first small, alternative venue in Prague and quickly progressed to the position of one of the city's most respected experimental stages. Its artistic director, Jan Grossmann, presented productions by international dramatists such as Beckett, Ionesco, Arrabal, Jarry and Mrozek, thus paving the way for the Czech Theatre of the Absurd. In 1963, the theatre was the stage for the premiere of Havel's first full-length play, *The Garden Party*, which also established the author's international reputation. In 1965 the Theatre by the Railings presented a guest performance of the play – in Czech – in West Berlin. It was not long before it was being performed in theatres all over the world. The play represented an undisguised challenge to the socialist ideology of the time and made the authorities aware that both Havel

THEATRE TICKETS

Theatre ticket prices in Prague have risen recently, but are still very cheap compared to the West. Tickets are available from box offices or from ticket agencies.

Nobel Prize for literature) they formed their own highly subversive mime company. The dark humour and scruffy appearance of the three men led one newspaper to dub them "the three black beetles of Prague".

Hybner went on to found the Reduta Theatre, which opened a few months after the Soviet invasion in 1968. It became a focus of political protest but inevitably it was soon closed down. Hybner continued working in Prague when he could, and now runs the Studio Gag mime theatre.

and the Theatre by the Railings needed to be kept under observation.

Havel's most frequently performed play, a one-act work called *Audience*, was based on his own experiences when, forbidden by the regime to publish his plays, he was forced to earn his living in a brewery – one of many manual jobs which the writer, and many others in his position, took on during the years of censorship. While working at the Na zábradlí Havel met Boris Hybner, a young mime artist. Together with Bohumil Hrabal (later nominated for the

LEFT: performance of Smetana's *The Bartered Bride*.
ABOVE: theatre sign in Prague.

Hybner had been inspired by the popular mime artist, Ladislav Fialka, whose imagination and inimitable style influenced a whole generation and helped make Prague a world centre for this form of theatre.

Fringe theatre

The kind of avant-garde theatre presented by these "alternative" dramatists, actors and directors of the 1960s represented a risk to the communist regime, especially after 1968, when the social climate became noticeably colder. Ewald Schorm, a producer with an established reputation in the film world, was able to steer Na zábradlí through the cultural-political problems of the era by mixing a repertoire of classics (Strindberg, Beaumarchais, Jonson, Ostrovsky, Goethe, Ibsen) with contemporary plays (Hrabal, Albee, Steigerwald).

This helped prevent an enforced closure of the Czech fringe theatre, which was in everyone's interests: actors and dramatists could continue with their creative output, audiences could see high-quality, stimulating works, and the regime avoided the loss of face and reputation which a forcible closure of the fringe scene would have brought in its wake.

Now that the ghost of the Cold War has been exorcised, and the countries of Eastern Europe

have been opened up to the West, Czech theatre has entered a completely new era.

Modern theatre

The first step was a radical change in cultural policy and the break-up of the large theatrical companies, which were generously subsidised by the regime as long as they toed the party line. Many private theatrical enterprises are mushrooming, ranging in output from conventional musicals and operettas tailored to the taste of tourists to totally avant-garde productions which attract a smaller audience.

It is a time to search for new authors as well, for the failure of the old system has robbed

plays such as those by Václav Havel of their frame of reference, making them virtually unperformable. It is important for Czech theatre to decide now on a new subject matter. The future certainly looks very hopeful and bright. Prague has a number of small, forward-looking theatres including the Reduta and the Kolowrat. The Archa is dedicated to producing plays written by new, young Czech dramatists, while Czech and Slovak history and culture forms the basis of programmes put on by the Ungelt Theatre Club.

The established theatre, too, has a lot to offer. In 1991, after eight years of renovation, the Estates Theatre was reopened – naturally enough, to the strains of *Don Giovanni*. Its classical performances are a close second to those at the National Theatre, and its operatic performances rival those at the Prague State Opera. Also waiting to be rediscovered are important, long-neglected writers of the pre-war years. A step in this direction was taken by the little Ha Divadlo *(Ha Theatre)* in Brno, with a new production of *The Human Tragicomedy* by Ladislav Klima (1878–1928). Klima was an existentialist, whose work was regarded by the socialist authorities as a shocking example of bourgeois decadence. Only during the brief flowering of the Prague Spring were any of his plays performed. The development of the Ha Theatre itself is typical of many of the little avant-garde stages throughout the former Czechoslovakia, ample evidence that enthusiasm for the theatre is not confined to Prague. Founded in 1974 in Prostějov in the Hána (hence the name) as an experimental stage, it moved seven years later to Brno. It is a typical writers' theatre which produces its own scripts. It is a small venue which sees its role as a cultural centre and its programme includes music and poetry readings as well as drama.

Two typically Czech theatrical forms are black light theatre *(see opposite)* and puppet shows. Puppet theatre has a long tradition in Czech culture (the Charles University in Prague offers a degree course in puppeteering and theatre design) and is very popular. The most ingenious productions, such as *Orpheo and Euridice* or *Don Giovanni* (complete with baroque-style marionettes) are presented by the National Marionette Theatre. ❏

LEFT: puppet theatre performance.

Laterna Magika

Open any newspaper or listings magazine, read the posters plastered all over Prague and you will realise how important theatre is to people of this city. Prague is perhaps best known for its puppet performances but mime and a speciality, Laterna Magika, are top on the list of attractions for many tourists.

Under the socialist regime the theatre was regarded primarily as a service industry designed to provide the population with approved cultural entertainment. The authorities instituted a strict diet of dull traditional, realistic plays and conservative productions.

At the end of the 1950s, however, an experimental theatre group struck a completely new tone in Czech theatre. The ensemble – initially created by members of the National Theatre for the World Exhibition in Brussels, EXPO 58 – was known as the Laterna Magika. It aimed to present visitors to the Czech pavilion with a first-hand impression of life in the socialist republic, its art and its culture. Such was its success that the former cinema of the Adria Palace in Národní třída was placed at the troupe's disposal.

It has since moved to the Nová scéna, Národní 40, which now bears its name. Laterna Magika has played to full houses virtually non-stop ever since, and has become one of the main tourist attractions in Prague. No doubt one reason for its success is that no knowledge of Czech is necessary in order to follow the performance.

The quaintly old-fashioned name "Magic Lantern" has been retained. The troupe's performance is based on a cinematic projection procedure in which the actors on stage become directly involved. Through a skilled combination of projections, movable screens and stage props, the players move between light and darkness, uniting film and theatre, mime and dance into one extraordinary stage experience. The disparate sections never have an independent role, but work together as a synchronised whole.

At the centre of the spectacle is the visual impression, the dialogue between stage and screen. The protagonists work with additional screens, on to which films or slides are projected. The often confusing actions of the performers on various levels of the stage in combination with the ever-changing projections give the audience the feeling of being transported to a world in which the laws of time and place have lost their meaning. The traditional theatre genres, such as tragedy and comedy, are fused into a drama of light and shadow which has entranced countless audiences, and left its mark on the development of international drama.

The performances of the Laterna Magika are among the most original on offer in the Czech capital. Programmes such as *The Magic Circus*, *The Tales of Hoffmann*, *The Odyssey* or the ballet *Minotaurus*, choreographed after a libretto by Dürrenmatt, have lost none of their fascination over the

years. The founder of the Laterna Magika, producer Alfred Radok, suffered the same fate as many other artists and men of letters. In 1968 he was forced to flee the country. When he died in exile in Sweden in 1976, the media in his native country did not consider the fact worth mentioning.

As a theatre of illusion, Laterna Magika makes no attempt at a political statement, but it was nonetheless involved in the events of the Velvet Revolution. The Civic Forum established its first headquarters in the troupe's original theatre, and it was in the dressing room that Václav Havel wrote the appeal which ultimately forced Miloš Jakeš to resign from the office of General Secretary of the Communist Party. ❏

RIGHT: Laterna Magika, the "Magic Lantern", in full swing.

CZECH FILM

*The Czech film industry is known throughout the world for its creativity,
technical excellence and the talent of its actors and directors*

After the Velvet Revolution, the Czech film industry was supposed to die a painful death. Tinsel Town movies from Hollywood would smother all before them in a commercial tidal wave which the proud doyens of Prague cinema could not hope to resist. Hollywood has certainly made its mark. Arnold Schwarzenegger even came to Prague in the 1990s to open a branch of the Planet Hollywood restaurant chain of which he is a part owner. The top American actors are as well known in the Czech Republic as anywhere else in the world. But the doom merchants for home-grown Czech film-making have been proved wrong. The patient has conspicuously refused to die. Czech film is not only thriving at home but winning plaudits around the globe.

Talent and tradition

The high point since 1989 was undoubtedly Jan Svěrák's *Kolya*. The 1997 Oscar winner for best foreign film tells the story of a five-year-old Russian boy left with an ageing Czech cellist after a marriage of convenience goes horribly wrong. Witty, fatalistic, beautifully shot and with just enough commercial accessibility to give it a chance in the West, it brought new prominence to a national cinematic culture oozing with talent and tradition.

Film enthusiasts will be aware that Czech and Slovak cinema has made its mark before. First successes at the Oscars came in the 1960s with Jan Kadar and Elmar Klos's *Obchod na Korze* (*Shop on the High Street*) and Jiří Menzel's *Ostře Sledované Vlaky* (*Closely Observed Trains*).

The film industry, like the cultural life of the country generally, is dominated by the position of the Czech lands as a crossroads at the centre of Europe. Meshed in somewhat awkwardly between western democratic traditions and eastern absolutism, the national culture, whether

expressed through literature, theatre or cinema, is shot through with images of helplessness and isolation. Assertiveness gives way to passivity. Resignation takes the place of enthusiastic ambition. Perhaps this helps explain the success of *Kolya*. Kolya's mother, a Russian, uses the main character Louka, played by Zdeněk Svěrák

(the director's father) as a stepping stone to flee westwards to Germany. He, like his country, has been dumped on. There is nothing he can do but adapt himself to a fate he has not chosen but for which he is, nonetheless, now responsible. Prague offers images of external beauty while daily life abounds with quiet desperation.

One common theme which is not used widely in *Kolya* is the village life portrayed in Saša Gideon's debut movie *Indian Summer* and later in his Oscar-nominated *Return of the Idiot*. Described by the critics as one of the most original movies to come out of Central Europe for many years, *Return of the Idiot* echoes Dostoevsky's classic novel in which a simpleton

LEFT: a still from the film *Closely Observed Trains* by Jiří Menzel.
RIGHT: a scene from *Kolya*, awarded an Oscar for Best Foreign Film Production in 1996.

Film Festival

For two weeks in summer, usually in the month of July, the Film Festival brings an international flair to the little Bohemian spa town of Karlovy Vary. Since 1950 the festival has been held biennially, attracting film makers and cinema enthusiasts from all over the world. It is the second-oldest festival of its kind in Europe – younger than Venice, but founded before those of Cannes, Locarno and Berlin.

Paradoxically, the origins of the Karlovy Vary Festival lie in neighbouring Mariánské Lázně. Immedi-

ately after the Czech film industry was nationalised in 1946, the first festival was held there. Originally there was no element of competition, but in 1948 a jury, at first drawn just from within the country, began to judge the films that were shown. In 1950 the first international committee of judges was formed and the festival became linked to an annual theme. During the early years the festival also included short films and cartoons, and for a while there was a special section for films from the Third World. The competition also introduced a new category for first films by young directors. From the beginning, the Karlovy Vary Festival showed a strong bias towards films on social themes. At the same time, it offered cinematographers from socialist and developing countries the chance to present themselves on an international stage. The quality of the films chosen confirmed the value of the concept: among the prize-winning works were *Auschwitz*, by the Polish director Wanda Jakubowská (1948), *No Peace under the Olive Trees* by the Italian director Santini (1951), *The Children of Hiroshima* by Japan's Kanet Schindó (1954), the Soviet film classic *Nine Days in a Year* by Michail Romm, *Diary of a Lady's Maid* by Luis Buñuel (1964) and Antonio Saura's brilliant film version of Lorca's *Blood Wedding* (1980). On the negative side, it was clear that the organisers were often guided by ideological rather than artistic motives in their choice of winning films. Nonetheless, the Karlovy Vary Film Festival was the only such event within the former Eastern bloc to achieve the highest international "A" rating.

The 27th festival in 1990 was held under very different conditions within Czechoslovakia. On this occasion, the organisers had moved away from the previous, rather pompous framework. Nevertheless, all the national film critics were unanimous that the festival had not gained in quality. Only the retrospective on Czech film production during the 1960s and some examples of the later works of Miloš Forman compensated for the lack of interesting new films. Despite some early concerns about the festival's viability, it is now rapidly becoming one of the most respected in Europe, attracting a host of top-class directors and actors from Europe and the United States. As a sign of Karlovy Vary's growing stature in the world of film, representatives are talking to their counterparts in the French town of Cannes on a partnership agreement on a variety of cultural activities.

Prague's film festivals are smaller but are developing an international following. In January there is the week long FebioFest, devoted to highlighting new Czech film and work for television. The festival also shows a selection of stridently socialist films from the not-so-distant Czech past. March brings the Days of European Film, a popular festival which offers the best in new European film productions from each of the EU member states. So, far this is the only festival of its kind in Europe. In November, Prague's ambitious Indies Film Festival takes place. It usually includes a section of works by filmmakers from the former Yugoslavia, in cooperation with a similarly independent-minded festival in Sarajevo. ❏

LEFT: Philip Kaufman, who directed the film version of Milan Kundera's *The Unbearable Lightness of Being*.

upsets the sensibilities of people around him. A small-town setting is used to concentrate the idiosyncrasies of the characters while, typically for Czech film, sexuality is used exemplify the absurdity of everyday life.

ANIMATION EXHIBITION

The Renaissance Kratochvíle Castle, some 20 km (12 miles) from Prachatice in southern Bohemia, serves an an exhibition centre for animated Czech films.

In their desire to achieve recognition in the West, Czech film-makers have not fully compromised the intellectual content of their films. Rather they have sought to channel them in a direction which can please both domestic and foreign audiences. In this respect, Svěrák's latest endeavour, *Dark Blue World*, is a classic. The film traces the lives of two young Czech men who, like hundreds of their compatriots, joined the Royal Air Force as fighter pilots during World War II. Many of those who returned to their homeland were persecuted by the communists after the coup d'état in 1948.

It is also a love story but one of some sophistication. Both pilots fall in love with the same English girl, straining their friendship to the limits. It has been a stunning success both at home and abroad. Although it cost just US$6.5 million to make it qualifies as the most expensive Czech film ever made. Czech films overall now account for around a quarter of the national gross box office total revenues of around 500–600 million crowns a year.

International directors

Perhaps the best known film about the former Czechoslovakia was Philip Kaufman's *The Unbearable Lightness of Being*. It was based on a novel of the same name by the Czech writer Milan Kundera. The film, starring Daniel Day Lewis and Juliette Binoche, was either a beautiful portrait of hedonistic life after the tragedy of the Soviet invasion or a romantic trash film for intellectuals, depending on your point of view. But it was inspirational for many of the young American and British backpackers who came to Prague in the early 1990s seeking free love and finding nothing remotely unbearable about the lightness of being.

Most foreign audiences simply fell in love with film's setting, something they had in common with the makers of the first *Mission Impossible* (1996) which was partly shot in

Prague, as was Miloš Forman's *Amadeus* (1984). But Prague offers more than stately homes, atmospheric old cobbled streets and magnificent vistas suitable for the Hollywood money-making machine. The Barrandov film studios, sprawling over the hills at the edge of the city, were once as busy as any of their counterparts in Berlin and Paris.

Along with the physical infrastructure came a wealth of talent. Perhaps the most famous son of the Czech film industry is Miloš Forman (*see page 112*), the emigre Czech

director of the Oscars winners, *One Flew over the Cuckoo's Nest* and *Amadeus*. The acting profession is widely respected. President Václav Havel's wife, Dagmar, is a well known Czech actress.

Communism and fairy tales

Under communism, the fortunes of Czech film-making swung in tandem with the vicissitudes of politics. The new freedoms of the 1960s brought with them a "new wave" bristling with originality. Prominent among the emerging talents of the time was Miloš Forman himself and the Oscar-winning Jiří Menzel. The 1968 invasion clamped down firmly on unorthodox culture and Czech

---

RIGHT: a scene from *The Unbearable Lightness of Being* starring Daniel Day Lewis and Juliette Binoche.

film went down with it. Little of any great merit was produced, or at least seen, for more than 20 years. One exception was Karel Kachyňa's 1970 film *Ucho (Ear)* which centred on the communist regime's obsession with listening in on their citizens' private lives. Unsurprisingly it was banned and did not receive an airing for another two decades.

Anyone who spends much time living in the Czech Republic quickly becomes aware of one curiosity of the country's film tradition – the extraordinary number of fairy tale movies made. This is explained by the fact that it was an easy, non-controversial way for young actors to earn a living under communism without compromising themselves by taking roles in propaganda films. But it was also an escape from the dull, stultifying reality of life under communism. The films are usually shot in the country side using the country's vast array of unspoilt castles and medieval villages. Tales of sentimental simple romance are set against an unreal world in which the audience could lose themselves for a couple of hours. The artistic value, as with all fairy tales is debatable, but the acting was often top rate.

Where to see Czech film

Many of the most well regarded and popular Czech films can be rented out from good video stores in the West. Art house cinemas will also offer occasional showings. Once in the Czech Republic, ironically enough, your options may be more limited. Wenceslas Square boasts a host of cinemas, most showing Hollywood blockbusters in English for a couple of dollars a ticket. There is also a multiplex cinema right outside the stop at the end of the red metro line (line C). But unless you speak Czech you may have problems with the domestically produced films. *The Prague Post*, the country's top English language newspaper has a culture section which will direct you to any such films which are being shown with English subtitles. But if you are really enthusiastic, time your trip to coincide with the Karlovy Vary film festival where translations are often available. ❏

LEFT: director Miloš Forman.
RIGHT: *Shop on the High Street*, directed by Jan Kadár and Elmar Klos.

MILOS FORMAN

The most famous son of the country's film industry, Oscar-winning director Miloš Forman, was born in Czechoslovakia in 1932. Within 12 years both of his parents had died in Auschwitz and Buchenwald concentration camps. He was raised as an orphan by other family members. As a young adult under communism, the great challenge for Forman and others of his generation was to maintain artistic integrity in a totalitarian state where culture was put under strict political control. He studied at Prague's illustrious Academy of Music and Dramatic Art and found friendship and support from friends such as Václav Havel and Milan Kundera. His three main Czech films – *Black Peter* (1963), *Loves of a Blond* (1965) and *The Fireman's Ball* (1967) – are considered comic masterpieces of the communist era. Following the 1968 Russian invasion, Forman left his homeland and, via France, made his way to the United States, where he achieved international celebrity. His first film in the US was *Taking Off* (1971), followed by *Hair* (1979). But the two films for which Forman is best known are his highly acclaimed Oscar-winners, *One Flew Over the Cuckoo's Nest* (1975) and *Amadeus* (1984). He has made other feature-length movies such as *Valmont* (1989), *The People vs. Larry Flynt* (1996) and *Man on the Moon* (1999).

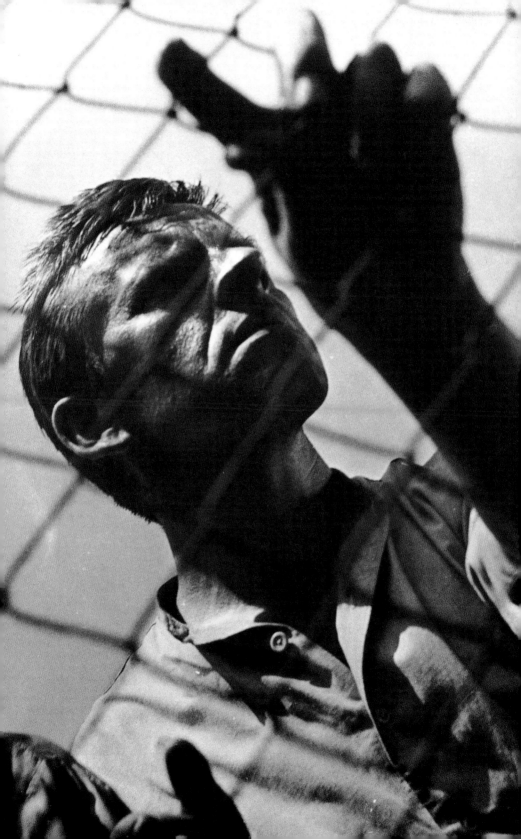

PRINCEZNA HYACINTA

Mucha

ART NOUVEAU IN PRAGUE

In Prague the avant-garde used revolutionary ideas to shape architectural styles in a way that would reflect their ideals and reject tradition

"Homage to Prague" is the motto written in colurful mosaic above the main entrance of the Municipal House, a monument to Prague's own brand of art nouveau architecture. The building was designed and built between 1906 and 1912 by the architects Osvald Polívka and Antonín Balšánek near the Powder Tower, on the site of the medieval royal palace and thus at the beginning of the traditional Royal Way. It was within its walls that the First Republic was proclaimed in 1918.

Conceived as a multi-purpose community centre with assembly chambers, ballrooms, exhibition halls and the magnificent Smetana Concert Hall, home of the Prague Symphony Orchestra, the Municipal House (Obecní dům) has now reopened to the public after an extensive and painstaking restoration. The Brazerie Mozart and the Café Nouveau will give visitors an idea of what the rest of the building is like but for the more curious there are regular guided tours through the Mayor's Chamber and other ceremonial rooms. Information about tours, concerts and exhibitions can be obtained from the foyer.

The most important Czech artists of the time were involved in the realisation of this city landmark. Karel Špillar provided the design for the mosaic by the entrance; the sculptures illustrating *Humiliation and Renaissance of the Nation* were the work of Ladislav Šaloun; Karel Novák produced the main decorative elements on the facade, including the light-bearing figures of Atlas gracing the balconies.

The work of Alfons Mucha

Particularly eye-catching are the large-scale allegorical portraits in the Primator Hall by Alfons Maria Mucha (1860–1939), the leading representative of the Prague secessionists and one of the most popular of all the art nouveau artists. Mucha worked primarily as a painter and graphic artist, but was also active in arts

and crafts. After studying in Vienna and Munich, in 1894 he moved to Paris, where he achieved artistic recognition almost overnight for the posters he designed for the actress Sarah Bernhardt. His sophisticated portraits of women – their hair and garlands of flowers elaborately entwined around their faces merging with the

ornamentation of the background or the picture frame – set a new trend.

Jiří Mucha, the artist's son, describes his father's commercial success: "After the phenomenal success of the Sarah Bernhardt posters, which became sought-after collector's items as soon as they were published, the printing firm of Champenois began to produce so-called 'panneaux'. They were really posters too, but without the advertising text. They were printed on good-quality paper or silk, and people either had them framed like pictures or used them to decorate screens. Within a short space of time, screens already decorated with these pictures were also being produced, and an

---

LEFT: a poster by Alfons Mucha.
RIGHT: an art nouveau doorway.

entire chain of shops sold nothing but the works of Mucha, in every imaginable variation.

"The decorative panels were all characterised by the long, narrow shape typical of his theatre advertisements. Unfortunately they were not all well made. It was a question of whether my father himself carried out all the corrections. Sometimes the printers were in such a hurry that there was no time for this. In such cases you needed only to glance at the original to realise how many details of drawing or colour had been lost in the lithographic process."

Mucha's success seems to have come quite naturally. As his son comments: "It is typical of the paradoxes which were forever occurring in father's life that he achieved fame as a result of precisely that aspect of his work which happened to be most fashionable at the time. He was not really aware of this fact himself; in not a single one of his lectures or writings about art does he make even the briefest reference to the way in which he arrived at his style in those days…" Exhibitions in Paris, Munich, Brussels, London and Prague followed.

In 1904 Mucha travelled to America, where he worked for some time as a stage designer and teacher at the Art Institute of Chicago. Shortly before the outbreak of World War I he

STREET OF ALL STYLES

A stroll down Celetná, radiating from Old Town Square, is the starting point for a whirlwind tour of Prague's architectural history. Along this street it is possible to see a series of Gothic and Romanesque foundations (originally ground floors) lying below baroque facades. The street also features a leading example of Cubism, in its House at the Black Madonna. Continue down Celetná to the Gothic-style Powder Tower and turn right onto Na Příkopě, then take in examples of other architectural styles, from the art nouveau Obecí dům to the neo-Renaissance Živnostenska banka at No. 20, and the modernist Palác Koruna.

returned to Prague, where he created his "Slavic Epic", a series of 20 monumental pictures dedicated to Slavic mythology. In 1913 Mucha designed a magnificently colourful window depicting episodes from the lives of the Bohemian saints for the New Archbishop's Chapel in St Vitus's Cathedral. He was finally laid to rest in the Vyšehrad Cemetery, the pantheon of Czech artists.

Architecture and sculptors

There is no doubt that Czech art nouveau drew its greatest inspiration from Paris. Most Prague artists visited the French capital in addition to Vienna and Berlin, the other great artistic centres of the time. Nonetheless, art nouveau in Prague developed into an independent artistic form of expression, as witnessed by numerous architectural elements throughout the city. In the early years it represented a reaction against the contemporary predilection for over-emphasising historic forms in architecture.

The main trendsetter as regards the new range of forms was the Prague Academy of Applied Art, which also achieved international acclaim with its contributions to the World Exhibitions in Paris (1900) and St Louis (1904). Using local folkloric elements, it developed a canon of expression which architects and craftsmen often followed down to the last detail. C. Klouček's ceramic and stucco ornamentation of facades was soon so widely copied that it was to become a characteristic of art nouveau buildings in towns all over Bohemia.

In architecture, Jan Kotěra, a pupil of the Viennese architect Otto Wagner, was one of the prime influences. He moved on from the originally naturalist conception towards a strong geometric and constructivist formal style. His most impressive works in Prague are the carefully restored Hotel Evropa and the Peterka House, with its elegantly ornamental facade, both on Wenceslas Square.

Apart from the sketches for the Municipal House, Osvald Polívka designed the house U Nováků (Vodičkova 36), the building housing the former Prague Insurance Company (Národní 7), the Bank of the Provinces (Na příkopě 20) and the New Town Hall on Mariánské náměstí.

The grandfather of Václav Havel designed and built the Lucerna Palace of Culture on Wenceslas Square as well as the family home on the Rašín Promenade.

With their new design for the main railway station (the Wilsonova) in 1980, architects Jan Šrámek and Alena Šrámková succeeded in integrating a historic building complex with a modern transport concept. The art nouveau building erected by J. Franta between 1901 and 1909 was remodelled around a massive ticket hall and departure area and linked to an underground railway without damaging the original fabric in any way. Further impressive examples of art nouveau architecture are the Koruna

House on Wenceslas Square and the steel Palace of Congress in the Exhibition and Trades Fair Park. The Hotel Paříž (U obecního domu 1, immediately behind the Municipal House) was declared a national monument in 1984.

The Svatopluk Čech Bridge and the magnificent facades of Pařížská Street form a remarkable urban ensemble. The bridge was constructed by J. Koula in 1908. Although the bridge with the shortest span in the city, it is certainly one of the most decorative.

The most outstanding sculptors of the era were Ladislav Šaloun, who was responsible for the vast monument to Jan Hus on the Old Town

Square, which was unveiled on 6 July 1915 to mark the 500th anniversary of the death of the Bohemian reformer; and Stanislav Sucharda, who created the Palacký Monument on the bridge of the same name.

True art nouveau sought to establish a balance between man and nature by using artistic symbols to add a cosmic dimension to personal experience. The artist could fuse a complex living environment with an idealised creative sphere. The fact that he was attempting to achieve an ideal which has become topical again today may be just one reason why, in Prague, art nouveau has lost nothing of its original fascination almost 100 years later. ❑

FAR LEFT: angel above a door in Celetná.
LEFT: the facade of the Hotel Evropa.
RIGHT: a decoration in Carp Street.

THE NATIONAL PARKS

These play an important part in the life in the Czech and Slovak Republics
and are supported and protected by thousands of locals on a voluntary basis

The national parks of the Czech and Slovak Republics are a both a source of national pride and a well spring for environmental regeneration. The locals take the matter seriously. In the Czech Republic there is a voluntary environmental guard of around 25,000 people looking after the forests and rivers and ensuring the observance of hunting and fishing regulations. They have achieved some remarkable successes, not least among which is the cleaning up of the waterways. The first adult salmon are expected to reappear in Czech rivers by 2003. Cross-border cooperation has been instrumental in protecting the national parks. Since the mid-1990s there have been annual meetings of young people from Germany and the Czech Republic.

In 2000, one such gathering was held in the Šumava and Bavarian national parks which meet at the border between the two countries. It was designed to address environmental issues in one of Europe's finest and best preserved forests. The Czech Republic created the Šumava National Park on 20 March 1991. Together with the National Park of the Bavarian Forest in Germany, a total of 81,000 hectares (200,000 acres) of countryside now stands under the strictest protection laws. The area covered by the National Park includes the largest self-contained forest in Central Europe. It is also – uniquely in Europe – an area of more than 80,000 hectares (198,000 acres) free of any major roads.

Unspoilt nature

The Šumava National Park is just one of many areas within the country's boundaries where there are strict limitations on the way land is used. Reports about the severe environmental damage to the industrial areas, especially in Northern Bohemia, have tended to eclipse the fact that the Czech and Slovak republics form one of the few regions in Europe in which

people are still be able to live in unspoilt natural surroundings. It is also a land in which animals that have been long extinct in other countries – brown bears, wolves and lynxes – are still to be found in their natural habitat.

Despite their relatively small area, the topography of the Czech and Slovak republics is

extremely varied. The upland regions include a wide range of scenery, attracting tourists from home and abroad. Cable cars and signposted footpaths lead up to the highest peaks and various recreational centres in the mountains. In order to limit the negative effects of intensive tourism, the authorities have drawn up a strict code of conduct governing visits to the national parks. For example, it is forbidden to leave the marked footpaths or to light fires or camp except within the specially designated areas. These regulations are strictly enforced and you will be fined for breaking them.

National parks and nature parks are large areas of untouched or largely unspoilt country-

LEFT: Slovakian paradise near Nová Ves.
RIGHT: canoeists can find ideal stretches of water in both republics.

side which are of scientific or general educational importance. Including as they do a great number of lakes and a well-developed network of signposted footpaths, they are rewarding for walkers and other nature-lovers.

There are designated routes to suit every taste and ability. In some protected areas distinctive nature trails have been laid out, marked by a white square with a green stripe. Information boards provide details of local flora and fauna to aid quick identification at regular intervals.

THE RIGHT EQUIPMENT

It is essential to have the right equipment for backpacking and camping in the republics. Although it is possible to buy gear when you arrive, it is better to bring the important items with you.

The seven national parks

Before 1987, six major areas had been declared national parks. Together with the 1,679 nature conservancy areas within the country, they cover an area of 17,272 sq km (6,669 sq miles) – in other words, 13 percent of the total land area. By comparison, the national parks of the US cover an area of 65,000 sq km (25,097 sq miles) – 0.6 percent of the total land area. No country in Central Europe could boast larger expanses of unspoilt natural habitats in which flora and fauna are preserved and studied in a scientific manner. Although most of the national parks in the former Czechoslovakia are situated within Slovakia (which now has seven

national parks of its own), it was in fact in the Czech lands that the very first attempts were made to preserve valuable natural habitats.

As early as 1838 two nature conservation areas were set up here: the forest areas of Hojná Voda and Žofinský in Southern Bohemia. Twenty years later, the forest conservation area of Boubínský prales was added. After World War II a systematic programme was launched to preserve typical scenery, archaeological sites and topographical formations.

The largest and most important national parks are the High Tatras National Park in Slovakia and the Krkonoše (Giant Mountains) in Northern Bohemia. The High Tatras National Park was founded in 1948 and joins the Polish Tatrzanski Narododowy National Park in the north. It covers an area of 770 sq km (300 sq miles); the protected area totals 510 sq km (200 sq miles). The Polish frontier is now open to traffic. The twin national parks of the High Tatras are administered jointly by both countries. The Vysoké Tatry (High Tatras) are the highest mountain chain in Slovakia; Mount Gerlachovský (2,655 metres/8,711 ft) and Mount Lomnický (2,632 metres/8,635 ft) are the highest peaks in the country. The topography of this alpine region, with its fissured craggy summits and picturesque mountain lakes, is typical of high-altitude landscapes and includes glacial valleys, moraines and more than 100 cirque lakes. It is ideal walking country and a popular skiing destination in winter, which means that it can get overcrowded.

The High Tatras form the northernmost section of the 1,200-km (750-mile) arc of the Carpathian Mountains. During the Quaternary Era the mountains were largely covered by glaciers; the present topography is the result of glacial erosion. Robert Townson, a Scottish physicist and geographer, studied the region in detail and described it in his book *Journeys through Hungary in 1793* (Slovakia belonged to Hungary at the time).

Brown bears and marmots

The land within the boundaries of the National Parks is subject to fairly heavy tourist traffic (the Polish section of the High Tatras is a fully developed tourist region). Nonetheless, the importance of nature conservancy has been recognised and afforded a high priority. There have been bans on the construction of new hotels in the High Tatras, and in some areas general bans on motor traffic.

The High Tatras are still the habitat of a large number of species which are extinct in most other European countries, or which are only able to survive in zoos. The mountains harbour brown bears, wolves, lynxes, wildcats, marmots, otters, wild horses, martens and mink. Most of these animals are hunted, but in the national parks they are protected all the year round. For many years the chamois was con-

The Krkonoše National Park was founded in 1963 and extends over an area of 385 sq km (150 sq miles). The region bears traces of the ice sheets which once covered it. Corries, moraines and glacial valleys are evident, as are the remains of more northerly flora (such as cloudberries). Characteristic species include monkshood, swallow-wort gentian and white hellebore. The spruce trees planted during the 17th and 18th centuries have been badly damaged by pollution and acid rain.

In one of the areas most badly affected by acid rain in the whole of Europe, 10,000 hectares (25,000 acres) of pine forest are losing

sidered a threatened species; nowadays they are more common. The chamois living in the High Tatras are a particular species only found here; the increase in tourism poses a threat to their habitat. Among the birds indigenous to the area are pheasant, partridge, wild geese and a number of species of duck. They may be hunted, but rarer large birds, such as golden eagles, vultures, ospreys, storks, eagle-owls, bustards and capercaillies are protected.

LEFT: experiencing the summit in the High Tatras, Slovak Republic.
ABOVE: this breed of chamois is unique to the High Tatras.

ROCK CLIMBING

Excellent training for rock climbing can be found on the sandstone crags around the Labe (Elbe) Valley in Northern Bohemia, in the locations of Rájec, Ostrov, Tisá and Bělá. Further challenges to climbers are provided by the impressive needle-shape rock towers of Český ráj (Czech Paradise), the triangle of land in Northern Bohemia between Turnov, Jičín and Mnichovo Hradiště, which includes the Prachovské skály and the Hruboskalsko. Another climbers' playground is the Moravian Karst in Southern Moravia. Many of the accessible rock terrains are situated in the protected regions in which visitors are urged to observe the principles of nature conservation.

their needles although steps have been taken in recent years to rectify the situation by replanting. The stocks of beech are restricted to the lower slopes. The entire national park area suffers from too many leisure visitors.

Slovakian paradise

The Slovenský raj National Park was established east of Poprad in 1988. The wild upland landscape extends over 140 sq km (54 sq miles) in an area which has been under a protection order since 1964. Wind, water and time have worn away the limestone plateau to form ravine-like gorges with waterfalls, cascades and

to west. It forms the heart of the Lower Tatras National Park (Národný Park Nízke Tatry), which covers a total area of 811 sq km (313 sq miles). The highest mountains are Mount Ďumbier (2,024 metres/6,640 ft) and Mount Chopok (2,024 metres/6,640 ft). There are dripstone caves (such as the Demänovské caves) which are accessible to tourists. The past few years have seen a number of hotels and chairlifts built and ski slopes prepared. Nonetheless, the eastern sections of the chain remain very peaceful and show few signs of human intervention. This is ideal walking country, since there are fewer steep gorges than in the High

karst. It is the habitat of many rare and protected plant and animal species.

The region has been made accessible to walkers and climbers by handrails, ladders and bridges (often consisting only of a tree trunk) where necessary. The main attractions of the park include the narrow defile at the rise of the River Hron and the Dobšinká ice caves. For keen walkers, Slovenský raj is a true paradise.

The Lower Tatras form the second-highest mountain chain in Slovakia, extending over a much larger area than the High Tatras. The long main ridge of the range, characterised by dense forest and bare, rounded mountain peaks, is no less than 80 km (50 miles) in length from east

CONFLICTING INTERESTS

A balance has to be struck between protecting wildlife and preserving economic interests, and each side has its energetic defenders. Slovakia in particular continues to suffer from governmental economic reform programmes. Early attempts to limit armament production and the export of weapons cost a large number of jobs which, in the main, have not been replaced. It must be tempting to compensate by expanding and developing tourism, a course which would inevitably be at the expense of the habitats of rare animal and plant species. It is remarkable that the Slovak authorities in regions such as the High Tatras have refused to build new hotels.

Tatras. Here, too, you may still meet bears, lynxes and wolves. Birds of prey are a frequent sight. You can also go fishing in the Čierny Váh River and in the large reservoir near Liptovský Mikuláš. The Lesser Fatra National Park (Malá Fatra) in Western Slovakia occupies an area of 200 sq km (77 sq miles) in the northeastern section of the mountain range of the same name. The highest peaks soar up to 1,709 metres (5,607 ft). A variety of rock types are present, in particular granite, sandstone and dolomite. The park also contains an extremely varied selection of flora and fauna; among the plants are warmth-loving as well as high-altitude species. The lower slopes, interspersed with canyon-like gorges, are ideal walking territory.

Covering an area of only 21 sq km (8 sq miles), the Pieninský Národný Park is the smallest of the national parks. It comprises a limestone mountain range dissected by the deeply eroded valley of the River Dunajec, which has become increasingly popular for rafting trips. In addition to the national parks, both the Czech and Slovak republics have an impressive number of extensive conservation areas. The Beskid Conservation Area, for example, extends over an area of 1,160 sq km (450 sq miles) and includes the Moravian and Silesian Beskids, part of the Javorníky Mountains and the Vsetínské vrchy. The area is protected for its primeval forests and environmentally precious mountain meadows. Also of interest is the architecture of the area.

A model national park region

The development of the joint national park region comprising the Bavarian Forest and the Bohemian Forest (Šumava) may help find a compromise between conflicting interests by preserving nature in cooperation with local residents. This was the idea behind the Biosphere Conservation Area, which originated in the proposal put forward in July 1991 by the environmental and nature protection agencies of the Czech Republic, Bavaria and Austria as "a united multi-national development concept to be agreed for the entire area". The authors saw the "only chance for the Bohemian Forest and the

Bavarian Forest in the preservation of the natural potential of the entire region as the basis for an environmentally-oriented development within the framework of a model ecological region".

Part of the scheme includes the modernisation or revival of the railway system, and the encouragement of small and medium-sized businesses in an environmentally-conscious way, as well as developing tourist facilities in harmony with the National Park, the natural surroundings and history of the area. Major industrial projects and the promotion of through traffic and goods traffic by the improvement of the road network are thereby rejected. The

opinions of those directly affected are divided. Many village mayors have voiced opposition to the project: "They want to send us back to the jungle so that people are forced to leave their homes once more."

The opposite view is taken by Peter Pavlik, who was persecuted after the Prague Spring and subsequently found a new home in the depths of the Bohemian Forest. He has transformed a farmhouse and goat shed into a restaurant. Just as he once wrote pamphlets against the Prague regime, he now writes letters to German newspapers: "I beg you, help us to preserve our common natural heritage; there is nothing like it left in Europe!" ❑

LEFT: strict rules apply to all visitors to the national parks and nature reserves.
RIGHT: a bubbling stream deep in the Bohemian Forest, Czech Republic.

Environmental Concerns

I t was not until after the bloodless revolution of November 1989 that the population of the then Czechoslovakia was confronted with black-and-white evidence of what many of them had suspected for a long time: that they were living in what was, ecologically speaking, one of the most severely threatened countries in Europe. The Danube canalisation scheme for the power station at Gabčíkovo in Southern Slovakia, which has caused

hearts…" Thus ran one of the songs which Czechoslovakian children used to learn at school. For many years the black smoke belching from the factory chimneys was seen as a symbol of progress in the country.

The main cause of air pollution lies in heat and power generation, which are heavily dependent upon fossil fuels leading to the release of oxides of sulphur, carbon and nitrogen as well as heavy metals. A particularly threatened area is northwestern Bohemia, where pollution levels exceed all safety limits. Environmental experts used to describe the situation here as catastrophic.

The region is the country's brown coal (lignite)

a major international outcry and petitions to international courts, is but one of the environmental catastrophes bequeathed by the communists. The decision of the Slovaks to see the project through to completion demonstrates just how difficult it is to halt the trends of the past.

It could be pointed out that rivers have been harnessed in this part of the world ever since the beginning of the Middle Ages. But such arguments cannot be used to justify the biggest environmental problem faced by the Czech and Slovak republics, namely air pollution.

"The chimneys are smoking and a band of children is playing on a heap of sand. Life blossoms forth in a thousand things and grows in our

mining centre; almost 70 percent of the total Czech production of this natural resource comes from local opencast seams. Most of the coal, which has a high sulphur content, is burned in the thermal power stations in the area. One-third of the total electricity generated in the Czech and Slovak republics comes from here. The industry has turned the district surrounding the town of Most into a barren lunar landscape and rehabilitation of the fields will take many years. The power stations lack adequate filters for the removal of excess sulphur, which means that local inhabitants constantly breathe in foul-smelling, poisonous fumes.

The sulphur emissions have also been found to be responsible for destroying forests on the mountain slopes of the Ore Mountains and the Krkonoše (Giant Mountains). Experts have estimated that the average life expectancy in the region is five years less than that of other areas within the Czech and Slovak republics. In some particularly endangered towns in northern Bohemia the authorities have at times distributed gas masks to children in the hope that at least some of the pollutants will be filtered out.

Northern Moravia occupies second place in the league of provinces severely at risk. Worst hit are the areas around Ostrava and Karviná. The Ostrava region is predominantly a manufacturing area, with heavy industry and hard coal mining. The worst air pollution comes from the iron foundries and the coke furnaces.

The third most polluted region in the Czech Republic is Prague. The concentration of industrial plant and exhaust fumes from the many antiquated vehicles has resulted in a pall of smog that sometimes hangs above the rooftops. Catalytic converters were made compulsory on newly registered cars in 1993, but in the opinion of many environmentalists this is not enough. At times of heavy smog during the 1990s, cars were even banned from the centre of the city.

Another serious problem is the pollution of the lakes and waterways. The River Labe (Elbe) is the dirtiest in Europe. The towns and villages along its course are the main culprits, for many of them do not process their effluence.

The Czechs have made big efforts to address some of these problems since the liberation from communist rule. But in nuclear power, they have picked up a double-edged sword. Clearly, the full activation of the Temelín nuclear power plant in Southern Bohemia could reduce the usage of fossil fuels. But, as domestic environmentalists and the government in neighbouring Austria have been quick to point out, it carries risks of its own. With memories of the Chernobyl disaster looming in the background, few in the former Czechoslovakia are entirely happy about the new reliance on nuclear power stations originally designed according to Soviet engineering standards.

Similar problems are faced by the Slovaks. The drive to transform what was traditionally an agricultural and deeply Catholic land into a modern industrial socialist state has also left its poisoned legacy. From the iron-ore works of Košice to the

arms factories of Dubnica and Martin, the pall of pollution hangs in the air. As Slovakia confronts the reality of independence and the leadership struggles to maintain employment, there seems little chance that such carbuncles will soon disappear from the landscape.

While the modernisation of industrial complexes will depend on the ultimate success of economic reforms, there is no way that the republics will be able to meet the cost of the big clean-up on their own. The European Union is financing some environmental rescue programmes, and the United States and Switzerland have also offered assistance. A number of loans from the World Bank and

Scandinavian banks have been allocated for projects of this nature. It is also hoped that money generated by the booming tourist industry will help finance environmental projects.

With around 100 million border crossings into the Czech Republic in 2001 alone, and a growing number of visitors to Slovakia, tourism has become a major resource.

It would be misleading to give visitors the impression that the region is permanently veiled in a thick vale of smog and its countryside crossed by polluted, dying rivers. There remain vast areas of countryside, including broad stretches of virgin forests and pristine mountains, where nature can still be enjoyed. ❑

LEFT: a tarnished idyll.
RIGHT: lignite mining near Most.

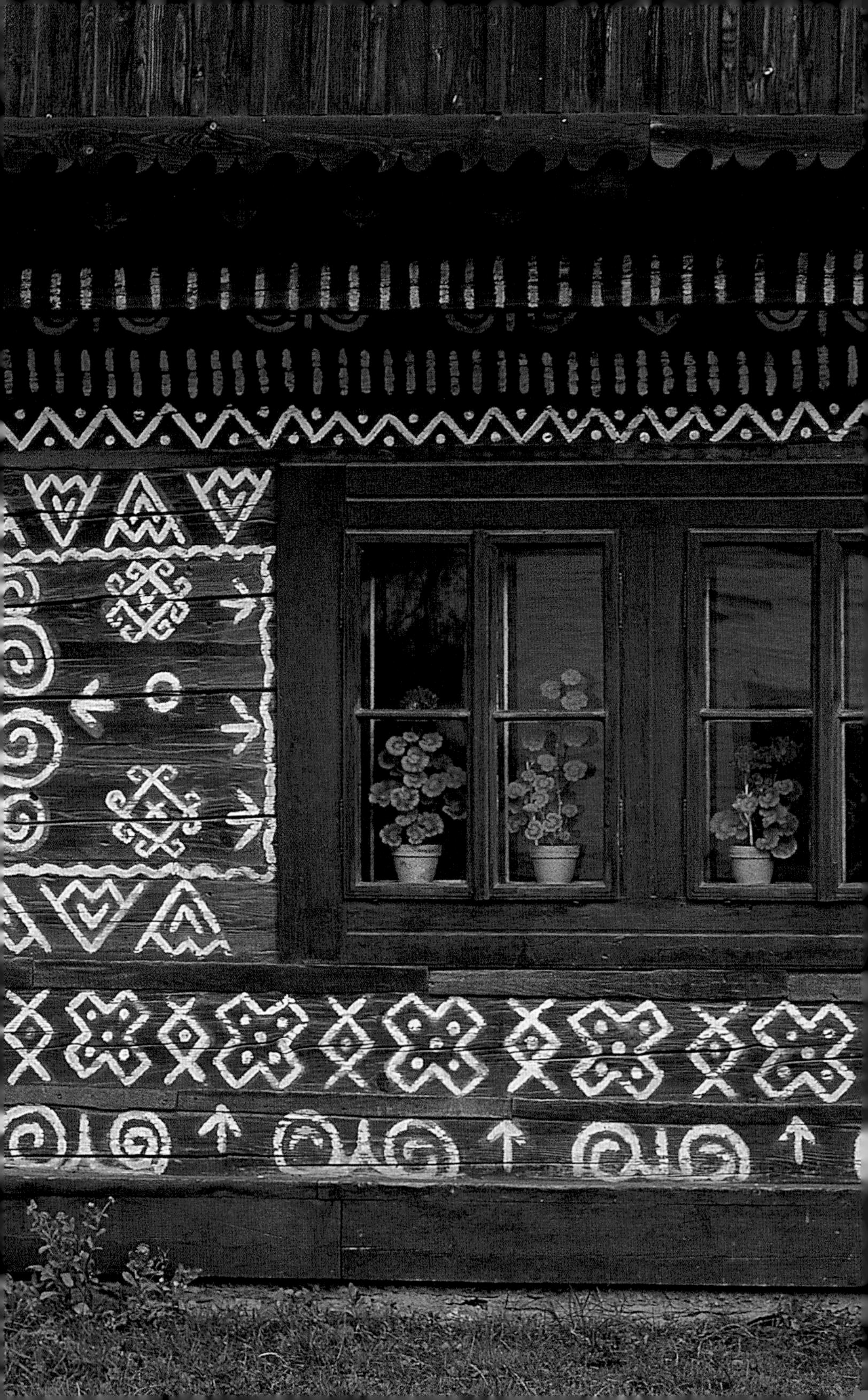

THE CZECH REPUBLIC

*A detailed guide to the Czech Republic, with principal sites
clearly cross-referenced by number to maps*

After years of ideological isolation, the Czech Republic has
emerged as one of Europe's most fascinating destinations.
While the larger cities are by now well used to the demands
of the tourism boom – and four of the country's airports are being
enlarged to meet the demands of international traffic – it often
seems that life out in the country has stood still. But even here
there are increasing signs of change; and it isn't only the facades,
neglected for so many decades, that are suddenly being returned to
their former glory.

The Czech Republic can look back on a long and eventful history
and in recent years the state has made enormous efforts to preserve
its rich cultural heritage. Many of the old town centres have been preserved as historical monuments, while Prague, Telč, Český Krumlov
and Kutná Hora all feature on the UNESCO world heritage list. Scattered throughout the republic are more than 2,000 castles and
chateaux, 200 of which are open to the public, while in Moravia the
pilgrims' church of St John of Nepomuk at Žďár nad Aázavou, and
the Lednice-Valtice chateau, have recently been added to the tally of
preserved monuments. Nature lovers will be delighted to learn that
10 percent of all Czech territory is protected from development, including the three national parks: Krkonoše (Giant mountains),
Šumava and the valley of the river Dyje, home to many rare species.

For a region with such a wealth of things to see, any description
must be selective. The journey begins in the Czech Republic, in the
historical Crown Lands of Bohemia, and its magnificent capital
Prague. We continue by exploring some delightful destinations in
Prague's environs and then follow a large arc from Southern
Bohemia to Western Bohemia and its famous spa towns, and then to
Northern Bohemia before travelling east of Prague into neighbouring Moravia. Having visited its capital, Brno, we head off into the
countryside again. Whichever route you take, you will not only encounter beautiful countryside filled with countless historical and
architectural gems, but also generous measures of the hospitality for
which the people are rightly renowned.

In both the Czech Republic and Slovakia, many of the towns have
a history of German as well as Slavic settlement. In this guide, therefore, some of the Slavic names are followed by their German
versions in brackets. ❏

PRECEDING PAGES: Southern Moravian wine cellars have small entrances;
historical houses in central Slovakia; Old Town Square in Prague.
LEFT: the Matthias Gate of Hradčany, Prague.

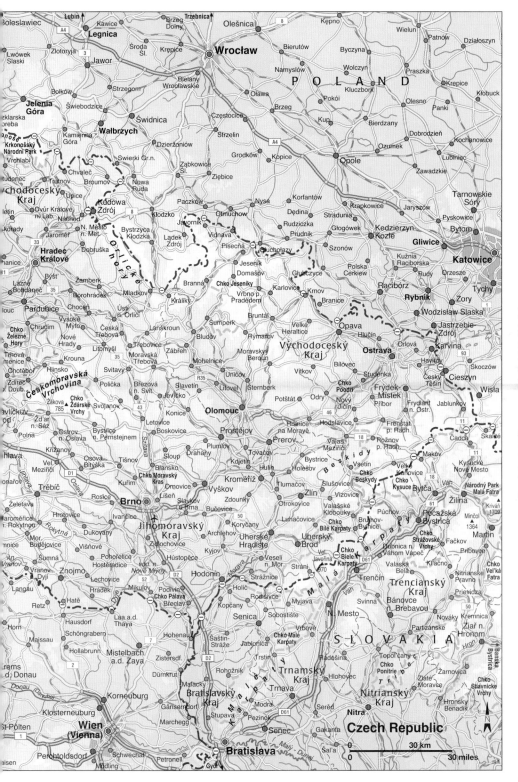

THE GOLDEN CITY

*Prague, one of the most beautiful cities in Europe,
has become a major tourist destination*

Viewed from the castle hill, the historical centre clings to the gently curving bend in the Vltava, its rooftops reflecting the golden patina of the midday sun. Its banks seem to be only just held together by the filigree constructions of its bridges: on the one side the Lesser Quarter and on the other the Old Town.

Anybody who looks over Prague from the parapets of Prague Castle must surely consider it to be one of the most fortunate of all European cities; fortunate because its skyline was never touched by the ravages of war and because its essential appearance was never scarred by the addition of any modern eyesores. After years of painstaking restoration, important architectural ensembles such as the Old Town Square have now been returned to their former glory. Today, Prague is a living architectural museum, vividly documenting succeeding phases of development, from its Romanesque origins, its mighty Gothic churches and monasteries, to the baroque palaces and the magnificent art nouveau boulevards of the "foundation years" laid out towards the end of the 19th century.

Every year in May, the memory of Prague's most famous composers, Mozart, Smetana and Dvořák, whose names are so closely linked with the history of the city, is resurrected when the elegant concert halls, churches and palaces open their doors for the Prague Spring Festival. It is a time when great international ensembles perform in the city, as well as renowned native orchestras such as the Czech Philharmonic or the famous National String Quartet. But good music can be heard in Prague all the year round: from jazz to rock to opera, all musical tastes are catered for.

The daily life of Prague is best experienced in its pubs. And it doesn't have to be the full-to-bursting U Fleků or U Tomáše, whose reputation is somewhat better than merited; or even the Chalice (U Kalicha), the local of Jaroslav Hašek's *Good Soldier Schweik*. No, the best beer, the most fortifying dumplings and the tastiest goulash continue to be served in more cosy, hidden establishments.

Where does the city's pulse beat? Is it in its historical buildings around which big city and medieval atmospheres seem to fuse? Or in the magical squares, with their mysterious play of light and shade, in which one might almost expect to bump into Rabbi Löw's monster, the Golem? Does the legendary ambience created by Prague's writers and artists still exist? Does the pulse of the city beat stronger today on the boulevard of Wenceslas Square, with its shopping by day and its bustling entertainment by night? The truth is that Prague is made up of so many different facets, and visitors must discover for themselves the secret of its appeal. ❏

PRECEDING PAGES: the Mayor's Chamber in the Municipal House in the New Town, decorated by Alfons Mucha between 1906 and 1911.
LEFT: Hradčany at dusk.

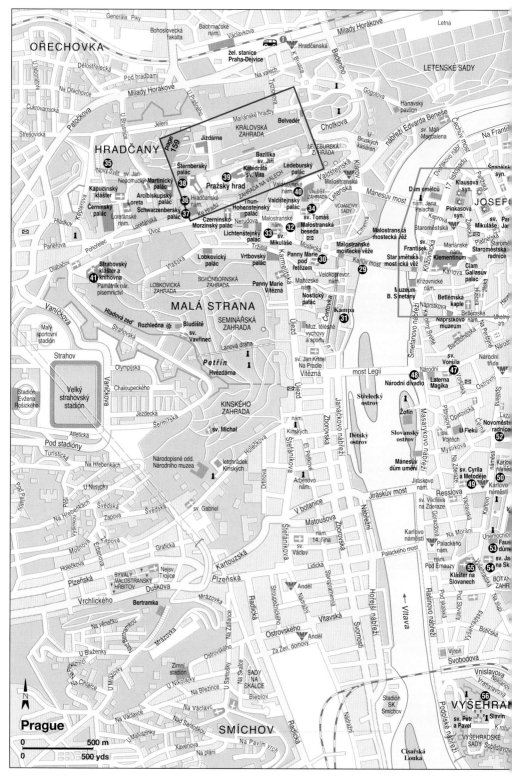

Prague

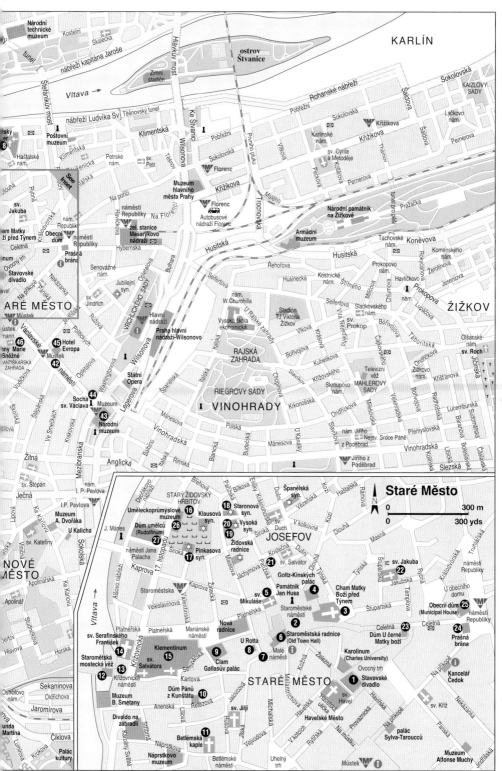

KARLÍN

ostrov Štvanice

Národní technické muzeum

Kostelní
Skalecká
tunel
nábřeží kapitána Jaroše
Zimní stadión
Štefánikův most
Vltava →
nábřeží Ludvíka Sv. Těšnovský tunel
Klimentská
Poštovní muzeum
Haštalské nám.
Petrské nám.
sv. Petr
See inset
Na poříčí
Muzeum hlavního města Prahy
Florenc
Florenc
Autobusové nádraží Florenc
žel. stanice
Masarykovo nádraží
náměstí Republiky
Obecní dům
náměstí Republiky
Prašná brána
Senovážné nám.
Husitská
Armádní muzeum
Národní památník na Žižkově
Koněvova
Husitská
Řehořova
Husinecká
Kostnické nám.
Prokopovo nám.
Prokopova
ŽIŽKOV
ARÉ MĚSTO
Můstek
Václavské
Hotel Evropa
Můstek
Hlavní nádraží
Praha hlavní nádraží-Wilsonovo
nám. W.Churchilla
Stadión TJ Viktoria Žižkov
sv. Prokop
Televizní věž
MAHLEROVY SADY
sv. Roch
Socha sv. Václava
Muzeum
Národní muzeum
RAJSKÁ ZAHRADA
RIEGROVY SADY
VINOHRADY
Žitná
Anglická
Vinohradská
nám. Jiřího z Poděbrad
Vinohradská
Slezská
Ječná
nám. I. P. Pavlova
I.P. Pavlova
Muzeum A. Dvořáka
U Kalicha
sv. Kateřiny
STARÝ ŽIDOVSKÝ HŘBITOV
Uměleckoprůmyslové muzeum
16 Klausova syn.
18 Staronová syn.
Španělská syn.
Dům umělců (Rudolfinum) 26
20 Vysoká syn.
19
sv. Duch
JOSEFOV
Staré Město
0 300 m
0 300 yds
náměstí Jana Palacha
27
17 Pinkasova syn.
Židovská radnice
sv. Jakuba
náměstí Republiky
NOVÉ MĚSTO
Kaprova
21 sv. Salvátor
Goltz-Kinských palác
Cham Matky Boží před Týnem
U obecního domu
Obecní dům (Municipal House) 25
Staroměstská
Památník Jan Husa 4
Mikuláše 5
Staroměstské náměstí
3
Nová radnice
2
Staroměstská radnice (Old Town Hall)
Dům U černé Matky boží 23
Prašná brána 24
sv. Serafinského František
Klementinum
Karolinum (Charles University)
Kancelář Čedok
Staroměstská mostecká věž
sv. Salvátora 15
Malé náměstí
Muzeum B. Smetany
Dům Pánů z Kunštátu 10
Clam Gallasův palác
STARÉ MĚSTO
Stavovské divadlo 1
sv. Havel
Divadlo na zábradlí
Betlémská kaple 11
Náprstkovo muzeum
Betlémské náměstí
Uhelný trh
Müstek
palác Sylva-Taroucců
Muzeum Alfonse Muchy

Map on pages 140–41

STARE MESTO

*Prague's historic Old Town has retained much of its original
character, with the Old Town Square forming a
natural centre and true heart of the city*

The dividing line between the Staré Město and the Nové Město – the Old and the New Towns – lies at the far side of **Václavské náměstí** (Wenceslas Square). To the right and left, wide pedestrian thoroughfares follow the line of the medieval town wall dating from the time before Charles IV had the New Town built in a semicircle around the historic city centre. The little street Na můstku leads to the heart of the Old Town. After a few paces visitors will come to a flea market – the traditional **Havelské Město** (St Gall Market) area – to the left, which leads directly into the **Uhelný trh** (Coal Market) one block further on.

To the right, in the background, is the silhouette of the **Kostel sv. Havel** (Church of St Gall). Originally Romanesque in style, the church was given its baroque facade between 1690 and 1700. It marks the hub of the district as it was first planned in the 13th century.

One block further on again is the **Stavovské divadlo ❶** (Estates Theatre, box office open Mon–Fri 10am–6pm; Sat–Sun 10am–12.30pm, 3pm–6pm; tel: 2490 1448) scene of the premiere of Mozart's opera *Don Giovanni* on 29 October 1787 and the oldest theatre building in Prague. It has been rebuilt several times and after major restoration it was reopened in 1991 with a performance of *Don Giovanni*. The concert scenes of the film *Amadeus* were filmed here.

The **Karolinum** (Carolinium), next door to the theatre, was originally a palace purchased by King Wenceslas IV from the Rotlev family for the Charles University. Across the centuries the university expanded to take over other buildings; all that remains of the original Gothic college is an arbour and the magnificent oriel window created by the Parler School. The building is now used for official ceremonies and is closed to the public.

Old Town Square

The **Staroměstské náměstí ❷** (Old Town Square) forms the natural centre of the Old Town and the true heart of the city. Occupying pride of place in the middle is the massive **Památník Jan Husa** (monument to Jan Hus). It was erected on 6 July 1915 to mark the 500th anniversary of the reformer's death. The surrounding buildings, dwarfed by the towers of the Týn Church, form an imposing backdrop.

At the base of the church towers lies the Týn School, which houses changing exhibitions. You can go through the school to the **Chram Matky Boží před Týnem ❸** (Our Lady Before Týn Church; opening hours erratic due to reconstruction, try between noon and 2pm), whose treasures

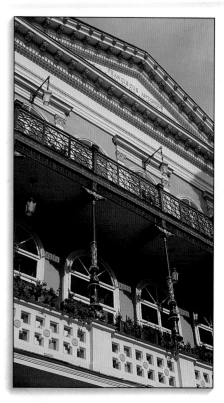

include the oldest font in Prague (1414) and a series of baroque paintings, such as the main altarpiece *The Assumption* by the first great master of Bohemian baroque, Karel Škréta (1610–74). The building, which was erected between 1365 and 1511 on the site of a small Romanesque church of St Mary, was the Hussites' main place of worship until their crushing defeat by the Catholics at the Battle of the White Mountain in 1620.

Although the varied architectural styles of the surrounding houses blend harmoniously, one or two buildings are nonetheless outstanding. The first of them is the early neoclassical house, U bílého jednorožce (The White Unicorn), followed by the Týn School and the Gothic Dům u Kamenného zvonu (House at the Stone Bell) which holds exhibitions and classical concerts in its restored interior. Last in the row is the **Goltz-Kinských palác ❹** (Kinský Palace; currently closed), whose fine facade reveals rococo elements. It was built between 1755 and 1765 by An-

selmo Lurago according to the plans of the Bavarian architect Kilián Ignaz Dientzenhofer, who died in 1751. In the 19th century, it housed a German school which was attended by Franz Kafka. It was here that Prime Minister Gottwald made his speech to the nation that brought in the communist regime. Today it is the home of the National Gallery's splendid collection of prints and drawings, and also houses temporary art exhibitions.

The smaller part of the square behind the Town Hall is dominated by the magnificent facade of **Kostel sv. Mikuláše ❺** (St Nicholas's Church; open Tues–Sun 10am–5pm). German merchants erected the first place of worship on this site during the 13th century; the present church was completed in 1735. Once again the architect was Kilian Ignáz Dientzenhofer who, together with his father Christoph, was in large part responsible for the city's baroque appearance.

The **Staroměstská radnice ❻** (Old Town Hall) is now used only ceremonies.

BELOW: the astronomical clock was mounted on the Old Town Hall by Nikolaus von Kaaden in 1410.

Map
on pages
140–41

The North Wing was burned down in 1945 during the last days of German occupation; a memorial plaque recalls the event. The building had formed the political hub of the capital since King John of Luxembourg granted the citizens rights of self-government in 1338. The chapel, council chamber and a number of other buildings in the western and northern corners were erected in rapid succession. In 1896 the corner house of U Minuty, adorned with antique and biblical murals, was absorbed into the complex. Among the tenants who were served notice to quit was the family of Franz Kafka. A photographic exhibition of his life story can be seen at U Radnice 5 (open Tues–Sun; entrance fee), the site of the house where he was born.

The most notable feature of the exterior is the amazing **orloj** (astronomical clock), dating from 1410 and situated to the right of the main late-Gothic portal. This wonderful timepiece consists of two clock faces: the calendar, below, which moves on a day every time the clock (above) strikes midnight. The signs of the zodiac and the rural scenes depicting the months were painted by Josef Mánes in 1864. At the very top is the Procession of Apostles, which was only installed in the 19th century. The view from the hall's tower (open daily 9am–6pm; entrance fee) is a popular attraction.

Opposite the Old Town Hall at No. 26, the **Muzeum českého skla** (Museum of Czech Glass, open daily 10am–9pm; entrance fee) has an exhibition of Czech glassware on the upper floor, and below a forge where various glassblowing techniques are demonstrated to visitors.

The southern Old Town

Leading off from U Minuty is the **Malé náměstí ❼**, the Little Square, evocative of medieval Prague. Surrounding the fountain with its pretty Renaissance railings are a number of fine houses, each with its own history. In No. 11, a Signore Agostino of Florence established the first documented apothecary's shop in the city (1353), and during the reign of Emperor Charles IV No. 1, which bears the twin

names In Paradise and At the Sign of the Angel, was the home of a herbalist from Florence. Most spectacular is the **U Rotta ❽** (Rott House) at No. 3, whose cellar was once the lower floor of a Romanesque town house. The first Czech Bible was printed here in 1488; at the turn of the 20th century an ironmonger had the building renovated, painting the facade with the original sign – three white roses – and some of his wares. The house now contains an excellent delicatessen.

Past the bend in the Karlova ul., on the right-hand side of the Husova, is the **Clam Gallasův palác ❾** (Clam Gallas Palace), a beautifully restored nobleman's house. The building, dating from the high baroque period, now houses the town's archives. Despite the cramped location, the facade is very impressive; it is framed by two decorative portals comprising pairs of Titans apparently bearing the weight of the entire world and the building. In the opposite direction, Husova Street leads to the **Dům Pánů z Kunštátu ❿** (House of

the Lords of Kunštát and Poděbrady, closed Mon; entrance fee) whose entrance lies in Řetězova No. 3, and which is devoted to George of Poděbrady, the only king of Bohemia to be elected by the people. The palace retains its Romanesque features, especially the simple barrel-vaulted rooms on the ground floor and in the cellar. Further to the left stands **Kostel sv. Agidia** (St Aegidius's Church; open daily), the severe Gothic church of the Dominican friars. In marked contrast to its unadorned exterior, the hall church is magnificently appointed inside. Baroque paintings displaying a masterful command of perspective and colour adorn the vaulted ceiling.

Bethlehem Chapel Square

Taking the third turning on the right off Husova, you will come to the **Betlémská kaple ⑪** (Bethlehem Chapel; open daily 9am–6pm; entrance fee) in the square of the same name. One of the most important shrines of the Czech people, its simplicity serves as a memorial to the sermons of Jan Hus, who used this chapel to fulminate against bigotry and love of splendour. Other great religious reformers also preached here, including Hus's contemporary and fellow rebel Jakobellus von Mies (Jakoubek ze Stříbra), who introduced the administration of the communion in both forms, and much later (1521), the radical Thomas Münzer.

The focal point in the chapel is the pulpit rather than the altar. The walls were used to illustrate the preacher's message in large letters and pictures before a congregation of up to 3,000 of the faithful. Ironically, after the defeat of the Hussites, the church passed into Jesuit hands; in 1786 it was completely gutted, but from 1950–54 was rebuilt in the original style to serve as a national monument.

The Preacher's House next door is also open to the public; it contains an exhibition documenting the life and works of the great reformer. On the west side of the square, surrounding a pretty courtyard, is

BELOW: the rococo staircase in the Clam Gallas Palace is the work of M.B. Braun (*circa* 1730).

Map
on pages
140–41

the well-stocked **Náprstkovo muzeum** (Ethnological Museum; open Tues–Sun; entrance fee). Náprstkova leads to the River Vltava, where – on the far side of the promenade – a little café in front of the **Muzeum Bedřicha Smetany** (Smetana Museum; open Wed–Mon; entrance fee) offers good views of the Charles Bridge and Hradčany Castle. The museum displays exhibits illustrating the life and works of the famous Czech composer *(see page 90).*

Crusader Knights' Square

Beyond the former millhouses is the **Staroměstská mostecká věž ⓬** (Old Town Bridge Tower; open daily; entrance fee) the last work that Peter Parler bequeathed the city. In spite of its slender form and invitingly high archway it was originally designed for defensive purposes, proving its worth in 1648 when the Swedes spent two weeks vainly trying to capture the Old Town. The west side of the tower was destroyed, but on the Old

Town side the gallery of sculptures has survived, including that of the national patron saint. St Vitus is portrayed protecting the bridge between two kings – Charles IV and Wenceslas IV.

Most of the 30 statues of the saints which now dominate the bridge were added during the baroque period, although the ensemble was only completed in 1928 with the statue of St Cyril and St Methodius. The earliest statue (1683), on the northern central pillar, is that of St John Nepomuk, who was tortured then thrown into the Vltava by Wenceslas IV because he spoke out against the latter's religious policies. A pious legend maintains that the king's wrath had been aroused by Nepomuk's brave refusal to break the sanctity of the confessional by betraying the secrets of the queen.

The **Křižovnické náměsti ⓭** (Crusader Knights' Square) was originally charged with the defence of the bridge and enjoyed high esteem within the city; between 1561 and 1694 the leaders of the order were ex

officio the Archbishops of Prague. Their **Kostel sv. František**  (St Francis's Church; closed Sat), with its magnificently painted dome, was no doubt designed to vie with the pomp and circumstance of the Jesuits' Klementinum nearby. The exhibition of jewelled monstrances and other exquisite items from the knights' treasury also includes an opportunity to view the medieval crypt and a surviving span of the 12th century Judith Bridge. The monument to Charles IV, standing outside the church was erected to commemorate the 500th anniversary of the founding of the university and portrays allegorical representations of the first four faculties at the feet of the founder.

On the far side soars the baroque facade of the **Kostel sv. Salvátora** (Church of St Saviour; open for services). It forms a part of the **Klementinum**  (Clementinum; open for classical concerts). The college was established by the Jesuits after they were summoned to Bohemia in 1556 and it became the bastion of the Counter-Reformation in the Hussite capital. The Society of Jesus took over a former Dominican monastery and a 2-hectare (5-acre) plot of land and set up a first-class educational establishment with a school, library, printing works and theatre. The university was soon granted the right to award doctorates and thus gained equal status with the Hussite Charles University. In 1622, after the Catholic victory on the White Mountain, it was able to absorb the troublesome competition and remained for many years the only university in the Czech capital.

Today the Klementinum houses a number of libraries, including the Národní knihovna (National Library); the magnificent rooms can be visited upon request.

Josefov, the Jewish quarter

The first Jewish community was founded in Prague in 1091. In 1255 King Otakar II granted the Jewish Privilege, thus guaranteeing Jews security within the law for the first time. In return, thanks to their

BELOW: the House of the Stork on the Old Town Square.

Map on pages 140–41

success as craftsmen and traders, Jewish people provided the king with a considerable income from the taxes that they paid. Their relationship with the authorities alternated between acceptance and hatred, and they frequently suffered at the hands of Prague's citizens. But the most terrible persecution was perpetrated by Hitler, as part of his "final solution". He intended to create a "museum of an extinct race" in Prague, and it was only because of this cynical plan that the synagogues and cemeteries were not destroyed. The heart of the **Josefov** grew up after 1250 around the Old-New Synagogue. In 1382 Wenceslas IV pronounced the district a protected ghetto.

Behind the Klementinum, the Platnéřská leads almost back to the Old Town Square. Shortly before this point you can turn left into the Maislova and left again opposite the Old-New Synagogue into the U starého hřbitova to the **Starý židovský hřbitov** ⓰ (Old Jewish Cemetery; open Sun–Fri 9am–6pm; entrance fee), where

weathered gravestones stand under gnarled trees. At the **Hrobka rabína Lowa** (tomb of Rabbi Low), pious Jews honour one of their great teachers who, during the 16th century, the Golden Age of the Jewish community, directed a Talmudic school in Prague. The rabbi is also known as the creator of the Golem, the artificial creature which he brought to life by mysterious magical practices, but which turned against its master.

At the entrance to the cemetery is the **Klausova synagóga** (Klaus Synagogue; open daily; entrance fee), in which old manuscripts and prints are displayed. Adjoining the synagogue is a hall of remembrance containing a moving collection of drawings by Jewish children in the concentration camp at Terezín.

On the opposite side of the cemetery is the **Pinkasova synagóga** ⓱ (Pinkas Synagogue; open daily; entrance fee). Now open as a memorial, its walls are painted with the names of the 77,297 Bohemian and Moravian Jews who perished in the

BELOW: graves the Old Jewish cemetery.

Holocaust. The **Staronová synagóga**
(Old-New Synagogue; open Sun–Fri
9am–6pm; entrance fee) is Europe's oldest Jewish place of worship. Begun in
1270, the building has an elaborate brick
gable and demonstrates evidence of the
severe Cistercian Gothic style, although a
number of elements were purposely
altered in order to avoid too much resem-
blance to the symbolism of the Christian
Church. Inside, the roof covering the main
area is supported by twin columns; only
men were allowed access to this part of
the synagogue, where readings from the
Torah took place. The galleries were added
during the 17th century so women could
to participate in the acts of worship.

Opposite is the baroque-style **Židovská
radnice** (Jewish Town Hall; closed to
the public). Eyes are drawn to the gable
with its unusual clock adorned with
Hebraic symbols: strangely but correctly,
the hands turn anti-clockwise. The building is still the headquarters of Prague's
Jewish community; it also houses a kosher
restaurant called Shalom, which is open
for lunch only. The building at the back
houses the **Vysoká synagóga** (High
Synagogue; open daily; entrance fee), so
named because of its location on the second floor of the building. Adjoining it is a
little park flanked by 19th-century houses
with imposing facades and a wealth of
ornamental detail. On the left the Cubist
facade of the Inter-Continental hotel
strikes a creative note on a functional
modern building.

Returning to the Old Town Square, it is
pleasant to stroll along **Pařižká** (Paris
Street). This was created over a century
ago within the framework of a restoration
programme to alleviate insanitary conditions in the Josefov. Its magnificent art
nouveau facades make it the most spectacular street in the entire city.

To the Powder Tower

From the earliest days of the city's history Celetná was an important trading street.
Even though its buildings were frequently

BELOW: door
detail, Pinkas
Synagogue.

Map
on pages
140–41

rebuilt in accordance with the tastes and fashions of the times (the predominant accent today is baroque), the visitor will be able to discern a number of medieval elements, such as the groin vaulting of No. 2, the **Sixt House** and the wooden roof trusses of No. 3 (The Three Kings).

On the left-hand side, immediately behind the Týn Church, the Štupartská leads down to the **Kostel sv. Jakuba** ㉒ (St James's Church; open daily). This was originally built by the Minorites during the reign of Charles IV, but it was later the subject of a particularly successful rebuilding in the baroque style. The expressive reliefs of the facade and the alteration of the interior to create a theatrical setting provide a fine stage for the frequent concerts held on the ornamental and powerful organ, dating from 1705.

Returning to Celetná, you can continue your exploration of the city along a stretch of the former Royal Way. Almost by the junction with the square, you will find the **Kavárna Egona Erwina Kirshe** (Egon

Erwin Kisch Cafe), named in memory of the German-Jewish writer who became famous during the 1920s as a roving reporter. Examples of his work can be found in the two bookshops on the left-hand side of the road, or in the second-hand shops under the arcades.

A little further on, where an alley joins the main road from the right, stands the house known as the **Dům U černé Matky boží** ㉓ (House of the Black Madonna; open Tues–Sun; entrance fee). Its rondo-cubist style lends the little square a distinctive note and demonstrates that even in 1912 it was possible to renovate and build anew in the modern idiom without destroying the optical harmony of an entire district.

The end of Celetná is dominated by the **Prašná brána** ㉔ (Powder Tower; open Apr–Oct daily 10am–6pm; entrance fee). In 1475, King Vladislav Jagiello had a fortified building erected beside his royal residence, on the site of a defensive gate which had marked the boundary of the

BELOW: exterior detail of the Municipal House.

Old Town since the 13th century. Badly damaged by the Prussians during the Seven Years' War, it was rebuilt in neo-Gothic style at the end of the 19th century. It was during the 18th century, when it was used as a powder magazine, that the tower acquired its present name.

Next door – where the former royal court was situated – stands the **Obecní dům ㉕** (Municipal House; guided tours daily; entrance fee) home to the Prague Symphony Orchestra. Architects Antonín Balšánek and Osvald Polívka produced the preliminary designs for this art nouveau building in 1903 and work was completed in 1911. It was conceived as a cultural as well as a civic centre.

The best Czech artists of the period were called on to contribute to the lavish interiors which are sumptuously decorated with inlaid floors, stained glass windows, wrought iron work and panels of wood and marble. Conducted tours of the art nouveau splendours of Alfons Mucha's Mayor's Chamber and other rooms are

available. Immediately behind the Municipal House is another notable building, this one dating from 1907: the **Hotel Paříž** which displays a mixture of neo-Gothic and art nouveau styles.

Returning to the centre of the Old Town via the street 17.listopadu, you will come to the **Uměleckoprůmýslové muzeum ㉖** (Museum of Decorative Arts; open Tues–Sun; entrance fee), which has a collection of Czech and European crafts from the 16th to the 19th century, in particular Bohemian glass, as well as rotating exhibitions and a small gift shop.

Diagonally opposite the museum is the **Dům umělců ㉗** (Rudolfinum; box office Alšovo nábřeží 12, tel: 2489 3352; art gallery: open Tues–Sun; entrance fee), an impressive building in neo-Renaissance style, facing Náměstí Jana Palacha (Jan Palach Square). During the years 1918–38 it was the seat of the Czechoslovakian parliament, but today it has returned to its original use, as the home of the Czech Philharmonic Orchestra. Many concerts in the Prague Spring Festival take place in the Dvořak Hall concery hall and the Rudolfinum's gallery is an important venue for foreign artists.

Map
on pages
140–41

The St Agnes Convent

The **Anežský klášter ㉘** (St Agnes Convent; open Tues–Sun 10am–6pm; guided tours; entrance fee) lies on the banks of the Vltava, off the beaten tourist track yet only a few minutes' walk further along the river. After years of restoration work, the convent, the oldest Gothic building complex in Prague, was reopened in 1980. The convent contains a permanent exhibition of 19th-century Czech painting and sculpture, including works by Mikuláš Aleš, as well as excellent rotating exhibitions and frequent evening concerts of classical music.

The cloister is adorned with plain early-Gothic vaulting and simple capitals, but unusually fine and expressive stone carvings are found in the Chapter Room and the adjoining Church of St Saviour to the right. The archway is decorated with five crowned heads on each side – men to the right and women to the left.

LEFT: resident of Prague. **RIGHT:** the magnificent facades of Paris Street.

Map on pages 140–141

THE MALA STRANA AND HRADCANY

One of the best-preserved areas of Prague, the Malá Strana abounds with baroque architecture and landscaped gardens, while the silhouette of Prague Castle is the best-known view of the city

On the other side of the Vltava, Prague reveals a very different - character from that of the bourgeois Old Town. In the vicinity of the river, the **Malá Strana** (Lesser Quarter) was previously the home of skilled workers, carters and fishermen; even today, it is a quarter inhabited mostly by diplomats, foreign business people and pensioners. Dominating the area is the residential district on the slopes of Hradčany, where the magnificent palazzi of the aristocracy rise amid wealthy monasteries and churches. Towering above it all is the imperial - cathedral and the castle – the seat of the rulers of Prague for over 1,000 years.

The Charles Bridge

The **Karlův most** ㉙ (Charles Bridge) remains the main link between the two halves of the city even today. In contrast to the thundering traffic on the other bridges, the Karlův most is an oasis of calm, apart from the tourists of course. Charles IV had the fine stone bridge constructed by his master builder, Peter Parler. There had been a stone bridge here before, the Judith Bridge, constructed during the latter half of the 12th century and named after the wife of King Vladislav I. But, like its wooden predecessors, it could no longer stand the force of the Vltava and collapsed in 1342.

Charles then wanted to create a permanent link between the two settlements on opposite sides of the river, which in those days were frequently at loggerheads with each other. Begun in 1357, the bridge itself represents the central section of the "Royal Way", along which in medieval times the sovereign walked to his coronation. Upstream from the Old Town Bridge, the dramatic weir vividly evokes Smetana's symphonic poem *The Moldau*.

Ahead and to the right, the view is dominated by the Cathedral of St Vitus, the crowning the summit of Castle Hill, and at the end of the bridge the Malá Strana is framed between the two **Malostranské mostecké věže** (Lesser Quarter Bridge Towers; open April–Oct daily 10am–6pm; entrance fee). The northern tower was built at the same time as the Charles Bridge, but the southern one is a remnant of the old Judith Bridge.

After passing under the arch, carry on along Mostecká (Bridge Street) before turning left into the Lázeňská. Continuing past the former hotels, The Spa and The Golden Unicorn (where Beethoven

LEFT: the nave of St Vitus's Cathedral.
RIGHT: the Charles Bridge connects the Old Town with the Lesser Quarter.

once stayed), you will soon reach the oldest place of worship in the Lesser Quarter, the **Kostel Panny Marie pod řetězem** ⓾ (Church of St Mary Beneath the Chains; open for services and concerts), dating from the 12th century. The massive facade combines both Romanesque and Gothic elements. The adjoining Velkopřevoské nám. is bordered by the elegant palazzi; the **Velkopřevorské náměstí** (Maltese Grand Prior's Palace; open daily; entrance fee) houses an interesting collection of historical musical instruments.

During the last decade of communist rule, the palace garden and the island of **Kampa** ⓛ next door, accessible via a small bridge over the Čertovka Channel, became the favourite meeting place for the flower children of Prague. They left behind lovingly executed murals, including one of John Lennon, in the district of the city known as Little Venice on account of its beautiful water mills and gardens. Retracing your steps, cross the **Maltézské náměstí** (Maltese Square), site of the

noble **Nostický palác** (Nostiz Palace), which is now the home of the Dutch Embassy, and the **Turbovský palác** (Turba Palace), now the Japanese Embassy. Turning into Karmelitská, where the Vrtbovský Palace at No. 25 is notable primarily for its baroque terraced garden, the route returns to Mostecká.

Around Lesser Quarter Square

The **Malostranské náměstí** ⓜ (Lesser Quarter Square) has been the focal point of the busy settlement under Hradčany Castle since the 10th century. It used to be the site where the daily market was held, and the meeting place of trading associations. The Jesuits transformed the predominantly bourgeois air of this town centre. Exactly as they did when building the Klementinum on the other side of the Vltava, they purchased a large tract of land, had all its buildings razed to the ground – an entire street, two churches and a cemetery – and started building the massive **Chrám sv. Mikuláše** ⓝ (Church of St Nicholas; open Apr–Sept daily, Oct–Mar Sat–Sun; entrance fee for concerts).

It is regarded as the masterpiece of Christoph and Kilian Ignaz Dientzenhofer, and its monumental baroque architecture is a lesson in history. Every detail – from the powerful ceiling frescoes to the forbidding statues of the four Fathers of the Church to the elaborately decorated pulpit – expresses the power and absolute authority of the victorious Catholic Church.

A comparison with the simple and austere Bethlehem Chapel, in which the heretic Jan Hus preached his sermons, clearly illustrates the full significance of the Counter-Reformation in this Protestant country.

In the immediate vicinity, in Letenská, which opens onto the square on the northern side, stand the **Klášter a Kostel sv. Tomáš** ⓞ (Monastery and Church of St Thomas; open for services). The foundation and construction of the Augustinians' Gothic basilica dates from the 13th century, and Kilian Ignaz Dientzenhofer gave the church its present appearance, including its imposing facade and the bright interior. The former town hall

LEFT: a veteran of the times looks on.

Map
on pages
140–141

(No. 21) was the administrative centre of the Malá Strana until the creation of Metropolitan Prague. It is now a cultural centre, **Malostranská beseda** and a popular venue for jazz and pop music.

Nerudova (Neruda Alley) is lined with Renaissance, baroque and neoclassical palazzi reflecting the prosperity of the nobility, who chose to build their residences on the approach road to the castle. There are some delightful house signs, especially The Three Violins (No. 12), The Golden Goblet (No. 16), The Golden Horseshoe (No. 33), The Black Madonna (No. 36) and The Two Suns (No. 37). The latter was the home of the poet Jan Neruda (1834–91), the author of the *Tales of the Lesser Quarter*.

Along the lower section, at No. 5, is the imposing **Czerninsko-Morzinský palác** (Czernin-Morzin Palace) on the left, dating from 1714, with an impressive door and a balcony supported by statues of Moors. The palace is home to the Romanian Embassy. Built at about the same time

was the **Thun-Hohenstejnský palác** (Thun-Hohenstein Palace), diagonally opposite at No. 20 which now houses the Italian Embassy.

Next door are the **Kostel a klášter sv. Kajetán** (Church and Monastery of St Cajetan), creating an architectural unity typical of the end of the 17th century. At its upper end, the Nerudova gives way to a romantic stairway leading to the castle. To the left, the Loretánská leads out to the Loreto Shrine and the district Nový Svět.

The Loreto of Prague

Loreto is a place of pilgrimage in Italy. It was believed that angels transported the sacred home of the Virgin Mary from the Promised Land to Loreto in the 13th century. When the Catholic Habsburgs tried during the Counter-Reformation to convert their Hussite subjects back to the "true faith", they used the pious legend to serve their cause. They had replicas of the Santa Casa built throughout the land. The best known and most attractive of these

BELOW:
the Lesser
Quarter and
St Nicholas
viewed from
the castle.

is the **Loreta** (Loreto of Prague; open Tues–Sun; entrance fee) built between 1626 and 1750. Unlike the simple original, the shrine became, over the centuries, an entire complex consisting of various buildings with a chapel, cloisters several storeys high, and the Church of the Nativity. Dominating the group is the early baroque tower, into which a carillon, which chimes every hour, was built in 1694. The Loreto's main attraction is the **Komora pokladů** (treasure chamber), in which are stored the precious votive gifts presented by pious pilgrims to the statue of the Virgin Mary.

The castle quarter

Nový Svět ❸ (New World) is a picturesque alley leading off Loreto Square. For many centuries it was the poorest district of the **Hradčany** (castle quarter). Today, however, the tiny, lovingly restored cottages with their doll's-house windows and tiny front gardens have made it a popular residential area for local artists,

if they can afford the rent. For a long time, the **Hradčanské náměstí** ❸ (Castle Square), enclosed by magnificent buildings, formed an independent community, albeit under the control of the lords of the castle. Beside the stairs leading up from the Nerudova, the former town hall, dating from 1598, is adorned with both the imperial and municipal coats of arms.

The southern side of the square is dominated by the stucco facade of the **Schwarzenberský palác** ❸ (Schwarzenberg Palace; open Apr–Nov Tues–Sun; entrance fee), with its distinctive sgraffito patterns. Completed in 1563, it is regarded as one of the finest examples of Bohemian Renaissance, and today houses the **Vojenské historické muzeum** (Museum of Military History).

Beside the entrance to the castle, the **Arcibiskupský palác** (Archbishop's Palace; open on Maundy Thurs only) adds an additional note of architectural splendour and contains the exquisite French Gobelin Tapestries and other treasures.

BELOW: the entrance to the first courtyard of Prague Castle.

Maps:
page 140
& below

The **Sternberský palác** ❸❽ (Sternberg Palace; open Tues–Sun 10am–6pm; guided tours; entrance fee) behind contains the National Gallery's priceless collection of European paintings from the 14th–20th century and is well worth a visit.

Prague Castle

Pražský hrad ❸❾ (Prague Castle; open summer 9am–5pm, winter until 4pm; entrance fee) is more than 1,000 years old; the first Czech rulers, the Přemyslids, established their main residence here, on a strategic site dominating the ford over the Vltava. Since then, succeeding generations of rulers have enlarged the complex with chapels, palaces, defensive structures and residential buildings.

A tour of Prague Castle begins in front of the **Matyášova brána** Ⓐ (Matthias Gate) in the first courtyard, the most recent of the three. To the right, a flight of steps leads up to the former Throne Room; today this is where state receptions are held. The second courtyard, with its beautiful baroque fountain, is more extensive. The **Kaple sv. Kříže** Ⓑ (Chapel of the Holy Cross) is to the right, built by Anselmo Lurago in 1753. The cathedral treasure, including reliquaries, monstrances, crucifixes, and mementos of Bohemian saints and kings, has been on view here since 1961.

Sharp left, in the northwest corner, is the **Hradní galerie** Ⓒ (Castle Gallery), which since 1964 has housed rediscovered works of art collected by the Habsburgs in the 16th and 17th century; above this are the **Španělský sál** (Spanish Room) and **Emperor Rudolf's Gallery**. Rudolf II, the last ruler to bring imperial glamour to Prague, was an eccentric collector. To the wry amusement of his contemporaries, he showed no interest in politics, but assembled a curious collection of artefacts, including stuffed exotic animals, alchemists' tools and objects for use in shamanistic rituals. Although this remarkable collection was dispersed by war and plundering, and at one stage

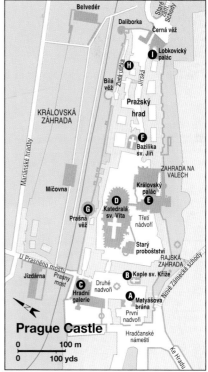

Prague Castle

largely removed to Vienna, what remains is still well worth seeing. Through the north gate of the second courtyard, a causeway leads across the old moat directly to the landscaped **Královska zahradá** (Royal Gardens, open Apr–Sept 9am–5pm), known today as the Presidential Gardens.

Head straight for the beautiful Renaissance **Belvedér**. In front of the building stands the so-called Singing Fountain, from which there is an attractive view of the magnificent cathedral across the moat, now transformed into a deer enclosure.

St Vitus's Cathedral

The **Katedrála sv. Víta** (Cathedral of St Vitus; open daily), a Gothic basilica 124 metres (405 ft) long and 60 metres (196 ft) wide, was begun in 1344 on the instructions of Charles IV. The first of his inspired architects, Matthew of Arras, was trained in the French Gothic school and his basic design for the cathedral reflects this background. After his death, Peter Parler and his sons continued the work, but gave the building their own individual stamp. Since it is impossible to step back and admire the facade from a distance, the visitor can only take it in as a steeply vertical wall. Consequently, entering the vast nave can be disorienting. There are no mysterious shafts of light as in other great cathedrals, for the original glass was replaced by modern panes. At first glance, too, the cathedral seems to lack a unity of style – partly because of the numerous extensions and additions across the centuries, the last being as recently as 1929, and partly because the church was planned from not only as a place of worship but also as a coronation church, mausoleum and destination of national pilgrimage. The statues on the triforium record the important figures associated with the cathedral, ranging from Charles IV to more contemporary personalities.

The magnificent **Kaple sv. Václava** (Chapel of St Wenceslas; entry not possible, must be viewed from the entryway),

BELOW: view of St Vitus's Cathedral from Novy Street.

Map on page 159

in the south transept, is dedicated to the life and works of the saint. Two arches further on, in the chapel of the Holy Cross, a staircase descends to remnants of the early medieval building, and to the Royal Crypt, with the sarcophagus of Charles IV. Don't forget to look upwards to admire the lozenges adorning the roof of the choir, the work of architect Peter Parler. His extraordinary skills are also evident on the south side of the choir, where the interplay of columns and struts and the remarkable complexity of the tracery are especially impressive.

Unusual in both position and execution is the **Zlatá brána** (Golden Door) and the remarkable entrance hall on the south flank. It is the main entrance to the cathedral and it was through here that monarchs passed en route to their coronation. A monarch's journey was not a long one, as the **Královský palác** ❺ (Royal Palace) lay directly opposite. The visitor enters the majestic **Vladislavkýz sál** (Vladislav Hall) via the Riders' Staircase, made wide

enough for rulers and guests to enter the room on horseback for tournaments. The intricate vaulting, spanning the whole width of the hall, makes it one of the most remarkable architectural achievements of the late Gothic era in central Europe.

The **Bohemian Chancellery** was situated in the adjoining rooms. On 23 May 1618, the furious citizens of Bohemia entered the room of the imperial governors Martinic and Slavata and threw them, and their secretary, out of the window. Although they all survived the 15-metre (50-foot) drop into the moat, this Second Defenestration of Prague sparked off the Thirty Years' War.

Opposite the eastern choir lies the Romanesque **Bazilika sv. Jiří** ❻ (St George's Basilica). Despite extensions and rebuilding schemes during Renaissance and baroque times, the church has retained its original early medieval appearance and, following a recent renovation, has been restored to its former glory. The adjoining convent houses a rich

BELOW: the stained-glass window of St Vitus's Cathedral.

collection of Czech Gothic and baroque art. Behind the cathedral, the late Gothic castle fortifications are dominated by the massive **Prašná věž ❻** (Mihulka Powder Tower) containing, among other curiosities, an alchemist's workshop.

Circumnavigating St George's and then turning uphill to the left, the route continues into the atmospheric **Zlatá ulička ❼** (Golden Lane), also known as Goldmakers' Alley, with antique shops, bookshops and a pub. The tiny houses, tucked into the arches of the battlements, have been the homes of craftsmen, goldsmiths and tailors for four centuries, conveniently situated to serve their exalted neighbours. Franz Kafka lived for a short while at No. 22, and the museum there is usually full of curious visitors.

From here, continue downhill, past the former burgrave's office – now the Children's House – to the **Lobkovický palác, ❶** (Lobkovic Palace; gardens partly open to public daily, palace open Tues–Sun), housing exhibitions on Czech history.

Through the East Gate, in the shadow of the **Černá věž** (Black Tower), is a terrace with a panoramic view. From here, you can descend the Old Castle Steps.

Waldstein Palace and gardens

Down below, the route turns right and then right again into a second alley, the Letenská. The first section runs alongside a blank wall, until a gateway suddenly provides access to the lovely gardens of the **Valdštejnský palác ❹** (Waldstein Palace, also called Wallenstein; gardens open May–Sept 9am–7pm). This was the very first baroque palace in Prague, built by the legendary general Albrecht von Wallenstein (1581–1634).

The massive building, is not open to the public, but the tranquil garden with its fountains and groups of statues is, and open-air concerts are sometimes held here. Unfortunately, when the Swedes conquered the Malá Strana and with it the palace of their former enemy, they removed the magnificent bronze figures by

BELOW: houses along Golden Lane.

Maps:
City 140
Castle 159

the mannerist sculptor Adriaen de Vries. Nonetheless, some have been replaced by replicas, including the Laocoon group. The park extends as far as the Garden Room, where the unusual barrel-vaulted ceiling is decorated with illustrations of the Trojan War – an allegorical portrayal of Wallenstein's military zeal in the Thirty Years' War.

Valdštejnské náměstí (Waldstein Square) is dominated by the broad facade of the palace. Next door stands the **Lede-burský palác** (Lebedour Palace, No. 3). Construction commenced in 1588, as the date carved above the doorway indicates, but the building assumed its present form during the 19th century.

Other buildings of note in the square and in the adjacent Waldstein Street are the **Pálffy Palace** (No. 14), **Kolovratský palác** (Kolovrat Palace, No. 110) and, at the far end, the **Furstenbergský palác** (Furstenberg Palace). Virtually all received their elegant facades during the 18th century. Even more attractive are the

BELOW:
blossom in
Strahov Park.

gardens on the slopes of Castle Hill, designed by baroque landscape architects. Sněmovní (Parliament Street) leads back to the Malostranské náměstí.

At No. 4 is the **Thunský palác** (Thun Palace), converted into the local parliament building in 1801. A memorial plaque recalls the fact that the first parliament of the Czechoslovak Republic met here on 14 November 1918 and officially deposed the Habsburg emperors.

Around Petřín Hill

If you board the No. 22 tram by the National Theatre and travel across the Vltava as far as Holeckova, you will see, just opposite the tram stop, a signpost announcing the Lanová dráha and indicating the way to the cable car up **Petřín** (Petřín Hill; tower open Apr–Oct daily, Nov–March weekends).

This ancient cable car runs every 20 minutes, but it is far more pleasant to walk through the orchards and meadows. At the beginning the route passes a monument

to the writer Jan Neruda; above the first cable car station, the rambling café terrace of the Vinárna Nebozízek offers a breathtaking panorama.

On the summit of the hill are a number of interesting sights: the **Kaple sv. Vavřinec** (Chapel of St Lawrence; open daily), originally Romanesque but now almost entirely baroque, the **Bludíště** (Labyrinth of Mirrors), and the **Rozhledna** (Observation Tower) – a small-scale replica of the Eiffel Tower, which offers a remarkable view over the city. The tower and the labyrinth were both built for the Jubilee Exhibition of 1891.

Strahov Monastery

Another important landmark lies only a few minutes' walk away. By passing through a baroque gateway, you can reach the **Strahovský klášter a knihovna** ④ (Strahov Monastery and library; open Tues–Sun 9am–noon, 1–5pm). The oldest buildings in this complex were completed after 1143, but completely destroyed by a

fire in 1258. The wars of the following centuries also left their mark, with the result that very little remains of the original Romanesque building. Today the monastery is predominantly baroque in style, but it contains early Gothic and Renaissance elements.

Only **Kostel sv. Marie** (St Mary's Church; same opening hours as the monastery) retains traces of the Romanesque original. The monastery library is one of the most beautiful and comprehensive historic libraries in Europe. The basis of the collection of over 130,000 volumes, including 2,500 first editions, was established by a perspicacious abbot in the middle of the 18th century. The secularisation under Emperor Joseph II led to the dissolution of a large number of monasteries, but Strahov was spared. The abbot took advantage of the dissolution to purchase a number of valuable collections. In 1945 the collection was enriched by the addition of works from other monasteries which were being closed down by the new regime.

Among the greatest treasures are the *Strahov Gospels*, dating from the 10th century (the book on display is only a replica: the original is in safe keeping), and a first edition of *De Revolutionibus Orbium Coelestium*, the work in which Copernicus first expounded his heliocentric theory of the universe in 1543.

The library's true fascination lies in the exquisite form of the two main rooms. The **Teologický sál** (Theologians' Hall), with baroque frescoes in the stucco cartouches, is particularly attractive. Here you will find a small, barred shrine which contained books banned by the church's censors. In the middle of the room stand a number of valuable globes from the Netherlands, dating from the 17th century. The Theologians' Hall is currently undergoing renovation but is due to reopen in the near future.

The **Filozofický sál** (Philosophers' Hall) is notable for its rich gold inlay on the walnut cupboards and the elaborate ceiling frescoes depicting the harmony of philosophy, science and religion, by the rococo artist Anton Maulbertsch. ❑

Map on pages 140–141

LEFT: the Philosophers' Hall in the Strahov Monastery Library. **RIGHT:** guard outside the first courtyard of Prague Castle.

Master Builders

Charles IV, the scion of the Přemyslids who attained the imperial crown in 1355, transformed Prague into the political and cultural centre of his vast empire. Under Charles, the city was dubbed the "Mother of All Cities", and the Gothic Prague that is admired by visitors today bears his stamp. The Charles University, the New Town clustered around Wenceslas Square and Charles Square, the Charles Bridge and – towering above all – the Cathedral of St Vitus – were all part of Charles's legacy.

Peter Parler

On 1356 Peter Parler was summoned to work on the Cathedral of St Vitus as the successor to Matthew of Arras. In choosing the young Parler, Charles provided Prague with a master builder of genius, entirely equal to the task of reflecting his imperialist aspirations. Parler came from a German family of builders and sculptors who made a significant contribu-

tion to the development of Central European Gothic art and architecture. The family name, Parler, stems from Parlier or Polier, the title of the second-in-command of a team of builders. As their master's trademark, the family used an angle bar in the form of an S-rune interrupted in two places. Parler, the undisputed supreme master builder of the family, was born in 1330 in Schwäbisch Gmünd and buried in 1399 in St Vitus's Cathedral. Charles IV recognised his exceptional talent in the church of the Holy Cross in his home town. The young architect's task in Prague was to prove the most important of his career: the completion of the Gothic cathedral in the Bohemian capital, which in 1344 had been elevated to the rank of archiepiscopal see. The new church was to be used as a coronation cathedral and royal burial place.

Parler's genius can best be appreciated in the Golden Portal and in his design of the chancel. The monumental fan vaulting was the first of its kind in Central Europe and became the model for all German vaulted roofs until the end of the Gothic era. Parler assumed sole responsibility for the completion of the main building begun by his predecessor; by allowing light to flood through the upper walls he created a powerful contrast to the relatively dark lower section of the nave. A further trend was set by the cuboid shape of the building, which arose from the juxtaposition of the smaller units representing the various storeys. The angling of the transept towards the imperial palace provided a powerful link between the sacred and secular worlds.

The Old Town Bridge Tower, built for defence as well as ornament, is one of the loveliest and least corrupted examples of this building-block principle. Marking the entrance to the Charles Bridge, it has a rib-vaulted viewing gallery, and a collection of sculptured figures which include St Wenceslas and St Vitus.

Parler's seminal influence in the field of sculpture is also demonstrated in the row of busts in the cathedral triforium which represent an important stage in the development of medieval portraiture. Parler was also responsible for the All Saints' Chapel in Hradčany Castle, the chancel of the Church of St Bartholomew in Kolín and the Church of St Barbara in Kutná Hora, noted for its beautiful fan vaulting.

LEFT: Peter Parler's statue of St Wenceslas in the cathedral.

The Dientzenhofers

By the time the Dientzenhofers, the second of the great German families of builders, made their artistic mark on Prague, the importance of the former metropolis had degenerated into that of a provincial backwater in the shadow of Vienna. While the magnificence of the monumental Gothic buildings reflected the glory of the reign of Charles IV, the baroque splendour of a later age stood in crass contrast to the cultural and economic decline that the country had suffered since the disastrous Battle of the White Mountain in 1620. The architectural excesses of the baroque era lent the city an illusion of new vitality, but at the same time they testified in stone to the triumph of the Habsburg Counter-Reformation.

This impression persists today, when you walk alongside the wall of the Jesuit Klementinum, which seems to tower over the former Royal Way between Charles Street and the Charles Bridge like a massive fortress. That the powerful ensembles of baroque Prague should be regarded as an architectural triumph is due in no small measure to the influence of the Dientzenhofer family.

Born in the village of Aibling in Upper Bavaria, the five brothers moved to Prague in order to study architecture. Four of them left the city over the years in order to return to South Germany, where they left their mark on a number of important sacred buildings, but Christoph Dientzenhofer (1655–1722) lived the rest of his life in Bohemia, becoming known, with Fischer von Erlach, as one of the fathers of late German baroque. He was influenced by the Italian architect Guarini, and flowing curved facades blend with the traditional Bavarian pilaster system in his churches.

Examples of Christoph Dientzenhofer's skill can be found all over Bohemia. His supreme masterpiece is considered to be the church of St Nicholas in the Lesser Quarter of Prague, which he designed with his son Kilian Ignaz Dientzenhofer (1689–1751).

St Nicholas's, the church commissioned by the Jesuits, was a piece of collaborative work by the Dientzenhofers. The father was responsible for the nave, and the son for the choir and the dome. This jewel of baroque architecture took almost 60 years to complete; it is one of the masterpieces of the era, and its silhouette dominates the skyline of the Lesser Quarter. Both Dientzenhofers died before it was finished, leaving the work in the hands of Anselmo Lurgo.

The younger Dientzenhofer was born in Prague and is regarded as one of the leading architects of late baroque, eclipsing even his father. Although he was responsible for a large number of secular buildings (such as the Villa Amerika, now the Dvořák Museum, and the Palais Kinsky in Staroměstské nám.), Dientzenhofer the Younger's main interest lay in churches. Whilst his father favoured a longitudinal plan, Kilian Ignaz preferred a centralised building, which he laid out in the form of a double shell.

This principle can be seen in the twin-towered centralised design of the church of St John Nepomuk on the Rock in the Nové Mesto. He was also responsible for the reconstruction of the Church of St Thomas after it was struck by lightning in 1723; and for another St Nicholas's, this one in Staroměstské nám., as well as the Church of St Mary Magdalene in Karlsbad (Karlovy Vary). ❑

RIGHT: the dome of St Nicholas is the work of Kilian Ignaz Dientzenhofer.

NOVE MESTO

Despite its name, much of the "New Town" actually dates from the 14th century, and it is the area of Prague that witnessed many of the country's 20th-century upheavals

Map on pages 140–41

Václavské náměstí **42** (Wenceslas Square) is not really a square and could hardly be called beautiful. It is rambling rather than intimate, a long, shrill market place rather than a chic boulevard. But this is in keeping with its original purpose, for it was designed as a horse fair, and was intended to serve as the bustling axis of the Nové Město, the New Town, which Charles IV constructed in a semicircle surrounding the Old Town (Staré Město), which was bursting at the seams.

Although the New Town was founded 600 years ago, much of what we see today dates from the 19th and early 20th centuries, when elegant buildings mushroomed in place of the wooden shacks and dilapidated tenement blocks. Prague's revolutions, the great popular uprisings against despotism and foreign oppression, from the 15th-century Hussite Rebellion to the Velvet Revolution of November 1989, have all begun here; at various times the square has been the stage for displays of national military strength, bitter defeats and jubilant victory parades.

Around Wenceslas Square

The most prominent building on the square houses the **Národní muzeum** **43** (National Museum; open daily except first Tues of each month 10am–6pm; entrance fee). It was constructed between 1885 and 1890 at the instigation of the Bohemian Patriotic Association. It was the Czechs' impressive answer to the nearby German Theatre (now the State Opera House) which had opened a few years previously to the strains of a Wagner opera.

Another reminder of the proud era of Bohemian independence is the equestrian **Socha sv. Václava** **44** (Statue of St Wenceslas), a massive monument erected in 1913. Further down, the square loses its civic character and turns into a lively shop-

ping and pedestrian area. On the left-hand side is the modernist **Palác Alfa** (Palais Alfa), built in 1928. One of the finest examples of art nouveau architecture in Prague is the **Peterkův dům** (Peterka House) situated at the far end of Wenceslas Square. Architect Jan Kotěra built this private residence in just one year (1900). On the other side of the square are the splendid art nouveau **Hotel Evropa** **45**, the Zlatá Husa Hotel, and the Ambassador. The Evropa, dating from 1904, is a popular location for period films. Each floor of the hotel is decorated with floral motifs, mosaics and ornaments. The elegant café has been renovated in the original style.

At the far end of the square, next to the row of hotels, stands the Palais Koruna.

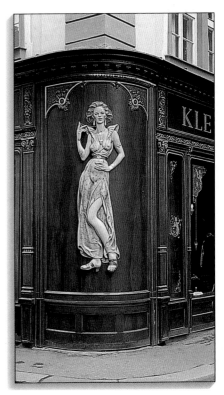

LEFT: facade of the Grand Hotel Europe.
RIGHT: New Town shop front.

Constructed shortly before the war, its architecture demonstrates early constructivist elements combined with the elaborate decorative features of art nouveau.

Na příkopě (The Moat) is a lively pedestrian street, packed with strollers and shoppers. No. 10 is a magnificent baroque palace; it has a garden restaurant and holds cultural events. The **Kancelář Čedok** (Čedok Office; open Mon–Fri 8.30am–6pm) at No. 18 sells plane and train tickets, and the **Pražská informační služba** (Prague Information Service; open Mon–Fri 9am–7pm, Sat–Sun 9am–5pm, closed Sun in winter) is next door, at No. 20. The former aristocratic town house at No. 22 is now a cultural centre with a good restaurant and bistro.

Back on Wenceslas Square, the Alfa Passage leads to the **Kostel Panny Marie Sněžné** ㊻ (Church of Our Lady of the Snows), founded in 1347. It was actually commissioned by Emperor Charles IV as a coronation cathedral, but as a result of the Wars of Religion which broke out a

few years later, only the chancel was completed. The church became famous as the arena of the radical Hussites. In 1419, incited by their preacher, Jan Želivský, they marched to the New Town Hall to demand the release from prison of their brethren and threw two of the imperial councillors from a window.

Street of the Nation

Národní třída (Street of the Nation) is, like Na příkopě, a wide and busy pedestrian area. On the right stands is Tesco; to the left is the enchanting **Kafkův dům** (Kafka House, No. 16) and the baroque **Kostel sv. Voršila** ㊼ (Church of St Ursula, No. 8), with fine frescoes and statues and a dynamic altar painting of the Assumption. The end of the street is dominated by the **Národní divadlo** ㊽ (National Theatre). Built on the banks of the Vltava, this is a fine example of Czech neo-Renaissance architecture and embodies the national enthusiasm for culture in the second half of the 19th century. Funds

BELOW: the National Theatre and the Vltava Bridge.

Map on pages 140–41

to build the theatre were raised mainly by public contributions, and in 1883, the curtain was raised on a gala performance of Smetana's opera *Libuše*, based on the myth of the founding of Prague. The adjacent New Theatre has now become the home of the **Laterna Magika** and has taken the company's name *(see page 107)*.

Slovanský ostrov (Slavic Island), which lies below the theatre, is so called because it was the venue of the first Slavic Congress held in 1848. It is now the site of a popular garden restaurant and cultural events are held here during the evening. The **Mánesův dům umění** (Mánes House of Fine Art; open Tues–Sun; entrance fee) on the banks of the river is interesting: the building itself reveals the influence of the Bauhaus movement, and exhibitions are organised inside by the Artists' Association. There is also an attractive cafe with a splendid view of the river.

In Jiráskovo náměstí, beside the Jiraskův most (bridge), a controversial new building, the work of American architect Frank

Gehry, draws brickbats and bouquets in roughly equal measure. From the square, the Resslova ul. leads away from the Vltava. At the second crossroads stands the Romanesque **Kostel sv. Václava** (Church of St Wenceslas), a Hussite place of worship.

Diagonally opposite, the exuberant baroque facade of the **Kostel sv. Cyrila a Metoděje** ❹ (Church of St Cyril and Methodius; open Tues–Sun) was the scene of a tragic incident in the summer of 1942. The conspirators responsible for the assassination of the hated Reichs protector Reinhard "The Hangman" Heydrich hid in the crypt, but were betrayed to the SS, who surrounded the entire block. The conspirators on guard in the nave held out for two hours before being killed; those remaining in the crypt shot themselves before the Germans reached them. In reprisal, the Nazis destroyed the village of Lidice, 25 km (16 miles) from Prague, shooting all the men and sending women and children to concentration camps.

BELOW: the New Town Hall.

Charles Square

Karlovo náměstí ㉚ (Charles Square) was planned as the hub of the New City from its inception. Today it is dominated by the mighty **Kostel sv. Ignáce** ㉛ (Church of St Ignatius) which served as the headquarters of the Jesuits from 1677. The stately **Novoměstská radnice** ㉜ (New Town Hall, closed to the public), where the Hussite Revolution began in 1419, occupies the northern end of the square. The Town Hall remained the political hub of the New Town until 1784, when the four constituent towns which made up Prague at that time were joined together to form a single administrative unit.

To the south lies the **Faustův dům** ㉝ (Faust House), which has been associated with alchemists since the 14th century. The present building dates from the 16th century, when it was owned by Edward Kelley, who served as alchemist to Rudolf II. It became associated with the legend of Faust in the 18th century, when Count Ferdinand Mladota conducted chemical

Map on pages 140–41

experiments here, arousing great suspicion. A few paces further on stands the **Kostel sv. Jana na Skalce** ㉞ (Church of St John on the Rock). An extravagant staircase leads up to the entrance, flanked by slightly protruding towers which curve away from the main axis of the building. Unfortunately, the church is often locked when services are not in progress.

The **Klášter na Slovanech** ㉟ (Slavonic Monastery, also known as the Emmaus Monastery; open daily) to the south of the square deserves even closer attention. Founded by Charles IV, mass was celebrated here according to the rites of the Old Slavonic Church – an obvious attempt on the part of crown and church to gain influence over the Orthodox Christians of Eastern Europe. Shortly before the end of World War II, many medieval works of art were destroyed when the monastery was bombed, but the fine cloisters, with frescoes dating from about 1360, are well worth seeing.

For visitors in need of refreshment, the **U Fleků**, situated in the Křemencova near the Town Hall, is the ideal choice. One of Prague's most famous taverns, the U Fleků has been brewing its own dark beer since the 15th century. For a more local atmosphere and a fine glass of Budar, try U Medvídků across the road from Tesco.

Vyšehrad

Above the Vltava stand the ruins of **Vyšehrad** castle (gardens open daily) in the district of **Vyšehrad** ㊱. Legend has it that this was the home of Princess Libuše who prophesied the founding of the city. It became the political and religious centre of the country until the construction of Hradčany. Apart from the tiny, Romanesque **Rotunda sv. Martina** ㊲ (St Martin's Rotunda), there remains little evidence of the glorious early years. More interesting is the adjoining **Hřbitov** (cemetery; open daily), where outstanding contributors to Czech cultural life and scientific advances lie buried, and where the **Slavín**, or tomb of honour, stands. The graves of composers Antonín Dvořák and Bedřich Smetana and poets Karel Hynek Mácha and Karel Čapek are here. ❏

LEFT: St Martin's Rotunda.

RIGHT: the church of St John on the Rock.

Map
on page
176

TRIPS FROM PRAGUE

*The excursions in this chapter can all be recommended as day trips
from the capital; the castle of Karlštejn, for example, less than
an hour from Prague, is one of the country's most famous sites*

Every year, **Hrad Karlštejn ①** (Karlštejn Castle), lying some 30 km (19 miles) southwest of Prague on the railway line to Plzeň, is stormed by thousands of tourists in coaches, cars and trains (castle guided tours daily Nov–Mar 9am–3pm, Apr–Oct 9am–4pm, May–June, Sept 9am–5pm, Jul–Aug 9am–6pm; entrance fee).

They achieve what their ancestors never managed, for the fortress, protected by massive walls and protruding cliffs, was impregnable to attackers. But Charles IV did not have Karlštejn built as a military stronghold – strategically speaking, it would have served no useful purpose on this site. It was planned with the sole purpose of safeguarding the holy relics and coronation insignia of the kingdom.

In medieval times these relics were of immense significance: they included two thorns from Jesus's crown, a fragment of the sponge soaked in vinegar offered to him on the Cross, a tooth of St John the Baptist and the arm of St Anne. To possess such treasures was seen as a sign of God's favour, a blessing for the emperor and his subjects. Even if Charles had felt no regard for this precious legacy personally, it would have been regarded as an unpardonable sin if they had not been used to further the greater glory of the emperor and the Holy Roman Empire.

Charles's collection of relics was presented once a year for public worship. On the Friday after Easter, the Day of the Holy Relics, the people flocked to the Karlštejn, and on 29 November, the anniversary of the death of Charles IV, Mass is still celebrated in the Chapel of the Cross, where the most precious items are preserved.

It was built in the 14th century by Matthew of Arras and Peter Parler, but much of what we see today is a reconstruction, dating from the 19th century.

You can reach the castle by road along the Berounka Valley, or – best of all – by one of the frequent slow trains from Prague's Smíchov Station. From Karlštejn station the castle is a pleasant stroll across the river, through the village and uphill through the castle grounds.

A tour of Karlštejn Castle

Tours start at the **Císařský palác** (Imperial Palace), before proceeding to St Mary's Tower, the Great Tower and, highest of all, the Chapel of the Cross. The palace, which includes the **Velký sál** (Great Hall), the Audience Chamber and the private apartments of the sovereign and his wife, are lavishly appointed. The ornamentation of the rooms housing the relics, however,

LEFT: Karlštejn Castle.
RIGHT: at a folk festival in Jihlava.

is almost beyond imagination. In the **Kostel Panny Marie** (Church of Our Lady), Charles's court painter, Nikolaus Wurmser, portrayed the emperor with the sacred relics of the Passion beneath a heaven filled with an angelic host. The **Kaple sv. Kateřiny** (Chapel of St Catherine), adorned with semi-precious stones, is where Charles IV spent days and nights in silent meditation. Above the door to the chapel is a portrait of the emperor with his second wife, Anna von Schweidnitz, carrying a massive cross.

The **Kaple ostatkového kříže** (Chapel of the Cross) itself is decorated with over 2,000 semi-precious stones. It is divided into two sections by a golden railing; the precious relics were preserved in the sanctuary, which only the emperor or the priests were allowed to enter. The walls are covered with over 100 paintings by Master Theoderic, dating from the mid-14th century; more relics are set into the picture frames. Owing to recent damage, this chapel is no longer open to the public

for viewing. After so much pomp and splendour, a short walk in the attractive surroundings of the castle provides a welcome contrast. The Bohemian karst (limestone) on which it is built is the setting for a number of romantic lakes nestling in forests inhabited by a wide range of wildlife. In summer these lakes are popular with swimmers. The nearby caves of **Koněpruské jeskyně** are also open to the public; in medieval times they were used as workshops by counterfeiters.

Lidice

Twenty-five km (16 miles) to the west of Prague, off the main road to Slany, is **Lidice** ❷ (memorial and museum open daily; entrance fee), the site of a World War II massacre carried out by the SS in retaliation for the assassination of the Reichsprotector Reinhard "The Hangman" Heydrich by members of the Czech resistance on 4 June 1942. It is believed that the SS received false information that Lidice had harboured the assassins. On

LEFT: a promising pub sign.

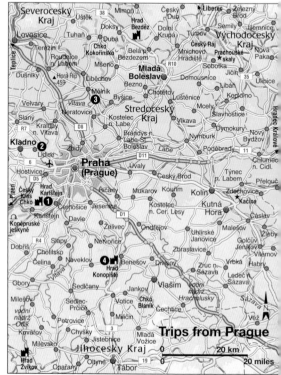

Trips from Prague

Map on page 176

the night of 9 June, all 95 houses were burned to the ground. All 192 adult male occupants were shot on the spot; the women were taken to Ravensbrück concentration camp, where many of them were tortured to death. The 105 children were transported to Lodz, and many of them died in the gas chambers. After the war, a new village was built next to the ruins of the old. A rose garden was planted and the site became a memorial. The museum to the left of the entrance shows films of the destruction and reconstruction of Lidice.

Terezín

The former Nazi concentration camp of **Terezín** (Theresianstadt), northwest from Lidice, makes for another sombre journey. Originally a garrison town established by Empress Maria Theresa (hence its name), it was used during World War II as a detention centre for Jews, political prisoners and prisoners of war. Although not an official extermination camp, those who did not die here of disease or starvation were sent off to more lethal camps such as Auschwitz. Some 140,000 people passed through Terezín. The camp also had the bizarre distinction of being used by the Nazis for propaganda in 1942 as a "model concentration camp" which fooled even the Red Cross.

Visitors today can see numerous exhibits documenting Terezín's sad past. Especially illuminating is the **Muzeum Ghetta** (Ghetto Museum; open daily; entrance fee) just off the main town square. More authentic still is a tour of the **malá pevnost** (Small Fortress; open daily; entrance fee) 2 km (1 mile) south of town, which contained the prison.

Mělník

During the 9th century the Slavic Pšovan dynasty constructed a castle at **Mělník ❸** (tours daily Mar–Sept; entrance fee), where the Vltava flows into the Labe (Elbe), about 32 km (20 miles) north of Prague. The castle served as a dowager

residence for the princesses of Bohemia and the settlement grew into a flourishing trading centre. Under the direction of Charles IV vineyards were established on the slopes above the Elbe. Not only was the red Burgundy-type wine popular at the imperial court, but it also brought considerable revenues to the town. The town sided with the moderate reformers during the Hussite rebellion and found themselves on the winning side at the end of the wars. As the hosts to three national Utraquist conferences between 1438 and 1442, the town enjoyed the special favour of George of Poděbrady, the leader of the faction, who rose to the position of king of Bohemia. Fortunes declined when his widow died in the Residence of Mělník.

Under a succession of further rulers the castle was rebuilt, fell into decay again and during the baroque era acquired its current character as a château. The architecture of the château reflects its historical development – each of the three main wings is characterised by a different style.

In the west wing the Gothic influence is dominant, displaying a certain strictness of form; in the north, the Renaissance is clearly evident in the imaginative arcaded walks and ornamental facades, and in the south the opulence of the baroque style unfolds. The centre of Mělník is very picturesque, although much of it is in need of repair. The market place, with its fountain commemorating the grape harvest, is framed by a curving arc of arcaded town houses. The clock tower on the Radnice (Town Hall) and the Church of the Fourteen Auxiliary Saints complete the harmonious effect. On the far side of the square, a busy street leads down to the Prague Gate and the impressive remains of the town fortifications.

Map on page 176

Konopiště Castle

About 40 km/25 miles southeast of Prague is **Hrad Konopiště** ❹ (open Tues–Sun, May–Sept 9am–noon, 1–4pm, Oct closes 3pm; entrance fee) dating from the 13th century. In 1423, in the midst of war, the two Hussite factions negotiated over liturgical details here.

After plundering by the Swedish army during the Thirty Years' War, the entire complex – originally built in Gothic style – was rebuilt as a baroque residence. It was Archduke Franz Ferdinand, however, the heir to the Habsburg throne who was assassinated in Sarajevo in 1914, who converted it into a fine private palace, which he proceeded to embellish with an extravagant collection of works of art.

Visitors are greeted by a solitary baroque gateway in front of the moat; the high walls are dominated by the **Východní věž** (East Tower). Of particular note is the large banqueting hall, with two Gobelíny (Gobelin tapestries) from Paris, and the sketches made for Cervantes' *Don Quixote*. The smoking room, the library and the chapel on the second floor, as well as the countless hunting trophies adorning the corridors and staircases, bear witness to the sophisticated pleasures of the lord of the castle and his guests. The vast castle grounds with their rose garden, ponds and game enclosures are open to visitors (tours Tues–Sun; entrance fee). ❑

LEFT: Konopiš has an Englis style park. **RIGHT:** panel paintin in the Chapel of the Cross in Karlštejn Castle.

Map on page 184

SOUTHERN BOHEMIA

Dotted throughout the Bohemian Forest landscape of woodland,
mountain ranges and lakes are the exquisite villages
and castles of this historic region

Jan Hus and the Hussites have frequently cropped up in this guide, with Hus himself portrayed as a God-fearing reformer, an eloquent opponent of splendour and bigotry, and a social revolutionary. But in Prague – the Bethlehem Chapel and Jan Hus memorial notwithstanding – evidence of his movement, which for centuries determined the history of the country, is rather hard to find.

In **Tábor ❶**, some 90 km (56 miles) south of Prague, every stone recalls the Hussite era. The town itself is easily reached on the E55 trunk road towards České Budějovice (Budweis) and Linz. According to the Bible, Christ's Transfiguration took place on Mount Tábor. The Hussites had this in mind when, in 1420, they gathered in their thousands near Kotnov Castle. It was five years after the execution of their teacher Jan Hus and a few months after their rebellion in Prague.

Men, women and children took up arms against the imperial army to fight against Catholic bigotry. The camp required fortifications, and from it grew the new town of Tábor. It was the starting point for a long campaign which culminated in the glorious victories at Vítkov in 1420 and Deutsch-Brod in 1422. However, after their brilliant leader, Jan Žižka, fell in 1424, a schism rent the movement in two – the moderate Utraquists and the radical Taborites. Divided, their strength inevitably waned. A crushing defeat for the Taborites at Lipany in 1434 finally put an end to their hopes and allowed George of Poděbrady to take power.

After the war Tábor grew into a bustling town. All Christian sects, including the Catholics, were tolerated and the inhabitants coexisted peacefully as Bohemian Brethren, Waldensians and moderate Utraquists. The spirit of rebellion was still burning bright, however, and whenever the citizens of Bohemia rose up

against serfdom and usury, the Taborite flag with its black background and red chalice would be seen fluttering among the rebel ranks. They were drawn into the defeat at the Battle of the White Mountain in 1620, after which they were forced to pay tribute to the Habsburgs.

A tour of Tábor

Nonetheless, the little town still offers a fascinating glimpse of life in this stormy era. From the main road you should turn off to the right and park in the car park near the ruined castle. From here you can visit the mighty **Válcová věž** (Round Tower) and the **Bechin Gate**, which houses a small historical exhibition. The streets were deliberately made narrow and

winding for defensive purposes. A fascinating tour of the cellars can be taken from the Town Museum. They climb up to **Žižkovo náměstí** (Žižka Square), which – like most of the rest of the town – has cellars and subterranean passages, sentry posts and storage areas. Since the Czech Nationalist Movement in the 19th century discovered its precursors in the proud Taborites, the square has been dominated by a monumental statue of the leader of the Hussite legions.

Nearby are the **Rolandova fontána** (Roland Fountain) and two simple stone tables, at which Holy Communion used to be distributed. The lofty tower of the Church of the Transfiguration dates from Hussite times. It soars above the former **Radnice** (Town Hall; open Apr–Oct Tues–Sun, Nov–Mar Mon–Fri, May–Sept daily; entrance fee), now a museum dedicated to the Hussite Movement, with its huge municipal coat of arms and a two-storey council chamber.

Pražská ulice, which has a number of attractive Renaissance houses, starts in the southeast corner of the square. During the past few years the side streets have undergone their own miniature renaissance; artists have established studios here, and a number of new galleries, antique shops and bookshops have opened. The old town wall should also be seen: the northern section is still in good repair. From here you can enjoy a panorama across the Jordán Reservoir. Created in 1492, it is the oldest construction of its kind in Bohemia.

East of Tábor

Halfway to Pelhřimov is **Hrad Kámen** (Kamen Castle). It is no coincidence that it houses a **Muzeum motorcyklů** (Motorcycle Museum; open Tues–Sun; entrance fee), for the International Motorcycle Federation was formed in 1904 in Pacov, and in 1906 the first Motor World Championships were held here.

The architecture of **Pacov** (Patzau) blends with the hilly scenery. Where a stronghold and later a fortress once stood

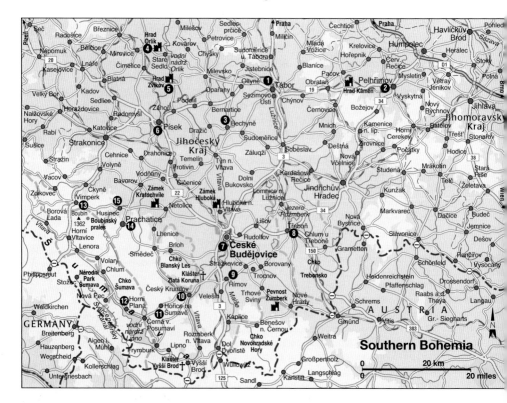

Southern Bohemia

Map on page 184

you can now see a Renaissance palace, its former defensive walls transformed into a magnificent promenade.

Pelhřimov ② (Pilgram) nestles by the River Bělá. The heart of the old town mirrors its history, with its Renaissance and baroque buildings (early Gothic traces are still found under the facades). A few kilometres south of Road No. 19 lies the village of **Včelnice**, with a glass foundry famous for the red glass known as Bohemian Garnet. Another attraction here is the narrow-gauge railway, which replaced an earlier horse-drawn tram, linking the town of Kamenice nad Lipou with Obrataň in the north and Jindřichův Hradec in the south.

Southwest of Tábor

The spa town of **Bechyně ③** has a tradition of pottery making which goes back to the 15th century and is the basis of the town's ceramics industry. Since 1884 it has been the home of a well-known college of ceramics, from which many artists

have graduated. Following the River Lužnice the route returns to the Vltava and the Orlík barrage, which is 60 km (38 miles) long. Dominating the central section of the lake, on the west bank, is **Hrad Orlík ④** (Orlík Castle; open April–Oct Tues–Sun; entrance fee). Originally an early Gothic fortress, the castle was rebuilt on a number of occasions. Surrounded by an attractive garden, the castle contains furniture and memorabilia dating from the time of the Napoleonic Wars.

Another popular castle is **Hrad Zvíkov ⑤** in a romantic setting further south, at the confluence of the Otava and the Vltava rivers. **Písek ⑥**, some 20 km (12 miles) south has a colourful history. A stone bridge dating from 1265, the oldest in Bohemia, crosses the Otava at this point. It formed a part of the Golden Path, the trading route to Bavaria. The settlement prospered on the gold-rich sands of the river bed.

Strakonice is often wrongly described as being an exclusively industrial town.

BELOW: spiral staircase detail inside Orlík Castle.

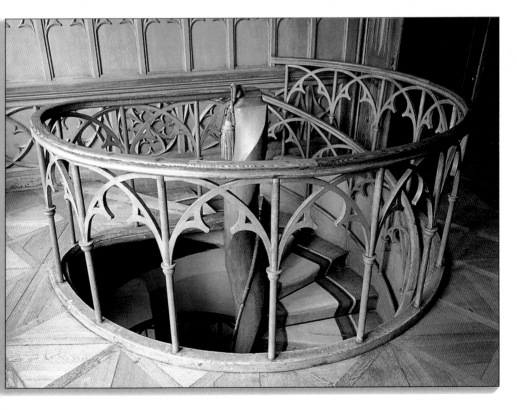

In fact, it has preserved many attractive medieval buildings and is the traditional setting for the International Bagpipe Festival. To the north of the town is the moated castle of **Blatná** (open Tues–Sun; entrance fee), an architectural jewel constructed at the end of the 14th century. The town itself is famous for its rose plantations. Many new varieties were developed here, though the innovative five-petal rose was produced by the horticulturists of Rožmberk in southern Bohemia.

České Budějovice

The 19th-century Czech writer Jan Neruda described the town of **České Budějovice ❼** (Budweis) at the confluence of the Vltava and the Malse as "Bohemia's Florence".

In 1265 the village, established by German settlers, received its town charter from Otakar II, and in 1358 Charles IV granted it staple rights. The discovery of silver deposits during the 16th century increased the wealth of the community and

made it the economic and cultural centre of southern Bohemia. The old town was laid out on the rectangular grid pattern typical of German settlements; the site of the original walls and moat is now a broad belt of parkland. At the centre lies the **Žižovo náměstí** (Zizka Square, named after the Hussite leader), with the main streets radiating from its four corners. In spite of a certain amount of damage over the centuries, its medieval origins are still apparent.

The pretty arcaded houses bordering the square have been meticulously restored. Only a few steps from the massive octagonal fountain, graced by a statue of Samson the lion-tamer, one of the paving stones (distinguished by a cross) marks the spot where, in 1478, the 10 men who murdered the local mayor were executed. Legend has it that anyone who steps upon the *bludný kámen*, the "madmen's stone", after 9pm will be led to hell.

Within the town itself, it is hard for visitors to lose their way. In the southwest of the town, beyond the baroque **radnice** (Town Hall) and the **Biskupský palác** (Bishop's Palace) are the ruins of the town fortifications. In the west, the former **Dominikánský klášter** (Dominican Monastery) lies on the defunct arm of the Vltava; it was founded by the King of Bohemia in 1265 and completed during the 14th century in Gothic style along with the Church of Our Lady of Sacrifice. Also nearby is the former arsenal, built in 1531, and the **Solná brána** (Salt House), the facade of which is liberally decorated with masques.

On the Hroznová to the north of the market place, make a point of visiting the former Masné krámy. The 16th-century "Meat Shops" have been converted into a restaurant and serve as a favourite rendezvous for experts and aficionados of the famous Budvar, the Budweis beer which is exported to 21 countries throughout the world. Suitably refreshed, one can continue to the **Kneislův dům** (Kneisl House) in the northwest corner and the baroque **Kostel sv. Mikuláše** (Church of St Nicholas). Finally, climb the 360 steps of the **Černá věž** (Black Tower), a freestanding belfry which soars above the

LEFT: the Bohemians enjoy music.

Map on page 184

rooftops and affords a bird's-eye view of the other places of historical interest within the town.

The view unfolds as far as **Zámek Hluboká** (Hluboká Castle; open Apr–May, Sept–Oct Tues–Sun 9am–4.30pm; June Tues–Sun 9am–5pm, July–Aug daily 9am–5pm; entrance fee) some 10 km (6 miles) away. The 13th-century former royal stronghold rises majestically from its rocky perch above the River Vltava. Its design has changed numerous times over the years. Today it resembles nothing so much as Windsor Castle. It is worth visiting for the collections of wood carvings, porcelain, tapestries, paintings and furniture collected by the imperial princes of Schwarzenberg.

The castle riding school and the elegant conservatory form the **Jihočeská galerie umění** (Southern Bohemian Gallery of Art; open Tues–Sun; entrance fee), housing an exhibition of southern Bohemian Gothic and Flemish art. The permanent display is supplemented by regular travelling exhibitions, usually of a high standard. The hunting lodge lying a mile or so to the southwest is also of interest; its attractive house and grounds contain the **Lesní a lovecké muzeum** (Museum of Forestry and Hunting; open Tues–Sun; entrance fee) as well as a zoo.

Třeboň

Extensive woodland, meadows, peat bogs, artificial canals, ponds and lakes are characteristic of the countryside surrounding **Třeboň ❽**. Many of the lakes were dug during the 16th century; the largest, covering an area of more than 500 hectares (1,200 acres), is **Jezero Rožmberk** (Rožmberk Lake) to the north of the town.

The lakes made Třeboň the fishery centre of Bohemia, and the local carp are still considered a delicacy. Every three years, a non-stop carp angling competition is held over a period of three days. To the south of Rožmberk Lake is the attractive **Jezero Svět** (Svět Lake), where you can hire a sailing boat or go for a trip on a steamer.

BELOW: communal fishing on a lake near Třeboň.

The healing powers of the peat moors were exploited during the last century in medicinal baths and sanatoria.

The town fortifications, including the old town gates and walls, enclose a medieval town centre where many houses date from Gothic and Renaissance times.

Třeboň château (open Apr–Oct, Dec Tues–Sun; entrance fee), sections of which date back to the 14th century, is one of the largest château in the country. Visitors can join as 45-minute guided tour of the château and see examples of Renaissance furniture and paintings.

Chlum to Nove Hrady

The village of **Chlum** near Třeboň, is famous for its glass-making; the blown and cut glass products are exported all over the world. The little town of **Jindřichův Hradec** is worth visiting, since attractive religious buildings and a large number of late Gothic, Renaissance and baroque houses have been preserved. The town's medieval castle (open Apr–Oct Tues–Sun; entrance fee) was enlarged in Renaissance style by Italian architects in the 16th century. The Gothic chapel of St George contains a cycle of frescoes depicting the slaying of the dragon. Here, too, the skills of an ancient craft are practised: a local workshop still produces hand-made Gobelin tapestries.

The route from České Budějovice leads in a southeasterly direction along the Malse to **Trocnov**, the native town of the Hussite leader Jan Žižka. The former gamekeeper's house has been turned into a museum. Only a few miles further on lies the village of **Římov ❾**, surrounded by a Way of the Cross marked with 25 little chapels decorated with exquisite wood carvings and sculptures.

Near the village the valley has been dammed to create a reservoir serving two-thirds of southern Bohemia. No bathing is allowed here, and for once the prohibition is accepted without demur as the area offers a large number of attractive alternatives. **Pevnost Žumberk** (Žumberk Fortress;

BELOW: famous Bohemian glass is produced in Chlum near Třeboň.

Map on page 184

guided tours May–Sept Tues–Sun, Apr–Oct Sat–Sun; entrance fee), southeast of Trhové Sviny, containing original furniture, provides an evocative picture of what life must have been like in these ancient castles, when the flickering of pinewood torches were the only light and open fires the only heat. The village of **Nové Hrady**, near the Austrian border, was built during the 13th century. Particularly interesting is the exhibition of unusual black glass, known as hyalite, which was produced in the surrounding foundries.

Following Route 156 west from Nové Hrady, the **Klášter Zlatá Koruna** (Golden Crown Monastery; open April, May, Sept, Oct Tues–Sun 9am–4pm, June, Aug 9am–5pm; entrance fee) lies a few miles north of Český Krumlov. The chief attractions of the monastery are the extensive library and the triple-naved basilica dating from the 14th century. Legend has it that the linden tree growing in front of the monastery produces unusual leaves in the shape of a hood, recalling the unfortunate

Cistercian monks whom Žižka hanged from its branches after he had set fire to the monastery buildings. Přemysl Otakar II founded the religious community here in 1263 in order to protect his royal interests in the region against the incursions of the Vítkovci (Wittigo) family.

Český Krumlov

The town of **Český Krumlov ❿** (Krumau) has retained its medieval character better than any other place in southern Bohemia. Every alleyway and hidden corner is an invitation to explore. The entire town has been declared a historic monument and, although restoration work during the past decades has made only slow progress, and some architectural treasures are still crying out for renovation, a leisurely exploration is recommended.

In 1240, the Vítkovci dynasty built their castle overlooking the Vltava. They were followed by three families of German nobles: the Rosenbergs (1302–1611), the Eggenbergs (1622–1717) and the

BELOW: view of the old town of Cěský Krumlov.

Schwarzenbergs (1717–1945). The original fortress was rebuilt as an aristocratic palace, from which the lords of the castle administered their economic and political interests in southern Bohemia. German colonists settled on the far side of the bend in the River Vltava and were awarded a town charter in 1274. Silver deposits in the nearby Bohemian Forest brought wealth to the noble rulers and diligent burghers alike; even when the mines were exhausted during the 16th century, the town was able to retain its prosperous air.

In the middle of the Old Town lies the Ring, bordered by charming Renaissance houses and the richly decorated **radnice** (Town Hall). To the south and west you can see sections of the original fortifications, topped by the slender tower of the **Chrám sv. Víta** (Church of St Vitus). The latter contains Gothic wall paintings and an elaborate early baroque altar. Of particular interest in the east of the town are the Curate's House and the **Městské muzeum** (Town Museum). Forming part

of the former Jesuit College (now in use as a hotel) is a theatre completed in 1613.

In the suburb of **Latrán** on the other side of the bridge across the Vltava is the Convent of the Minorites and the Sisters of the Order of St Clare. Both communities used the adjoining Corpus Christi church. A long-established brewery occupies a 16th-century arsenal. The **Hrad** (castle; tours Apr–Oct Tues–Sun; entrance fee) sprawls high above the town – less extensive than Prague Castle, but no less attractive, thanks to its moat, now the home of a colony of bears.

The upper castle was designed as a feudal residence. The Maškarní sál (Hall of Masks) is decorated with wall paintings and the Čínský salónek (Chinese Cabinet) contains a collection of exquisite porcelain from the Chang Dynasty. The massive tower belongs to the earliest period of the medieval castle, although the arcade was not added until 1590.

A bridge flanked with statues of saints leads across to the baroque Hradní divadlo

BELOW: Český Krumlov.

Map
on page
184

(Castle Theatre), built in 1767. The castle gardens contain an open-air theatre with a revolving stage which hosts a wide range of imaginative productions during the summer season.

The rich variety and quality of the manuscripts and books in **Rožmberk Castle** (tours May–Sept Tues–Sun; Apr–Oct Sat–Sun; entrance fee), 17 km (10½ miles) south east of Český Krumlov on Route 160, has made them well-known throughout the literary world. Paintings and weapons are also on display.

From the Lipno Reservoir

Like Rožmberk Castle, **Klášter Vyšší Brod** (Vyšší Brod Monastery; open May–Sept Tues–Sun 9am–5pm; entrance fee) was founded by Vok von Rožmberk in the first half of the 13th century, along the trading route to Austria. The community soon prospered and expanded. Before World War I its estates comprised more than 4,000 hectares (9,800 acres). Part of the monastery was returned to the Cistercian order in 1990.

The road to the Lipno Dam on the Vltava leads to **Hořice na Šumavě ⓫**. This village was traditionally famous for its passion plays, performed by the local residents (largely of German extraction), which continued to be staged throughout the war years. The tradition broke down after the German residents were expelled, but now the community is endeavouring to revive it.

The little medieval town of **Horní Planá ⓬** (Oberplan) lies directly on the shores of the lake. It is the birthplace of the poet and painter Adalbert Stifter (1805–68). The house where he was born now contains a small museum.

The **vodní nádrž Lipno** (Lipno Reservoir) is 44 km (27½ miles) long and up to 16 km (10 miles) wide in places. A steamer service links the lakeshore communities of Lipno, Frymburk, Černá v Pošumaví and Horní Planá. For many years, a considerable stretch of the long strip of land between the lake and the Czech–Austrian border was fenced off with barbed wire, which enabled it to retain much of its wildlife. A footpath

leads from Nová Pec to the **Jezero Plešné** (Plešné Lake), above which a monument to Adalbert Stifter stands on a high cliff.

The Bohemian Forest

The **Šumava** (Bohemian Forest), in particular the sections adjoining Germany and Austria, are less suited to a touring holiday than to a peaceful stay in unspoilt natural surroundings. The **Schwarzenbergský kanál** (Schwarzenberg Canal) is a remarkable construction dating from the end of the 18th century. In times past it served as a means of transporting felled logs; today it links the sleepy villages and isolated farmsteads of the Bohemian Forest.

The Iron Curtain tolled the death-knell of the border regions. Now, with the creation of a national park spanning the frontiers, new life is blossoming in the area. For some years now it has attracted country lovers keen to save the lovely old farmhouses from decay. Thanks to them a number of the typical 17th-century wooden cottages are still standing, and the

RIGHT: canoeing in the Bohemian Forest.

Map on page 184

wooden chapel on the hillside near **Stožec** has been faithfully restored. In the Upper Vltava Valley you will notice encouraging signs of careful tourist development designed to attract visitors seeking peace and quiet in restful surroundings. Here you can wander at leisure through the forests (though some sections of the Bohemian Forest are under strict protection and not accessible to tourists).

South of Vimperk (Winterberg), at the foot of Mount Boubín (1,362 metres/ 4,358 ft), lies the **Boubínský prales** (forest), a conservation area since 1933. Some of the trees here are 400 years old, and the rare flora and fauna of the region attract botanists and zoologists.

Zlatá stezka (The Golden Pass) was the name of the trading route from Bohemia to Bavaria. During the Middle Ages it brought considerable prosperity to the towns in the Bohemian Forest.

Volary (Wallern), the best-known resort in the area, was founded by settlers from the Tyrol. Even today you can see the occasional wooden chalet with sloping roofs weighted down with stones, which is so typical of alpine regions.

Vimperk ⓭, also along this route, is the gateway to the Bohemian Forest. In 1264 Přemysl Otakar built a fortress above the Volynka Valley to protect the trading route.

The town is noted for its printing works, founded in 1484. It produced elaborately decorated missals, copies of the Koran and other books. Fine examples are on display in the municipal museum and the Bohemian Forest Gallery in the castle, along with an exhibition of cut glass characteristic of the region. Above Vimperk, the cross-country ski tracks lead to Zadov and Churánov, the winter sports centres of the Bohemian Forest.

All the old routes of the Golden Pass converge on **Prachatice** ⓮, a little town where luxury goods, cloth and weapons were stored until their sale or onward transport had been arranged. The most important trading commodity was salt; until the 17th century the town was the biggest repository of salt in Bohemia. When the Habsburgs introduced a monopoly and diverted the salt routes through České Budějovice (Budweis) and Gmünd, Prachatice declined into an economic and cultural backwater.

Remains of the 14th-century town walls are still standing today. There is also a Gothic church housing a number of treasures, and a Town Hall constructed in 1570 and reconstructed during the 19th century with elaborate graffito decorations. The grammar school on the market place was where Jan Hus, a native son of neighbouring **Husinec** ⓯, was educated.

At the end of the 16th century, Wilhelm von Rosenberg (Rožmberk) ordered the building of the Renaissance **Zámek Kratochvíle** (Kratochvíle Castle; open Apr–Oct Sat–Sun 9am–4pm, May–Sept Tues–Sun 9am–5.15pm; entrance fee) some 20 km (12 miles) from Prachatice. His brother, Peter Vok, embellished the property with a park, surrounded by a wall and bastion. Today the castle serves as an exhibition centre for Czech animated films.

LEFT: the Bohemian Forest in winter. **RIGHT:** the smoking room in Hluboká Castle, north of České Budějovice. ❑

Map on page 198

WESTERN BOHEMIA

This area is dominated by the town of Plzeň – home to the famous Czech beer – but other villages, bordering Germany, have traditions and history that make them worth a visit

Bohemia's historical and cultural development mirrors that of its capital, Prague. The area has always been subject to both Slavic and German influences and this is particularly true of the region of western Bohemia. A journey through this scenically attractive region can be combined conveniently with a tour of the world-famous spa towns described in the next chapter *(see pages 205–213)*.

Plzeň

Plzeň ❶ (Pilsen) is the second-largest town in Bohemia, with a population of 180,000. It is famous for the local beer, *Prazdroj* (Pilsner lager, *see page 200*). Plzeň rose to international importance soon after receiving its charter from King Wenceslas II in 1295. Lying at the confluence of four rivers – the Mže, the Radbuza, the Úhlava and the Úslava – and at the crossroads of four long-distance trading routes, the town rapidly established itself as a trading centre. In addition, the locally mined raw materials (kaolin, mineral ores and hard coal) helped to make it a centre for crafts and industry.

It was in Plzeň that the first Czech book, the *Kronika Trojánská*, was printed and published in 1468. From 1420, following the voluntary departure from the city of the Hussite military leader Jan Žižka, Plzeň was loyal to the Catholic emperors. To show his thanks, Emperor Sigismund relieved the town of all feudal dues; Plzeň thus acquired the privileges of a tax haven and entered a new era of economic prosperity. In 1599, when the plague was rampant in Prague, Emperor Rudolf II moved his official residence here for nine months. The entire court and all foreign representatives follow suit, and once more the town boomed.

The stormy period of industrialisation during the 19th century was accompanied by the expansion of Plzeň to a cultural centre for the surrounding region. The first theatre opened here in 1832, and today Plzeň has three major dramatic stages, including a Children's Theatre and a Loutkové divadlo (Marionette Theatre) where Josef Skupa, creator of the legendary puppets Špejbl and Hurvínek *(see page 107)*, once worked.

Plzeň is also the home of the famous Škoda Works, founded by the engineer and industrialist Emil von Škoda at the end of the 19th century. The enterprise grew from the modest base of a small machine factory to become one of Europe's greatest industrial complexes, known for its arms production in both world wars. The company was for decades the town's largest employer, and would probably

LEFT: the spa baths at Karlovy Vary.
RIGHT: golden statue in Plzeň's Market Square.

have continued to expand according to the values of Western capitalism had the American troops under General Patton, who liberated the town in 1945, not subsequently withdrawn in accordance with an agreement with the Soviet army.

The Gothic heart of the city takes the form of a rectangular chessboard, with a large square, known today as the **náměstí Republiky** (Square of the Republic), in the centre. In the middle of the square is the early Gothic **Kostel sv. Bartoloměje** Ⓐ (Church of St Bartholomew), whose spire (103 metres/ 427 ft) is the tallest in Czech Republic. The interior is decorated with murals dating from before 1400. Dominating the high altar is a Gothic statue, the **Plzeňská Madonna** (Plzeň Madonna), completed in about 1390.

With its flying buttresses and pendant keystone, the **Šternbergská Kaple** (Sternberg Chapel) on the southern side of the chancel is a good example of late-Gothic architecture. The **radnice** Ⓑ (Town Hall), built in the Renaissance style between 1554 and 1558, is decorated with extravagant *sgraffito* ornaments, making it by far the most conspicuous building in the entire square. When Rudolf II came to the city, he resided in the Emperor's House next door. House No. 234, opposite the main entrance to the church, dates from the Middle Ages. Since its renovation in 1770 it has been considered one of the finest baroque buildings in Bohemia. The architectural magnificence continues around the square and along the narrow alleys of the **Staré město** (Old Town) where the facades of the houses are decorated with fine frescoes and sgraffito, the work of Mikuláš Aleš, an esteemed Czech artist of the 19th century.

In the midst of all this splendour, only the solitary **Morový sloup** Ⓒ (Plague Column) erected in 1681, is a reminder that the residents of Plzeň did not escape the dreadful pestilence. In the southeastern corner, the Františkanská ul. leads to the former **Františkánský klášter** Ⓓ (Franciscan Monastery) with its pretty **Kapel**

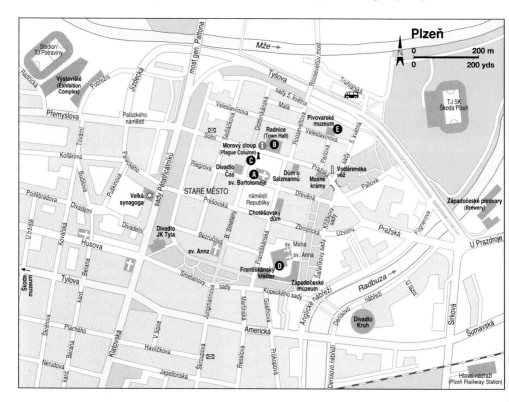

Maps:
City 196
Area 198

sv. **Barbory** (Chapel of St Barbara) and its late Gothic frescoes illustrating the lives of the saints. In the northeast of the Old Town, by the Perlova, are the former butchers' stalls, the **Masné krámy** (meat market), a recently converted exhibition hall and concert auditorium. The water tower nearby is 450 years old. A few yards further on, in the Veleslavinova ul., the **Pivovarské muzeum** ❺ (Museum of Beer Brewing; open Sept–May Tues–Sun, Jun–Aug daily 10am–6pm) is also worth a visit, particularly as it is the only such museum in the country.

Around Plzeň

During the Middle Ages a community of Cistercian monks settled near **Plasy** ❷, some 15 km (9 miles) north of Plzeň. They built a vast monastery complex, one of the largest in Bohemia. The most impressive building is the convent itself, which was constructed on oak stilts because of the marshy conditions. The two-storey **Královská kaple** (Royal Chapel) is a particularly fine example of the Gothic masons' art.

Following the course of the Střela in an upstream direction, you will reach **Rabštejn nad Střelou** ❸, the smallest town in Central Europe, with only 40 inhabitants. It perches on a rock above the swiftly flowing river, which is spanned by a magnificent Gothic bridge. From the 13th century onwards a fortified castle protected this important crossing on the long-distance trading route to Saxony and Northern Europe; the remains of the stronghold can still be seen today.

The little town of **Manětín** ❹ lives up to its reputation as the best place to see baroque architecture in Western Bohemia. It lies 30 km (19 miles) from Plzeň. During the 18th century, Manětín was given a complete facelift. Surrounding the palace – the work of the Italian architect Giovanni Santini – are numerous examples of baroque sculpture.

Also worth mentioning are the fine paintings by the Czech baroque master Petr Brandl, which hang in the town's two churches. Some 9 km (5 miles) southeast of Plzeň lie the ruins of the former **hrad** (castle), mentioned in records as early as 976. After the foundation of the town of New Pilsen, the site of the fortress was rechristened Old Pilsen; it later came to be known as **Starý Plzenec** ❺. The castle was built by the Přemyslid dynasty as a cultural and administrative centre. Its fortifications included a 10-metre (32-ft) wall – a section of which is still standing today – and the oldest intact monument in the Czech Republic, the **Rotunda sv. Petra** (Rotunda of St Peter), which dates from the late 10th century.

A few miles further on, rising on a hillside to the east of the village of **Stáhlavy**, stands **Lovecký zámek Kozel** (Kozel Palace; tours May–Sept Tues–Sun Apr, Oct Sat–Sun). This classical-style building nestles in magnificent woodland; the main section was completed between 1784 and 1789. Several years later a number of additions were made, following plans drawn up by the master architect Ignác Palliardi. Today the palace houses a collection of 18th- and 19th-century art.

Plzeň to the German border

The E53 from Plzeň leads south to the little town of **Švihov** ❻, where there is a magnificent moated castle built in a mixture of Gothic and Renaissance styles. It houses a collection of medieval weapons (tours May–Sept Tues–Sun; Apr, Oct Sat–Sun; entrance fee).

The town of **Klatovy** ❼ is known as the gateway to the Bohemian Forest. It is also famous as a cultivation centre for carnations. The **Černá věž** (Black Tower) soars to a height of almost 80 metres (256 ft) above the Renaissance-style Town Hall and the market square. Its airy gallery

affords a fine view of the historic town walls and the surrounding hills. Those with a liking for the macabre can gaze at the mummified corpses of Jesuits in the catacombs beneath the early baroque **Kostel sv. Ignáce** (Church of St Ignatius). Also worth visiting is the **Bílí věž** (White Tower), a free-standing belfry belonging to the early Gothic **Kostel svaté Marie** (Church of St Mary). Visitors should also take a look inside the former chemist's shop (*lékárna*) on the Town Square, which still contains its original, baroque shop fittings. In this it is unique. It is listed in the UNESCO catalogue of historic monuments.

Map on page 198

The beautiful countryside of the central Bohemian Forest also deserves protection. Particularly attractive is the valley of the thundering Bystřina Vydra (Vydra torrent), which is 7 km (4 miles) long, and which lies a few miles southeast of Klatovy. Beyond Sušice, where the river flows more quietly, stand the ruins of **Hradní zřícenina Rábí ❽** (Rábí Castle; tours Apr–Oct Tues–Sun; entrance fee), built in the mid-14th century to protect the local gold-panning industry. This, the most powerful ruined castle in Bohemia, was captured twice during the Hussite rebellions; it was later destroyed by fire and finally abandoned.

To the west of the Bohemian Forest is **Železná Ruda ❾**. The most interesting sight in this small town is a little church topped by the onion-shaped domes typical of high baroque architecture in the region. In the vicinity is a ski circuit as well as a cable car to the summit of **Hora Pancíř** (Mount Pancíř; 1,213 metres/3,885 ft). Shortly before the German border, the ancient trading road turns in a southwesterly direction towards the Bavarian towns of Furth im Wald and Regensburg, cutting through the Chodsko region.

The Chodsko region

The Chods – the name is derived from the Slavic word for "patrols" – are a Slavic ethnic group whom the rulers of Bohemia allowed to settle in the district some 1,000 years ago. Their task was to defend the border and to offer protection to travellers and traders. They accomplished this with such efficiency that they were awarded special privileges, which they continued to enjoy until the region came under the rule of the Habsburgs after the Battle of the White Mountain in 1620. To this day, on the weekend following 10 August, the Chods make their annual pilgrimage to the **Svatý Vavřineček** mountain, where they take part in an age-old festival of song, dance and bagpipe music, dressed in their bright traditional costumes.

The town of **Horšovský Týn ❿** is an-

BELOW: the Bohemian Forest in autumn.

Pilsner Lager

Few Czech products are as famous as Czech beer. The brewing tradition in Bohemia extends over many centuries – in Prague, the oldest written record of the brewer's art is found in a document dated 1082. And yet the capital does not produce the country's best beer; that honour is almost certainly held by Plzeň (Pilsen), although Budvar is surely a strong competitor. Although the Prazdroj Brewery was founded as recently as 1842, the town's brewing tradition stretches back much further. When Plzeň was founded in 1290, the town was granted the right to brew its own beer. Numerous exhibits in the Museum of Beer Brewing testify to a thriving brewing industry here in the Middle Ages. Before the new Prazdroj brewery opened, beer was produced in various private houses throughout the town.

Like every other beer, Pilsner is produced by heating ground malt with water and hops before allowing the liquor to ferment at low temperature by the addition of a special yeast, the *saccharomyces carlsbergensis*. Despite all this, the flavour of Pilsner lager remains unique and many attempts have been made to discover the secret. The water used in the brewing process clearly plays an important role in the determination of quality and taste; the local water is very soft and has an exceptionally low level of salinity.

Another reason for the beer's success lies in the preparation of the malt; only barley with a low protein content is used. But the characteristic taste and headiness of the beer is achieved by the addition of first-class, oast-dried hops from Žatec.

All these basic ingredients have been employed in numerous foreign breweries but to date, not a single one has succeeded in producing an authentic-tasting Pilsner Urquell.

Another secret must lie in the cellars in which the beer ferments and matures. They were driven deep into the sandstone cliffs and extend over a distance of 9 km (5½ miles). Throughout the year, they are maintained at a constant temperature of 1–2°C (33–35°F). The walls of the cellars in which the beer is kept for two to three months are coated with a fungus similar to penicillin. Many "spies" have tried to kidnap the fungus from the Plzeň cellars in order to introduce it to the cellar walls of their own breweries. So far, nobody has been able to find a suitable habitat; sooner or later it always died. Fourteen years after the brewery was set up, local lager was sold for the first time outside the country. In 2000, the brewery, now owned by South African Breweries, exported over 560,000 hectolitres of beer, pushing Budvar into second place in the country's beer exporting league.

The citizens of Vienna were the first to try Pilsner Urquell; by 1865, three-quarters of the brewery's total production was destined for export. From 1 October 1900, a "beer train" left Plzeň daily for Vienna. Somewhat later, a similar train travelled regularly to Bremen; there the lager was loaded on to ships for transportation to America.

Today the Prazdroj Brewery, now including the Radegast and Velké Popovice breweries, produces almost 8 million hectolitres of beer a year. Exports are flooding into Western Europe and new global markets are opening. ❏

LEFT: advertising poster.

Map on page 198

other Chode settlement. It was protected by a mighty fortress, built during the second half of the 13th century. Some parts of the early Gothic castle are still standing. Following a devastating fire in the mid-16th century, the fortress was rebuilt in the style of a Renaissance palace. It is surrounded by an extensive, landscaped park.

Domažlice ⓫ (Taus), the capital of the Chodsko region, lies only a few miles from the German border crossing at Furth im Wald. The town was established around 1260 as a customs post. The fortifications are still visible in places; the **Dolní brána** (Lower Gate) leads directly on to the long, narrow market square of this pretty little town, fringed by attractive arcaded houses of various periods. A massive belfry rises up above the deanery church. Every evening, an ancient Chode trumpet melody rings out from its panoramic viewing platform.

The **hrad** (castle) itself was built during the 13th century; it was later completely destroyed by fire and rebuilt in 1728. Of the original fortress, only the **Kulatá věž** (Round Tower) remains today; it houses collections from the **Chodské muzeum** (Chodsko Regional Museum; open daily except Mon).

The **Jindřichovo muzeum** (Jindřich Museum), named after the well-known composer and expert in Chode folklore, provides an introduction to the particular character of the customs and culture of the area. There is also an interesting and comprehensive display illustrating the traditional craft of glass painting.

Visitors wishing to learn more about the folklore of the Chodsko should pay a visit to the surrounding villages. Draženov, Mrákov and Újezd are typical of the local architectural style; particularly attractive are the traditional Chode log cabins.

There is plenty to see on the E50, which runs in a westerly direction from Plzeň (most drivers move too fast to appreciate the sights and villages). The first town along the route is **Stříbro** ⓬, founded in 1240 in the vicinity of a silver mine. Parts of the late-Gothic fortifications are still visible, including a Gothic bridge with a Renaissance tower, and Renaissance-style

houses – including the town hall – surrounding the market place. It is worth making a short detour to the south to visit the important monastery at **Kladruby**; its cathedral is the work of the 18th-century architect Giovanni Santini.

A few miles before the border stands **Přimda** ⓭, originally built in Romanesque style during the 12th century as a look out fortress. The little township nestling beneath the castle used to be inhabited by the Chods. **Tachov** ⓮, a former royal town, is considered to be the centre of the region. Remains of the medieval town wall and a good number of fine old houses testify to its illustrious past.

Cheb

From Stříbro you can turn north along the main road leading up to Cheb in the northwest of Bohemia, a route which provides access to the Bohemian spa towns *(see pages 205–213)*. **Cheb** ⓯ (Eger), a lovely town on the bend in the river, always lay right in the firing line of two opposing

cultures. The town bears traces of a turbulent history, originating in the 10th century when the Slavs built a stronghold on the rock overlooking the ford. Soon afterwards, German merchants settled around the fortress, founding the town of Egire which acquired market privileges in 1149. A young Swabian duke carried off and married Adelheid, the fair maid of the castle. In 1167, as the Emperor Frederick Barbarossa, he became ruler of the fortress and township, and embarked upon an ambitious scheme to enlarge its base. He held court here on three occasions; his son often celebrated Christmas here, and even his grandson, the Emperor Frederick II, despite his preference for Apulia, summoned his vassals to this imperial palace on several occasions.

Chebský hrad (Cheb Castle), therefore, is not only the oldest well-preserved building in the Czech Republic, it has also served as a stage for European history on various occasions. The town has one more claim to fame – or notoriety. During the period when the country was subject to Habsburg rule, it fell into the hands of the Bohemians. Albrecht von Wallenstein, the brilliant general in charge of the imperial army stationed his troops in Cheb during the Thirty Years' War.

In the interests of a united Germany, with himself as its supreme authority, he was considering the possibility of negotiating peace with Sweden – a course of action which would have saved many hundreds of thousands of lives and prevented the devastation of vast tracts of land. He demanded that his officers, who were under oath of loyalty to the emperor, swear allegiance to him personally. The emperor naturally saw this as an act of high treason and declared the general an outlaw. The Irish cavalry officer Walter Devereux led an attack on Wallenstein in February 1634; the general's troops were overpowered and Wallenstein himself was assassinated in his house by the market square. Cheb is a much quieter place today. The market square is the focal point

BELOW: the old apothecary in Sušice.

Map on page 198

of this little town of some 20,000 inhabitants. Surrounding the square (named after King George of Poděbrady, the first Hussite sovereign of Bohemia), beneath the arcades of the half-timbered houses, are a number of pretty shops and cafes.

A tour of Cheb

Some of the buildings are particularly striking: the former **Radnice** (Town Hall), a splendid example of baroque architecture, dominates the eastern side of the square. The **Schillerův dům** (Schiller House) next door was where the famous German dramatist (1759–1805) stayed whilst gathering material and impressions for his famous *Wallenstein* trilogy. The **Hotel Hvězda** on the corner has a restaurant, bar and overnight accommodation.

The broad market place is graced by the Roland Fountain on the south side and the **Herkulova fontána** (Hercules Fountain) to the north. In the centre is the **Špalíček**, a collection of market stalls (formerly constructed of wood, which could be extended as required). Of special interest are the **Schirndingův dům** (Schirnding House) behind, with a high gable, and the **Gablerův dům** (Gabler House), which was originally Gothic in style. Tucked away at the top of the square is the **Městské Muzeum** (Municipal Museum; open Tues–Sun; entrance fee) – the house in which Wallenstein was assassinated.

On the southwestern and northern periphery of the Old Town, comfortably reached on foot through the picturesque alleyways, lie five interesting churches. All were built by religious communities which took up residence in the town during the 13th century. To the south lie the Gothic Church of Our Lady of the Ascension and the baroque **Kostel sv. Kláry** (Church of St Clare); to the north are the churches of **Svatý Václav** (St Wenceslas) and **Svatý Mikuláš** (St Nicholas), the portal and towers of which display elements from the original Romanesque period. The latter was substantially altered by the master of German baroque, Johann Balthasar Neumann, who was born in Cheb in 1687, and went on to design many outstanding secular and religious baroque buildings

all over southern Germany. The **Kostel sv. Bartoloměje** (Church of St Bartholomew), lies directly on the River Ohře; from here it is only a few steps to the fortress.

The **Černá věž** (Black Tower), the massive keep of lava stone, is perched on steep cliffs overlooking the river dominating the Romanesque **hradní komplex** (castle complex).

The showpiece of **Chebský hrad** (Cheb Castle; open Apr–Oct Tues–Sun; entrance fee) is the painstakingly restored two-storey **Románská kaple** (Romanesque chapel). It looks unassuming enough from the outside, and the gloomy lower floor which housed the guards and servants confirms the initial impression.

The airy upper floor, however, which was also reached by a wooden bridge from the palace proper, is a miniature gem of late-Romanesque architecture. Graceful columns with exquisitely carved capitals support the elegant ribbed vaulting of the ceiling – a fitting setting for the emperor and his retinue. ❏

RIGHT: fine residences line the market place in Cheb.

Map on page 198

THE SPA TOWNS OF WESTERN BOHEMIA

The restorative natural spa waters that abound in the region towards the German border have given Bohemia international renown since the 18th century

I n the spas of Western Bohemia, visitors have the chance to immerse themselves in an atmosphere belonging to the long-vanished era of the Austrian empire. Since the Velvet Revolution of 1989, this has acquired even greater nostalgia value. Sadly, the architectural sins of the recent past are not so easily undone; here and here, grey concrete buildings characteristic of the communist period rise between the faded "imperial yellow" of the residences and sanatoria.

Karlovy Vary

Karlovy Vary , formerly called Karlsbad (Charles's Spa), is the oldest of the Bohemian spa towns. Legend has it that Emperor Charles IV discovered the healing spring on which it is centred quite by chance, whilst chasing a stag on a royal hunting expedition from his nearby castle of Loket. The exhausted animal sprang from a cliff straight into a bubbling hot spring, with the baying hounds close on its heels. Despite the scalding temperature of the spring, the emperor's personal physician declared that it possessed healing properties. In 1349 Charles founded a settlement here; and in 1370 he granted the town its municipal charter.

But it wasn't until the latter part of the 17th century, following a period of devastating fires and damage during the period of Swedish occupation in the Thirty Years' War, that the town's golden age began. Under the generous patronage of the Habsburgs, Karlsbad rose to supremacy as the most elegant spa town in the world, offering every refinement essential for fashionable amusement at the time. Competitions and plays, gossip and political intrigue, exhibitionism and witty conversation were its hallmarks. Everyone wanted to be a part of the scene. The

sins and vituperations of the nights of riotous drinking and extravagant parties were washed away by morning constitutionals and bathing in the healing waters.

Crowned heads, literary luminaries and great musicians were all attracted by this heady mixture. Peter the Great put in an appearance on two occasions – under the pretext of engaging in discussion with philosopher Gottfried Leibniz over the progress of science and art in Russia. Among the visitors to the spa were great men of letters such as Gogol, Goethe and Schiller, and composers including Bach and Wagner, but Karlsbad also attracted the new tycoons of Europe, who tended

LEFT: Karlovy Vary.
RIGHT: taking the waters at Karlovy Vary.

to stay in the high-altitude Sanatorium Imperial. Aristocratic visitors preferred the
velvet-and-plush Grand Hotel belonging
to the former confectioner Johann Georg
Pupp. Even Karl Marx took the waters in
Karlsbad; in fact, the town provided him
with inspiration for several chapters of
Das Kapital.

World history was also made in Karlsbad. Matters reached a head in 1819,
when the frenzied times of the French
Revolution and the Napoleonic Wars gave
way to the Congress of Vienna. The Austrian Chancellor, Prince von Metternich,
invited representatives of those German
states he considered to be "reliable" to
join him in determining the Karlsbad
Decrees. These represented a joint agreement to repress all attempts at greater civil
liberty within Europe, an aim which
would be achieved through the use of
police informers and censorship. Metternich and his decrees were largely responsible for the tension that ultimately led to
the European revolutions of 1848.

In the spa's heyday the journey to
Karlsbad – by carriage through the Bohemian Forest and then down into the
narrow Teplá Valley – was much more
difficult than it is now. But at least there
was no shortage of parking spaces, and
the lords and ladies were not forced to
abandon their carriages by the roadside.
Today, vehicles are prohibited within the
historic spa district itself. The easiest
approach is from the south; if you are
lucky you may be able to leave your car
by the bend in the Teplá, or even on the
promenade by the river.

Around the town

The row of stately buildings begins on the
left bank of the river with the **Galerie
umění** (Art Gallery) and a magnificent
kasíno (casino). Together with the Park-
hotel, the Grand Hotel Pupp is impossible to overlook as it extends across several
blocks along the esplanade. Its main
entrance, much less conspicuous, is set
back on a square where the Teplá takes a

BELOW: spa
colonnade in
Karovy Vary

Map
on page
198

bend to the right. Behind the hotel, a cable car climbs some 200 metres (640 ft) to the Friendship Heights where there is an observation tower and the Restaurant Diana. The station halfway up is the starting point for a number of clearly marked walks such as the tranquil footpath to the Petrova Výšina (Peter's Heights) and the steep cliff known as Jelení skok (Stag's Leap), at the top of which a bronze chamois stands sentinel. From the numerous clearings in the woodland, fine views of the town and the surrounding hills can be enjoyed.

Returning to the valley, a favourite walk is along the **Stará louka** (Alte Wiese), an avenue containing the most elegant and expensive shops in town. Particularly tempting is a factory outlet selling locally made Moser glass and porcelain; the factory's vases and dinner services are internationally known. Here, too, you can buy other typical souvenirs from Karlovy Vary, including Lázeňské oplatky (Karlsbader Oblaten) – wafers which have been popular for over a century – and Becherovka, a herbal liqueur prepared since 1805 from 19 different herbs, in accordance with a traditional recipe drawn up by the imperial count's personal physician, Dr Frobzig. It is known locally as Karlovy Vary's 13th spring. The appropriate antidote in cases of excessive consumption is Karlsbad Salts, also locally produced and offered for sale in every shop. Beware, though, they are a powerful laxative.

On the opposite bank of the river, which can be reached comfortably by one of the many little footbridges, stands another famous hotel, the **Kaiserbad**, which was built before the turn of the century by Viennese architects in French Renaissance style. Nearby is the **Městské divadlo** (Municipal Theatre), built in 1886 and carrying on a theatrical tradition that has flourished in the town since 1602.

The promenade leads to the market place. It is hoped that future renovation work here will take into account the mistakes of the past, the most glaring

examples of which are the hideous **Pump Rooms** opposite. The magnificent **Kostel Maří Magdalény** (Church of St Mary Magdalene) is well worth a visit; completed in 1736 on the orders of the Knights of the Cross, it is another fine example of the work of the Bavarian architect Kilian Ignaz Dientzenhofer. It invites comparison with his famous church of St John on the Rock in Prague.

The focal point of the spa town is the **Mlýnská kolonáda** (Mill Colonnade; springs can be sampled all day every day), built from 1871 to 1879 by Josef Zítek, who was also responsible for the National Theatre in Prague. Here you can sample one of the four thermal springs upon which the town's reputation rests.

There is no need to extend the tour to include the other spa and medicinal bath complexes further to the north, unless you want to indulge in long-term therapy in what is the largest balneological establishment in the country. Instead, take the left-hand fork, which leads to the **Ruský**

kostel (Russian Church), completed at the end of the last century. By following the steep incline up the Savodá třída – Park Road – bordered by towering, ancient trees and charming villas – you can quickly escape the noise and bustle of the promenade and look down over the spa quarter with its hotels and baths.

Spa treatments

The basis of the treatment at Karlovy Vary is its 12 thermal springs, each possessing a high mineral content. They gush out of the earth at high pressure, at a rate of almost 3,000 litres (660 gallons) per minute. The best-known spring, Vrídlo, produces more than 3 million litres (660,000 gallons) of water daily at a constant temperature of 73°C (163°F). The most important part of the cure is drinking the water, but the baths are also believed to be beneficial. In former times only baths were prescribed and the patients were obliged to lie in the water for two days and two nights without interruption.

BELOW: a café in Kalovy Vary.

Map on page 198

Today's cures are less rigorous, and treatments, whether they are for metabolic disorders, digestive complaints, chronic malfunction of the liver and gall bladder, infectious hepatitis, diabetes or gastric and duodenal ulcers, by no means preclude taking advantage of all the leisure facilities and attractions that this lively spa town provides. Karlovy Vary also has plenty to offer on the cultural side. As well as theatre and opera performances, exhibitions and promenade concerts, the summer film festival provides exciting variety.

Jáchymov

Jáchymov ⑰ (Joachimsthal) lies in the foothills of the Ore Mountains (Erzgebirge), a few miles north of Karlovy Vary on the road to Chemnitz in Germany. The first settlement was founded here in 1516 following the discovery of rich silver deposits; three years later, the town acquired a royal charter. The founder of Jáchymov, the Imperial Baron Schlick, was granted the privilege of minting the famous Joachimsthaler guilders, which were soon recognised as international currency, giving their name first to the *Thaler* – the silver coin formerly used throughout Germany and Austria – and ultimately to the leading monetary unit of the modern world, the dollar.

In the 16th century, Jáchymov, then with a population of some 20,000, was the largest town in Bohemia, after Prague. At times, as many as 1,000 miners were employed underground. After just over a century of intensive exploitation, however, the silver seams were exhausted; by 1671, even the mint had to close down. The little town, having lost its *raison d'être*, was given a new lease of life by the worldwide scientific revolution.

For a while, the people of Jáchymov eked out an existence manufacturing porcelain and glass. The dyes were extracted from pitchblende, a waste product of silver mining. But in 1896, the French physicist Antoine Becquerel discovered radioactivity in these mineral deposits. Shortly after that, the physicists Marie and Pierre Curie demonstrated the existence of the elements polonium and radium, which they were able to isolate from the heaps of waste. The town became the site of the first radium baths in the world. A baker was the first to open a bathing establishment. The next complex was more elaborate, and by 1906 Jáchymov was recognised as a medicinal spa town.

Today the little town's main source of income remains its medicinal baths and cures. The healing properties of the radioactive waters from the mines, which bubble forth from galleries more than 500 metres (1,600 ft) below the earth's surface at a pleasantly warm temperature, have been found particularly efficacious in the case of disorders of the locomotive and nervous systems and cardiovascular disease. The spa buildings are concentrated in the south of the town, surrounded by woodland and lying some distance from the road. The **Radium Palace**, the magnificent spa rooms built in 1912 in the secessionist style (a variation of art nouveau which began in Vienna and spread

RIGHT: marble elegance in the historic Grand Hotel Pupp.

to Bohemia), contains a concert hall and a number of elegant restaurants. In the nearby park stands a fine monument to the scientific pioneer Marie Curie-Sklodowska, erected by the grateful citizens of Jáchymov. The modern spa rooms, the Akademik Běhounek, are named after one of Curie's pupils, and further testify to the town's economic expansion.

To the north, the **Staré město** (Old Town) marks the historic centre of the mining community. Characterised by its octagonal tower and terraced gables, the late Gothic **radnice** (Town Hall) dominates the central square. The long, narrow market place is bordered by a number of distinguished, well-preserved houses in a mixture of Gothic and Renaissance styles. Despite frequent renovation, the parish **Kostel sv. Jáchyma** (Church of St Joachim) is worth a visit. The former mint behind the town hall now contains the **Numizmatické muzeum** (Museum of Mining and Numismatics) and provides an interesting insight into local history. To gain the best overall view of the town, take the chair lift to the top of the **Klínovec** (1,244 metres/3,980 ft), the highest peak in the Ore Mountains and a spectacular vantage point.

Some 10 km (6 miles) southwest of Karlovy Vary on a minor road to Cheb, **Hrad Loket** (Loket Castle; open daily Tues–Sun; entrance fee) is a favourite destination for an outing and worth the visit. The royal fortress is built on a high cliff overlooking a bend in the River Ohře, which explains the appropriateness of its name: *loket* means elbow. The first documented reference to the stronghold was in 1239; the oldest section of the building still standing, a Romanesque-style rotunda, was probably built towards the end of the 12th century. The main tower is constructed of granite blocks; the gateways and the margrave's residence were added during the 14th century.

Also of interest is a collection of locally manufactured glass, porcelain and pewter. There is also the Goethe Museum.

BELOW: Františkovy Lázně has been a spa town since 1793.

Map on page 198

Protected by the castle, the settlement has survived until the present day, and the medieval houses grouped around the market square continue to charm visitors.

Františkový Lázně

Františkový Lázně ⑱ (Franzensbad), lying a few miles north of Cheb, is the odd one out among the spas of Western Bohemia, because the little town with its 24 icy mineral springs was conceived in a unified style in the late 18th century. Taking the waters here, or undergoing a course of baths in the radioactive moorland mud, is beneficial in treating coronary and rheumatic disease and a wide variety of gynaecological complaints. Františkový Lázně has an international reputation. The healing water comes from the Ohře, an acidic spring whose curative properties were well known even in the 16th century. It was a local physician, Dr Vinzenz Adler, who introduced the spa to an international public at the beginning of the 19th century. Emperor Franz I of Austria discovered the benefits of the spring and gave his name to the town.

The town centre is laid out on a regular grid pattern and surrounded by spacious parks, containing the springs, spa rooms and baths. The Národní třída, or National Street, is bordered along its entire length by attractive 1900s houses, although the House of the Three Lilies at No. 10, one of the first boarding houses, is 100 years older. Standing off centre in the southwest corner is the Nám. mírů, the main square, with colonnade, meeting rooms, gas baths and the elegant Frantisek Spring Pavilion, which was built in 1832.

Adjoining it on the west side, in Dvořákovy sady (Dvořák Park), is the Bath House I and the massive wooden pavilion housing two further springs, the Luisin pramen (Luisenquelle) and the Studený pramen (Kalter Sprudel).

In the vicinity are two Glauber's salt springs, the source of an efficacious laxative which, together with the spring water, constitutes one of the spa town's principal export commodities. The other springs are to the southeast near the Hotel Imperial, still one of the best addresses in town,

which enjoys a splendid location and can be reached by a pleasant walk. To the north and east is the Městské muzeum (Municipal Museum; closed Mon; entrance fee), the theatre and the Hudební pavilon (Music Pavilion), the setting for frequent promenade concerts.

Only 6 km (4 miles) from Františkový Lázně lies a bizarre landscape. The peat moor of Soos-Hájek has been declared a nature conservation area. Poisonous carbon dioxide issues from funnel-shaped hollows; the bubbling mud, like a landscape in a science fiction film, recalls the volcanic origins of the region. This is even more in evidence in the nearby Přírodní Rezervace Komorní Hůrka (Komorní Hůrka Nature Reserve), where traces of the region's last volcanic eruption during the Quaternary Period can still be seen.

Mariánské Lázně

Situated at a height of some 600 metres (1,920 ft) in a protective arc of wooded hills stretching to the north, west and east,

Mariánské Lázně (formerly Marinenbad) makes a good base for a tour through western Bohemia, not only for its favourable geographical location but also for its well-developed tourist infrastructure. One of Europe's most scenic spas, Mariánské Lázně's long list of famous visitors includes Edward VII, king of Great Britain from 1841 to 1910. The town possesses more than 40 mineral springs, whose highly saline waters are used for the treatment of bladder disorders, respiratory problems, heart ailments, rheumatism and blood and skin diseases.

The Premonstratensian monks from nearby **Teplá** must have been aware of the healing properties of the water when they established the village of Auschowitz near the springs in 1341, creating a sort of *dépendance* of their abbey, which lay some 13 km (8 miles) to the east. In 1710 the abbot had a pilgrims' lodge built to provide shelter for the steadily growing band of invalids who came in search of a cure. At the same time, the springs were tapped; the monks decanted the water into barrels which they sold for a handsome profit to prosperous cities and noblemen's estates. In 1749 an inventive apothecary at the abbey found a convenient way of cutting the transport costs by evaporating the water and marketing the much more convenient Teplá Salt. The mineral baths were added a few decades later. The water from the Stinking Spring (Stinkquelle) – named for its high hydrogen sulphide content – proved particularly efficacious, and thankful patients dedicated votive pictures to the Virgin Mary. The spring's name was changed to Mary's Spring (Marienquelle), and in 1818 it became known officially as the Spa Town of the Austrian Monarchy, although it did not receive its town charter until 1868.

Mariánské Lázně is full of fascinating stories. In 1820, at the age of 74, Goethe drove over by coach from Karlovy Vary. He returned the following year, the constant companion of the charming Baroness Ulrike Levetzov, who was only 19 years old. Their relationship developed into a passionate romance, but when the potential mother-in-law refused to give her consent to a marriage, Goethe withdrew and never visited the spas again.

Goethe was only the first of many writers and composers to be inspired by the springs of Mariánské Lázně. He was followed by Frédéric Chopin, Richard Wagner, Mark Twain and Henrik Ibsen. In 1833, the violinist Ludwig Spohr composed his romantic waltzes entitled *Memories of Marienbad*, and in the 1960s Alain Resnais made the film classic *Last Year in Marienbad*, which rapidly gained cult status.

Around the town

A popular venue for international congresses and symposia, Mariánské Lázně has developed into the most comfortable and modern of all the spas, expanding far beyond its modest origins. Today the southern approach leads through several miles of uninspiring modern suburbs before the elegant spa district unfolds. On the left-hand side, the central avenue, **Hlavní třída** (formerly Kaiserstrasse), is

LEFT: a statue of Goethe.

Map
on page
198

bordered by a variety of shops, attractive restaurants and several large hotels. The hotels include the **Bohemia**, which underwent renovation a few years ago and now combines art nouveau elegance with modern facilities and comfort.

On the right, the spa gardens extend towards the horizon across gentle hills. On its southern boundary stand two fine buildings dating from the turn of the century – the **Nové lázně** (New Baths) and the former pump rooms, now known as the **casino** and used as a cultural centre. From here you pass the **Ambrožův pramen** (Ambrosiusquelle), the **Centrální lázně** (Central Baths), the **Mud Baths** and the **Mariin pramen** (Marienquelle).

Ascending the hill, the road passes the **Kostel nanebevzetí** (Church of the Assumption) before reaching the spa promenade. The rotunda housing the **Křížový pramen** (Kreuzbrunnen) was built in 1818 when the town was first recognised as a spa. The cast-iron structure of the **Nová kolonáda** (New Colonnade; open daily with waters offered from 6am–noon and 4–6pm) is fascinating both optically and technically. The filigree struts forming the framework of the finely proportioned Promenade Hall were produced by a Moravian foundry in 1884–89; they lend the open construction, with its lively ceiling frescoes, a wonderful light airiness.The computer-controlled **Zpívající fontána** (Singing Fountains) – a series of playful water sculptures immediately in front of the building, completed in 1988– cannot really compete

Climbing up to the next terrace, you reach the **Goetheho dům** (Goethe House; open Wed–Sun). Today the neoclassical building serves as municipal museum. The square in front is dominated by the old-fashioned **Hotel Kavkaz**. Its rooms appeal to lovers of faded elegance who are prepared to ignore the dripping taps, musty carpets and warped window frames. A stroll along the northern perimeter of the park will lead past a number of other hotels and bath houses and then back to the upper end of the Hlavní třída.

It is worth checking the programme at the **Městské muzeum** (Municipal The-

atre). Nature-lovers will also find plenty to enjoy in the immediate neighbourhood of the town. There are many delightful woodland walks along a total of 70 km (40 miles) of paths.

A few miles northwest of Mariánské Lázně is **Lázně Kynžvart** ❷⓪ (Bad Königswart), another little spa town, known for its therapeutic, iron-rich, acidic waters, and specialising in the treatment of childhood illnesses. The town, which came into the possession of the dukes of Metternich in 1630, is dominated by a massive castle. In 1690, the dukes proceeded to erect a mighty baroque palace over the old castle walls. Chancellor Metternich (1773–1859) then had the building renovated in the Empire style at the beginning of the 19th century. Goethe and Beethoven both stayed here. Visitors can enjoy the castle's collections which include such diverse treasures as Egyptian mummies, and oriental and Gothic paintings, as well as a display of curiosities. The castle is surrounded by an extensive, landscaped park. ❏

Map on page 218

NORTHERN BOHEMIA

Famous for its fruit, hops and wine this region is also a mining district containing great scenic beauty as well as rich history and culture set amid the southern slopes of the Ore Mountains

L eaving behind the relaxed spa towns of western Bohemia, the next stage of the tour strikes out from Karlovy Vary in a northeasterly direction towards **Klášterec nad Ohří ❶** (Klosterle), on the River Ohře (Eger). This ancient little town was originally the possession of the Benedictine order; the Bohemian king Přemysl Otakar II later presented it to the aristocratic Cumperk family.

The Renaissance **zámek** (castle; open Apr–Oct Tues–Sun; entrance fee) acquired its pseudo-Gothic appearance after being gutted by fire in 1856. Today it houses an extensive porcelain collection with exhibits ranging from Chinese antiquities to contemporary items. Another interesting town is **Kadaň**, on the Ohře. The medieval town square with its arcades, elaborate gabled roofs and stone portals is especially attractive. The **radnice** (Town Hall), with a Gothic tower and pretty oriel window, was rebuilt in the baroque style following a fire, as was the church opposite, also originally Gothic.

On the southern slopes, overlooking the river, stands the former **Klášter** (monastery), now housing the municipal archives. Apart from a large number of Gothic remains and baroque additions, it has cellar-like vaulting and the sarcophagus of the monastery's founder, Johann Hassenstein von Lobkowitz.

No visit to northern Bohemia, the cradle of hop-growing, would be complete without sampling the local beer. A pleasant aroma and a spicy, resinous quality characterise the type of hop grown in the area surrounding the town of **Žatec** (Saaz). Fertile soil and favourable climatic conditions guarantee the supremacy of hops from this region, grown here since the 10th century. Today 60 percent of the total production is destined for the export market. **Chomutov** (Komotau) has a number of architectural sights, including

the historic town square which has an unusual arcade, and the 16th-century Collen-Luther House. A number of magnificent medieval chambers have been preserved. The little **Kostel sv. Kateřiny** (Church of St Catherine) in the vicinity is a fine example of the early Gothic style.

The medieval town of **Most ❷** (Brüx), lying on the trading route from Bohemia to Saxony, has become a thriving mining community. A new town has gradually replaced the original settlement. The relocation of the Gothic deanery church in 1975 was an impressive technical achievement. For the first time in Europe, a total mass weighing 12,000 tons was moved in one piece. Only the altar, 17.5 metres (56 ft) high and 8 metres (26 ft) wide, was

PRECEDING PAGES: the Pravčická brána, the largest rock arch in Europe. **LEFT:** heading upcountry. **RIGHT:** a Bohemian miner.

dismantled. Of particular interest is the nearby **Zámek Jezeří** (Jezeří Castle). The remarkable architectural ensemble includes baroque buildings, a Renaissance palace and a Gothic fortress. Nonetheless, since 1973 the entire complex has been the subject of violent controversy. The coal lobby demands that the castle be demolished and the rock upon which it stands blown up, since they stand in the way of mining the brown coal. Cultural historians and ecologists object violently to these plans, and geologists have pointed out that if coal mining goes ahead the entire mountain would suffer from a landslide.

The castle in **Duchcov** ❸ (Dux) is the former residence of the von Waldstein family *(see page 33)*. It contains a rare collection of historic gems. At the end of the 18th century, Giovanni Giacomo Casanova wrote his memoirs here.

The district town of **Teplice**, housing the **Krušnohorské divadlo** (Krušnohorské Theatre) and an interesting museum, is the oldest spa town in Bohemia. The baths, with their radioactive springs, are used to treat circulatory disorders and malfunctions of the motor system. A visit for refreshments in one of the town's many attractive restaurants, wine bars and cafes is recommended.

The Labe Valley

Litoměřice ❹ (Leitmeritz) and its hinterland are often described as the Garden of Bohemia; fruit and vines flourish here. The former Royal City also offers the visitor a wealth of historic sights and architecture. The town is characterised by its Renaissance and baroque buildings. Setting the scene are the chalice-shaped roof of the **Mráz dům** (Mráz House) and the **radnice** (town hall), of Gothic origin but rebuilt in Renaissance style.

The town's skyline is dominated by **Katedrála sv. Štěpána** (St Stephen's Cathedral). Visitors should also make a point of visiting the **Severočeská galerie** (Gallery of Northern Bohemia; open Tues–Sun; entrance fee). This attractive region has

Map on page 218

had its fair share of suffering at the hands of history. A particularly harsh fate befell the town of **Terezín** ❺. It was founded in 1780 by Emperor Joseph II as a bastion against the Prussians and named in honour of Empress Maria Theresa. During the last war, the German occupying forces established the notorious concentration camp of Theresienstadt here. A memorial recalls the thousands of Jews who suffered and died *(see panel on page 42)*. The moving **Muzeum ghetta** (Museum of the Ghetto; open daily; entrance fee) records the horrors of the Nazi regime. A branch of the museum is also to be found at the former Magdeburg Barracks.

A few miles further upstream lies **Roudnice nad Labem** (Raudnitz), site of a baroque castle. An interesting gallery is housed in the former riding school. **Hora Říp** (Mount Říp) rises above the gentle hill landscape to the south. According to legend, Čech, founding father of the nation, and his entourage paused on the mountain's summit and, enchanted by the

view, decided to settle in the region. The **Kaple sv. Jíří** (St George's Chapel) on the mountain was built in honour of a celebration marking the victory of Prince Soběslav over Emperor Lothar in the Battle of Chlumec in 1126.

Downstream from Litoměřice, the next town is **Ústí nad Labem** ❻ (Aussig). Its well-developed industry has made it the economic centre of the region. Enjoying a favourable location on the medieval Salt Road and at the confluence of the Bílina and the Labe, Ústí nad Labem became a Royal City in the 13th century.

The approach to the city is marked by **Hrad Střekov** (Střekov Castle; open Tues–Sun; entrance fee), perched on a high basalt cliff overlooking the Labe (Elbe) just outside the city. A number of famous people have visited this fortress, and in 1842, Richard Wagner composed his opera *Tannhäuser* here. The town centre has a number of other interesting sights. Since a bomb attack during World War II, the tower of the Gothic **Kostel**

BELOW: hops from Žatec give Czech beers their special flavour.

nanebevzetí (Church of the Assumption) has had a small list. The entire building has had to be underpinned and is regarded as one of the architectural curiosities of Europe. The neighbouring baroque ensemble, comprising the **Kostel a klášter sv. Adalberta** (Church and Monastery of St Adalbert), has been restored and now serves as a concert and exhibition hall. In 1972 an organ with 3,572 pipes was installed. In the vicinity of Ústí nad Labem is **Tiské skály**, a romantic labyrinth of bizarre sandstone rock formations. A few miles further upstream, **Zámek Velké Březno** (Velké Březno Castle) is worth visiting for its interior, which retains its original features, and for the attractive 5-hectare (12-acre) park.

Also worth mentioning is the village of **Stadice** in the **Údolí Bílina** (Bílina Valley), the setting for *Kosmas*, the first Czech chronicler's account of Přemysl Oráč, founder of the ruling dynasty of Bohemia. According to legend, Princess Libuše married this simple farmer and inspired him to found the city of Prague. In memory of the event, the inhabitants of Stadice are said to have supplied hazelnuts for the royal table. Today the town square, with its ancient memorial stone, is a national monument. Interesting in a very different way is the toxic waste tip in **Chabařovice**, to the west of the town. There are no precise details concerning the exact composition of the tip, which was commissioned in 1905. It is suspected that the contents of the entire Mendeleev periodic table are represented here, offering the possibility of hitherto unknown compounds. The American government provided funds for the disposal of 40,000 tons of highly toxic hexachlorobenzol.

Near to the town of **Děčín** ❼ is **Zámek Děčín** (Tetschen Castle), situated on the Labe just before the German border, was occupied under communism by the Soviet army; following the 1968 invasion, they established a permanent garrison here. Concerts are held here during the summer and the castle now contains a puppet

BELOW: Most has its fair share of environmental problems.

Map on page 218

museum (open Wed–Sun). Nature-lovers have a special affection for the area surrounding Děčín. Two Swiss artists, the painter Adrian Zingg and the engraver Anton Graff, were so enchanted by the beauty of this landscape that when they surveyed the picturesque rocky cliffs, deep ravines and narrow defiles they felt themselves transported back to their native land and lost their desire to return home. That was in 1776; since then, the area surrounding Děčín, and in particular the sandstone region near **Hřensko**, has been dubbed "Bohemia's Switzerland".

One of the thrills of the area is a trip through the foaming spray of the mountain torrents in a narrow boat – with a local wild water expert at the helm, of course. Also popular is a detour to **Pravčická brána**, a remarkable natural rock formation in the sandstone plateau around Hřensko. The sandstone mountains were formed 130 million years ago, but the region is in grave danger from today's air pollution. One crumbling sandstone block weighing about 800 tons is poised above the main road from Hřensko. It will probably have to be blown up to avoid the risk of a major catastrophe.

The Česká Lípa region

The **Česká Lípa** ❽ (Böhmisch Leipa) region is rich in unusual natural phenomena. These include the **Sloupské skály** (Sloupské skály cliffs), occupied by the sandstone castle of Sloup, and the **Panské skály** (Panské skály cliffs), which consist of thousands of basalt pillars. Observed from the air they resemble a honeycomb; from the side, they look more like organ pipes, which explains their local nickname: *varhany*, "the organ".

Southeast of Česká Lípa, the ruin of **Hrad Bezděz** (Bezděz Castle; open Apr–Oct Sat–Sun; May–Sept Tues–Sun; entrance fee) soars heavenwards; it is an important example of Bohemian Gothic defensive architecture. Never rebuilt, it includes an early Gothic chapel. Emperor Charles IV had **Máchovo jezero** (Máchovo Lake) created near the castle. The lake is known for its carp, but it is also a popular resort with beaches and warm water.

Jizerské Mountains area

With a population of 100,000, the town of **Liberec** ❾ (Reichenberg) is famous for its cloth production, which was begun in the Middle Ages by Flemish weavers. The weaving tradition led to tremendous prosperity in the middle of the last century, when a succession of textile factories was established. Today, a number of well-preserved historic buildings still testify to the town's Golden Age. More than 40 of them are national monuments.

Among the most important is the **Renesanční palác** (Renaissance palace; open Tues–Sun; entrance fee), whose chapel is noted for its beautifully carved altar and coffered ceiling. Impressive, too, is the **Radnice** (Town Hall); built in the style of the Dutch neo-Renaissance, it was designed by the Viennese architect Frans von Neuman and has definite similarities to the New Town Hall in Vienna. A wonderful view of the town and the **Jizerské hory** (Jizerské Mountains) beyond can be enjoyed from the central of the three

RIGHT: the Labe Elbe near Litoměřice.

Bohemian Glass

There is evidence that the Bronze Age settlers of what is now the Czech Republic manufactured glass in the form of beads for necklaces and bracelets. During the Middle Age the first glass drinking vessels windows, panes of glass and wall mosaics were produced.

In 1370, under Charles IV, artists created the monumental mosaic of the Last Judgment on the South Portal of St Vitus's Cathedral. The magnificent windows of the Church of St Bartholomew in Kolín date from about 1380. Domestic use of glass included bottles and flasks, in shades of green or brown.

By the turn of the 15th century there were eight glassblowers' foundries in Bohemia, five in Moravia and a further eight in territory which belonged to Bohemia at the time. The glass factory in Chřibská (Kreibitz), a town in the Lusatian hills, was first mentioned in 1427. It exerted a considerable influence on the development of the glass industry. Dur-

ing the 16th century the rough-and-ready glassware produced in the Bohemian Forest no longer satisfied the refined tastes of the worldly aristocrats in the first years of Habsburg rule. Following the Venetian glass-blowing tradition, production moved towards thin glass in the harmonious forms of the Renaissance.

After 1600, cylindrical tankards served as a basis for the famous enamel painting. Between 1600 and 1610 the gem-cutter Caspar Lehmann from Uelzen (1563–1622) experimented with the cutting of glass at the court of Rudolf II in Prague. The manufacture of cut glass did not become widespread in Bohemia until 1680.

Nowadays, Bohemian crystal is exported all over the world. The classic form of the Bohemian baroque wine glass with a cut pedestal foot, and the many-faceted beaker of fine, thin glass was traditionally adorned with ornate floral bouquets, garlands or grotesque decorations. After 1720 the range was enlarged by the addition of gilt glass and the black engraving in the style of Ignaz Preissler (1676–1741). Along with the local cut and polished glass, Bohemian chandeliers with cut glass prisms were also much sought after. During the 18th century crystal lustres were exported to the courts of the King of France and the Tsar.

After a period of decline at the end of the 18th century, Bohemian hyalite glass with its coloured enamel decoration established an independent reputation. Around 1800 the range of glass was further enlarged by the trend towards less ornate, finely polished and engraved Empire and Biedermeier glassware. The thick-walled coloured glass discovered by Friedrich Egermann in about 1820 revived interest in the craft further: black hyalite glassware, agate glass, Lithyalin glass and new uses for ruby glass all became popular.

The status of Bohemian crystal was boosted during the 19th century by the manufacture of mirrors and tableware as well as glass coral. The latter survived until recent times in Jablonec nad Nisou (Gablonz) under the trade name Jablonex. During the 20th century the names of Loetz, Lobmayer and Jeykal ensured the worldwide reputation of Bohemian crystal through their adaptation of the fantasy, colour and metallic effects characteristic of the art nouveau style. ❏

LEFT: art nouveau glass from Bohemia.

Map on page 218

towers. On the **Staroměstské náměstí** (Old Town Square) beneath, the 16th-century Deanery Church of St Antony was rebuilt in neo-Gothic style in 1879. From here the narrow Věterná ulice (Wind Alley), with its beautiful 17th-century, half-timbered **Wallensteinské domy** (Wallenstein Houses), leads to the **Malé náměstí** (Small Square).

The **Severočeské muzeum** (Museum of Northern Bohemia; open Tues–Sun; entrance fee) is situated in the north of the town. It contains a fine collection of tapestries, furniture, pottery and glass, plus a historical and folklore section. Between 1938 and 1945, Liberec (then known as Reichenberg) was the largest town in the so-called Sudetenland. It was also the home of Konrad Henlein, the Sudeten German leader who demanded the Anschluss (union) with the German Reich and subsequently became the Gauleiter of Sudetenland and civil commissioner for Bohemia.

Some 20 km (13 miles) north of Liberec stands the forbidding fortress of the town of **Frýdlant** ❿ with its **hrad** (castle; open Tues–Sun; entrance fee), featuring an impregnable round tower. It was built in 1241, on a rock above the Smědá, by a knight named Ronovec; later owners converted it into a Renaissance castle. After the Bohemian uprising of 1619, the castle's Lutheran lord, Christoph von Redern, sided against the Habsburgs; his fate was sealed after defeat at the Battle of the White Mountain. In 1620 Albrecht von Wallenstein (Waldstein; *see page 33*) bought the estate and made the castle his home.

As a token of gratitude, Ferdinand II elevated his diligent General Wallenstein to the rank of duke. But the moment of glory was to be short-lived; in 1634 Wallenstein was assassinated and the Friedland estate passed to Count Gallas, another general in the imperial army. His heirs opened the castle to the public. One of the first castle museums in Europe was created almost 200 years ago in response to the considerable interest aroused by Schiller's dramatic trilogy *Wallenstein*, written in 1799. The Lower Castle, with its meticulously renovated Renaissance facade, is linked by the Knight's Bridge

to the original Gothic fortress. The latter contains luxuriously appointed salons and halls as well as a well-stocked art gallery.

Also worth visiting is **Zámek Sychrov** (Sychrov Castle; open Tues–Sun; entrance fee), 20 km (13 miles) south of Liberec. It was built at the end of the 17th century, but did not acquire its romantic Gothic appearance until the last century.

Today's visitors to the castle tread in the footsteps of two of the greatest Czech composers, Antonín Dvořák and Josef Suk, who were frequent guests. One of the most prominent landmarks in the region is undoubtedly the elegant tower of the television transmitter on the summit of **Hora Ještěd** (Mount Ještěd). It can be reached by cable car, and the tower restaurant offers a panorama across the Krkonoše and the Jizerské mountains.

Bohemian Paradise

Adjoining the district to the south lies the nature reserve **Český Ráj** (Bohemian Paradise), where between Turnov (Turnau)

and Jičín the massive sand deposits left by a sea covering this land during the Cretaceous Period have remained until this day. Near Jičín, there is the famous nature reserve of **Prachovské skály**, with its bizarre sandstone cliffs, vertical walls and deep, narrow grottoes.

Jablonec nad Nisou ⓫ (Gablonz), the principal town in the Jizerské mountains, stands in the shadow of the highest peak in the area, the **Černá hora** (1,084 metres/ 3,556 ft) and is primarily important for its glass and jewellery production. During the 16th century the area was settled by German glass-blowers because the wooded slopes of the Jizerské Mountains provided them with copious supplies of the charcoal needed for their craft.

During the 18th century they rose to fame with their glass imitations of pearls and precious stones, and the community experienced an economic boom. Today the **Muzeum skla** (Glass Museum; open Tues–Sun; entrance fee) documents the town's glorious heyday and the history of this traditional craft *(see page 222)*. Walkers and skiers find ample recreation possibilities in the Jizerské Mountains in both summer and winter. Especially popular is the annual cross-country ski competition known as the Jizerská padesátka (the Iser Mountain Race), which starts in the resort of **Bedřichov**.

The Krkonoše

To the east rise the peaks of the **Krkonoše** – the Giant Mountains – which as the highest mountains in Bohemia form the natural boundary between the Czech Republic and Poland. The mountain crest extends over a length of 36 km (23 miles); the highest peak, at 1,602 metres (5,126 ft), is the **Sněžka** (Schneekoppe).

Weathering and ice have produced a succession of strangely shaped seas of rock and bare pillars of stone, providing a fitting scenario for the fantastic stories of Rübezahl and other legendary characters. Almost the entire region was declared a national park in 1963; together with the

BELOW: people have been skiing in the Krkonoše since 1894.

Map on page 218

adjoining area across the Polish frontier, it forms one of the largest nature conservancy areas in Europe. The domestic buildings of the Krkonoše display a unique variety of styles, demonstrating the skill of the carpenters and builders in this mountainous region.

Also worth visiting in the area are the museums in Vrchlabí (Hohenelbe), Jilemnice, Vysoké nad Jizerou and Trutnov (Trautenau), which house extensive folklore collections and natural exhibits.

The main winter sports centres, with ski lifts, cross-country ski tracks and downhill pistes are **Špindlerův Mlýn** (Spindlermühle), **Pec pod Sněžkou** and **Harrachov**. The *Turné Bohemia,* international ski-flying championships, are held here each year. The highlight of the winter sports season in Harrachov is the ceremonial entry of Rübezahl, the legendary ruler of the Krkonoše, at the beginning of March. The brightly costumed parade fills the streets with a lively atmosphere of festivity and celebration.

Towards eastern Bohemia

East of **Trutnov**, the area surrounding **Police nad Metují** and **Teplice nad Metují** is well known to mountaineers. Erosion of the sandstone cliffs has resulted in an intricately shaped skyline, resembling the silhouettes of town buildings.

Particularly popular are the **Adršpašsko-teplické skály**, but the more remote **Broumovské stěny** also offer spectacular views. The little town of **Broumov** is the ultimate backwater. The Benedictine monastery here – just one of the works of the Dientzenhofers in this part of the country – is a superb example of baroque architecture. On the journey from the Krkonoše to **Hradec Králové** it is worth stopping in **Dvůr Králové**. A zoo, later expanded into a safari park (open daily; entrance fee), was established here in 1946. The park is stocked with a wide range of animals, including rare species such as the white rhinoceros.

A few miles to the south lies the small spa town of **Kuks**, notable for the impressive baroque statues of the 18th-century artist Matthias Braun surrounding the

Kostel sv. Trojice (Church of the Holy Trinity). Two rivers, the Tichá Orlice and the Divoká Orlice, both free of industrial pollution, flow through the little towns of Letohrad, Lanškroun, Litice, Jablonné and Žamberk. Providing the backdrop are the **Orlické hory** (Orlicke Mountains), a relatively low chain covered in spruce. They reach a maximum altitude of 1,155 metres (3,789 ft). Below, in the picturesque valleys, glitter countless lakes. The most popular one lies near **Pastviny**, north of Letohrad; the best-known ski centres, with lifts, are **Deštné** and **Říčky**.

Zámek Rychnov and Kněžnou castle contain a regional exhibition. The town itself, a regional centre, was traditionally the home of clothmakers and weavers; its textile manufacturing industry is still very important. From here you can make excursions into the mountains or to the large number of castles concentrated in the vicinity. Particularly recommended are **Častolovice** and **Doudleby**, as well as the imposing baroque castle in **Litice**. ❑

RIGHT: downhill skiing in the Krkonoše.

EASTERN BOHEMIA

Map on page 228

This region is characterised by contrasting scenery, including natural sandstone rock formations, forested uplands, broad lowlands and the highest massif in the country

From Prague the national road No. 2 leads to the town of **Kutná Hora ❶** (Kuttenberg). This attractively situated regional centre is today a rather sleepy but back in medieval times it was the most important town in Bohemia after Prague. As the centre of silver mining and the royal mint, the town generated such enormous wealth that it placed the Bohemian kings among the most influential rulers in Europe, and they frequently resided here.

At the insistence of Jan Hus, Wenceslas IV signed the Kuttenberg Decree, a major reform of the constitution of Prague University in favour of Czech nationals. With the victory of Jan Žižka's troops over the emperor's army of mercenaries before the city gates in 1422, Kutná Hora entered the annals of the Hussite Wars. Approaching from Prague, your first impression on entering the town will be of the richly decorated stone fountain in the Rejskovo nám. The attractive baroque **Kostel sv. Jana Nepomuckého** (Church of St John Nepomuk) lies in the Husova *třída*, leading into the Palackého nám, bordered by fine Renaissance houses which, along with the **Staroměstská radnice** (Old Town Hall), forms the heart of the Old Town.

The late Gothic **Kamenný dům** (Stone House; open Tues–Sun; entrance fee) on Náměsti 1máje is of particular interest. This unusual townhouse was constructed by an unknown master builder towards the end of the 15th century; most of the statues are

BELOW: Hradec Králové is famous for its production of brass instruments.

ascribed to Brixi, a famous stonemason from Wroclaw. The building underwent major renovation at the beginning of this century and today serves as the municipal museum. On the way down to the River Vrchlice lies the Gothic **Kostel sv. Jakuba** (Church of St James), with an 82-metre (262-ft) high tower. During the baroque period an onion dome was added; at the same time the interior acquired its share of baroque features.

Next door lies the **Vlašský dvůr** (Italian Court; tours daily; entrance fee), originally built as the Královská mincovna (Royal Mint) around 1300. Florentine craftsmen minted the silver coins which served as legal tender throughout Europe: the Prague pennies. The cellars house an extensive exhibition documenting the trade. When supplies of silver ran out the mint was forced to close (mid-18th century) and later became the town hall. In about 1400, Wenceslas IV had the East Wing redesigned as a royal residence. Forming part of this complex is the **Kaple sv. Václava** (St

Wenceslas's Chapel), demonstrating a surprising blend of architectural styles: under the Gothic ribbed vaulting, and framed by medieval winged altars, the art nouveau artist František Urban has executed a series of paintings narrating the well-known legend of St Wenceslas.

The Barborská ul. leads south past the fort – also formerly used as a mint – and the powerful Jesuit college to the Gothic **Chrám sv. Barbory** (Cathedral of St Barbara; open Tues–Sun). The mine owners of Kutná Hora financed this magnificent place of worship and dedicated it to the patron saint of miners. Peter Parler began the building work in 1388, and Benedikt Ried designed the nave at the end of the 15th century, but the project was not completed until 1558.

Apart from the valuable frescoes in the **Smíškova kaple** (Smíšek Chapel), the references to the cultural and economic history of the city are of interest. The spaces between the vaulting of the choir roof are decorated with the coats of arms of the

BELOW: Kolín hosts the world's largest meeting of brass ensembles each June.

craft guilds of the town. On the west wall of the south aisle, workers in the city's mint are depicted; a wall statue portrays a miner with tools and lamp. In **Sedlec**, a suburb of Kutná Hora, is the 14th-century church of Panna Maria. Nearby, at the bottom of the hill, is the **kostnice** or ossuary (open daily; entrance fee) decorated with the bones of thousands of victims of the 14th-century plague and the Hussite Wars a century later. Items made from bone include a huge chandelier made from one of very bone in the human body.

Situated about 3 km (2 miles) to the northeast of Kutná Hora, **Kačina** ➋ is the finest Empire-style palace in the whole of Bohemia. Built between 1802 and 1822, it is surrounded by an attractive park, which contains a large number of rare trees. The attractions of the palace itself include the library and the theatre, as well as an agricultural museum.

In the nearby town of **Kolín** ➌, the Old Town is laid out on a grid pattern of equal squares, a piece of town planning characteristic of the Germans who settled here in the early 13th century. The **Church of St Bartholomew** was begun a little later; Peter Parler subsequently added a magnificent choir. With its radiating chapels illuminated by elaborately traced windows it is one of the loveliest churches in Bohemia. The town once housed one of the largest Jewish communities in the land.

Today, the only traces of Kolín's former ghetto are a semi-ruined **Synagóga** (synagogue) and a medieval **Hřbitov** (cemetery). In 1757 Kolín was the site of a major battle in which the imperial forces, under Field Marshal von Daun, defeated the army of Frederick the Great, forcing the Prussians to withdraw from Bohemia. Each June a rousing **Festival dechové hudby** (brass band festival) is held in memory of František Kmoch, a composer and native son of the city. Brass bands from all over the world come to take part. Further down the Labe lies the spa town of **Lázně Poděbrady** (Bad Podiebrad), whose most valuable asset is

LEFT: inside the "Bone Church" at Sedlec.

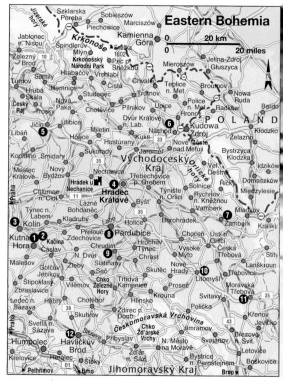

Map on page 228

the iron-rich mineral spring discovered at the beginning of this century. The spa subsequently became famous for the treatment of cardio-vascular complaints. Renowned, too, is the Bohemian lead crystal from the glass foundries of Poděbrady. The town's other claim to fame is as the birthplace of its namesake, the first Hussite king of the Bohemians, George of Poděbrady, who was born in the castle in 1420.

Following the E67 in an easterly direction, you will see the Gothic castle of **Karlova Koruna** (Charles's Crown; open daily; entrance fee) in the little town of **Chlumec nad Cidlinou**; it is the work of the Italian architect Giovanni Santini. Chlumec went down in history as a centre of the Peasants' Revolt, which occurred here in 1775. A memorial some way outside the town bearing the popular Czech proverb "Fallen like a Peasant at Chlumec" recalls their defeat. Continuing eastwards, the route passes the pretty little castle of **Hrádek u Nechanice**, which lies a few miles north of the E67.

Hradec Králové ❹ (Königsgrätz) grew up on the site of a prehistoric settlement at the confluence of the Labe and the Orlice. During the 14th century it became the dowager property of the queens of Bohemia. Dating from this period is the brick Gothic **Katredrála sv. Ducha** (Cathedral of the Holy Ghost), which in 1424 served as the temporary burial place of the Hussite leader Jan Žižka. As a centre of the reform movement, two years after the Battle of Lipany, in which the Hussites were defeated, the town was bold enough to defy Emperor Sigismund.

The **Bílá věž** (White Tower), which has the second-largest bell in Bohemia, the baroque **Kostel sv. Marie** (Church of St Mary), the Jesuit College and the **Biskupský palác** (Bishop's Palace) all date from the 16th century.

Northwest of Hradec lies the little town of **Chlum**, best known for the battle fought here in 1866 in which the Prussians defeated the Austrians and their Saxon allies. The 300 graves scattered between the villages of **Hořiněves**, **Číštěves** and **Sadová** are a moving lega-cy of the battle. On a mound near Chlum is a neo-Gothic charnel house and a memorial to the fallen.

Further north

Further to the north is the old royal city of **Jičín ❺**, founded by Václav (Wenceslas) II, which at various times belonged to a number of Bohemian noble dynasties. After the Battle of the White Mountain, it fell to Wallenstein who incorporated it into his Friedland estate. He wanted to make Jičín the political and cultural centre of his empire, but his plans to do so were only partially realised. But despite that, this period (early 17th century) was the most important in the town's history.

The only town gate still standing is the 50-metre (164-ft) **Valdická brána**, built in 1568. It provides a fine view of the tree-lined avenue leading to the park of **Libosad** in which Wallenstein had an attractive pleasure palace built for himself and his retinue. Further to the north are the towers of the Carthusian monastery

which he founded; it was converted into a prison in 1783. Next to the gate, the Church of St James was also built on the orders of Wallenstein, but was only completed in the 19th century; the general's daughter is buried here. The town square is surrounded by Gothic, Renaissance and baroque houses. On the south side stands **Waldstein zámek** (open Tues–Sun), built by Italian architects in 1624–34. It was here, in 1813, that the Holy Alliance of the allies against Napoleon was sealed.

The region is also characterised by its remarkable volcanic features, for example the basalt cliffs which rise above the bizarre ruins of the Gothic castle in **Trosky** (open Tues–Sun). Further on the road to Turnov is the remarkable cliff town of **Hrubá Skála**, with the ruins of another medieval castle nearby. The area retains economic significance because of the presence of extensive deposits of Bohemian garnet and other precious stones. **Turnov** (Turnau) is internationally famous as a centre of gem-polishing and

the production of garnet jewellery. The district museum with its collection of precious stones is well worth seeing.

Following the Jizera valley to the north of Turnov, the visitor will soon arrive at the town of **Železný Brod** (Eisenbrod), which is renowned for the manufacture of ornamental glass. The town gets its name from the iron ore which has been mined here ever since the 17th century. A number of old wooden buildings are preserved, including the belfry next to the church of St James. Železný Brod is a good base for excursions into the Český Ráj.

The origins of **Náchod** ❻ lie in a Gothic watchtower built to protect the long-distance trading routes. A succession of historical figures left their mark here: George of Poděbrady, Albrecht von Wallenstein, the Trčka family and the Piccolominis. During the last century Náchod was also the native town and periodic place of work of the writer Josef Škvorecký. The region provides the background for his well-known novel, *The Cowards*. South of Náchod, you can swim in the **Rozkoš u České Skalice**, the largest reservoir in Bohemia. In Nové Město it is worthwhile visiting the castle and the market place, which is fringed by Renaissance-style townhouses. Another interesting destination is Opočno, with its magnificent arcaded Renaissance castle.

Among the little towns in the foothills of the Orlické Mountains, **Žamberk** ❼ (Senftenberg) is of most historical importance. During the 17th century, Magdaléna Grambová introduced the art of lace making to the town from Italy. The traditional family workshops gradually expanded, until there was a flourishing industry in the town, and the delicate work of today's lacemakers is in demand. The municipal museum (open Tues–Sun) has an exhibition dedicated to lace production; the town also has a training centre for lace workers.

Towards Moravská Třebová

The second most important town in eastern Bohemia, and for many years the rival of Hradec Králové, is **Pardubice** ❽. The Renaissance-style town centre reflects its golden age under the Pernštejn family.

LEFT: foal at the stud in Kladruby.

Map on page 228

Among the many architectural attractions of the town are the late Gothic **Zelená brána** (Green Gate), the Church of St Bartholomew and the Church of the Annunciation.

The **Hrad** (castle), originally built for defensive purposes, was later converted into a palace; it now accommodates the **Severočeská galerie** (North Bohemian Gallery; open Tues–Sun; entrance fee).

Today, Pardubice is a modern town with an excellent university for students of chemistry and technology. Nearby is the Semtín chemical plant, which produces Semtex. The main local event is the annual steeplechase held in Pardubice for the first time in 1874 *(see page 233)*.

Also in the vicinity lies **Kladruby** – location of a famous **Hřebčinec** (stud farm) where Spanish and Italian thoroughbreds, the so-called Kladruby Greys, are bred. In the mid-16th century the first horses were supplied for the Pernštejns' estate by Emperor Maximilian II. South of Pardubice, the countryside becomes more varied, with dense forests covering the hills. In July the town of **Chrudim** ❾ attracts puppeteers from all over the world to the **Loutkový festival** (Marionette Festival). The **Muzeum loutek** (Museum of Puppets; open daily; entrance fee) occupies the former Soap Boilers' House – a magnificent Renaissance building, despite its prosaic name.

The Renaissance castle in **Slatiňany**, a few miles further south, contains a remarkable gallery of paintings, engravings and sculptures on the subject of horse breeding. The idyllic artificial lake of **Seč** in the upper reaches of the Chrudimka is surrounded by hills. The scenic beauty of the region has been protected by nature conservation areas, such as that surrounding **Polom**, which retains the essential character of the primeval forests which once covered the area. Also typical is the rural architecture, examples of which are displayed in the **Vysoãina Open-Air Museum** west of Hlinsko.

To the east of Chrudim, passing through

BELOW: the little wooden church at Slavanov near Nachod.

a varied hilly landscape, the route leads to **Vysoké Mýto**, which still bears traces of the original grid pattern (around the market place) as well as three 13th-century town gates.

Further along the E442 is **Litomyšl** . For centuries this town has been a trading and cultural centre, and has played a dominant role in the Czech national revival during the last 200 years. Today, a **Renesanční zámek** (Renaissance castle; open daily; entrance fee) stands on the site of the former fortress. This was one of the many magnificent residences of the Pernštejns. Also of interest in Litomyšl is the **Presbyteriální kostel** (Presbytery Church), the **Univerzita** (college), the **Piarist Church** and the main square. The latter is bordered by stately baroque, Renaissance and Empire-style buildings and was once one of the main centres on the Bohemia to Moravia trading route.

Although the town has lost much of its historical, economic and social significance, it still retains some of its former

glamour. Famous musicians and guests from all over the world flock here each year for the **Festival opery a klasické hudby** (Festival of Opera and Classical Music), for Litomyšl was the birthplace of Bedřich Smetana. The brewery houses a museum of Czech music and a special exhibition illustrating the life and works of the renowned 19th-century composer.

The local regional centre of **Svitavy** (Zwittau) lies to the southeast of Litomyšl. Of the villages in the vicinity **Moravská Třebová** is of particular interest. It has a magnificent Renaissance-style town hall, an imposing fortress and a palace.

Sázava Valley towards Brno

There is a motorway linking Brno with Prague, but travellers who prefer a more leisurely pace or who like to travel by train can follow the alternative route along the thickly forested **Udolí Sázava** (Sázava Valley). Further downstream the river is tamed by a number of locks. In the upper reaches, however, particularly the section between **Světlá nad Sázava** and **Ledeč nad Sázava**, it finds its own way, tumbling from rapid to rapid.

The writer **Jaroslav Hašek**, author of *The Good Soldier Schweik*, lived and died in the shadow of the fortress in **Lipnice nad Sázavou**, to the west of Havlíčkův-Brod. He was buried in the local cemetery and his house has been turned into a memorial museum. Within the castle, an exhibition covers his life and work.

The little villages surrounding **Havlíčkův Brod** (Deutsch-Brod) are the home of glass-blowers and miners. It is a poor but attractive region. The town itself was rechristened in 1945 after the Czech poet and satirist Karel Havlíček Borovský; the old name, however, recalls the German miners who settled this ford (*brod*) from the 13th century. A fine portal of the Gothic Church of the Assumption still stands. The baroque **Svaté rodiny** (Church of the Holy Family), some fine townhouses dating from the same period, and the rococo facade of the Křenovský dům set the tone of the Old Town. One unusual touch is the skeleton which adorns the tower of the town hall. ❑

LEFT: rape is an important cash crop.

The Pardubice Steeplechase

Josef Pírka, a photographer from Pardubice, vividly described the start of the hunt in the 19th century: "In the distance we could discern through the mist horsemen in formal attire, grooms, roughriders and stable lads; some of the horses bore side-saddles. In the distance we could see the bright red riding habits of the master of hounds and his two assistants, together with the pack."

The hunt soon developed into a race in which speed was what really counted. Following the English tradition, the huntsmen followed each other in hot pursuit; their goal was usually a church tower (steeple), which gave this type of race its name. This led to the founding of the Pardubice Hunt Club in 1848, and on 5 November 1874 the signal was given for the start of the first race across a specially prepared course.

The Great Steeplechase in Pardubice is one of the most difficult, dangerous (for the horses) and dramatic horse races in Europe. Winning it ranks with winning England's Grand National at Aintree and is every jockey's dream. Racing fans, punters and tipsters gather in their thousands on the last Sunday in March at Aintree and on the second Sunday in October in Pardubice; some try to attend both events. The two races, however, are completely different. The Grand National is run over a closely mown grass track. Runners complete two virtually identical laps with almost 30 artificial obstacles on terrain as flat as a snooker table. The course is 7,216 metres (7,770 yards) long and the race is over within a matter of minutes.

The Pardubice course, by contrast, reflects the very different personality of the Czechs: no grass, no artificial barriers, but hedges, sand and water-filled ditches and rough ground with 31 obstacles. The course is 6,990 metres (7,456 yards) long.

In the entire history of the two races, so far only one jockey – the British professional G. Williamson – has succeeded in winning at both Pardubice and Aintree. He gained the trophy in Pardubice four times, between 1890 and 1893, but at Aintree he won on just one occasion – in 1899. The speciality of Pardubice is the Taxis Ditch, the fourth obstacle, which is rather like Beecher's Brook at Aintree. Whoever stumbles here has already lost the race. During the 1880s it was mooted that the Big Ditch, as it was then known, should be made less difficult, but the Count of Thurn und Taxis, the Postmaster-General of the Royal and Imperial Monarchy, defended the ditch, and in his honour it was renamed the Taxis Ditch.

In the mid-1990s, the Taxis was finally altered after angry protests from animal rights activists. Before 1994, more than 20 horses had lost their lives here.

It remains a tough race, though. The Irish Bank, a natural embankment 2 metres (6 ft) high and 2 metres wide with small ditches on either side, the Snake's Ditch and the deceptive jump called The Gardens are all feared by riders and ridden alike.

In 2000 the favourite, Peraun, ridden by Zdeněk Matysik, won the Velká Pardubickaá, for the third year in a row. The only foreign horse threw his rider early in the race. ❏

RIGHT: the leap over Taxis Ditch jump at the Pardubice Steeplechase.

Maps:
City 236
Area 246

BRNO

This modern city has some good museums, a rich cultural life and a handful of historic sites. It's possible to escape the crowds in Prague by spending a couple of days here

Brno ❶ (Brünn), the capital of Moravia, nestles in attractive rural surroundings at the confluence of the Svratka and the Svitava rivers. Over 30,000 years ago, settlers of the Aurignacian culture settled in this congenial place, and a few centuries before the dawn of the Christian era, Celtic tribesmen founded a town here, which they called Brynn. The Slavs, who arrived here in the 6th century, changed the name to Brno; in about 800 they built a fortress on Mount Petrov. The earliest documented records of the castle date from the 11th century, when it is cited as the seat of a margrave of Moravia.

The stronghold guarded the crossroads of the trading routes to the Baltic and the Black Sea. A community soon grew up in its protective shadow, expanding during the 12th and 13th century due to the influx of new citizens from Germany. In 1243 it was granted a municipal charter by Wenceslas I. The town's importance grew under Charles IV; from 1350, the Moravian provincial parliament met here and local assizes were held. It was not until 1462, however, that Brno was finally proclaimed the capital of Moravia in place of Olomouc. Charles IV issued a decree that all traders following the royal route from Austria to Poland via Moravia had to stop in the town and offer their wares for sale. This encouraged science and the arts to flourish too, a trend strongly reflected in the foundation of new monasteries.

First textile factories

Cloth manufacturers set up factories in Brno towards the end of the 18th century. Sheep farming flourished in the surrounding grazing land, providing the raw materials. The fast-flowing rivers and local coal deposits provided the energy. Soon cloth woven in Brno penetrated the important markets of the Habsburg empire and even established itself in Western Europe in competition with fabrics produced in England. Before long, Brno was being described as "the Manchester of Moravia".

The demolition of the town fortifications during the 18th century provided space for a major rebuilding scheme including generously laid-out parks and boulevards. The architects Adolf Loos and Bohuslav Fuchs (the founder of Czech functionalism) were responsible for shaping the town's modern configuration. The best examples are found in the gracious 19th-century residential districts outside the park belt. The Vila Tugendhat in the Černá pole district was built in 1930 to designs by Ludwig Mies van der Rohe. In 1928 an exhibition of contemporary art and culture in the Pisárky district received

LEFT: fine detail on Brno's town hall by Master Pilgram.
RIGHT: street scene in Brno.

attention from the international press. The exhibition halls erected for this event today form the centre of the **Mezinárodní výstavní komplex** (International Trades Fair Complex), which hosts the International Machine Fair in autumn and the International Consumer Goods Fair in spring. Brno has emerged as a centre of the machine-building and electronics industries as well as textiles, and these fairs are important for the country's exports.

The Old Town

The site of the original Slavic fortress is occupied by **Katedrála sv. Petra** Ⓐ (St Peter's Cathedral; open Mon–Wed, Fri–Sat 6.30am–6pm, Thurs 6.30am–7.30pm, Sun 8.30am–6pm). Built in the high-Gothic style, the cathedral suffered severe damage when the town was besieged by the Swedish army during the Thirty Years' War. During the 18th century it was renovated in baroque style. At the beginning of the 20th century it was renovated again, this time in neo-Gothic style, and acquired

twin towers. The cathedral contains a number of notable frescoes and statues, including the massive Gothic sculpture, the *Madonna with Child*. One particularly interesting detail is the exterior pulpit on the north side of the church. From here, in the 15th century, the Italian Franciscan monk John of Capestrano harangued the faithful gathered in the square below. Visitors may wonder why the church bells are rung twice daily – at 11am and again at noon. It is a tradition dating from 1645, when the Swedish troops under General Linart Torstenson laid siege to Brno. The leader of the army had sworn he would scale the town walls by noon, or else withdraw. Hearing of this, the beleaguered citizens, no longer able to resist the force of the Swedish attack, had the bells of St Peter's chime 12 o'clock when it was only 11am and the town was saved.

The winding Petrská ul. (St Peter's Street) leads down to the secular centre of the old town, the former **Horni trh** Ⓑ (Herb Market), dominated by the **Sloup**

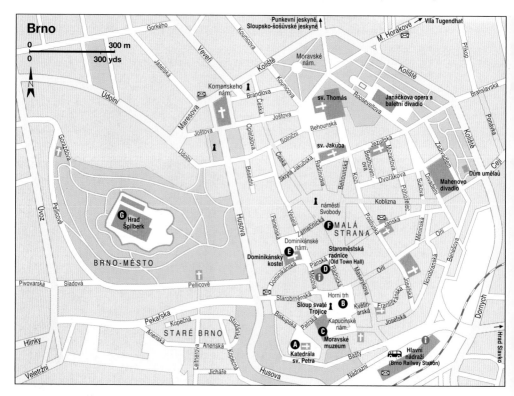

Map on page 236

svaté Trojice (Trinity Column). The market square is always an animated spot, with stalls and stands grouped around the elaborate **Parnassusova fontána** (Fountain of Parnassus), a baroque fantasy of mythical figures and allegorical representations of the four seasons.

At the point where the Petrská ul. opens onto the square, the most striking complex is the **Moravské muzeum** ● (Museum of Moravia; open Tues–Sun; entrance fee), housed in a succession of medieval palazzi. The famous **Věstonická venuše** (Venus of Vestonice), at 30,000 years the oldest extant Stone Age clay figure, forms the pièce de résistance of a comprehensive archaeological and scientific exhibition. Also worth a visit is the art gallery, containing works by Rubens and Cranach as well as Moravian painters from the 15th century to the present day. In the southeast corner lies the Reduta, opened in 1670 and thus the oldest theatre in the town. In the north, only a few steps away along the Radnická ul., stands the oldest

BELOW: Brno is dominated by its cathedral.

secular monument in Brno, the **Staroměstská radnice** ● (Old Town Hall). Dating from the 13th century, it is famous for the entrance designed by the master builder Antonín Pilgram. The Town Council held its meetings here until the end of World War II. Guarding the passage through to the courtyard is the **Brněnský drak** (Dragon of Brno), which according to local legend once gobbled up all the virgins in the city. In fact, the creature is a stuffed alligator, presented by a passing group of Turkish jugglers to Archduke Matthias, who visited Brno in 1608 to drum up support for a conspiracy against his brother, the Emperor Rudolf II. Before leaving he decided to donate the creature to the city fathers, who displayed it in a place of honour in front of the Town Hall.

Following the Mecova ul. the visitor reaches the former fish market. The baroque **Dominikánský kostel** ● (Dominican Church); the former monastery next door has served since 1945 as the New Town Hall. The Renaissance building

Moravian Wine

It seems likely that grapevines were brought to Moravia by the ancient Romans. By the time the Kingdom of Greater Moravia was established, wine was certainly produced in the region. Excavations of settlements dating from this period have revealed evidence of grapes, so wine production in Moravia must be at least 1,100 years old.

The vine-growing regions of Southern Moravia extend over an area of more than 26,000 hectares (64,200 acres). They lie at the northern limits of the wine-producing area of Central Europe. Moravia has neither the intense sunshine of Dalmatia nor the tranquil and humid climate of the Moselle or Rhine valleys. For this reason, vines are grown only on south-facing slopes in hilly districts protected from frost and wind, and predominantly on dry, sandy soils. Despite these limitations, Southern Moravia produces light wines which are often sweeter than those from the famous wine-producing areas of

France. During the first weeks after the grape harvest, the cellarmen supervise the process of maturation until the *burčak,* the new wine, is ready. It is allowed to "cook", as this process is known, for only a couple of hours before the vintners themselves drink a good litre of it each, on the pretext that it will cleanse their blood and provide them with the life-giving energy of the soil and the sun.

Months will pass by before the wine has settled in the barrels and it is time to taste it. Unless a vintner decides to treat a novice to his "three-man wine" – allegedly, one person actually drinks the wine while the other two have to hold him firmly to stop him from falling over – a wine tasting is a dignified procedure.

Before taking the first little sip one should appreciate the colour and savour the bouquet. After the first reaction to the unexpected sharpness, let the full taste slowly develop on the tongue. The entire procedure is repeated several times standing in front of a number of barrels, until the preferred wine is determined.

Two of the oldest and most famous wine cellars are Valtice and Přimětice near Znojmo. Both were established during the baroque era and have magnificent cross vaulting. The arches were built so wide that the lord of the manor could drive through in his coach and even turn round.

Another impressive cellar is in Satov, which is also near Znojmo; its walls are adorned with some amusing frescoes. During the 16th century the Archbishop of Olomouc received his supplies of red wine from the village of Pavlov near Mikulov. And for many years the wine served in the Town Hall cellars in Vienna came from the community of Satov. Jan Amos Komensky (Comenius) was a guest in Blatnice, and even Napoleon was a fan of Archlebov wine; he celebrated his victory at Austerlitz with a Southern Moravian vintage.

Now Moravian wineries are aiming to get their produce into the lucrative markets of the West. Membership of the European Union could be a double-edged sword as a ban on planting new commercial vineyards to stop overproduction could be a major obstacle when the Czech Republic joins. The Czech Ministry of Agriculture is fighting to gain an exemption. If it does not, the future of this ancient wine-growing area is far from certain. ❑

LEFT: grape-picking in Southern Moravia.

Map on page 236

erected above the cloister was used as long ago as 1582 as the assembly hall for the Moravian estates.

The Lower City

Further to the north, surrounding the nám. Svobody (Freedom Square), lies the **Malá strana G** (Lower City). The square served as the lower market place of the medieval town, but all that remains from this period is the former merchant's residence in the southwest corner. It dates from 1596 and has a fine entrance and inner courtyard.

The **Kostel sv. Jakuba** (Church of St James) was rebuilt following a fire during the 15th century. Under the window on the south face of the high tower, Antonín Pilgram placed a little manikin who points his naked backside at the cathedral – the church of the wealthy inhabitants of the Upper Town – embracing a girl as he does so. Continuing in an easterly direction, the route passes the Jesuit church, dedicated in 1734 and regarded as the finest baroque church in town, before reaching the ring of parkland.

To the left stands the modern **Janáčkova opera a baletní divadlo** (Janacek Opera House and Ballet Theatre), to the right the Mahenovo divadlo (Mahen Theatre), built over a century ago in the style of the French Renaissance and famous as the first stage in Europe to be lit by electric light. Behind stands the lovely **Dům umělců** (Artists' House), built in 1911.

Spilberk Castle

Hrad Špilberk G (Spilberk Castle; open Tues–Sun; Mar–Oct; entrance fee), dominating the town from a high plateau, is a conspicuous landmark. It was built about 1270 by King Přemysl Otakar II because he thought the old Slavic stronghold on Mount Petrov provided insufficient protection. By the time the Swedish army began its memorable siege during the Thirty Years' War, Italian military architects had transformed it into a virtually impregnable citadel. It withstood attack by troops from a number of countries; in 1742, Frederick the Great failed to storm the fortress, but eventually Napoleon was successful in 1809. From the 17th century

the castle was one of the most feared prisons in Europe. Among the incarcerated were unrepentant heretics, peasant revolutionaries and members of the aristocracy who had fallen into disfavour at the imperial court, such as the Croatian leader, Baron Trenck. The tolerant Emperor Joseph II closed it in 1783, but after the French Revolution the Habsburgs reopened it, to house their many political opponents. The Italian poet Silvio Pellico, for example, spent 15 years in Spilberk.

At the foot of the fortress lies the former Augustinian monastery with the Church of the Assumption, containing a charming *pietà* ascribed to Heinrich Parler the Younger and dating from about 1385. The monastery was the home of the father of genetic science, the abbot Gregor Johann Mendel (1822–84). Mendel established a tradition of learning in the city.

Today, its six ancient establishments of higher education within the city have over 20,000 students. Viktor Kaplan, the inventor of the hydraulic turbine, lectured at the

RIGHT: the market place.

Techniká universita (Technical University), and the founder of the **Hudební fakulta** (College of Music) was the composer Leoš Janáček. His works are the focus of the autumn festival of classical and contemporary music.

Towards Southern Moravia

On 2 December 1805, the armies of three emperors faced each other in the Battle of Austerlitz, 20 km (13 miles) east of Brno. The French forces under Napoleon confronted the allied regiments of Austria and Russia under Emperor Francis II and Tsar Alexander I.

On **Hora Žuráň** (Mount Žuráň), two trees mark the position of Napoleon's command post. From here he directed 741,000 men and 250 cannons against an army far superior in numbers. Some 40,000 men fell in the ensuing battle. In 1911 a monument to them was erected on top of the Mohyla míru Heights near the village of Prace, where the slaughter was thickest. After his victory Napoleon set up his

headquarters in the baroque **Hrad Slavkov** (castle) nearby. It was here, on 6 December, that he signed the peace treaty acknowledging his supremacy as the most powerful ruler in Europe. Each year, on 2 December, the **Bojiště u Slavkova** (Battlefield of Austerlitz) becomes the arena for a reconstruction of the battle. Thousands of enthusiasts come from France and other European countries to take part in the Battle of the Three Emperors.

The Moravian Karst

North of Brno, between **Blansko** and **Sloup**, lies the **Krasová oblast** (Karst region) of Moravia (Moravský Kras), a landscape of romantic gorges and some 400 caves both large and small, carved out of the solid limestone by underground rivers. There is a spectacular view down into the **Propast Macocha** (Macocha Abyss), 138 metres (453 ft) deep. A marked footpath leads down the almost vertical walls to the twin lakes at the bottom.

Those with a poor head for heights are recommended to visit the **Punkevní jeskyně** (Punkevni jeskyne caves; tours every 15 minutes; closed Dec; entrance fee) by boat. The breathtaking magnificence of the vaulted roofs is heightened by the forests of stalactites and stalagmites. The largest cave is the **Kateřinská** (concerts are held here to take advantage of its acoustics). The Balcarka Caves are particularly stunning. The **Sloupsko-šošůvské jeskyně** complex, on the northeastern edge of the karst region has been the site of a number of interesting archaeological finds; the **Jeskyně Kůlna** (Kůlna Cavern) bears traces of human occupation some 100,000 years ago.

The settlement in the **Byčí skála** cavern dates from the Palaeolithic era, and remains of a royal burial place from the 7th–6th century BC have also been found. Much evidence of early iron smelting furnaces can be found all over the Moravian karst region. The rich iron ore deposits and the ease with which charcoal could be obtained made the area a valuable source of raw material for armaments. Iron tools and jewellery were made here, as well as swords and armour. ❏

Maps:
City 236
Area 246

LEFT: Moravian Karst region. **RIGHT:** the lush scenery of the Moravian Karst.

Map
on page
246

SOUTHERN MORAVIA

In this landscape there are no mountains, just hills and very little woodland. The region contains some fine castles and wine estates, and most people here make their own wine

The tour described here runs in a clockwise direction around the region. It starts by taking the E461, which leads due south from Brno towards the Austrian border, following the Svratka to the lower reaches of the River Dyje (Thaya). The rolling landscape is reminiscent of parts of Italy; to the south rise the **Pavlovské Vrchy** (Pavlovské vrchy Mountains), with Devon limestone cliffs and the **Chko Pálavká** (Pálava Nature Reserve), famous for its rare steppe flora. In past times the silhouette of the Pavlovské vrchy served as a landmark for merchants; today, it is reflected in the waters of the **vod. n. Nové Mlýny** (Nové Mlýny reservoir).

Just to the north of the Austrian border, in a vine-growing area, is **Mikulov ❷** (Nikolsburg). Since the 16th century this little town has been connected with the dukes of Dietrichstein-Mensdorff. Their castle, dating from medieval times, was rebuilt on a number of occasions and ended up as a baroque palace. One of the main attractions here is the so-called "tenner" barrel dating from 1643, which has a capacity of 1,010 litres (269 gallons).

An old synagogue in the oriental style demonstrates the importance of the Jewish community here. Dominating the scene is the **Kaple sv. Sebastiána** (Chapel of St Sebastian), on the Svatý Kopeček, the Holy Mountain.

The chateau in **Lednice ❸**, a few miles to the east on the River Dyje, is visited by up to half a million tourists each year. It was built in the English Gothic style and is surrounded by an attractive landscaped park. Also of interest are the cast-iron framed greenhouses dating from 1834, the 60-metre (197-ft) minaret, replicas of historic churches and the **Janohrad**, an artificial ruin.

Further south, the little town of **Valtice** has a well-known vintners' school, and the 17th-century palace of the Dukes of Liechtenstein, which is famous for its wine cellars. Also well worth visiting is the parish Church of the Assumption, whose altarpiece of the Holy Trinity is a Rubens original.

To the south of **Břeclav ❹** (Lundenburg), an important railway junction, excavations have revealed a vast old Slavic defensive settlement which was an important centre of the Kingdom of Great Moravia. The **Archeologické muzeum** (Archaeological Museum; open Tues–Sun; entrance fee) here merits a visit.

Southwest of Brno

The little town of **Ivančice ❺** was the birthplace of the famous art nouveau painter Alfons Mucha. Although he spent

much of his life in France, in nearby **Moravský Krumlov**, Mucha reveals to what extent he remained faithful to his Czech homeland. His famous *Slovanská epopej*, 20 vast canvasses depicting themes based on Slavic history and mythology, is exhibited in the Knights' Hall of the Renaissance castle.

The road rejoins the River Dyje as it irrigates the fertile Znojmo plain to the southwest of Brno. The main crops in the valley are fruit and vegetables; the slopes are reserved for the production of fine wines. The town of **Znojmo** ❻ was the first community in Moravia to receive its town charter, in 1226. It has successfully preserved its medieval character over the succeeding centuries. The city walls still stand, along with numerous houses and churches from the Gothic, Renaissance and baroque eras.

Beneath the market place (Nám. Míru) there is a vast cellar for the storage of wine; the square itself is dominated by the fine Gothic tower – all that remained of the Town Hall at the end of World War II. The **hrad** (castle) occupies the site of a former 11th-century border fortress dating from the Přemyslid kingdom. It houses the **Jihomoravské muzeum** (Museum of Southern Moravia; open May Sat–Sun, June–Sept Tues–Sun; entrance fee).

The Romanesque **Kostel sv. Kateřiny** (church of St Catherine) contains a series of wall paintings dating form the early 12th century. After the Cold War ended, the magnificent tract of land on the banks of the Dyje was officially protected as a joint Austrain-Czechoslovakian national park. Numerous footpaths and tracks lead through the Dyje valley, and the region is popular with anglers and walkers.

The Upper Dyje Valley

Further upstream, the Dyje has been dammed to create a vast reservoir. One mile from the barrier itself, perched on a crag above **Vranov nad Dyjí** ❼, stands the magnificent Castle of Frain (tours daily; entrance fee). Originally built as a

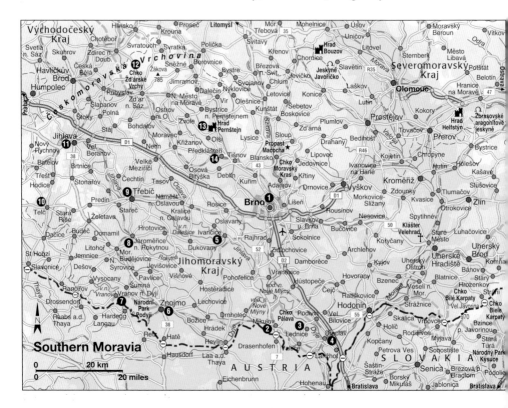

Map on page 246

fortress, it was later converted into a splendid baroque residence. It is worth joining a tour just to see the splendid baroque **Sál předků** (Ancestral Hall), not to mention the castle chapel and the lovely audience rooms. The whole building has been wonderfully restored.

A fine castle stands sentinel over the little town of **Jaroměřice** ❽, equally famous for its lovely bridge across the River Rokytná. The castle includes its own theatre, in which the premiere of the first Czech opera, *L'origine de Jarmeritz en Moravie* (The History of the Town of Jarmeritz in Moravia) was performed in 1730. The work was composed by František Václav Míča, a valet who had been commissioned by the lord of the castle to assemble a servants' orchestra. He even arranged a number of ambitious productions of Italian operas. The tradition is perpetuated to this day in the **Výroční festival klasické hudby** (annual festival of classical music) held in Jaroměřice each summer, when the extensive castle grounds and the pretty little town are thronging with international visitors.

West of Brno

Třebíč ❾ is known primarily as an industrial town, but its **Bazilika svatého Prokopa** (Basilica of St Procop; open Tues–Sun), dating from the 13th century, is well worth a visit. The triple-naved building is the most important example of the transition from Romanesque to Gothic architecture within the lands of the Bohemian crown. The basilica forms part of a monastery, in which the **Opátská kaple** (Abbot's Chapel) also contains a magnificent series of 13th-century wall paintings. Part of the monastery was converted into a palace during the Renaissance period. Today it houses the **Západomoravské muzeum** (Museum of Western Moravia; open Tues–Sun; entrance fee), including unusual collections such as a picturesque selection of crib figures.

In the town centre, only a handful of houses and doorways remain from the Gothic era; a hint of the Renaissance is visible in the gables of the monumental townhouses. The **Malovaný dům** was adorned with sgraffito by the Venetian merchant Francesco Calliardo; the Black House, dating from 1637, bears an allegorical depiction of Virtue, and many other buildings display fine decorative features.

Nestling amidst woodland close to **Náměšť nad Oslavou**, a charming little town west of Brno, lies a vast Renaissance castle which served Tomáš Garrigue Masaryk (first president of the Czechoslovak Republic in 1918) as a summer residence. Today a precious collection of Gobelin tapestries is displayed here.

In the neighbouring village of **Kralice nad Oslavou** there is a memorial museum dedicated to the Kralická bible, the Czech Bible, produced between 1579 and 1593. The bible is linked with the Community of the Moravian Brethren, who were known as religious reformers in Bohemia during the Middle Ages.

Telč ❿ (Teltsch) is undoubtedly one of the most beautiful towns in the whole Czech Republic. Dating from the 16th century, the central square is surrounded

RIGHT: grapes growing in Velice.

by historic houses linked by continuous arcades. After the Great Fire of 1530, the entire town was rebuilt in a unified Renaissance style. The region was originally covered by marshes, but during the 12th century the founding fathers of the city had these drained. By the beginning of the 14th century Telč had been awarded royal privileges; still standing within the old town centre are various late-Gothic gateways and a large number of fine old houses which date from this period.

Most important among the town's religious buildings is the **Kostel nanebevzetí** (Church of the Assumption), built during the 15th century.

The **Renesanční palác** (Renaissance palace; open Apr–Oct Tues–Sun, Apr, Sept and Oct closing at 4pm; entrance fee) stands immediately next to the market place. It was built to replace the original fortress at the end of the 16th century, at the behest of the lords of Hradec, who were inspired by their frequent trips to Italy. They added columned arcades, audience rooms with statues, paintings and stuccoed walls and ceilings in imitation of the Italian buildings they admired.

Visitors approaching via the Prague motorway, or planning to return to the capital by the same route, should make a point of breaking their journey in **Jihlava** ⑪ (Iglau). The town was founded in 799 on a former trading route; it rose to prosperity during the 13th century when extensive silver ore deposits were discovered in the vicinity. In 1249 the town received its charter; 20 years later the citizens were awarded staple rights and permission to mint their own coins.

In the **Court of Appeal of Iglau**, the ultimate authority in mining law for the entire Holy Roman Empire, cases were tried according to the Iglau Mining Laws, which were regarded as binding in many parts of the world even centuries later.

When silver mining was abandoned some 300 years later, cloth production, a complex industry introduced by Flemish weavers and dyers, became the principal

BELOW: market place with fountain in the romantic border town of Slavonice.

Map on page 246

driving force behind the town's economy. Jihlava is, however, particularly proud of its reputation as a centre of the arts. Its most famous native son is the composer Gustav Mahler (1860–1911), although he spent much of his life in Vienna.

Remains of the town walls, and the Náměstí Míru, whose area of 3,700 sq. metres (almost an acre) makes it the largest town square in Central Europe, bear witness to the town's historical importance. On the east side of the square, bordered by townhouses with painted arcades, stands the **radnice** (Town Hall). Dating from 1426, it provides access to the catacombs, constructed during the Middle Ages as storerooms and defensive passages. The miners' court met in the corner house, and the mint was housed in the building opposite. Also on this square was the headquarters of the clothmakers' guild; it is now a museum.

The parish **Kostel sv. Jakuba** (Church of St James) is the real jewel among an array of fine churches. Begun in 1257, the building was completed at the end of the 14th century. Dating from the same period is the exquisite statue of St Catherine.

Into the mountains

North of the motorway from Prague to Brno extend the Bohemian–Moravian Mountains. It is a landscape of wooded slopes reflected in the waters of countless lakes. Those who follow the route from Prague along the Sázava Valley will pass through Deutsch-Brod before coming to **Žd'ár nad Sázavou**.

The town serves as the starting point for a visit to the **Chko Žd'árské Vrchy ⓬** (Žd'árské Vrchy Nature Reserve) on the crest of the Bohemian–Moravian ridge. Here the visitor will find expanses of primeval forest, Ice Age peat moors and more than 280 lakes both large and small. In this remote region you will find the last evidence of many of the country's oldest and most interesting traditions, and in the villages the old wooden farmhouses, the so-called *dřevěnice*, can still be seen.

On **Mount Žákova** 785 metres/2,575 ft), by the source of the Svratka, the local inhabitants welcome spring by ceremoni-

ously opening the well. The associated celebrations are a delight.

Following a branch line of the rail link to Brno, the traveller comes to **Nové Město na Moravě**, famous for the **Horácké Museum** (open Tues–Sun; entrance fee) and its 16th-century castle. The town is a good base for hikes in the mountains.

The enchanting **Hrad Pernštejn ⓭** (Pernštejn Castle; open Apr–Oct Sat–Sun, May–Sept Tues–Sun: entrance fee) perches above the **Údolí Nedvědička** (Nedvědička Valley). The massive walls have survived the march of time remarkably well. You may find your visit coincides with that of film crews and production teams filming at the castle.

Visitors should also visit the **Porta Coeli** (Gate of Heaven) monastery in **Předklášteří ⓮** near Tišnov, a few miles before Brno. Founded in 1233, the complex includes a majestic church with a cross vaulted roof. The cloisters and the chapter house are among the finest works of Gothic architecture in Moravia. ❏

RIGHT: Pernštejn, one of the largest and best-preserved castles in the Czech Republic.

Map on page 254

NORTHERN MORAVIA

"Black Gold" has been mined in this region for centuries but Northern Moravia isn't dominated by this industry. Among the mountains there are skiing and hiking trails and historic towns

Northern Moravia has about 2 million inhabitants, virtually all of whom are concentrated in the two conurbations around Olomouc and Ostrava; the remaining regions are rural in nature and sparsely populated. In the south lies the fertile Haná plain (Hannakei), with Olomouc at its centre. Passing through the Moravská brána (Moravian Gate) the traveller reaches the northeastern industrial area centred upon Ostrava. To the north, the Jeseníky Mountains form a natural boundary; in the southeast the Moravian and Silesian sections of the Beskid Mountains separate the region from Slovakia.

Olomouc

The town of **Olomouc** ❶ has a long and colourful history. The first written references to this settlement in the shadow of a Slavic fortress were in 1055. Eight years later, Olomouc was elevated to the rank of diocesan town. Its spiritual rulers awarded the community municipal and staple rights and encouraged the diligent Premonstratensian order to settle here along with German craftsmen and merchants, so that the town soon became the capital of Moravia. It was occupied by Swedish troops for a number of years during the Thirty Years' War, an event which saw the start of the town's slow decline.

Brno, its rival in Southern Moravia, then became the provincial capital; in 1778 the university was also transferred there. Olomouc's reputation as a bastion of Catholicism loyal to the ruling Habsburgs remained but it was surrounded by an increasingly rebellious hinterland. For this reason the town was often referred to as the Salzburg of Moravia.

This may explain why so many historic buildings have survived in the **Staré město** (Old Town). On the náměsti Míru, the former Upper Square, the most conspicuous is the magnificent **radnice** (town hall). To the former town clerk's office were added a splendid banqueting hall and the late-Gothic Chapel of St Jerome; during the Renaissance came the elaborately decorated external staircase and the loggia. A popular attraction is the **orloj** (astronomical clock) dating from 1422, whose figures move in a similar manner to the apostles on the town hall clock in Prague. Characteristic of the area is the massive 18th-century **Sloup sv. Trojice** (Trinity Column). Half a dozen baroque fountains grace the Old Town. Two of them stand on the **Náměstí Míru** (Square of Peace); others are found on the Lower Ring, immediately adjacent to the south side of the square, and to the north, on the square in front of the Church of St Maurice.

PRECEDING PAGES: a view of the Moravian-Silesian Beskids. **LEFT:** a church near Střilky. **RIGHT:** a happy reaper.

Construction of the latter, a hall church housing a fine baroque organ, began in 1412; it was the place of worship of the ordinary citizens. The episcopal church was the **Katedrála sv. Václava** (St Wenceslas' Cathedral), which dates from 1107, and gained a 13th-century Gothic cloister that was decorated with a fine series of murals in about 1500. The cathedral treasury can be viewed in the crypt.

Litovel ❷ (Littau), to the northwest of Olomouc, is called the "Venice of the Hannakei". It is a pretty little town spread across the six arms of the River Morava. Its principal historic monuments include a

Gothic chapel, St Mark's Church and the **Morový sloup** (Plague Column) erected in 1724. The local museum displays traditional folk costumes and prehistoric archaeological finds. In the hills to the west of the town is the 13th-century **Hrad Bouzov** (castle; open Apr–Oct Tues–Sun, Nov–March Sat and Sun; entrance fee). After extensive damage during the Thirty Years' War, in 1696 the fortress and the attached estates were taken over by the Teutonic Order, which had the building converted into a palace. The **Jeskyně Javoříčko** (Javoříčko caves; tours Tues–Sun Apr–Oct; entrance fee) also attract visitors.

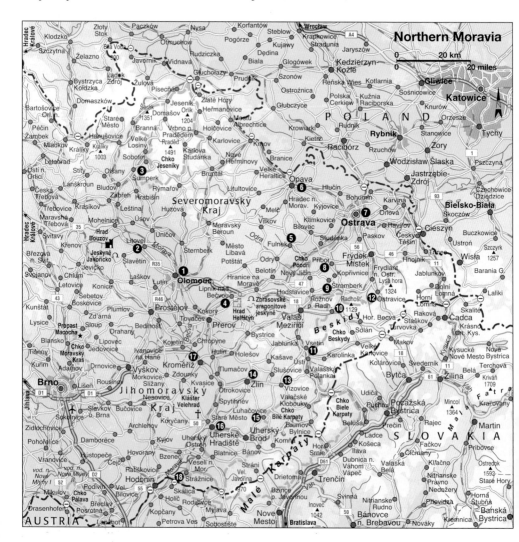

Map on page 254

The Jeseníky Mountains

The Jeseníky Mountains, to which the town of **Šumperk** ❸ serves as gateway, are rich in scenic beauty. A little further north lies the spa town of **Velké Losiny**, scene of one of the last witchcraft trials in Europe; an exhibition of instruments of torture recalls the fateful event. The best base for a tour of the region is without doubt the spa town of **Karlova Studánka**, to the east.

From here you can follow a variety of walking routes into the mountains. Particularly rewarding, if testing, is the path leading to the summit of the **Praděd**, the highest peak in the Jeseníky Mountains 1,491 metres (4,891 ft): the view stretches right across into neighbouring Poland. Another interesting path on the other side leads towards **Petrovy kameny**, and passes the scene of the Witches' Sabbath of Walpurgis Night – that is, if you believe the popular legend.

Through the Moravian Gate

Lipník nad Bečvou ❹, to the east of Olomouc, has preserved its medieval town centre and 15th-century fortifications. Also of interest here are the Renaissance castle and the Gothic church, which was rebuilt during the Renaissance and baroque periods.

A footpath leads from the town along the far bank of the River Bečva to the 13th-century **Hrad Helfštýn** (Helfsteyn Castle; open Tues–Sun; entrance fee), one of the most imposing ruins in the country. Fencing displays, performed in costume, are frequently held in the castle courtyard. A few miles south of Hranicena Moravě lies the spa of Teplice nad Bečvou. The town is popular not so much for the rather stale-tasting warm water produced by its springs as for the magnificent **Zbrasovské aragonitové jeskyně** (caves), which contain mighty stalactites, and miniature lakes emitting vapours.

Fulnek ❺ is well worth visiting for its castle, built in a mixture of baroque and Renaissance styles. It is also the site of the monument to Jan Amos Komenský, better known to foreigners under his Latin name, Comenius, who lived here from 1618 to 1621. Shortly before Opava lies the palace of **Hradec nad Moravicí** (Grätz), built on the site of a 10th-century Slavic fort. Following a devastating fire, the complex was rebuilt in the Empire style and subsequently rechristened The White Castle.

Great composers such as Paganini and Franz Liszt stayed here at the invitation of the music-loving Prince Lichnowsky. Each year the **Beethovenovy týdny** (Beethoven Weeks) commemorate two visits by the German master in 1806.

The name of **Opava** ❻ first cropped up in records in the 12th century. The town was the capital of the German-settled Silesian duchy of Troppau from the 13th century right up to 1918. Among the town's sights are the remains of the former town wall and the Gothic churches of St Mary, the Holy Ghost and St John.

From 1618, the tower on the so-called Butterfly House (Schmetterlingshaus) was where travelling merchants stopped with their wares, which they were required to

RIGHT: view from the garden of Hradec nad Moravicí, in which Beethoven often stayed.

offer for sale for a period of three days. The entrepreneurial spirit of Opava has been maintained to this day; it is regarded as a model for the development of privatisation within the newly capitalist Czech Republic. Because of its German roots, many of the inhabitants still have relatives or other contacts in Germany.

Ostrava , with 350,000 inhabitants, is the third largest town in today's Czech Republic, but its history reaches back into the mists of time. Traces of a camp left by mammoth hunters have been discovered on Landek Hill. However, its turbulent modern history began at the beginning of the last century, when extensive coal deposits were discovered. This led to a massive boom in the town, which became the centre of iron and steel smelting and heavy industry.

Since then, Ostrava has been the bearer of the ambiguous nickname "the steel heart of the Republic". Other industrial towns sprang up around Ostrava. Pitheads and vast factory complexes scar the landscape and noxious smoke, rarely filtered, belches forth into a leaden sky, casting a grey veil across what was once attractive foothill scenery.

The monuments worth seeing, such as the 17th-century Town Hall on **Masarykovo náměstí** (Masaryk Square), a little wooden church in **Ostrava Hrabová** dating from the 16th century, and the Renaissance palace surrounded by a magnificent park in **Karviná**, struggle bravely to maintain their attractions in the face of this pollution. In the Beskid foothills, on both banks of the River Ostravice, lies the twin town of **Frýdek-Místek**. It was founded in the 13th century as a Moravian border town. Its main attraction is a castle rebuilt in the baroque style.

The Beskids

The little town of **Hukvaldy**, with a wildlife park and shady avenues of chestnut trees, lies on the northern slopes of the Beskid Mountains in the shadow of a romantic ruined castle. The Czech composer Leoš Janáček (1854–1928) was born here. Worth visiting nearby for its Gothic church and the well preserved Renaissance buildings surrounding the market place is **Příbor** ❽, the town where Sigmund Freud first saw the light of day.

A few miles south lies **Štramberk** ❾, overshadowed by the tower of a medieval castle which looks more like a mosque. The town itself is one of the loveliest in the country, a maze of winding narrow streets. The local culinary speciality is the delicately spiced, cone-shaped waffle known as *Štramberské uši* (Stramberg Ears). The name is believed to relate to a period when the town was overrun by the Tartars. The neighbouring town of **Kopřivnice** is famous as the home of the Tatra car production plant. Further to the West, **Nový Jičín** is a Gothic jewel with historic townhouses, a Gothic church and a castle.

The **Beskidy** (Beskid Mountains) of Moravia and Silesia form a natural boundary to the Slovakian Republic. **Valašsko** (Wallachia) lies in the Western Beskids – without doubt one of the most fascinating

LEFT: Štramberk in the Moravian-Silesian Beskids.

Map on page 254

regions in the Czech Republic, especially for authentic folklore (a far cry from the performances offered in restaurants and nightclubs). Old customs are still treasured and the local people are welcoming. For sports enthusiasts the Beskids offer a wide range of activities throughout the year, from mountain walks in summer to ski tours and downhill skiing in winter.

The town of **Rožnov pod Radhoštěm** ❿ provides an excellent base from which to explore. In the interesting **Valašské muzeum** (Open-Air Museum of Wallachia; open daily; entrance fee) you can witness life as it used to be lived all over this part of the country, and hear the tinkling bells of the traditional horse-drawn carriages and the strains of dulcimer and violin playing the folk music of Wallachia.

The buildings which comprise the museum were removed from their sites in the immediate vicinity and rebuilt within the museum park. Later on, perfect replicas of other houses were added. In this way an entire little town of wooden build-

ings has been recreated, complete with a pretty church where services are held. The inn Na posledním groši serves good, satisfying meals. The newest section of the park includes a water-driven sawmill, a water mill and a smithy which echo to the sounds of paddle wheel, saw and hammer. The weekends are devoted to traditional customs. Music and dancing are performed by people in local costumes, and traditional crafts, from wood carving to pottery, are offered for sale.

From the nearby Ráztoka Valley it is possible to take a chair lift to the summit of the **Pustevny** (1,018 metres/3,340 ft), a local mountain whose flanks are dotted with typical Wallachian wooden houses and a number of mountain hotels. It is worth taking the hour-long ridge walk to the **Radhošt'** (1,129 metres/3,704 ft), which is dominated by a majestic statue of the Slavic god Radegast. According to legend, those who touch the statue's stomach are bound to return here one day.

The castle in the regional centre of

BELOW: relaxing at day's end.

Vsetín ⓫ in the Bečva Valley houses an exhibition portraying the customs and traditions of the area. Within easy reach to the southeast lies the winter sports and mountain walking paradise of **Soláň**. Equally attractive are the idyllic hamlets and wooden mountain huts. Sheep graze on the mountain slopes, and horses and oxen still draw the ploughs.

The **Lysá hora** (1,324 metres/4,344 ft) is the highest peak in the Beskids. It lies to the east and can be scaled easily from the little town of **Ostravice** ⓬. The ascent, which takes several hours, is rewarded by the enchanting view. On a clear day you can see the peaks of the **Malá Fatra**, the Lesser Fatra range in Slovakia. During the winter months, Lysá hora is very popular with both downhill and cross-country skiing enthusiasts.

Further to the east lie the remote mountain villages of **Dolní** and **Horní Lomná** – as yet an undiscovered part of Moravia. Both these small communities are famous for their annual folklore festivals. The high-altitude valley, enclosed on three sides, preserves its primeval forests in the form of a nature reserve. Another centre of the Valašsko is the little town of **Vizovice** ⓭. The romantic castle, built on the site of a 13th-century monastery, contains an art gallery with works by Dutch, Italian and French masters; there is also a collection of fine china. Vizovice is famous for its distillery, which produces the plum brandy *slivovice* (Slivovitz). At harvest time – and at other seasons of the year – the town holds colourful festivals.

Zlín ⓮ is often described as a town in the country. Originally of no particular importance, it enjoyed a boom towards the end of the 19th century, when Tomáš Bat'a had the idea of producing here the *bat'ovky*, simple and inexpensive shoes made of linen. The enterprise soon expanded to become an internationally known concern.

The town is a typical example of interwar development, constructed in a unified, functional style. Here, great modernist architects such as Le Corbusier and Franz

BELOW: the nave of the Cistercian monastery church, Velehrad.

Map on page 254

Gahura realised their concepts for residential and commercial districts. In 1949 the town was rechristened Gottwaldov, after the first communist president of Czechoslovakia. In 1990, after the Bat'a heirs' claims of ownership were recognised, the old name was readopted.

Luhačovice ⑮, a spa town to the east of Uherské Hradiště, basks in an atmosphere of peace and relaxation. Ten mineral springs, in particular the Vincert Spring, provide relief from disorders of the upper respiratory system. The composer Leoš Janáček is among those who have come to convalesce in this little town.

Greater Moravia

In the valley of the **River Morava** (March), in the heart of Moravian Slovakia, lies the town of **Uherské Hradiště** ⑯ (Hungarian Hradisch), founded in 1257 by Přemysl Otakar II to protect the trading routes. The name indicates that it was here, on the border of Upper Hungary (most of which now lies in the region of Slovakia), that a large group of Protestant refugees from Hungary made their home. They injected fresh life into the town. The Gothic town hall, a number of lovely churches, most of them rebuilt in the baroque style, and the **Lékárna** (apothecary) on the market place, reconstructed in the rococo idiom, all testify to Uherské Hradiště's glorious past.

The town's principal attraction, however, is the Staré Město (Old Town) on the West Bank. It is now a suburb, but very probably was once the site of **Velehrad**, the legendary capital of the first Slavic empire within the territory which today is the Czech and Slovak Republics.

During the 19th century, traces of an early Slavic settlement were discovered here; it was not until a systematic excavation was undertaken in 1948 that experts were able to establish that this had been an important town, if not the actual capital, of the Kingdom of Greater Moravia. During the 9th and 10th century its rulers established close links with Byzantium and, with the help of the Slavic apostles Cyril and Methodius, began the Christianisation of Central Europe.

Supporting such an assumption are the town's location near the Moravian Gate, at the crossroads between the Amber Road, one of the most important north–south routes in Central Europe, and the east–west trading route along the Morava valley.

Thousands of urn graves dating from the 6th and 7th century have already been examined. Living quarters and a two-storey cathedral have also been unearthed, and it is well known that Velehrad, with its 5-km (3-mile) fortifications, was well protected against attack from the landward side. Nonetheless, the archaeological investigations continue, and the results to date can be inspected in a specially created museum, the **Památník Velké Moravy** (open Tues–Sun; entrance fee).

The name of the capital of Greater Moravia has been preserved a few miles to the west, in the **Klášter Velehrad** (Cistercian Monastery of Velehrad). It was founded in 1205 by the margrave of Moravia, a brother of the king, Přemysl Otakar I. Its basilica, completed in 1238,

is dedicated to the two Slavic apostles, Saints Cyril and Methodius. Each year, on 5 July, the joint festival of the two saints, the monastery – now used as a sanatorium – is the focus of a folkloric pilgrimage.

The Haná Plains

The Haná Plains (the Hannakei) extend northwards towards Olomouc. The principal town in the region is **Kroměříž** (Kremsier), which has a beautiful historic centre that has been declared a national monument. The attractive central square, **Riegrovo náměstí**, stands on the site of an old Slavic settlement. In 1110 the little market town passed into the possession of the bishops of Olomouc and remained in their hands for centuries. Even a number of short-lived occupations by the Hussites had no effect on the the town's religious orientation.

Awarded a municipal charter in 1266, the town's advantageous location on the Morava trading route attracted a large number of new residents. A castle and a

Map on page 254

cathedral were built. Both the German colonists and an active Jewish community, which since the late Middle Ages had possessed its own chamber of trade and even a town hall, had an impact on the continued development. The Church of St Maurice, begun in the 13th century, was finished in about 1500.

In 1643, during the Thirty Years' War, the town, the castle and the cathedral were burned to the ground by invading Swedish troops, but it wasn't long after the cessation of hostilities that reconstruction began. Under the supervision of Italian architects, work commenced on the remodelling of the fortress to create a magnificent **palác** (palace; open May–Sept Tues–Sun, Apr and Oct Sat and Sun; entrance fee) in a combined Renaissance–baroque style.

Today visitors can inspect not only the meticulously restored apartments, but also one of the most important art collections in the country, including works by Titian (*Flaying of Marysas by Apollo*), Lucas Cranach and Pieter Brueghel, among others, and *King Charles of England and Queen Henriette*, which was painted by Antony van Dyck.

A flower garden was created just outside the estate gates; it is a stunning example of baroque garden planning. The Květná zahrada, a public park, is an oasis of calm in this bustling city. The Hudební festival (music festival) in August and the film festival, Ars-Film, which follows it, are the liveliest times to be in the city.

Following the Morava to the south of Uherské Hradiště, after 20 km (13 miles) the road comes to the little town of **Strážnice** ⑱. It's a sleepy place for most of the year, except for the end of June when it suddenly comes to life on account of the **Mezinárodní folklórní festival** (International Folklore Festival). Costume groups arrive from all over Europe and beyond, to take part in the singing and dancing competitions. In the castle itself there is an interesting folklore museum.

Twenty km (13 miles) further on, **Hodonín** is an industrial town that is only worth mentioning because it is the birthplace of the country's founder president, Tomáš G. Masaryk (1850–1937). ❏

LEFT: the imperial hall in Bučovice Castle. **RIGHT:** the blue Beskids.

SLOVAKIA

*A detailed guide to the Slovak Republic, with principal sites
clearly cross-referenced by number to the maps*

Slovakia has come a long way and been through a lot since
independence in 1993. After years of lagging behind its
neighbours in Hungary and the Czech Republic it is now
pushing hard to catch up with them in the race to join the European
Union. For visitors, this is opening up new possibilities in a country
which was once an unknown quantity.

City centres are being restored, big hotels and a wealth of smaller,
family run pensions now provide tourists with a range and a quality
which seemed unimaginable 10 years ago. And what a country it is.
With a wealth of natural sights second to none – vast tracts of
unspoilt woodland, high mountain peaks, hundreds of glacial lakes,
five national parks, castles, ravines, waterfalls – for adaptable, nature-
loving visitors willing to restrict their material needs,

Slovakia is a romantic, still relatively inexpensive holiday destination par excellence. It covers an area of 49,000 sq km (19,000 sq
miles), which makes it larger than Switzerland; within the most popular holiday region, the High Tatra Mountains (up to 2,650
metres/8,694 ft), an area of 770 sq km (300 sq miles) has already
been designated as a national park where no further tourist development is permitted. With its canyons, waterfalls and caves, it is ideal
walking territory. What is more, there are the extensive forests of
the Low Tatras (the habitat of bears, wolves and lynxes), plus 100 or
so castles to explore and traditional relaxing spa towns such as Piešt'.

The Slovak government, envious of the success of its neighbours
in attracting visitors, wants to accommodate the growing influx while
remaining conscious of the need to preserve the country's character.
Standards of services and facilities are now as good as anywhere in
the region while prices are generally low. And because of the relative
newness of the tourist phenomenon in Slovakia you can be sure of a
hearty welcome from the locals.

The journey through Slovakia begins with its fascinating capital,
Bratislava, a city with a delightful old centre and a flourishing cultural life. We then explore its environs: the castles and villages on the
banks of the River Danube, before sweeping across the country from
the towns of the Little Carpathians in the west through the Tatra
Mountains to the historic centres in the east where Slovakia borders
Poland and the Ukraine.

Wherever you go in the country you can be sure of encountering
magnificent and varied scenery, an intriguing history and culture but
also a warm welcome from a naturally hospitable people.   ❏

PRECEDING PAGES: Štrbské Pleso in the High Tatras; Spiš Castle, the largest in the
Slovak Republic.
LEFT: wooden dwellings near Zuberec in the Tatra foothills.

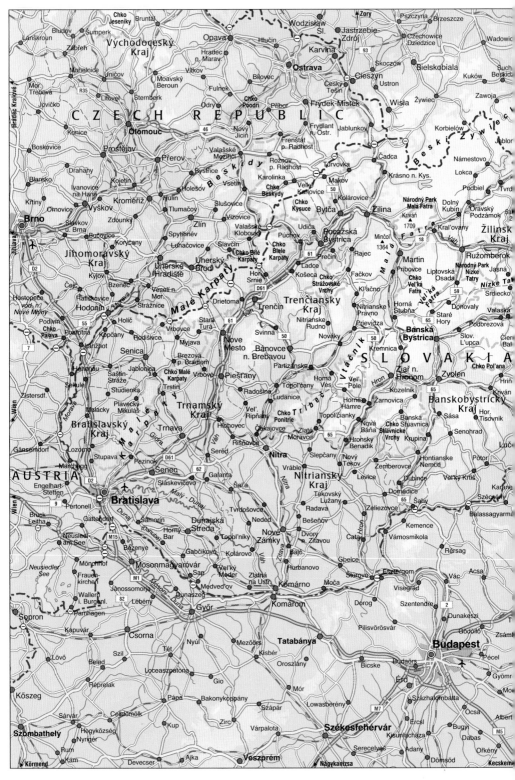

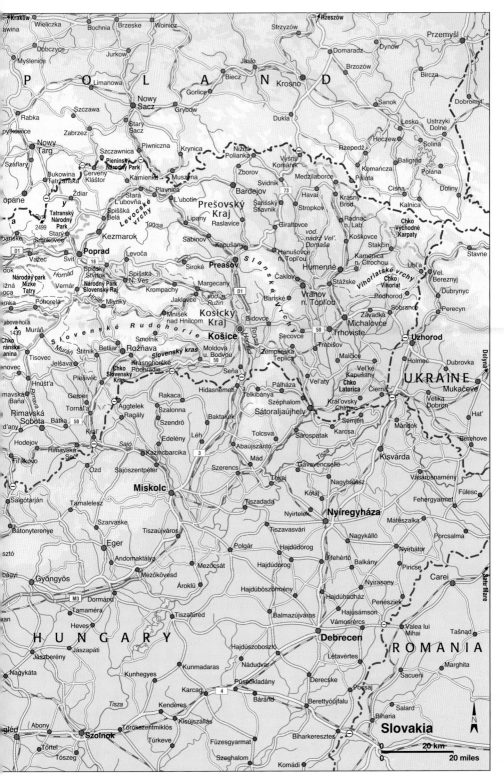

Map on pages 272–73

BRATISLAVA

The capital of the Slovak Republic has had a turbulent past, including 40 years of communist planning, but its restored Old Town and the rest of its attractions can be seen by a leisurely tour on foot

E ven in prehistoric times the fertile plain around Bratislava on the southern slopes of the Little Carpathians attracted settlers. The site had a further advantage in its strategic position at the intersection of two long-distance trading routes near the Hungarian Gates Gorge, where the Danube valley cuts between the Alps and the Carpathians. The Amber Road linked the centres of civilisation on the Mediterranean with those around the Baltic, and the Danube provided a means of transporting goods from Western Europe to the Black Sea.

A Celtic tribe, the Boii, made themselves a base in a fortified settlement near Bratislava. They minted coins and were active traders. After a short period of occupation by the Germanii, the Romans established camps along the southern bank of the river. The fortified natural boundary marked the limits of their empire, the *limes*, although they did build outposts on the far side of the river as well. During the 4th century the invasion of the Huns put an end to Roman rule, but neither the aggressive mounted tribes nor the Langobards and Avars who succeeded them left any traces of their stay. This, however, was not true of the Slavs whose migration brought them to the region from the 6th century.

In 623 they founded a tribal union covering the whole of what now constitutes the Czech and Slovak Republics, and during the 9th century the amalgamation of the Slavic principalities of Moravia and Nitra created the Kingdom of Greater Moravia, in which the area surrounding Bratislava played a crucial role.

Hungarian rule

The defeat of an army of Bavarian and Slavic troops in 906 marked the beginning of Hungarian rule. It was a historical turning point, described in chronicles as the Battle of Brezlauspurg which reveals the origins of the German name for the city, Pressburg, and can be traced back to Braslav, the Slavic ruler.

The Slavs soon reached a compromise with the new rulers, who were able to strengthen their position of supremacy despite temporary reconquest by the Czech Přemyslid dynasty and attacks by armies of the German empire.

The kings of Hungary granted Bratislava its municipal charter in 1217 and encouraged foreign workers to settle in the area. The arrival of Italian craftsmen and Jewish and Arabian traders soon turned Bratislava into an international city. During the dispute over the Austrian succession the population decided to offer

LEFT: an evening view of the Danube with the silhouette of the castle. **RIGHT:** a narrow street in the Old Town.

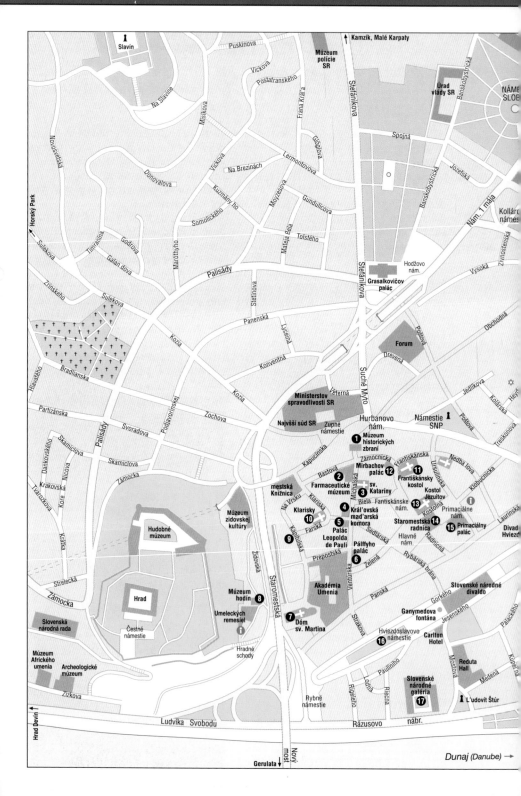

Slavín

Puškinova

Vlčkova

Postřanského

Na Slavíne

Mišíkova

Na Brezinách

Vlčkova

Lermontovova

Frana Kráľa

Gogoľova

Múzeum
polície
SR

Kamzík, Malé Karpaty

Štefánikova

Úrad
vlády SR

Banskobystrická

NÁME
SLOB

Spojná

Jozefská

Banskobystrická

Nám. 1 mája

Kollár
námes

Novosvetská

Donovalova

Kuzmányho

Somolického

Moyzesova

Gundulicova

Mateja Bela

Tolstého

Vysoká

Horský Park

Sulekova

Godrova

Timravina

Galan dova

Marótyho

Palisády

Šteřinova

Panenská

Lýcejná

Hodžovo
nám.

Grasalkovičov
palác

Štefánikova

Žilinstenská

Zrínskeho

Sulekova

Kozia

Konventná

Suché Mýto

Forum

Poštová

Obchodná

† † † † † † †
† † † † † † † †
† † † † † † †
† † † † † †
Bradlianska

Hlavatého

Partizánska

Podjavorinskej

Zochova

Svoradova

Skamiclova

Kozia

Veterná

Ministerstov
spravodlivosti SR

Hurbanovo
nám.

Námestie
SNP

Drevená

Jédlíkova

Koláŕská

Heyr

Treskonova

Dankovského

Nicova

Skamiclova

Zámocká

Najvšší súd SR

Zupné
námestie

Kapucínska

① Múzeum
historických
zbraní

Zámočnícka

② Mirbachov
palác

František

František

Nedba lova

Ursulínská

Klobučnická

Laurín

Tvarožkova

Kore

Krakovská

Palisády

Zámocká

Bastová

Michalská

Baštová

② Farmaceutické
múzeum

sv.
Kataríny

③

⑫

⑪ Františkánsky
kostol

Kostol
Jezuitov

mestská
Knižnica

Na Vršku

Klariská

Biela Fantiškánske

⑬

Kostolná

Primaciálne
nám.

Primaciálny
palác

Divadlo
Hviezd

Múzeum
židovskej
kultúry

Klarisky

⑩

Farská

④ Kráľovská
mad'arská
komora

⑤ Palác
Leopolda
de Pauli

Sedlárska

⑭ Staromestská
radnica

Radničná

⑮

Hudobné
múzeum

Hrad

Kollárská

⑨

Prepoštská

⑥ Pálffyho
palác

Zelená

Hlavné
nám.

Rybárská brána

Slovenská
národná
divadlo

Strelecká

Zámocká

Slovenská
národná rada

Čestné
námestie

Múzeum
hodín

⑧

Umeleckých
remesiel

ⓘ

Staromestská

Akadémia
Umenia

Ventúrska

Panská

Gorkého

Jesenského

Ganymedova
fontána

Palackého

Kúpel

Múzeum
Afrického
umenia

Archeologické
múzeum

Žižkova

Hradné
schody

⑦ Dóm
sv. Martina

Strakova

Hviezdoslavovo
⑯ námestie

Carlton
Hotel

Medená

Reduta
Hall

Hrad Devín

Ludvíka

Svobodu

Rybné
námestie

Rigeleho

Lóda

Riečna

Slovenské
národné
galéria

⑰

Ľudovít Štúr

Paulínho

Mostová

Ráznusovo

nábr.

Gerulata

Nový
most

Dunaj (Danube) →

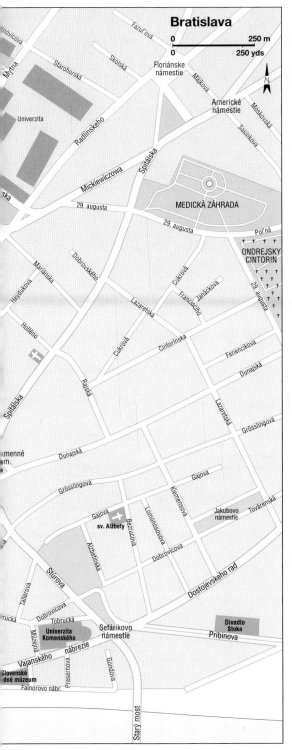

Bratislava

their support to Hungary rather than Austria. The king of Hungary, Andras III, demonstrated his grateful thanks by making Bratislava a free city on 2 December 1291 – an act which unleashed an unprecedented economic and cultural boom. The Gothic city, which has survived at least in outline until the present day, thus arose, protected by massive walls. The banks of the Danube benefited from the construction of a harbour; tolls and taxes on the principal exports – wine and cloth – were dropped.

An independent municipal administration, free election of judges and religious tolerance attracted new residents. Among the 5,000 citizens were a large number of Jews, who lived in their own district. Additional privileges, such as the right to mint coins and staple rights, the elevation to the rank of Free Royal City in 1405 and the founding of the Academia Istropolitana 1467, the first university in Hungary, encouraged further prosperity. The Turkish invasion came out of the blue; the Turks conquered the heartland of Hungary and the capital city of Buda. Consequently the Hungarian National Assembly chose Bratislava as its temporary capital in 1535. Originally intended as an interim solution, the situation lasted right up until 1784. In fact, no fewer than 11 kings and eight queen consorts had been crowned in St Martin's Cathedral by 1830.

Queen Maria Theresa

One of the queens was Maria Theresa, the Empress of Austria and Queen of Hungary, under whose rule Bratislava blossomed once again. The former fortress was converted into a magnificent palace, and while the Old City was being modernised in line with the baroque elegance fashionable at the time, the first factories were opened in the suburbs. Based on a long tradition of craftsmanship, Bratislava became a rapidly expanding industrial centre. The founding of the Danube Steamship Company in 1830 and the opening of the railway link with Vienna in 1848 revolutionised trade and business.

One more revolution was to shake the city, however. Under pressure from the

Hungarian Estates Council, the emperor signed a treaty in Bratislava on 11 April 1848 granting Hungary autonomy, with its own government and parliament. One year later the Emperor Franz Joseph I declared the treaty null and void, but in 1867 the Habsburg monarchs were forced to accept a compromise.

The capital of Slovakia

Under the leadership of Ľudovít Štúr, the Slovakian opposition was still on the Hungarian side in March 1848. However, they were soon forced to recognise that the revolutionaries, too, were only interested in pursuing a policy of Hungarian nationalism. For many, a new orientation became essential: exiled in America, Slovakian and Czech immigrant groups agreed on the foundation of a common state. On 1 January 1919 the troops of the Czechoslovak Republic marched into Bratislava. The town, in which about half the residents were Slovakian, became the capital of Slovakia. The first experience of living with the Czechs was not encouraging; between 1938 and 1945, the Slovaks even attempted independence with their own state under fascist rule.

On 4 April 1945, Soviet troops liberated the city from the Germans. During the second half of the 20th century Bratislava finally became a Slovakian city; today the Slovaks virtually have their capital to themselves.

An ambitious rebuilding and restoration programme has transformed the city. However, not all the developments have been positive; while the historic city centre has survived largely intact, Bratislava still bears all the scars of 40 years of communist planning and control. The sights can be savoured in the course of three leisurely walks.

A tour of the town

The 14th-century **Michalská brána** (St Michael's Gate; open daily 10am–5pm except Tues) is the only medieval town gateway still standing. The tower, which

BELOW: between 1541 and 1784, Bratislava was the capital of Hungary and was called Pozsony.

Maps on page 272-73

was given its baroque cupola in the 18th century, is surmounted by a statue of the archangel. Even visitors who are not interested in touring the **Múzeum historických zbraní ❶** (Museum of Historic Weapons; open May–Sept Mon and Wed–Fri, Sat–Sun, Oct–Apr open daily; entrance fee) should climb to the top of the tower, for the panorama from the platform provides a good view of the Old Town.

It is worth making a short detour through the outer gateway beside the little bridge which crosses what was once the town moat. House No. 28 contains the historic apothecary's shop, At the Sign of the Red Crab, and an interesting **Farmaceutické múzeum ❷** (Museum of Pharmacy; open Tues–Sun; entrance fee). Continuing along the Michalská, you will pass a fine Renaissance house at No. 7, built in 1648 for the town councillor Andreas Segner, whose family coat of arms still graces the entrance. Many visitors miss the unobtrusive **Kaplnka sv. Kataríny ❸** (St Catherine's Chapel), but those who do notice it and go inside are greeted by an attractive Gothic interior.

A few steps further on, house No. 4 contains a handicrafts shop and a Hungarian bookshop. The baroque mansion opposite is open in the evening, when its vaulted ceiling reverberates to the incongruous sounds of disco music.

The atmosphere in the adjoining palazzi is much more sedate, for they now serve as the university's library. The **Král'ovská mad'arská komora ❹** (Royal Hungarian Chamber), a magnificent baroque palace, was where the Hungarian Estates Council met from 1802 to 48. It was before this assembly that L'udovít Štúr made his stirring speech advocating equal rights for all peoples within the Austro-Hungarian Empire. A memorial plaque recalls the deeds of this forerunner of the Slovakian freedom movement. Beyond this point the Michalská leads into the Ventúrska.

The garden pavilion of the **Palác Leopolda de Pauli ❺** (Palace of Leopold de Pauli) was the setting for the celebrated concert début of Franz Liszt, when he was just nine years of age. In 1762 another

infant prodigy, the six-year-old Wolfgang Amadeus Mozart, enchanted the local *haute volée* in the **Pálffyho palác ❻** (Palace of Marshal Pálffy; open Tues–Fri 10am–6pm, Sat–Sun 10am–5pm) in the Ventúrska No. 10. This distinguished building was for a while the party college; ironically enough, after the revolution it served as the administrative headquarters for the movement Public Against Violence, the Slovakian counterpart of the Civic Forum in Prague. In 1467, on the other side of the road in Ventúrska No. 3, King Matthias Corvinus founded the Academia Istropolitana, the first Hungarian university. Today the building houses the **Akadémia umenia** (Academy of Fine Arts), which was a key centre in the Velvet Revolution. The café opposite has a reputation as a meeting place for students, intellectuals and artists.

This lively street was one of the town's main thoroughfares even in medieval times. In those days it was named the Ventura Alley after a family of Italian

tradesmen who lived there. It ends by the **Rokokový palác grófa Erdodyho** (Rococo Palace of Count Erdody). Turning right into the Panská, you reach **Dóm sv. Martina ❼** (St Martin's Cathedral; open daily except during services). Even the basic design of St Martin's Cathedral is unusual. The tower, surmounted by a golden crown and glittering roof tiles, formed a part of the medieval fortifications. For this reason the entrances had to be placed along the side walls. It is a triple-naved hall church which was finally dedicated in 1452 after a construction period of over 100 years.

The interior is dominated by Gothic fan vaulting, which shows the influence of the Viennese architectural style. A pillar within the chancel is adorned with the coat of arms of King Matthias Corvinus. The donor of the church received the bones of St John the Evangelist as a gift from the Turkish Sultan Mahmud I.

These relics are kept in a chapel in the north transept which was specially de-signed by Georg Raphael Donner between 1732 and 1734. Donner also created the baroque high altar and the lovely **Súsošie sv. Martina na koni** (equestrian statue of St Martin) which adorns the head wall of the south transept.

From 1563 to 1830 the cathedral of St Martin was the site of the coronations of the kings of Hungary. During the 18th century it was rebuilt at their behest, and baroque exuberance replaced the simple Gothic style of the interior. In the cathedral treasury above the canons' chapel on the north side of the tower, some original traces can still be seen. Of particular note is an exceptionally fine monstrance dating from 1449.

One of the most glaring eyesores in modern Bratislava is the urban motorway that cuts between the old city and the Hrad (castle) and then crosses the Danube by means of the **Nový most** (bridge). It is a remarkable construction in itself, but one is tempted to ask whether it was really necessary to sacrifice part of the historic

BELOW: medieval carvings on the door of St Martin's Cathedral.

Maps on page 272–73

town centre, including a Jewish synagogue, in order to make room for it. There is even talk of knocking the bridge down and moving it to restore this central part of the city to its former glory.

Once at the other side, the visitor mounts the **Hradné schody** (castle steps) to the fine Gothic gate. On the way it is worth making a short detour to visit the Dom U Dobrého Pastiera, the House of the Good Shepherd, which lies at the junction of Židovská ul. and Mikulášska ul. It is a delicate-looking house with a fine yellow stucco facade, which was built in 1760 in pure rococo style; each storey consists of a single room. It currently houses the historic **Múzeum hodín** ❽ (Clock Museum; open Oct–Apr daily except Tues; entrance fee).

The castle

The massive building of the **Hrad** (castle grounds open daily; treasury open Tues–Sun) rises above the city and the river. As early as the 9th century, the Slavs

built a border fortress to protect the ford at this point on the Danube. It was extended over the following centuries by the Hungarians. The Habsburgs recognised the strategic importance of the site as one of the outer defences protecting Vienna from the Turks, and between 1635 and 1649 they had the high walls with the protruding corner towers constructed upon a square ground plan by the master fortress builder Carlone.

Even Maria Theresa, in the following century, still kept the Hungarian crown jewels within the castle walls. The castle burned down a total of three times, the last occasion being in 1811, after which it was not restored until 1953. A glimpse into the corners of the **Hunger Tower** and the **Torture Chamber** (which is full of bats) provides a vivid impression of the cruel fate suffered by many of the prisoners incarcerated within their walls. The castle houses a branch of the Slovakian National Museum (closed Mon) with displays of weaponry, folk art and furniture.

BELOW: a sunset reflects on the bridge over the Danube in Bratislava.

Highly symbolic is the location of the city's new landmark, the headquarters of the **Slovenská národná rada** (Slovakian National Committee), immediately below the castle courtyard. The best way to return to the starting point of your route is along the northern side of the cathedral. In the Middle Ages the canons from the cathedral chapter lived in the **Kapitulská** ❾ (Priests' Alley). They were permitted to sell their own wine and were exempt from paying taxes. Accordingly, many of the houses in this quiet street are elaborately decorated, including the **Prepoštsky Palác** (Provost's Palace) at No. 19, the **Collegium Emmericianum** at No. 20 and the **Kanovnov Dom** (Canon's House) at No. 15, which has a Renaissance facade and a baroque door.

The next lane to the right leads to the **Klarisky** ❿ (Convent of St Clare) with its simple Gothic church, which now serves as a gallery for Gothic paintings and sculptures as well as forming an elegant setting for classical concerts. The

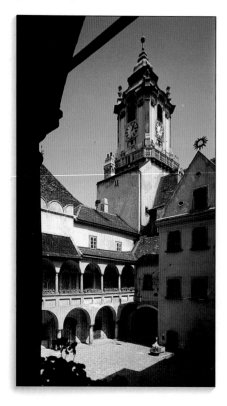

reason the strange pentagonal tower stands on the perimeter wall of the church is that it was the only way in which the nuns were able to circumvent the strict building regulations applicable to a begging order. After visiting the church, you should turn right into the narrow Baštová, previously known as Executioner's Alley. The incumbent of this honoured municipal post resided at No. 5. Passing the arsenal at No. 2, you will soon be back at St Michael's Gate once more.

To the Danube Esplanade

The second walk starts from the point where the first one ended. Opposite the Baštová is a romantic, winding street lined with lovingly restored houses, which leads towards the eastern section of the Old Town. The **Františkánsky kostol** ⓫ (Franciscan Church) on Františkánske nám. is the oldest church in the city; it was completed in 1297 and the unadorned chancel dates from this period. On the side altar stands a remarkable late-Gothic sandstone *pietá*. St John's Chapel on the north side, dating from 1380, is another masterpiece of the Gothic mason's art. The church was extended several times at later dates; during the 18th century it was even adorned with a Loreto chapel similar to the one in Prague.

The light-hearted rococo **Mirbachov palác** ⓬ (Mirbach Palace; open Tues–Sun; entrance fee) opposite the former home of a wealthy brewery owner; today the building is part of the Municipal Art Gallery.

Fringed by noble townhouses, the beautiful **Hlavné námestie** (Main Square) has formed the bustling hub of urban life since medieval times: it served simultaneously as market square, parade ground and place of execution. Its centre is occupied by a huge fountain. In the summer it is decked out with the chairs and tables of cafes and bars. A perfect place to sit, have something to drink and take in the beauty of the old city.

Bratislava is a religious centre, which explains the large number of churches in this part of town. Among the most magnificent is the **Kostol Jezuitov** ⓭ (Jesuit Church) standing on the northern side of

LEFT: the courtyard of the town hall.

Map on page 272–73

the square; at the time of the Counter-Reformation it was changed from Protestant to Catholic and subsequently acquired an imposing appearance. The fine rococo pulpit and **Stĺp sv. Márie** (St Mary's Column) in front are both witnesses to the zeal and skill of the architects.

The **Staromestská radnica** ⓮ (Old Town Hall) next door is the result of the amalgamation of a number of private houses. As long ago as the 14th century it was known as the Gothic House with the Tower, and from that time onwards became the seat of the municipal administration. The vaulted passageway leads into an attractive courtyard; even the Gothic chapel has been carefully restored. The building acquired its predominantly Renaissance appearance in the 16th century and the present tower was built in baroque style in 1732, the old one having been toppled by an earthquake. Inside, the beautiful coffered ceiling of the council chamber is impressive, as are the baroque stucco and frescoes adorning the courtroom. The

building also houses the city archives and a library. In addition, since 1948 the entire complex, together with the adjoining **Apponyi Palais,** has served as the Municipal Museum. It is impossible to overlook the Zelený dom (Green House), an old tavern in which the town's golden days were celebrated in style.

Between the Town Hall and the Jesuit church a little street leads directly to the elegant **Primaciálny palác** ⓯ (Bishop's Palace; open daily; entrance fee) in Primaciálne námestie built between 1777 and 1781 for the Archbishop of Esztergom. It served as winter residence for the first prince of the church and the holder of the highest religious office in Hungary. The building is open today as part of the Municipal Art Gallery, which permits the visitor to venture into the Hall of Mirrors where the Treaty of Bratislava was signed on 26 December 1805 after Napoleon's victory in the Battle of Austerlitz.

In former times the town moat ran between the Old Town and the Danube.

BELOW: interior of the National Theatre.

When the fortifications were removed by Maria Theresa, the space was used for public buildings. The top end of the lengthy **Hviezdoslavovo nám.** ⓰ (square) is dominated by the **Slovenské národné divadlo** (Slovakian National Theatre), in front of which stands the **Ganymedova fontána** (Ganymede Fountain).

Diagonally opposite, the **Carlton Hotel** still retains an air of the Roaring Twenties. From the Carlton, the Mostová leads past the Reduta Hall, which is the home of the Slovakian Philharmonic Orchestra, and then down to the bank of the Danube and the modern monument to Ľudovít Štúr, the creator of the written Slovakian language. This was previously the site of the Coronation Hill, where newly crowned kings would promise to protect the city against all its foes.

On the right-hand side of the road running along the river bank is the **Slovenské národné galéria** ⓱ (Slovakian National Gallery; open Tues–Sun; entrance fee), housing paintings from the past 200

years. Further downstream stands the **Univerzita Komenského** (Komenský University), the most important institute of higher education in Slovakia, and the **Slovenské narodné múzeum** (Slovakian National Museum; open Tues–Sun; entrance fee), which has an important archaeological collection. The landing stage for passenger ships to Vienna, Devín and Budapest is also here.

The modern town

Bratislava's dynamic present equals its past. The city's pulse beats fastest on the northeast side of the Old Town, on the Námestie SNP (the Square of the Slovakian Uprising). During the Velvet Revolution, tens of thousands of citizens braved the winter cold here. Even today, the square is the arena for protest meetings and, as a sign of the times, it also features a McDonald's restaurant.

To the southeast of this square lies **Kamenné námestie** ⓲ (Kamenné Square), lined with department stores, hotels and fine art nouveau buildings. To the north is the tree-lined pedestrian area, the Poštová, which crosses the busy Obchodná shopping street. At the end of the Poštová lies the Hodžovo námestie, location of the Grasalkovičov palác, a magnificent rococo-style summer residence built for the princes and presidents of the Royal Hungarian Council. Above a sweeping circular staircase is the Spanish Room where Franz Josef Haydn and his orchestra performed in 1772.

Next door stands the luxury hotel **Forum**, with cafés, restaurants and a casino. Further to the north is the city's prosperous villa quarter containing fine houses from the 1900s. The terrain climbs towards the **Slavín**, the huge monument to Soviet soldiers who fell in World War II. The Kostol na Kalvárii church once stood nearby, but the authorities demolished the tower to make the Slavín monument more prominent.

Beyond the city gates

Clearly signposted footpaths lead to the hilly **Horský Park**. Koliba and the television tower on the summit of the Kamzík

LEFT: tram in the town centre.

Maps on page 272–73

offer magnificent views of Bratislava. It can be reached by means of the trolley bus No. 213, and has the additional advantage of an excellent restaurant at the top.

The **Malé Karpaty**, the Little Carpathian Mountains, which extend in a northerly direction from Bratislava, are the city's nearest recreational area. Vineyards nestle between wooded hillsides; wine tastings are available almost everywhere. A number of picturesque wine-producing villages punctuate the Wine Route, including **Jur**, **Limbach**, **Pezinok** and **Modra**.

The restaurant **Pezinská Baba**, in the middle of the woods, is famous for its excellent wine and homemade specialities. Nearby stands a cottage, the Chata na Bielej skale, the former holiday home of the communist leaders. Trout and carp from the Netherlands were flown in for the dignitaries, while they went hunting for moufflons, wild boar and deer. Deer are still common; even packs of wolves occasionally roam these vast forests.

Excursions into the past

Further excursions in the immediate vicinity can be taken to **Červený kameň Castle** and the **Palace of Smolenický zámok**, which displays a number of interesting architectural details and fine interiors. But the most mysterious place in the environs of Bratislava is undoubtedly **Hrad Devín** (Devín Castle; closed Mon; entrance fee), which lies some 10 km (6 miles) upstream and can also be reached by river boat. The precipitous rock overlooking the confluence of the Morava and the Danube has been built upon for at least 5,000 years.

According to legend, the first castle was built here by Devoina, the daughter of the Duke of Moravia: it is first mentioned in records of the kingdom of Greater Moravia during the 9th century. The present fortress dates from the 13th century, although it was rebuilt in the 16th century by the Hungarian king of Poland and prince of Transylvania, Stephen Bathory. In 1809 it was almost completely destroyed by Napoleon's troops. But even in the late 20th century, Devín Castle continued to have its uses: those who failed in their attempt to

flee into nearby Austria were condemned to see their hopes of a better life end in the castle prison. The barbed wire and prison cells did not disappear until after the critical days of November 1989. In July the Slovaks celebrate an annual festival of peace in the ruins.

An alternative excursion follows the southern bank of the Danube to the unusual archaeological site of **Gerulata**. Only 15 minutes' drive from Bratislava, this Slovakian enclave just before the Hungarian border clusters around the three villages of **Rusovce**, **Jarovce** and **Čuňovo**. It was the only region within Slovakia which formed part of the Roman Empire for any length of time. Extensive excavations have shed new light on Roman culture and its interaction with neighbouring people in this far-flung province. The banks of the Danube are still a paradise for anglers and people who appreciate riverbank flora and fauna. There are many traditional inns and taverns which offer fish specialities and local wines. ❑

RIGHT: the Little Carpathians are an important vine-growing area.

Map
on page
286

WESTERN SLOVAKIA

Western Slovakia is home to many of Slovakia's spa towns,
but the region also provides good walking country
and ancient towns worth a visit

Lying in a fertile, vine-clad valley only 45 km (28 miles) to to he northeast of **Bratislava ❶** is the diocesan town of **Trnava ❷** (Tyrnau). It can be reached by means of the D61 motorway as well as by train. In 1988 the town celebrated its 750th anniversary and, in honour of the event, it received meticulous restoration. The architectural variety of Trnava reflects its significance as one of Hungary's religious and cultural centres during the long period of Turkish rule in the southern part of the country, and helps to explain why it has been dubbed "Slovakian Rome".

In 1238 Bela IV, the reigning king of Hungary, awarded the settlement its municipal and market privileges, placing it directly under the jurisdiction of the crown. The extraordinary advantages associated with its status and its favourable location at the intersection of two long-distance trade routes encouraged Trnava's rapid growth and prosperity. In 1543 the town became the religious centre of all Hungary when the Primate of the Hungarian Church, the Archbishop of Esztergom, took refuge here because his own town and most of the rest of the country had been overrun by Turks.

The foundation of a university less than a century later marked the transformation of the trading centre into a cultural metropolis. The transfer of the university to Buda in 1777 and the return of the primate to Esztergom after its liberation in 1822 would have probably resulted in Trnava's sinking into provincial oblivion once more, had Slovakian intellectuals not moved the seat of the "Company of Academics" to the town in 1792. This was the most important scientific and literary association in Slovakia, which at that time was still under Hungarian rule.

Topped by its massive twin towers, the **Dóm sv. Mikuláš** (Cathedral of St Nicholas) dominates the panorama of the Old Town. In 1380 the present Gothic church was constructed on the site of a Romanesque basilica; it was subsequently extended on several occasions. The **Univerzitný kostol sv. Jána Krstitl'a** (University Church of St John the Baptist) was constructed by Italian masters commissioned by the Jesuits. In eight years, between 1629 and 1637, they completed the largest religious building in Slovakia. Together with the **Archibiskupský palác** (Archbishop's Palace; open Tues–Sun; entrance fee), it sets the architectural tone on University Square.

Soaring above the long, narrow market place is the Town Tower, 69 metres (226 ft) high. The elaborately stuccoed facade of the classicistic town hall dates from

PRECEDING PAGES: the ruins of Strecno Castle stand above the Váh Valley.
LEFT: aerial view of the Váh Valley.
RIGHT: in the spa gardens at Piešet'any.

1793 and bears witness to the unshake-able optimism of Trnava in a time of threatened slump, as does the Municipal Theatre of 1831. Also worth visiting are a number of beautiful private houses in the Hollého ul. and the Kapitulská ul., as are the well-preserved town walls with the protruding bastions to the east and west of the Old Town.

Into the Váh Valley

Piešt'any ❸ (Pistyan) lies 35 km (22 miles) along the Váh Valley following the main road, No. 61, to the north. A statue in the spa quarter bears testimony to the great expectations of this world-famous spa town; it depicts a man throwing away his crutches. As much as 3½ million litres (700,000 gallons) of hot mineral water at a temperature of 67°C (152°F) gush out of the earth here every day; patients with rheumatic complaints appreciate the sul-phurous mud. There are first-class hotels and spa facilities available, and the nearby **Priehrada Slňava** ❹ (Slňava Dam) offers good opportunities for water sports. The town is delightfully peaceful and pro-vides a good base for excursions into the surrounding countryside. Because of the protection provided by the hills, the

Map on page 286

climate here is unusually mild. From the 17th century increasing numbers of visitors flocked to the spa, and in 1827 the Hungarian count Erdödy, whose family owned the entire town until 1940, decided to make capital of its natural advantages. Spa halls and parks were created on the north bank; the southern **Kúpeľný ostrov** (spa island) with the **Napoleónske kúpele** (Napoleonic Baths) and the town's principal spring, the **Prameň Adam Trojan**, was linked directly to the town by means of the colonnaded bridge.

Under the aegis of Alexander Winter, a private citizen who took on the general lease for the spa facilities, a number of art nouveau sanatoria were built. The enterprising businessman not only transformed Piešťany into a favourite meeting place of the fashionable world, but also encouraged a social conscience. In 1893 he founded a "workers' boarding school" and persuaded public health bodies to fund spa visits for the first time. During the past decades the municipal authorities have confirmed the town's international reputation by building modern spa facilities and the Art Museum.

It seems that a fondness for sitting in warm mud has a long, indeed ancient, tradition. Evidence of Neanderthal settlement has been found here. Even the local love of the arts, expressed during the International Music Festival each summer, and the open-air exhibition of plastic arts in the spa gardens, has ancient roots. In 1939 a farmer found the *Venus of Moravany*, a small sculpture carved from the tooth of a mammoth, which is one of the oldest sculptures ever found.

Near **Čachtice** ❺, situated 10 km (6 miles) further north, the remains of a vast castle rises out of the valley. It was formerly the residence of the mad Countess Elisabeth Bathory. Documents record that the "White Lady", as the countess was known, was responsible for the murder of 300 young girls. She believed that bathing in their blood was beneficial to her snow-white skin. The story has inspired a number of horror films. Tracks from the main road lead to the castle from where there are views of the surrounding nature reserve.

Trenčín

Trenčín ❻, a lively little town with a long history, lies further upstream. As long ago as the 6th century, the Slavs built a fortress on the huge rock overlooking the Váh Valley.

History here goes back even further, however, as the Roman inscription on the rock testifies. Dated AD 179, it records the victory of the locally stationed Roman legion over a tribe of Germanii; it is the oldest written record ever found in Slovakia. A settlement soon developed in the protective shadow of the fortress, and was awarded market rights in 1412. From 1302 the Hungarian magnate Matúš Čák had the complex remodelled into a prestigious, well-fortified castle, from which he ruled over the whole of Western Slovakia. John of Luxembourg and his son, the future Emperor Charles IV, chose it on several occasions as the site for negotiations with the kings of Poland and Hungary. King Sigismund strengthened the bulwark against the Moravian Hussites.

From the 17th century, the Counts Illésházy, who had received the town and its fortress in fief from the Habsburgs, rebuilt the complex in accordance with the latest theories of defensive architecture. Their descendants donated the entire fortress to the town in order to avoid the immense maintenance costs.

Trenčiansky hrad (Trenčin Castle; open daily for guided tours; entrance fee). A castle chapel with a rotunda and the central Matúš Tower are all that remain of the medieval structure. The entire complex is extensive and includes an arsenal, casemates and an oubliette as well as the Trenčín Gallery with a collection of paintings by old masters. The Gothic parish church was built in the shadow of the castle rock. It possesses a perfect example of a charnel house, and an elaborate alabaster altar adorns the baroque burial chapel of the Illésházys, added at a later date.

The central axis of the Old Town is formed by the Peace Square, fringed by well-kept private dwellings dating from Renaissance and baroque times. The brightly coloured frescoes in the early-baroque Church of St Francis are charming. The town gate with its octagonal tower provides access to an unusually large 19th-century synagogue, which reminds the visitor that the town's expansion into a cloth centre and fashion capital was a direct result of the efforts of the once flourishing Jewish community.

The thermal baths of **Trenčianske Teplice** ❼ lie barely 15 km (9 miles) further to the north along the Váh in the tributary valley of the Teplica, bordered by wooded hills. The hot springs, high in sulphur and chalk content, provide relief from rheumatism and neurosensory diseases; they were known during Roman times and the Middle Ages as Aqua Teplica but were seldom visited.

It was the enterprising Joseph Illésházy who had a pretty summer residence built here in 1729 and who subsequently attracted high society to the emerging spa town. In 1750 the fashionable **Hotel**

BELOW: the magnificent oriental bath house in Trenčíanské Teplice.

Map on page 286

Kaštiel, a grand hotel built in the style of a Renaissance castle, opened its doors. Under the direction of private individuals, bath houses, pump rooms and elegant restaurants were built beside the 11 springs. The most original contribution was provided by the architect Franz Schmoranz, who designed an **oriental bath house** in Moorish style.

The owner of the spa town, Iphigenie d'Harcourt, discovered the imaginative sketch at the Paris World Exhibition in 1878 and commissioned the architect to build the *hammam* as an intimate bath house with luxurious, individual cabins. Today, the oriental bath house is used as the men's changing rooms for the adjoining Sina spa house.

Nitra

The romantic **Nitra Valley** lies to the east of the Váh Valley and can be reached either by crossing the mountains from Trenčín, or by going back along the Váh and taking the main road from Trnava.

The venerable town of **Nitra** ❽, the oldest town settlement in the Czech and Slovak Republics, lies on a broad bend in the river. It is an attractive setting and must already have been inhabited for several generations when, in 829, the Slavic feudal lord Přibina persuaded Archbishop Adalram of Salzburg to dedicate a court chapel here. From this point onwards, the history of the place is easier to follow: Mojmír I, prince of the empire of Greater Moravia, conquered the town shortly afterwards and extended it considerably.

In 880, after the message of Christianity had been spread across most of the country by the two Slavic apostles Cyril and Methodius, who are still regarded as the patron saints of the Slovaks, the pope elevated Nitra to the rank of the first diocesan town in Slovakia. Under Hungarian rule in the 11th century, the town entered its Golden Age.

The castle served the bishops, who were simultaneously the local feudal lords, as their administrative seat. Even today it is

BELOW: selling vegetables and fruit from a road-side stall.

still the residence of Bishop Ján Chryzostom Korec, who established a reputation for himself within the Slovakian opposition. All the alleys leading uphill from the town open on to the Square of Slovakian Cooperation, dominated since 1750 by a column dedicated to the Virgin Mary and recalling the two cholera epidemics of the previous decades. A stone bridge lined with statues of saints leads to the first gateway and the courtyard, where a restored tower reminds us that this was a medieval stronghold.

The single-nave Gothic cathedral was extended on several occasions; in 1720, following a radical remodelling in the baroque style, it was adorned with original frescoes. A much older early-Romanesque church was discovered in 1930; the master builders of the intervening epochs had walled in this architectural jewel.

The upper classes and senior clergy lived in the Upper Town, in the shadow of the towering castle, while craftsmen and traders formed a community within the Lower Town. Now take the Východná, which leads to a quiet square. The **Great Seminary** appears to hover between the baroque and classical styles; today it houses the local museum with a collection of archaeological exhibits.

The Diocesan Library next door is the famous Nitra Codex dating from the 11th century. Opposite stands the classical-style Canons' House. The builder added an Atlas to one corner, but the citizens soon recognised that the statue fulfilled no structural purpose and christened him Corgoň the Rascal.

Follow the Samova ul. from here and you will arrive at the Franciscan monastery, which today houses the interesting **Slovenské Pol'nohospodarské** (Museum of Agriculture; open Tues–Sun 9am–5pm; entrance fee). The adjoining church contains wood reliefs illustrating the life of the order's founder.

The underpass beside the Studenie Gallery and the Academy of Art was once the only access to the castle. Beyond the

BELOW: eating lunch in Nitra's town square.

Map
on page
286

square, the Saratovská ul. forms the central axis of the Old Town. Only two blocks further on and standing in the centre of the **Mierové náměstie** (Peace Square), St Michael's Chapel recalls the town's two cholera epidemics. The surrounding cafés and the garden terrace of the Hotel Slovan provide a welcome chance to relax. The remainder of the Lower Town can be explored easily during a gentle stroll.

Turning towards the southwest, is a series of 11th-century frescoes in the simple Romanesque **Chapel of St Stephen**. The most notable buildings in the Gudernova ul. are the baroque ensemble formed by the Grammar School and the Piarist church, which possesses a remarkable double tower. To the east, on the former main square of the medieval Lower Town, the architectural tone is set by the Andrej Bagar Theatre and the town hall.

Around Nitra

The slopes of the Tribeč Mountains to the north of the town provide ideal vine-

growing conditions. The vineyards are interspersed with traditional roadside inns and attractive restaurants. The summit of the Zobor Peak (588 metres/1,929 ft) provides a magnificent panorama across the town and the valley.

Half way between Nitra and Bratislava lies the pretty town of **Galanta**, home of the legendary Esterházys. Despite its population of only 15,000, the town has no fewer than four castles. The oldest, in the centre of the built-up area, dates from the Renaissance; another, in neo-Gothic style, houses a museum of local history.

On the return journey, less than 20 km (12 miles) before Bratislava, lies the community of **Senec**, whose two lakes, crystal-clear and undeniably romantic, never fail to enchant visitors.

Travelling along the Danube

This southwest corner of Slovakia bears strong traces of Hungarian influence; in some villages, Hungarian is even the main language. Travellers who want to learn

BELOW:
Vlkolínec, a village built of wood.

Map on page 286

more about the cultural and historical influences of the region may be tempted to make a detour across the border to Hungary, to Esztergom or even to Budapest.

Behind Bratislava, to the right of the trunk road No. 63, are lush and lovely river meadows. Unfortunately, from **Šamorín** onwards they have been ruined by the construction of the reservoir and power station at **Gabčíkovo**, a scheme which has sparked off a row between Slovakia and Hungary. The Hungarians maintain that the completion of the dam and the diversion of the river along a canal will result in enormous damage to the environment, and have demanded that the Danube be made a protected area.

It is advisable to bypass the scene of the controversy by following road No. 63, along which the town of **Dunajská Streda** ❾ offers the first interesting opportunity for a break. The name of this town means Wednesday on the Danube, which alludes to the fact that since the 16th century this regional centre has been

permitted to hold a market every Wednesday. The **Žltý kaštiel**, the baroque Yellow Castle, is a well-stocked museum of local history (open Tues–Sun; entrance fee). This, and the Gothic Church of the Assumption, decorated with medieval frescoes, are both well worth visiting. The recent discovery of hot springs has given new impetus to local hotels and restaurants. The conservation area Zlatná na Ostrove, shortly before Komárno on the Danube, is still the habitat of the great bustard (*otis tarda*), the largest European scavenging bird resident in the steppes.

The history of **Komárno** ❿, which lies at the confluence of the Váh and the Danube, mirrors almost exactly the rise and fall of the royal and imperial monarchy. The home town of Franz Lehár, whose music reflects with such light-hearted élan the many national influences at work in his homeland, has been divided since 1918. The Danube serves as the frontier – just as it did in Roman times when the *limes* ran along its course, and later during the Turkish attacks on the fortress.

Among the many fine churches is the Orthodox Pravoslav Church, which has an exceptional collection of icons and liturgical items.

An idyllic spa town

The highlight of any visit to Southern Slovakia could well be a stay in Patince or **Štúrovo** ⓫, the idyllic spa towns lying downstream along the Danube. The region enjoys the highest average temperature in the whole of Slovakia, and it seldom rains here. Additional attractions lie in the area cradled by the arm of the Danube, in the solid comfort of the hotels and guest houses, and – a peculiarity of Southern Slovakia – in the so-called *Pussten*. These are a particular type of traditional Hungarian restaurant, where violinists play genuine gypsy music to accompany the flambéed specialities and fine wine.

In Štúrovo you can even try out an unusual form of transport – the *kompa* ferry, which takes you across to the other bank of the Danube, to the ancient town of **Esztergom** with its cathedral presided over by the Hungarian bishops. ❑

LEFT: storks are common in Western Slovakia.
RIGHT: a climber makes his ascent.

Map on page 298

CENTRAL SLOVAKIA

The centre of Slovakia is dominated by the mountains of the Lower Tatras as they gradually give way on all sides to gentle river valleys and rolling hills with small mining communities dotted among them

Banská Bystrica ❶ is certainly the most interesting of Central Slovakia's mining towns. The Slavic inhabitants of the sleepy hamlet of Bystrica were seized by gold fever during the 13th century, when gold, silver and copper deposits were discovered outside their very doors. Encouraged by the royal privileges, German miners flocked to the new eldorado from nearby Zvolen (Altsohl). The community soon prospered and was awarded a town charter in 1255.

The Fugger dynasty from Augsburg saw the potential of the mines and stepped in, investing vast sums of capital. At the beginning of the 16th century James II, nicknamed James the Rich, acquired a large proportion of the mines, both in the town and the region, for his family business, thus establishing what was actually a monopoly on European copper production. The Fuggers and their partners made Neusohl their administrative capital, thus enabling the town to earn huge profits not only from the extraction of the ore, but also from processing, related crafts and international trade in precious metals. In those days, however, the profits were anything but fairly distributed. In 1525 the miners came out on strike.

It was from Banská Bystrica, on 29 August 1944, that the message for the Slovakians to start their revolt against the Nazis went out over the radio. Since then, the old market place has been called the **Námestie národného povstania** (SNP, Square of the Slovakian Uprising). This has always been the focal point of the busy little town. Despite some rebuilding in the Renaissance style, most of the houses surrounding the square have retained many original Gothic elements.

The **Thurzo House** in the southeast corner of the long, narrow square is the most magnificent of all, for it served as the official headquarters of the mining company. Today it houses the **Múzeum mestskej histórie a folklóru** (Museum of Municipal History and Folklore; open Mon–Fri and Sun; entrance fee). **Benického dom** (Benický House; museum open Mon–Fri and Sun; entrance fee) diagonally opposite is notable for its elaborately decorated facade with a loggia supported by elegant Tuscan columns.

The **Orloj** (clock tower) points the way to the **Pevnost'** (fortress), a collection of buildings which gradually evolved into a single complex. The residence of the governor, appointed by the king to oversee the mining operations, also served as a storehouse. The building later became known as the Matthias House, for the Hungarian king Matthias Corvinus stayed

PRECEDING PAGES: winter in the Lower Tatras.
LEFT: a blacksmith at work.
RIGHT: the Square of the Slovakian Uprising in Banská Bystrica.

here on a number of occasions. The Gothic gateway tower and the **Banícky kostol** (Miners' Church) completed the castle complex; the barbican building was constructed at the start of the 16th century.

Other mining towns

In **Zvolen** ❷, too, you will find many buildings recalling its own Golden Age. The settlement received a town charter in 1244 and grew prosperous through the mining of its silver deposits. It is not the town itself which is of particular interest, however, but the magnificent **Hrad** (castle; open Tues–Sun 10am–5pm). It was

built in 1382 by King Ľudovít the Great, who planned to use it as a base for his hunting expeditions. King Matthias Corvinus also fell in love with the beautiful setting and made the hunting lodge his favourite residence. During the 16th century the Thurzos replaced the elegant lightness of the original building with massive defensive features; the Esterházys finally turned it into an imposing palace. The castle now serves as a museum exhibiting a remarkably valuable collection of medieval Slovakian art. In the town itself, little remains of the workshops that once made this an important centre of

Central Slovakia

Map on page 298

woodcarving. However, traditional crafts are kept alive by the Medzinárodný folklórny festival (International Folklore Festival) which takes place every summer, usually in July.

Banská Štiavnica ❸ (Schemnitz) about 25 km (16 miles) from Zvolen, traces its origins back to a mining village established in about AD 1000. During the 12th century, German miners added a number of pit shafts to the open-cast seams. The village subsequently expanded into a national mining centre. In 1244, Banská Štiavnica received its charter as a free royal city. Here, too, the Fuggers ensured that they retained the lion's share of the mining and, during the 15th and 16th century, the town became the most important supplier of silver in Hungary. Explosives were first used in Banská Štiavnica mines in 1627; the introduction of mechanical pumps was also an invention of local mining engineers, who from 1735 were trained in a university college.

The most interesting buildings in the town are the former houses of the wealthy mine owners; their Renaissance-style architecture, built upon Romanesque or early-Gothic foundations, reflects the prosperity that Banská Štiavnica achieved. Most of them are situated around the central Trojičné námesti (Trinity Square), dominated by a baroque column. The Miners' Court used to meet in house No. 47; its verdicts were based on the Schemnitz Mining Law, which was codified in 1217. Today the building houses an informative **Banícke múzeum** (Museum of Mines; open daily; entrance fee), where the industry of the Middle Ages is documented with tools, rock samples, models and a shaft leading some 70 metres (230 ft) underground.

Nearby stand the Renaissance building occupied by the former Chamber of Mines, the notable Parish Church of St Nicholas and the Old Town Hall.

Above the Old Town rises the **Hrad** (castle; open May–Sept daily, Oct–Apr Mon–Fri; entrance fee). During the 13th century a Romanesque church occupied the site, but with increasing prosperity in the 16th century the citizens converted the

strategically located place of worship in a fortress with thick walls and five tower The nave became a castle courtyard.

Historically speaking, **Kremnica** (Kremnitz) is one of the most importa towns in Slovakia. Mentioned in recor as a Slavic settlement in the 12th centur the town owes its rapid expansion and el vation to the status of a free royal city 1328 to the extensive gold and silv deposits in the nearby Kremnica Mou tains. Precious metals are still extracte from its pits today. From 1335, followir the award of special privileges by the kir of Hungary, Charles Robert, the town w permitted to mint its own gold ducats – tradition maintained by the mint in th Horná ul. until recent times.

Such was the town's prosperity that repeatedly attracted the attention of env ous conquerors; even the Hussites plu dered it during 1434. Nonetheless, th town has been able to maintain its trad tional appearance. The spacious Námest 1 mája (Square of 1 May) is bordered b

several dozen fine houses, mostly built during the 14th century and extended in contemporary style during the Renaissance. The **Mestské múzeum** (Municipal Museum; open Tues–Sun; entrance fee) at No. 7 provides the visitor with an insight into the history of the town. The square, built on a slight slope, is bordered by the **Zámok** (castle; open May–Sept Tues–Sun; entrance fee), which from the 13th century served both as administrative headquarters and as a repository for precious metals. The embankments and bastions surround a Gothic church and the forbidding castle keep.

Other castles of the region

Apart from its picturesque towns, this region has a large number of fortresses and palaces. Totalling no fewer than 70, some of them are in good condition whilst the others survive only as ruins. **Bojnický Zámok** (open May–Sept Tues–Sun 9am– 5pm, Oct–Apr 10am–3pm; entrance fee), west of the town of **Prievidza** ❺ (Priwitz),

is generally considered the finest in the whole of Central Europe. Historians claim that it was founded about AD 1000, during the reign of King Stephen of Hungary. The castle changed hands frequently over the years. The Lords of Pálffy assembled a unique collection of paintings here. Directly below the castle walls there is a popular thermal bath; the grounds contain the largest zoological gardens in Slovakia.

South of Martin, **Blatnický Hrad** (open Tues–Sun 10am–5pm; entrance fee) dominates the lovely Gaderská dolina valley. Hidden away in a large stretch of continuous woodland, the castle is first mentioned in records dating from the 13th century. Access is gained by a footpath; no cars are permitted.

The course of the Váh is rich in castles. **Budatínsky zámok** (Budatín Castle; open Tues–Sun 8am–4pm; entrance fee) lies at the confluence of the Kysuca and the Váh, just to the north of the town of **Žilina** ❻ (Sillein). Having grown up at the intersection of important medieval trade routes,

BELOW:
Oravský castle
stands sentinel
above the
Orava River.

Map on page 298

the town remains the busiest traffic junction in all Slovakia. Of particular interest is the little church of St Stephen, one of the oldest Romanesque churches in Slovakia, whose interior is adorned with a number of striking frescoes. Žilina makes a good base for exploring the attractive region of **Orava**, in the northernmost corner of Slovakia. A well-developed tourist infrastructure has arisen around the Oravská nádrž (Orava reservoir).

The romantic **Oravský hrad** (Orava Castle; open May–Oct Tues–Sun; entrance fee), boldly perched on a limestone crag above the river, was built to guard the trading route to Poland and was fortified on a number of occasions. It now houses a museum of local history. The entire region is famous for its traditional folk music and extravagant traditional costumes. Traditional crafts such as embroidery, ceramics and pottery, as well as the painting of furniture, also retain their place in modern society.

To the south of Žilina, **Čičmany** ❼ is famous for its richly embroidered costumes and its wooden houses decorated with colourful motifs.

Into the mountains

To the east of Žilina you can follow the course of the the romantic Vrátna Valley through Terchová and on to Vrátna, from where a cable car trundles up to the main ridge of the **Malá Fatra** (Lesser Fatra), beneath the highest peak of the range, Kriváň (1,709 metres/5,606 ft). The **Nízke Tatry** (Lower Tatras) are popular with walkers and skiers. In the western section, the long succession of peaks makes it possible to hike along the crest, where there are breathtaking views. One of the most rewarding hikes is from Šturec or Krížna in the **Veľká Fatra** (Greater Fatra) to Chabenec and on to the **Chopok**, the main ridge of the Lower Tatras.

In **Liptovský Mikuláš** ❽, the Slovenské krasové múzeum (Museum of Slovakian Karst; open Tues–Sun; entrance fee) provides a taste of the wonders of nature to be experienced in the **Demänovské jaskyne** (Demänovské caves; open mid-May–mid–Sept; closed Mon; entrance fee), 11 km (7 miles) to the south. Their cham-

bers and galleries are ornamented with stalactites and stalagmites and are linked by a series of underground lakes, streams and waterfalls. On the southern flank of the Chopok ridge, the village of **Tále** ❾ is a good base for less experienced walkers. The gentle ski slopes in the foothills of the **Bystrá dolina** valley are ideal for novices. The village also has an open-air swimming pool, restaurants, hotels, a motel and a campsite.

At 2,043 metres (6,703ft), **Mount Ďumbier** is the highest peak in the Lower Tatras. The ascent from **Čertovica** is equally rewarding in summer or winter: there is a magnificent view across the mountains of Slovakia from the Polish to the Hungarian frontier, from the Beskids to Branisko. The eastern section of the Lower Tatras, between Čertovica and the **Sedlo Popová** (Popová Ridge), is an unspoilt wilderness. The main crest is covered by continuous forest. The only reminder of civilisation is a transmitter on the summit of the **Kráľova hoľa**. ❑

RIGHT: many rare flowers in Slovakia are protected.

EASTERN SLOVAKIA

*No other region of the former Czechoslovakia offers visitors a
more varied and colourful combination of natural beauty
and historic sights than Eastern Slovakia*

Map below

Although the inhabitants of Spiš,
Šariš, Zemplín, Gemer and Košice
all feel themselves to be Eastern
Slovaks, there are clear differences in both
dialect and folklore. The variations are
most clearly reflected in the architecture
of the towns and villages.

Košice ❶ (Kaschau), situated in the
foothills of the Slovenské Rudohorie (Slovakian Ore Mountains), is the principal city
in Eastern Slovakia and the second largest
city in Slovakia. Founded by Saxon settlers, the community was awarded special
privileges by the King of Hungary in 1244.
In 1342 it was proclaimed a free royal city
and from 1369 it was the first city in Central Europe to be allowed to bear its own
coat of arms. The town became wealthy as
a result of its international trade with Hungary and Poland; the university, founded
in 1657, turned it into a cultural metropolis.
The Golden Age lasted only until the 18th
century, when internal strife, the Turkish
Wars and finally the split from Hungary
marked the beginning of a period of economic decline. The historic town centre,
which has been magnificently restored, is a
national monument. **Katedrála sv. Alžbety**
(St Elizabeth's Cathedral) rises above the
central Námestie Slobody (Freedom
Square); it is considered to be one of the
most beautiful Gothic churches in the
country. The north door, the *porta aurea,*
dating from 1460, frames a statue of the
patron saint; the magnificently carved
high altar, completed a few years later,

**PRECEDING
PAGES:**
carpenter and
traditional
wooden statue.

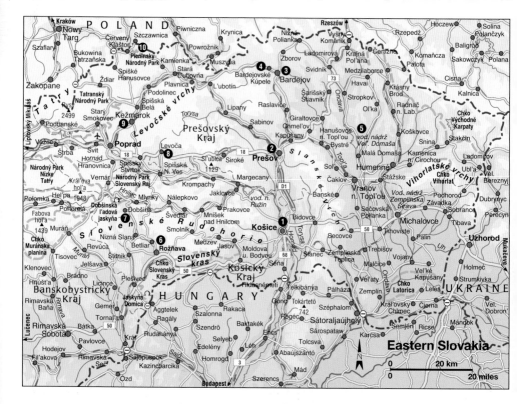

Eastern Slovakia

0   20 km
0   20 miles

describes 12 scenes from the life of Saint Elizabeth. The free-standing Zvonica (belfry), Urbanova veža, and the cemetery chapel, dedicated to St Michael, complete the architectural ensemble of the square. For modern citizens of Slovakia, Košice is the town of the Slovakian "magna carta", and the home of the Košice government protocol, which was proclaimed in the Committee House here on 4 April 1945, and which provided the basis of Czechoslovakia's postwar constitution.

The communist leadership decided to turn Eastern Slovakia into an industrial region. A vast iron and steel works was constructed near Košice, although there were lamentably inadequate supplies of water and iron ore. It proved to be the most blatant and, ecologically speaking, the most catastrophic false investment in the history of Czechoslovakia. The only positive step taken by the former regime was to set up the Technical University of Košice which produced a large number of well qualified steel and mining engineers.

In the northeastern corner of the region lie Prešov (Preschau) and Bardejov (Bartfeld), attractive towns which in medieval times enjoyed privileges as free royal cities, forming the Pentapolis League with Košice, Levoča and Sabinov. Fine Gothic and Renaissance houses with ornately decorated gables grace the town square of **Prešov ❷**, now an important centre of Slovakian and Ukranian culture, possessing both a Slovakian and a Ukranian theatre. The most attractive building is the **Rákoczyho palác** (open daily and Sat 9am–1pm; entrance fee), once the residence of Prince Rakoczy, which houses a museum of local history.

In **Bardejov ❸** near the Polish border, the medieval city centre, dating from the town's founding year (1219), has survived to this day. Almost all the fortifications, constructed during the 15th century, can also still be seen. The houses surrounding the central square reflect the town's heyday in Gothic and Renaissance times. The **radnice** (town hall) dates from 1509;

today it serves as municipal archives and museum. The Gothic **Kostol sv. Agídia** (Church of St Aegidius) has eleven magnificent altars as well as numerous paintings and statues. The neighbouring spa town of **Bardejovské Kúpele**  has operated as a spa since the 13th century. Its waters are famous for their efficacy in treating stomach disorders and illnesses of the digestive tract. It is the most important spa town in Slovakia after Piešt'any.

Wooden churches

The remote mountain villages of Eastern Slovakia are known for their traditional **Drevené kostoly** (wooden churches). Most of them were built during the 18th century and reveal an imaginative mixture of baroque and archaic elements. They frequently stand on some sort of eminence, their towers rising above the rooftops of the village. Their interiors bear witness to a Byzantine influence; many contain an iconostasis. The portraits of saints on the folding triptychs are mostly the work of anonymous local artists and craftsmen and depict religious subjects created in classical styles. The minor figures, however, are modelled on simple people, displaying the common features and ordinary clothing of the times. Also worthy of note are the decorative wall and ceiling paintings, the altars, pews and missals. There are 24 such churches in Eastern Slovakia and they are all national monuments.

In a hilly region further to the south, on the **Rieka Ondava** (River Ondava), lies the **vodná nádrž Vel' Domaša** ❺ (Domaša Dam) – a good tip for a longer stay. The reservoir is popular among anglers and offers water sports facilities of all kinds. Among the natural sights of the region are the Morské oko mountain lake in the **Vihorlatské vrchy** (Vihorlat Mountains) and the lovely **vodná nádrž Zemplínska Šírava** (Zemplínska Šírava Lake), also known as the East Slovakian Lake. Its location on the southern slopes of the Vihorlat ensures favourable climatic conditions. The bathing season lasts for

BELOW: house facade in the cloth town of Bardéjov.

Map on page 304

almost five months of the year, and there is an annual average of nearly 2,200 hours of sunshine. The passenger boats crossing the lake will take you on outings to the villages lining the shores and the town's restaurants have an excellent reputation for regional specialities.

A caver's paradise

The scenery of the **Slovenský kras** mountains, surrounding the mining town of **Rožňava ⑥** in the south of the region, is characterised by caves, gorges and karst landscape. The vaulted roof of the **Jaskyňa Domica** (Domica Cave; tours Tues–Sun; entrance fee) is covered with bizarre, coloured stalactites.

Equally impressive are the columns of ice in the **Dobšinská ľadová jaskyňa** (Dobšinská Ice Cave; tours mid-May–mid-Sept Tues–Sun; July-Aug daily; entrance fee), north of the town of **Dobšiná ⑦**. It lies adjacent to the **Slovenský raj**, the so-called Slovakian Paradise, an area of natural beauty marked by canyons, gorges

and waterfalls. Particularly spectacular is the **Kysel' Canyon**, which over a length of 5 km (3 miles) drops a distance of more than 350 metres (1,200 ft).

The most impressive of all, however, is the **Vel'ký Sokol**, also 5 km (3 miles) long and with walls rising up to 300 metres (1,000 ft) above the river, which in one place is only a metre (3 ft) across. On the edge of the Slovenský raj, the River Hornád forces its way through a 11-km (7-mile) gorge, traversable by boat.

Further to the west, the town of Švermovo provides a convenient base for hikes into the eastern end of the Lower Tatra range, specifically the ascent of the 1,948-metre (6,391-ft) high Kráľova hoľa.

Northeastern Slovakia

Culturally speaking, northeastern Slovakia is a largely independent region. Known to the Slavs as **Spiš**, it was christened Zips by the German migrants who settled in the area from the 11th century onwards. In 1271, 24 towns within the

BELOW: wooden church in Eastern Slovakia.

Map
on page
304

region joined forces to form a league of free cities, choosing the royal town of Levoča (Leutschau) as their capital. Five years later they were emulated by the Seven Mountain Towns of the Zips surrounding the free royal city of Göllnitz.

They prospered on their mining, trade and crafts, but the towns' history was a turbulent one. In 1412, the Emperor Sigismund pawned 13 of them to Poland for a few thousand silver pence, then refused to buy them back. The remaining towns came under pressure from the Hungarian nobility, and the Catholic Church tried to force their inhabitants to convert to the one true faith. In 1769 the Habsburgs conquered the entire region, annexing it for their empire. It was not until 1876, however, that the Hungarians finally put an end to all autonomy.

The magnificent Gothic and Renaissance churches of the region bear witness to this history, as do the elegant belfries, fine town halls, sprawling farms and mighty castles. Many of these monuments

have been turned into museums, but a considerable number of the churches were converted or even demolished by the communist regime. Nonetheless, the centres of the cities of the Spiš have maintained their medieval appearance. Four of them have been declared national monuments: Levoča, Kežmarok, Poprad, Spišská Sobota and Spišská Kapitula.

Levoča ❽ contains a unique work of art by the local master craftsman Pavol: a **Gotický drevený altár** (Gothic wooden altar, no less than 18 metres (59 ft) high. It stands in the 14th-century **Kostol sv. Jakuba** (Parish Church of St James; tours: summer every 30 minutes, winter every hour), the second-largest Gothic church in Slovakia, which is situated on the Mierové námesti (Peace Square), a spacious square bordered by splendid patrician houses. The lovely Renaissance **radnica** (town hall; open Tues–Thurs) was completed in 1559 and is adorned with a massive belfry and a series of fine frescoes, depicting bourgeois morality.

Kežmarok ❾ (Käsmark) is notable for its Romanesque-Gothic parish church of the Holy Cross, its Protestant wooden church and a fortress which was later converted into a palace. In the **Kostol sv. Agídia** (Church of St Aegidius) in **Poprad**, a series of 15th-century frescoes, in particular an enchanting panorama of the High Tatras, the mountains dominating the town, has been carefully preserved. In the **Spišská Sobota** district there are historic townhouses and a Gothic parish church. Exceptionally fine examples of popular architecture are found in the remote villages of the Levoča Mountains and the valley of the River Poprad.

The northern Spiš region includes the magnificent **Pieninský Národný Park** ❿, where the **Rieka Dunajec** carves its way through the Pieniny Mountains. One of the most exciting ways of exploring the river is to take a wild water trip on a *plte* (raft) in the company of a rafter from the Górale, a people living on both sides of the national frontier between Slovakia and neighbouring Poland. Raft trips, available from May to August, start from Červený Kláštor and end near Lesnica. ❏

LEFT: peppers thrive in the warm climate of Eastern Slovakia. **RIGHT:** raft trips along the Dunajec River.

Map on page 314

THE HIGH TATRAS

The High Tatras are popular with hikers and walkers. The mountain range contains such natural wonders as huge lakes, waterfalls and an abundance of wildlife

The most popular tourist region in Slovakia is a nature reserve: the **Tatranský Národný Park ❶** (Tatra National Park or TANAP). By following paths visitors can observe and experience a natural wilderness without damaging it. Almost all the mountain peaks in the park are accessible, and from almost any point in the park it is possible to enjoy unforgettable views of the main mountain ridge.

Extending about 64 km (40 miles) along the Slovakian–Polish frontier, the High Tatras (Vysoké Tatry) are the highest mountain range in the Central Carpathians. Although the range is much lower than the Alps and therefore lacks the permanent snowfields and glaciers, it nevertheless possesses an alpine character. The mountain slopes are covered with pine woodlands up to an elevation of 2,500 metres (8,200 ft), above which the alpine zone begins.

The High Tatras support a rich variety of fauna, including bears, chamois, marmots and eagles. Around 300 peaks are identified by name and elevation. Until an earthquake blew off its top in the 16th century, the highest peak in the range was the Slavkovský štít, with an elevation of more than 2,700 metres (8,850 ft). Evidence of the catastrophe can be seen in the massive outcrops of rock which were hurled down into the Vel'ká Studená dolina Valley. The highest mountain in the Tatras now is the Gerlachovský štít 2,655 metres (8,711 ft).

The highest peaks were originally over 3,000 metres (9,843 ft); during the Ice Age glaciers up to 200 metres (660 ft) thick wore away the summits and rent deep clefts in the mountain mass, thus forming the impressive hanging valleys, lakes and rock walls which characterise the Tatras today. Glacial remains can still be found on the north faces of the mountains, in the places where the sun never

penetrates. In some places there are large patches of snow which do not melt, even on the warmest summer days of the year.

Natural wonders

The 35 mountain lakes in the Slovakian Tatras have been left behind by the retreating glaciers. They are commonly referred to as "sea eyes", because the ancients believed that their deep, crystal-clear waters were directly linked with the sea. Some fill the hollows left in the rock by the ice sheets; others are contained by rock dams formed by the deposition of rocks and stones. The largest of the mountain lakes, the **Vel'ké Hincovo pleso**, has a surface area of almost 20 hectares (50 acres) and is over 50 metres (160 ft deep). The jewels

PRECEDING PAGES: the Gerlachovský štít is the highest summit in the High Tatras.
LEFT: climbers in the High Tatras.
RIGHT: an autumn hike up Mount Rysy.

in the crown of this mountain range are the picturesque waterfalls. The spectacular Kmet'ov Falls in the Nefcerka Valley thunder 80 metres (262 ft) into the depths below. The vast Studenovodské vodopády and the Skok Falls in the Mlynická dolina Valley, as well as the Obrovský Falls in the Studenovodská dolina Valley, are a magnificent natural spectacle.

An ideal climate

The Tatra Mountains have much more to offer than just scenic beauty; the towns and villages and the bracing mountain climate are equally inviting. The massif towers above the surrounding mountains, forming a watershed and creating a microclimate unique in Central Europe. The setting was ideal for the establishment of sanatoria for the treatment of tuberculosis, asthma, respiratory complaints and nervous diseases, all of which respond well to the oxygen-rich air. A stay in the Tatras is beneficial even during the cold, wet season, for the intensity of the healing

ultraviolet rays is largely dependent upon the purity of the air. Even during the main tourist season, when there tends to be a lot of haze in the Alps, the skies in the High Tatras are generally clear. There is a partial ban on the use of private cars in operation, which means that the range is largely spared pollution from exhaust fumes, smoke and water vapour. Above the tree line, after the fog or rain has cleared, there is virtually no trace of water evaporation. The number of hours of sunshine here is as high as on the sunny plains of southern Slovakia, and amounts to between 1,800 and 2,000 hours a year.

Characteristic of the region are sudden climatic changes. While the valleys are buried under a thick layer of cloud, the upper slopes of the High Tatras often enjoy brilliant sunshine. The cold air, which is relatively heavy, sinks into the valleys and the warm air, which is less dense, moves up to the higher altitudes. Among the climatic characteristics of the Tatra region are a number of unusual

LEFT: meteorological station at Lomnický štít.

Map on page 314

phenomena: a mirage effect caused by the mountains, flashes of lightning from an otherwise clear sky and *föhn* winds of up to 150 kph (94 mph). Even sand from the Sahara desert, brought by the high-altitude trade wind, is deposited on the snow-covered peaks of the High Tatras. Another attraction is the ever-changing play of light at dawn and during the evening.

Trekking and hiking

Autumn is probably the best time of year for hiking in the High Tatras. Although the days are shorter, the skies are at their most brilliant blue, and the forested slopes are a riot of colour. The highlight of exploring the High Tatras is to climb through the wild valleys, past mountain lakes and across strangely formed rock terraces. The 350 km (220 miles) of clearly marked footpaths provide even inexperienced walkers with access to the mountains. But the main ridge of the High Tatras is only accessible to experienced climbers; it extends for over 26 km (16 miles) from

Ľaliové sedlo to Kopské. The northern slopes are steep and cold, and present a tremendous challenge to mountaineers.

Even in winter, the High Tatras and the neighbouring White Tatra (Belanské Tatry) to the east are attractive destinations, for they offer ideal conditions for cross-country and downhill skiing. The guesthouses, however, are often fully booked during the winter sports season, so prior reservations (or plenty of patience) are necessary.

The Tatra Mountains can be easily reached from other parts of the country and offer a sensitively developed tourist infrastructure, with accommodation ranging from top-class hotels to mountain huts with basic facilities. A hundred years ago no direct roads led to this remote mountain district.

Today it can be reached via the scenic route Cesta Slobody (Freedom Trail), which links the main tourist centres – Štrbské Pleso, Starý Smokovec and Tatranská Lomnica. Buses and an electrified railway line provide additional means of transport.

BELOW: Mount Kriváň, one of the most spectacular peaks in the range.

Starting points

Tatranská Lomnica ❷ is an ideal base for a visit to the region, since many walking tours actually begin here. Visitors who prefer not to exert themselves unduly can take one of the two cable cars to the Skalnaté pleso, which lies at an altitude of 1,750 metres (5,741 ft).

The **Hotel Encián** and the observatory invite one to stay longer; additional cable cars provide a link with the highest peaks of the range. The village itself houses the **Múzeum Tatranského národného parku** (TANAP Museum; open Mon–Fri, weekend 8am–noon; entrance fee), where – apart from various exhibits on the region's folklore – visitors can admire the large collection of flora from the Spišská Magura.

From Tatranská Lomnica one can continue to **Tatranská Kotlina** and visit the impressive **Belanská jaskyňa** (Belanská Caves; hourly tours June–mid-Sept Tues–Sun, 9am–4pm; entrance fee). Nearby **Ždiar** ❸ is a typical Slovakian hill community extending 7 km (4 miles) along the slopes of the Spišská Magura. On Sunday and during folk festivals the locals wear their traditional costumes.

Štrbské Pleso ❹, the highest village in Slovakia, also makes a good base. It is the start of a number of interesting routes, including the popular climb to the top of Mount Rysy, whose summit provides a magnificent view of the entire Tatra range. Another much-visited destination is Mount Kriváň (2,494 metres/8182 ft), further west, the site of many national pilgrimages.

Routes through the mountains

Every visitor to the Tatras makes for the **Cesta Slobody**, the Freedom Trail, undoubtedly the loveliest mountain road in Slovakia. For more than 70 km (44 miles) it runs parallel to the mountains from Podbanské in the west, through Tatranská Lomnica to Podspády and Tatranská Javorina, from where it continues across the border into the Polish Zakopane. Less convenient, but every bit as attractive, is a journey by train from Poprad to Tatran-

BELOW: view of the mountain range in summer.

Map on page 314

ská Lomnica and on to Štrbské Pleso. The carriages chug slowly through the craggy mountain landscape and seem to stop beside virtually every barn.

The main footpath through the mountains, the so-called **Magistrale**, provides the best way of getting to know the region. The route is marked in red, is well maintained along its entire length, and traverses the area between Podbanské in the west and Tatranská Kotlina at an average height of 1,300–2,000 metres (4,260– 6,600 ft).

The first section passes along the shores of the Jamské pleso Lake to Štrbské Pleso, continuing to Popradské pleso and up the famous zig-zags to the summit of **Ostrava**, on over Mount Tupá, beneath Končistá and Gerlachovský štít to **Sliezsky dom**.

From here the marked route runs along the slopes of **Slavkovský štít** (Mount Slavkovský) and past the Sesterské pleso lakes to the **Hrebienok**. Skirting the mouth of the **Studenovodská jaskyňa** (Studenovodská cave), the path continues

past the waterfalls and uphill to Lake Skalnaté pleso, as far as the cable car leading up **Lomnický štít,** which at 2,632 metres (8,638 ft) is the second highest mountain in the range.

Then it is on to Veľká Svišť'ovka and down into the **Zelené pleso** (Zelené Valley). Near the Bielé pleso, the path starts to climb once more to the **Kopské sedlo**. Another path then traverses the ridge of the Belanské Tatry and leads the hiker down to Tatranská Kotlina.

Mountain climbs

Hiking along the Magistrale is an unforgettable experience, even for less practised walkers – especially when one combines the main walk with short detours to the nearby summits and valleys. But when attempting to climb a mountain it is imperative that the time it takes (shown on the signposts) is taken into account. The Tatras are not only a region of great beauty, they can also be a region of great danger. Many visitors overesti-

BELOW: photographing the peak of Lomnický štít.

Map on page 314

mate their strength, abilities and knowledge of the area and pay for their foolishness with an accident, frostbite or even death. Not only individuals but also organised groups are at risk. Before undertaking an ambitious touring programme, it is essential to check with the mountain rescue association, which has a branch office in all the larger villages. The following are some of the most popular routes from west to east.

From **Podbanské**, Tri studničky or the **Furkotská chata** mountain hut hike up to **Kmet'ov** and the **Vajanského vodopád** waterfalls in the shadow of **Kriváň** (Mount Kriváň). Two further routes of interest in this area lead over the Kôprovské sedlo mountain crest to lakes **Hincovo pleso** and **Popradské pleso**, and the **Furkotská dolina** (Furkotská Valley) with the Wahlenbergové plesá lakes.

From **Štrbské pleso** in the Furkotská Valley climb up Mount Kriváň and descend into the **Mlynická dolina** valley (ski area established in 1970), passing the Skok

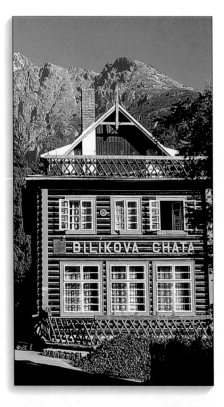

Waterfall, the **Vyšné Kozie** and **Capie pleso** mountain lakes. From there a route continues up the **Mengusovská dolina** valley, and past the **Popradské pleso** mountain lake, which is the starting point for the ascent to the summit of **Mount Rysy**, beneath which is situated the highest mountain hut in Slovakia. The mountain trail to **Vyšné Hágy** over Mount Ostrva is also pleasant.

From Vyšné Hágy walk to the **Batizovské pleso** lake, then continue west past the Popradské pleso to Štrbské pleso, or east to Sliezsky dom and from there to **Tatranská Polianka**. From Tatranská Polianka hike to Sliezsky dom and then continue from the **Velické pleso** mountain lake up to the **Poľský hrebeň** (Polish Saddle), before descending through the **Svišťová** and **Bielovodská dolina** valleys to **Tatranská Javorina**.

From Sliezsky dom you can also hike to the top of the Hrebienok. Another attractive route is from the Batizovské pleso mountain lake to Vyšné Hágy. Experienced walkers with a guide might also consider some of the routes up **Gerlachovský štít** or the **Východná Vysoká** from Sliezsky dom.

From **Starý Smokovec** take the cable car up the Hrebienok, and from there follow a not too arduous but long climb up the **Slavkovský štít**. An alternative is to follow the **Velíká Studená dolina** valley to the **Zbojnická chata** hut and then continue via Prielom and Poľský hrebeň to the Sliezsky dom. Another beautiful route leads to the **Studenovodské vodopády** waterfalls and to the **Téryho chata** mountain refuge.

Set off from **Tatranská Lomnica** to the Studenovodské vodopády waterfalls and up the Hrebienok, the **Skalnaté pleso** mountain lake and on to the **Hotel Encián**. From there, climb up to the **Vodopády Hrebienok** (Hrebienok Waterfalls) or down into the valley of the **Biele pleso** (White Lake) and the **Zelené pleso** (Green Lake) and return to Tatranská Lomnica. Experienced walkers will enjoy the route from Bielé pleso to Tatranská Kotlina but novices should not attempt it even in good weather conditions. ❑

LEFT: Tatranská Lomnica at the foot of Lomnický štít. **RIGHT:** a frosty ironwork gate.

INSIGHT GUIDES
TRAVEL TIPS

New Insight Maps

Maps in Insight Guides are tailored to complement the text. But when you're on the road you sometimes need the big picture that only a large-scale map can provide. This new range of durable Insight Fleximaps has been designed to meet just that need.

Detailed, clear cartography
makes the comprehensive route and city maps easy to follow, highlights all the major tourist sites and provides valuable motoring information plus a full index.

Informative and easy to use
with additional text and photographs covering a destination's top 10 essential sites, plus useful addresses, facts about the destination and handy tips on getting around.

Laminated finish
allows you to mark your route on the map using a non-permanent marker pen, and wipe it off. It makes the maps more durable and easier to fold than traditional maps.

The first titles
cover many popular destinations. They include Algarve, Amsterdam, Bangkok, California, Cyprus, Dominican Republic, Florence, Hong Kong, Ireland, London, Mallorca, Paris, Prague, Rome, San Francisco, Sydney, Thailand, Tuscany, USA Southwest, Venice, and Vienna.

INSIGHT GUIDES
The world's largest collection of visual travel guides

CONTENTS

Getting Acquainted

The Place

Area: the Czech Republic has an area of 78,886 sq km (30,500 sq miles); Slovakia an area of 49,035 sq km (18,933 sq miles).

Situation: The republics form part of Central Europe and are situated at a latitude between 48°–51° north and at a longitude between 12°–22° east. The Czech Republic shares its borders with Germany, Austria and Poland; Slovakia has Austria, Hungary, Poland and the Ukraine as neighbours.

Capital cities: Prague is the Czech Republic's capital; Bratislava is the capital of Slovakia. Brno is the capital of Moravia, which is part of the Czech Republic.

Time zone: one hour ahead of GMT and six hours ahead of EST. Clocks go forward in May and back in September.

Currency: The unit of currency is the crown (koruna česká or Kč in the Czech Republic; Slovenská koruna or Sk in Slovakia).

Weights and measures: the metric system is used.

Electricity: The electricity supply in both republics is mainly AC 220 volts, although very occasionally there are outlets supplied with just 120 volts.

International Dialling Code: Czech Republic: 420 Slovak Republic: 421

The Capital Cities

The Czech Republic: Prague

The Bohemian metropolis is situated on the River Vltava (Moldau), spread out between seven hills. It lies between 176–397 metres (577–1,302ft) above sea level, at 50° north and 14° east; about the same latitude as Frankfurt, Land's End and Vancouver. The city has a population of 1,210,000 (1999) spread over a total area of 497 sq km (190 sq miles). The historical part is made up of the Old Town (Staré Město), the New Town (Nové Město) and the Lesser Quarter (Malá Strana), and claims over 500 towers and steeples. Prague is divided into 56 districts, which are administered from town halls.

The Slovak Republic: Bratislava

The capital of Slovakia lies on the Danube, where the river has cut a broad path through the southern tip of the Little Carpathian Mountains. The Hungarian border is only 20 km (13 miles) to the southeast, and Vienna 56 km (35 miles) to the west. Of particular interest to the visitor is the Old Town, containing a large number of remarkably beautiful buildings dating from a variety of periods. They reflect the city's fortunes through 11 centuries of direct or indirect Hungarian rule. The castle stands some 80 metres (250ft) above the river and dominates the Old Town from its position at the other side of the Vienna motorway. Bratislava is much smaller than Prague, with a population of just over 400,000, but is nonetheless a major road and rail junction as well as river port. This importance is likely to grow as the city establishes itself in its new role as capital of an independent Slovakia.

Climate

Warm summers punctuated by occasional periods of rainfall and long, dry winters are typical of the moderate continental climate found in both the Czech and Slovak Republics. Considerable climatic variations are due primarily to differences in elevations. For example, whereas the annual precipitation in Prague measures 476 mm (19 inches), in the High Tatras the average amounts to 1,665 mm (66 inches) per year. The best times to visit Prague are the spring and autumn. May, when the gardens and parks are in full bloom, heralds the classical music festival "Prague Spring", while the mild autumn with its stable weather offers the best prospects for extended strolls around town.

Population

Over 10 million people live in the Czech Republic and around five million in Slovakia. There is a sizeable gypsy minority living in both the Czech and Slovak Republics. The largest minority in Slovakia are the Hungarians living in the south and making up nearly 11 percent of the population. There are also Polish and Ukrainian minority groups.

Government & Economy

The Czechs and Slovaks have resolved almost all of their outstanding differences arising out of the peaceful break-up of Czechoslovakia in 1993. Both countries are now looking forward to becoming the first former communist countries to join the European Union (EU) and policy making in all the most important areas is geared towards that aim. The Czech Republic still has a higher standard of living than Slovakia and its young democratic system has looked more stable for most of the time since the two went their separate ways.

Nevertheless, the promise of EU membership has kept some of Slovakia's more wayward politicians at bay in recent years and it is earnestly pushing through political and economic reform. The legacy of communism remains however. Unemployment in areas dominated by the old communist factories is high in both countries. Pensioners living on meagre state handouts face hardship. The health and education systems are poorly funded although the quality of the staff is generally high.

Religion

After World War II, religion – as was its fate in other communist countries – was stripped of all official significance. Religious services were only permitted within certain limitations. In the wake of 1989, however, chapels and churches throughout the two republics are in the process of being restored and revived. Of the 18 different religious denominations represented in the country, Roman Catholicism has the most adherents, especially in Slovakia. After the revolution there was an upsurge in the growth of sects, which attracted young people in particular, but the most conspicuous fact about religion in both the Czech and Slovak Republics is that it is becoming a less and less important part of daily life.

Public Holidays

Czech Republic
- **January** New Year's Day (1)
- **March/April** Easter Monday
- **May** May Day (1), Liberation Day (8)
- **July** Feast Day of SS Cyril and Methodius (5), Anniversary of the death of Jan Hus (6)
- **October** Independence Day (28)
- **November** (17)
- **December** Christmas (24–26),

Slovakia
- **January** New Year's Day (1), Epiphany (6)
- **March/April** Good Friday, Easter Monday
- **May** May Day (1)
- **July** Day of the Slav Missionaries (5)
- **August** National Day (29)
- **September** Constitution Day (1), Patron Saint's Day (15)
- **November** All Souls' Day (1),
- **December** Christmas (24–26)

Various Christian holidays, for example the Feast of Corpus Christi and The Assumption of the Virgin Mary, are celebrated in different regions but are not considered national holidays.

Planning the Trip

Entry Regulations

VISAS & PASSPORTS

You must check before you travel as requirements are apt to change, but at present no visa is required for either republic for citizens of most European countries as well as the United States and Canada. Nationals of other countries are advised to contact their respective Czech or Slovak embassies or consulates for information *(see Embassies Abroad, page 329)*.

Customs

Customs controls are quite rigid. Upon entering the Czech or Slovak Republic, you'll be given a leaflet explaining the customs regulations. Rules can change so you must check the regulations before attempting to import or export anything at all.

IMPORT

All items of personal use may be taken in duty-free; any electronic, photographic and filming equipment should be listed together with serial numbers and presented to the customs for confirmation. The list must be declared again upon departure. All items of personal use taken in to the country must also be taken out.

You are allowed the following items for your own consumption (goods restricted to persons 18 years of age or older): 200 cigarettes, 50 cigars or 250 grams of tobacco, 2 litres of wine, 1 litre of spirits and 50 grammes of perfume. Foreign visitors are permitted to take gifts into the country whose total value does not exceed reasonable amounts.

EXPORT

The following items can be taken out of the republics duty-free: 2 litres of wine, 1 litre of spirits, 250 cigarettes, 50 cigars or 250 grams of tobacco.

Health and Insurance

Citizens from EU countries are entitled to free emergency care under reciprocal arrangements with the Czech and Slovak republics but it is wise to take out an insurance policy to cover non-accidental care. Citizens from other countries should take out a health insurance policy during their stay.

Money Matters

CURRENCY

The unit of currency is the crown (koruna česká or Kč in the Czech Republic; Slovenská koruna or Sk in Slovakia). There are 20, 50, 100, 200, 500, 1,000, 2,000 and 5,000 crown notes and 1, 2, 5, 10, 20 and 50 crown coins and 10, 20 and 50 halér coins. There is no limit to the amount of currency that may be taken in or out of the country but only small amounts of crowns may be taken in or out. It is possible to change back your crowns, but in this case it is necessary to have an exchange receipt.

Eurocheques can be exchanged everywhere in the two countries and even on the border for a maximum of 6,500 crowns. Sometimes what looks like an exceptionally good rate may be accompanied by an inordinately high commission. Cash is still used for most transactions in the Czech and Slovak Republics. Travellers' cheques are accepted by some souvenir shops, hotels and restaurants as well as by banks, but rates are often poor. Credit cards are now widely accepted.

Black Market

Avoid all contact with people offering "good exchange rates" with "no commission" on the streets. In Prague, the bottom of Wenceslas Square is a particular favourite of such people. If they don't pick your pockets while talking to you they will almost certainly rip you off if you deal with them. Remember, the Czech (and the Slovak) crown is freely convertible, which means that you cannot get a better rate than in the banks and foreign exchange bureaux. Shopping around for a better commission rate is a good idea but dealing with black marketeers will end in tears.

EXCHANGE

In most shops and kiosks, payment is made in crowns. Shops and hotels accepting credit cards will normally have the requisite signs on the door. International exchange rates are published in newspapers and displayed at banks and exchange bureaux. There is no shortage of places to change your money in the city centre. Banks are usually open normal working hours.

Getting There

BY AIR

Czech Republic

Prague is now an established tourist destination served by airlines from around the world. Many airlines now fly from New York to Prague and in the case of ČSA, the Czech national carrier, the flight is non-stop. ČSA also flies from Chicago via Montreal as well as from Toronto. Prague is directly linked to virtually every European capital.

Prague Ruzyně airport lies 20 km (13 miles) northwest of the city. The public transport system affords the cheapest way to get from the airport to the city centre and vice versa. The number 119 bus runs between the Dejvická underground station and terminal north of

Prague-Ruzyně Airport (Stop-Nové letiště). The 119 runs every 20–40 minutes between 4am and midnight. The trip should take 30–40 minutes including waiting time. Before getting on a bus, buy a 12-crown ticket from a vending machine or a newsagent. Any taxi will drive you to the airport from the city centre. From the airport itself, there are taxis marked "Airport" on their roofs. There is a 25-crown boarding fee and you will then pay 17 crowns/km. The trip should cost no more than 500 crowns. There is also a minibus shuttle service between the airport and the city centre. Minibuses will stop at Namesti republiky, at the ČSA City Travel Centre, near the Renaissance and Marriott hotels. VW transporter minibuses take six passengers. The price is 90 crowns per passenger. For further information tel: (02) 2010 4111 or see the internet sites at ČSAS.

Slovakia

All ČSA flights to Bratislava go via Prague. Bratislava airport is for the most part still used only for charter flights and flights within the region. But fortunately Vienna International Airport is within easy reach of Bratislava, which is situated right on the Austrian border. There are several flights a day to Vienna from most major international airports. From Vienna Airport you can get a bus to Bratislava or take a taxi.

BY RAIL

Czech Republic

There are direct train connections to Prague from Germany and Austria. From Stuttgart and Munich, the journey takes approximately 8 hours, from Frankfurt 10 hours, Berlin 6 hours, Hamburg 14 hours and Vienna 6 hours. Generally speaking, "Eurorail" and such passes may be used only on the Czech sections of international routes, not on the domestic network. There is no through service from the channel ports. The service from Paris is known to the

French as the Paris–Praha Express and to the Czechs as the Zapadní Express. It leaves from the Gare de l'Est at 11pm and goes via Frankfurt and Nuremberg, arriving at Prague at 5.53pm the following day. The Donau Kurier from Cologne leaves at 7.58am, requires a change at Nuremberg, and reaches Prague at 9.55pm. All trains from Southern Germany and Austria arrive at the Main Station (Hlavní nádraží). Trains from the direction of Berlin come to a halt at the Masaryk Station (Masarykovo nádraží) or at Prague-Holešovice Station.

Travellers coming from Germany and wishing to see the spa towns of Western Bohemia can take the train to Cheb (Eger) from Nuremberg and there change over to other forms of transport. Other rail destinations in the Czech Republic as well as Slovakia can be reached via Prague. Travellers who do not have a ticket from the capital city to their ultimate destination may purchase one at the main train station in Prague. For information on Czech rail travel and for bus transfers, accommodation, sightseeing trips, etc, contact the offices of Czech Railways.

Slovakia

There are regular train services to Bratislava from Prague (around 5 hours), Vienna (45–90 minutes

Czech Railways

- V Celnici 6 110 00 Praha 1
  Tel: (02) 2423 9464/2423 5438. Fax: (02) 2423 2191.
- Žel. stanice Praha hl.n. Wilsonova 80, 110 00 Praha 1. Holiday sales.
  Tel: (02) 2421 4886.
  Fax: (02) 2422 4030.
  International ticket sales (train, bus, airline tickets).
  Tel: (02) 2421 4886.
  Fax: (02) 2421 7032.
- Žel. stanice Praha Holešovice 170 00 Praha 7 – Holešovice
  Tel: (02) 800 805 800 776.
  Fax: (02) 806 948.
  E-mail: CKcd915@quick.cz.

depending on the train) and Budapest (around 2½ hours). The journey from Vienna is the shortest and most convenient means of entering Slovakia by train; the international train services between Budapest and points west run through Slovakia.

BY ROAD

Czech Republic

Travellers arriving from Germany can reach Prague via the following main border crossings from:

Baryreuth via Schirnding/Pomezí
Nuremberg via Waidhaus/Rozvadov
Regensburg via Furth im Wald/Folmava
Passau via Phillipsreuth/Strážné

Munich via Bayrisch Eisenstein/Železná Rudá
Berlin via Zinnwald/Cínovec

If you're entering the Czech Republic from Austria (from west to east):
Salzburg via Linz Summerau/Horni Dvořiště
Vienna via Gmünd/České Velenice or Grametten/Nová Bystřice

Slovakia

Travellers arriving from Austria can reach Bratislava by taking the motorway from Vienna via Hainburg, which takes around an hour; from Hungary take the Budapest road along the Danube and either cross the border at Komárno or continue along the Hungarian side of the border past Gyor. The journey by road from Budapest to Bratislava takes around two hours. The most direct link to Bratislava from the Czech Republic is the motorway down from Brno via Kúty. You should be able to make it from Prague to Bratislava in around 3 hours.

Although there are not as many private cars as there are in Western Europe, drivers still have to reckon with delays, particularly in the Czech Republic. The main roads are generally in good condition, but the many lorries using them can make progress very slow, especially by day.

All drivers are required to be in possession of a valid national driver's licence, car registration documents and a car nationality sticker. The international green insurance card should also be taken along. At the border, "citizens of foreign countries" are handed a special vehicle licence, which is to be filled out and then shown with the other documents. If the driver is not using his own vehicle, he must provide written consent from the vehicle's owner. Caravans, trailers and boats require no special customs documents. Controls at the border crossings are often very thorough, so be prepared for long waits, particularly during the high season. This situation does not yet apply to the new international border between the Czech Republic and Slovakia; a customs union has been established enabling the free transportation of goods.

Unleaded petrol (95 octane) is obtainable at most larger filling stations. Note: neither petrol nor diesel bought in the country may be taken out in reserve canisters. If you're travelling by night you should make sure you have enough petrol, as it may be impossible to find a filling station open.

By and large, the international traffic regulations apply in both republics. The motorways are toll-free. The maximum speed limit within city boundaries is 60 kph (37 mph). On expressways it is 130 kph (80 mph), and on country roads 90 kph (56 mph). If you get caught exceeding the speed limit you can count on paying a fine of about 500

ČSA Airline Offices

Prague
City Service Centre
V Celnici 5
110 00 Praha 1
Tel: (02) 2010 4111, 232 4305, 2481 0513, 231 9995
Fax: (02) 2481 0426
E-mail: sales@upj.csa.cz
The offices are next to Náměstí Republiky metro station.
Flight information
ČSA Airtours
Kolejní 2
160 00 Praha 6
Arrivals
Tel: (02) 20 10 45 22-5
Fax: (02) 2010 45 26
E-mail: acr@airtours.cz
Departures
Tel: (02) 20 10 45 30
Fax: (02) 20 10 45 26
E-mail: pcr@airtours.cz

Abroad
Australia
Czech Airlines
ČSA – Czeslotour
Suite 809, Level 8
Australia Square Tower
264 George Street
Sydney NSW 2000
Tel: (02) 9247 7706
Fax: (02) 9252 5217
E-mail: csa@czeslo.com.au

Canada
ČSA
2020 Universite Street
Suite 2210
Montreal, QUE
Canada H3A 2A5
Sales: (514) 844 6376
Reservations: (514) 844 4200
Fax: (514) 844 5742
E-mail: czech_airlines_montreal@msn.com
www.czechairlines.com
UK
ČSA
72/3 Margaret Street
London W1W 8HA
Reservations: (020) 7255 1898
Sales: (020) 7255 1366
Office: (020) 7637 9152
Fax: (020) 7323 1633
E-mail: sales@czechairlines.co.uk
USA
ČSA
1350 Avenue of the Americas (on 55th Street)
Suite 601
New York 10019-4702
Sales: (212) 765 6545
Reservations: (212) 765 6022
Czech Vacations: (877) 293 4225
Fax: (212) 765 6588, 765 6108
E-mail: csanyc@rcn.com
Website
www.czechairlines.com

crowns. Driving while under the influence of alcohol is absolutely prohibited. Children under 12 years of age can not sit in the front seat. Seat belts must be fastened.

BY BUS

The following companies offer a wide range of international routes to and from the Czech and Slovak Republics.

Concord Praha s.r.o.
Praha – Strasbourg – Paris
Vídeňská 619, Praha 4
Tel/fax: (02) 4491 0649, 4491 2336
E-mail: concordpraha@post.cz

Eurolines Praha
Senovážné náměstí 6,
110 00 Praha 1
Tel: (02) 2423 9318

Slovenská Autobusová Doprava Bratislava š.p.
Mlynské nivy 31,
821 09 Bratislava 2
Information:
Tel: (+421) 984 22 22 22
International enquiries:
Tel: (02) 555 71 312
Fax: (02) 555 62 887
www.eurolines.sk

Capital Express
Czech Republic: U výstaviště 3,
170 00, Praha 7
Tel: (02) 2087 0368
Fax: (02) 2087 0249
E-mail: capital@comp.cz
www.capitalexpress.cz
Emergency: (+420) 606 619913
Great Britain: 57 Princedale Road
Holland Park, London W11 4NP

Tel: (020) 7243 0488
Fax: (020) 7727 3024
E-mail: desk@capitalexpressuk.com
Kings Court Express
Czech Republic: Havelská 8/521,
110 00 Praha 1
Tel: (02) 2423 4583, (+420-2)
2423 3334
Fax: (02) 2423 5245
Great Britain: 15 Balham High
Road, London SW12 9AJ
Tel: (020) 8673 7500/8673 6883
Fax: (020) 8673 3060

Useful Addresses

TRAVEL AGENCIES

Czech Republic (code: +420)

AVE Travel a.s. Main railway station, Wilsonova 8, 120 00 Praha 2 (metro station Hlavní nádraží)
Tel: (02) 2422 3226, 2422 3521, 2461 7568
Fax: (02) 2422 3463, 2423 0783
www.avetravel.cz
Open 6am–11pm year round.
Offers all kinds of accommodation services, transfers, exchange services, theatre ticket sales, monetary services of Western Union.

Bohemia Travel Service, Výstaviště Praha, LDS 1/6, 170 05 Praha 7
Tel: (02) 2010 3625,
Fax (02) 3337 4131
Offers 20 different cruises for foreign visitors in the Czech Republic, sightseeing tours in Prague.

PragueTravel 2000, Přílepská

1692, 252 63 – Roztoky u Prahy
Tel: (02) 3310 4331,
Mobile: (602) 200 051
Fax: (02) 3310 4332,
E-mail: info@praguetravel2000.cz
Toritour s.r.o. Václavské náměstí 17
110 00, Praha 1
Tel/fax: (02) 2400 9265
E-mail: info@toritour.cz
Accommodation in every town in the Czech Republic including spas, trips from and around Prague, spa treatment in Carlsbad, Marienbad and Jáchymov, and special student programmes.

Wittmann Tours, Mánesova 8
120 00 Praha 2
Tel: (02) 222 524 72/(603) 426 564
www.witmann-tours.com
A Jewish guide service in Prague which also offers trips to neighbouring countries.

Slovakia (code: +421)

Tour Operator, Ružová dolina 22,
821 09 Bratislava
Tel/fax: (02) 4342 6101
E-mail: dowina@dowina.sk
www.dowina.sk
CK Focus Travel
Tel: (02) 6446 2835
E-mail: Info@focustravel.sk
Satur Bratislava, Jesenského 5,
821 09 Bratislava
tel: (07) 5441 0077
CK NOVA, Námestie sv. Egídia 95
058 01 Poprad, Slovakia
Tel: 52 7723 309
Tel/fax: 52 7723 490
E-mail: nova@sinet.sk
Services include group programmes, hiking trips in the mountains, guides and accommodation.
CK Tatry, SNP 32, 058 01 Poprad
Tel/fax: (092) 776 7289
E-mail: cktatry@cktatry.sk

Čedok Offices Abroad

Austria: Čedok Reisebüro GmbH
Parkring 10, 1010 Wien
Tel: (01) 512 4372
Fax: (01) 5124 37285
France: Čedok-France
32 avenue de l'Opéra, 75002 Paris
Tel: (01) 4494 8750
Fax: (01) 4924 9946
E-mail: cedok@wanadoo.fr
Germany: Čedok Reisen GmbH

Breakdown Services

Breakdown: It's a good idea to purchase international travel cover from your own automobile association prior to your intended journey. The headquarters of the Czech Breakdown Service ("Yellow Angels") can be contacted at any time of the day or night in Prague at Limuzská 567, tel: (02) 154 for emergency towing and motoring information – the service is free to those with the necessary insurance cover; tel: 123 for 24 hour repairs.

There are a number of garages that will be prepared to do quick repairs:
BMW Praha 10, Průběžná 80,
tel: 781 1109;
Fiat Praha 4 - Branik, K Ryšánce 16,
tel: 420 164;
Ford Nissan Praha 4 - Spořilov, Severní 1/2458, tel: 766 753
Renault Praha 10 - Malešice, Limuzská 12a, tel: 772 770;
VW Audi Praha 5 - Jinonice, Mezi lány 22, tel: 5721 1648.

Leipzigerstrasse 60, 10117 Berlin
Tel: (030) 204 4644
Fax: (030) 204 4623
E-mail: cedok.reisen@berlin.de
Čedok Reisen GmbH
Kaiserstrasse 54, 60329 Frankfurt/M
Tel: (069) 274 0170
Fax: (069) 235 890
E-mail: vit.buchta@cedok.de
Italy: Čedok Italia S.R.L.
Via Piemonte 32, 00 187 Roma
Tel: (039) 648 3406
Fax: (039) 648 28397
Russia: Čedok
33/39, 4th Tverskaja-Jamskaja,
125047 Moscow
Tel: (095) 978 8932
Fax: (095) 978 9922
E-mail: cedok-moscow@mtu-net.ru
Switzerland: Čedok Reisebüro AG
Am Schanzengraben 11,
8002 Zürich
Tel: (01) 287 3344
Fax: (01)287 3345
E-mail: cedok@befree.ch
UK: Čedok Travel Limited
Suite 22–23, 5th Floor, Morley
House, 314/322 Regent Street,
London W1B 3BG
Tel: (020) 7580 3778
Fax: (020) 7580 3779
E-mail: travel@cedok.demon.co.uk
USA: Czechoslovak Travel Bureau Inc.
10 East 40th Street, New York,
N.Y. 10016
Tel: (212) 609 9720
Fax: (212) 418 0597

AIRLINES IN PRAGUE

Aeroflot, Pařížská 5, Praha 1.
Tel: (02) 2481 2682/3
Air France, Václavské nám. 57 110
00 Praha 1.
Tel: (02) 24227164
Austrian Airlines, Revoluční 15,
Praha 1.
Tel: (02) 2482 6199, 2482 7347
Fax: (02) 2482 8488
British Airways, Ovocný trh 8 117
19 Praha 1.
Tel: (02) 2211 4444
Delta, Národní 32, Praha 1.
Tel: (02) 2433 9309
KLM, Václavské náměstí 39, Praha 1.
Tel: (02) 2422 8678
Airport, tel: (02) 367 822
Lufthansa, Aviatická 1048/12,

PO Box 39, 160 08 Praha 6.
Tel: (02) 2011 4456
Malev Hungarian Airlines, Na
Příkopě 15, Dětský dům, vchod z
Havířské ul. 110 01 Praha 1.
Tel: (02) 2422 4471/2
SAS, Rytířská 13, Praha 1.
Tel: (02) 2421 4749.
Airport: Tel: (02) 367 817.
Swissair, Pařížská 11, Praha 1.
Tel: (02) 2481 2111

AIRLINES IN BRATISLAVA

Aeroflot, Laurinska 13, Bratislava.
Tel/Fax: (02) 5443 2174
Air France, Prievozska 6, Bratislava.
Tel: (02) 5341 9811
Air Slovakia, Pestovatelska 2,
Bratislava.
Tel: (02) 54342 2744
British Airways, Stefanikova 22,
Bratislava.
Tel: (02) 5245 0000; fax: (02)
5245 0003
ČSA - Czech Aerolines, Sturova 13,
Bratislava or Airport of M. R.
Stefanik, Bratislava.
Tel: (02) 4342 3667/5296 1073;
fax: (02) 5296 1070
Delta, Rajska 2, Hotel Kyev,
Bratislava
Tel: (02) 5292 0940, fax: (02)
5292 0939
KLM, Dunajska 4, Bratislava.
Tel: (02) 5292 1111; fax: (02)
59221215
Lufthansa, Sturova 4, Bratislava.
Tel: (02) 5292 0422
LOT, Spitalska 51, Bratislava.
Tel: (02) 5296 40 07

Practical Tips

Emergencies

SECURITY AND CRIME

The crime rate is significantly lower
than in western European countries.
However since 1990 the incidence
of offences like robbery and fraud
have increased measurably,
particularly in Prague. It's therefore
a good idea to deposit any
valuables in the hotel safe and if
possible to park your car at a
supervised car park. Also beware of
pickpockets. There are professional
gangs roaming busy shopping and
tourist areas as well as the metro,
trams and buses. In an emergency
either consult with your hotel
reception or contact the police
directly by dialling 158. If you either
lose or have your personal
documents stolen, contact your
embassy representative immediately
(see Embassies, page 329).

Emergency Numbers

Emergency	155
Ambulance	373, 333
Dental Emergency	374
Fire Brigade	150
Police	158

MEDICAL SERVICES

Western visitors will be treated in
any city clinic or hospital. It's a
good idea to take out a medical
insurance policy that will cover you
while travelling before setting out
on your journey. Chemists are open
during normal business hours. In
case of an emergency after hours,
you'll find the address of the
nearest chemist on emergency duty
posted in the window. You should,

of course, bring with you any special medications that you know or suspect you may need while visiting the country.

Business Hours

Most shops are open weekdays 9am–7pm, with speciality stores open 10am–6pm. Smaller shops frequently close their doors for a couple of hours during lunchtime. On Saturdays shops close at noon or 1pm with the exception of large department stores, which often remain open until 6pm. **Banks and Exchange Bureaux:** Most banks are open 9am–3.30pm although larger branches may stay open until 5pm. Exchange bureaux are open from 8am until at least 7pm; some even remain open until 10pm. Most hotels will exchange money around the clock, but be aware that their rates are slightly higher than at a regular exchange bureau or bank.

Media

NEWSPAPERS, MAGAZINES & BOOKS

Foreign news publications are available at the kiosks located in hotels as well as in many bookshops and at stands on the main streets in the centre of Prague and Bratislava. Weekly English- and German-language, locally published, newspapers have been available for several years now. The most useful is the *Prague Post* which contains a mixture of news, features and listings with the tourist and expatriate communities in mind. The Tourist Information Centre stocks restaurant guides and general information brochures in a number of languages. If you're looking for books written in German, French, Russian or English, your best bet is to make a trip to one of the international bookstores in Prague. An increasing amount of Western literature is also available in Bratislava.

RADIO & TELEVISION

Radio and television have undergone big changes since the revolution, with a high proportion of Czech and Slovak families and almost all hotels having cable services. Cable usually offers BBC World, CNN and Sky along with several German and Austrian channels. State-controlled CT2 in the Czech Republic sometimes shows English-language movies with Czech subtitles but everything on the highly successful private NOVA channel is dubbed into Czech. There are dozens of new radio channels but the English-language radio, Metropolis, closed down several years ago.

Postal Services

Stamps can be bought in post offices or at newspaper kiosks. Enquire about current postal rates for letters and postcards once you're in the country as they tend to go up frequently. In the larger towns, you'll find red letter boxes just about everywhere you look. The larger post offices are open 8am–7pm Mon–Fri and 8am–noon Sat; smaller post offices are generally only open 8am–1pm or 3pm at the latest Mon–Fri.

International Dialling

Code for Czech Republic: +420
Code for Slovakia: +421

Telecommunications

TELEPHONES

Since privatisation to a foreign consortium, the Czech telephone system has improved beyond all recognition. You can use coins or phone cards (which are available in most newsagents). The telephone system now operates according to Western standards, which means that public phones are not infrequently out of order! There are rows of telephones at most metro stations as well as on the streets.

As ever, bear in mind that hotels will charge considerably more than public telephones.

FAX AND INTERNET

In most of the larger hotels you can both send and receive a fax or take advantage of Internet facilities to send email. There are also centrally located Internet cafés springing up all over Prague, Bratislava and other major towns and cities in the Czech and Slovak Republics.

Tourist Offices

The Czech Republic especially is firmly on the tourist map and has a host of private and publicly funded tourist offices. It is still probably true to say that for information about where to go and how to get there and bookings the national travel agency **Čedok** remains the largest and most efficient agency. Its office is in Prague, at:
Čedok, a.s. Prague Na příkopě 18
111 35 Praha 1
Tel: (02) 2419 7111
www.cedok.cz.
CK Praha is also useful: Václavské náměstí 53, 110 00 Praha
Tel: (02) 2196 5243 – foreign trips.
(02) 2196 5244 – domestic trips.
For addresses of Čedok abroad *see Useful Addresses, page 326.*
In **Bratislava** the best bet is **Tatratour**, Mickiewiczova 2. `
Tel: (02) 5292 7965, 5293 2811-13; tel/fax: (02) 5292 7888,
PSČ: 811 07
E-mail: bratisl@tatratour.sk
   PIS, the Prague Information Service, also provides tourists with all necessary information. Their main office is at Na Příkopě 20, Praha 1, tel: (02) 264 022; other offices are at Staroměstské náměstí 1, Praha 1, tel: 2448 2562 and the Main Railway Station (Hlavní nádraží). Offices are usually open in the summer Mon–Fri, 9am–7pm, Sat–Sun 9am–5pm, with shorter hours Mon–Sat in the winter. A telephone information service is available on 187 or 544 444. The

Bratislava Information Service
(BIS) is located at Klobúčnická 2,
tel: (02) 16186, (02) 5443 3715.
Here you can find out about
everything that is going on in the
city, and book tours, interpreters
and translators *(see Useful
Addresses, page 326 for
accommodation).*

Slovak Tourist Board

SACR, the Slovak Tourist Board
can be contacted at: Namestie
L.Stura 1, PO Box 35, 974 05
Banska Bystrica, Slovak Republic
Tel: (421 48) 413 61 46-48
Fax: (421 48) 413 61 49
Website: www.sacr.sk
Email: sacr@sacr.sk

Foreign Embassies

EMBASSIES IN PRAGUE

Bulgaria: Krakovská 6, Praha 1.
Tel: (02) 2422 8647
Canada: Mickiewiczova 6, Praha 6.
Tel: (02) 2431 1108
France: Velkoprevorske nám. 2,
Praha 1.
Tel: (02) 5732 0352
Germany: Vlašská 19, Praha 1.
Tel: (02) 5732 0190
Hungary: Badeniho 1, Praha 6.
Tel: (02) 365 041
Italy: Nerudova 20, Praha 1.
Tel: (02) 5732 0011
Russia: Pod Kaštany 1, Praha 6.
Tel: (02) 381 945
South Africa: Ruská 65, Praha 10.
Tel: (02) 6731 1114
UK: Thunovská 14, Praha 1.
Tel: (02) 5732 0355
USA: Tržiště 15, Praha 1.
Tel: (02) 5732 0663

EMBASSIES IN BRATISLAVA

Czech Republic: Hviezdoslavovo
nám. 8, Bratislava.
Tel: (02) 5920 3303/59203304
Canada: Mišíkova 28D, Bratislava.
Tel: (02) 5244 2177/5244 2178
Croatia: Mišíkova 21, Bratislava.
Tel: (02) 54433647/54433657

France: Hlavné nám. 7, Bratislava.
Tel: (02) 59347
Germany: Hviezdoslavovo nám.
10, Bratislava.
Tel: (02) 5441 9640/5441 9641
Italy: Červeňova 19, Bratislava.
Tel: (02) 5441 2585/5441 3043
Poland: Hummelova 4, Bratislava.
Tel: (02) 5441 3196/5441 3174
Russia: Godrova 4, Bratislava.
Tel: (02) 5441 5823/5441 4436
Slovenia: Moyzesova 4, Bratislava.
Tel: (02) 5245 0005/5245 0009
UK: Panská 16, Bratislava.
Tel: (02) 5441 9632/5441 9633
USA: Hviezdoslavovo nám. 4,
Bratislava.
Tel: (02) 5443 0861/5443 3338

Czech Embassies Abroad

Australia
8 Culgoa Circuit, O'Malley
Canberra, ACT 2606
Tel: (02) 6290 1386
Fax: (02) 6290 0006
E-mail: canberra@embassy.mzv.cz
Bulgaria
ul. Panajot Volov
1000 Sofia
Tel: (02) 946 1110, 946 1111
Fax: (02) 946 1800
E-mail: sofia@embassy.mzv.cz
Canada
251 Cooper Street, Ottawa,
Ontario, K2P 0G2
Tel: (613) 562 3875
Fax: (613) 562 3878
E-mail: ottawa@embassy.mzv.cz
Croatia
Savska cesta 41/VIII
10 000 Zagreb
Tel: (01) 617 7246/612 1558
France
15, Avenue Charles Floquet
75343 Paris Cedex 07
Tel: (01) 4065 1301
Fax: (01) 4783 5078
E-mail: paris@embassy.mzv.cz
Germany
Wilhelmstrasse 44
10117 Berlin-Mitte
Tel: (030) 226 38-0, KO-2263
8121-4
Fax: (030) 229 4033
E-mail: berlin@embassy.mzv.cz
Hungary
Rózsa útca 61, 1064 Budapest VI.

Tel: (01) 351 0539
Fax: (01) 351 9189
E-mail: newdelhi@embassy.mzv.cz
Ireland
Embassy of the Czech Republic,
57 Northumberland Road,
Ballsbridge, Dublin 4
Tel: (01) 668 1135/6681343
Fax: (01) 668 1660
E-mail: dublin@embassy.mzv.cz
Poland
ul. Koszykowa 18,
00.555 Warszawa
Tel: (022) 628 7221-5/628 1759,
Fax: (022) 629 8045
E-mail: warsaw@embassy.mzv.cz
Slovenia
Riharjeva 1, 1000 Ljubljana
Tel: (01) 420 2450
Fax: (01) 283 9259
E-mail: ljubljana@embassy.mzv.cz
UK
26 Kensington Palace Gardens
London W8 4QY
Tel: (020) 7243 1115;
visas: (020) 7243 7943
Fax: (0200 7727 9654
E-mail: london@embassy.mzv.cz
USA
3900 Spring of Freedom Street,
NW, Washington DC 20008
Tel: (202) 274 9100
Fax: (202) 966 8540
E-mail: washington@embassy.mzv.cz
Yugoslavia
Bulevar Kralja Aleksandra 22,
11 000 Beograd
Tel: (011) 323 0133-4
Fax: (011) 323 6448
E-mail: belgrade@embassy.mzv.cz

Slovak Embassies Abroad

Australia
47 Culgoa Circuit, O'Malley
Canberra ACT 2606
Tel: (06) 290 1516/290 2405
Fax: (06) 290 1755
Telex: (06) 61807
Canada
50 Rideau Terrace
Ottawa
Ontario K1M 2A1
Tel: (613) 749 4442/7913716
Fax: (613) 749 4989
Croatia
Prilaz Gjure Deželica br. 10
41000 Zagreb

Tel: (01) 484 8941/275021
Fax: (01) 484 8943
Czech Republic
Pod hradbami 1
160 00 Praha 6
Tel: (02) 320502/320521
Fax: (02) 320401
France
125, Rue du Ranelagh
75016 Paris
Tel: (01) 4414 5120/4414 5600
Fax: (01) 4288 7653/45207875
Germany
Aussenstelle Berlin
Leipziger Strasse 36/Ecke
Charlottenstrasse 24
10117 Berlin
Tel: (030) 204 4007
Fax: (030) 208 2459
Hungary
Stefánia út. 22-24
H-1143 Budapest XIV
Tel: (01) 251 1660
Fax: (01) 251 1460
Poland
Litevska 6
00-581 Warszawa
Tel: (022) 628 4051-4/2294859
Fax: (022) 628 4055/418285
Slovenia
Tivolská cesta 4
61000 Ljubljana
Tel: (061) 125 2454/1257511,
Tel/fax: (061) 125 5425
Ukraine
ul. Jaroslavov val č. 34
252 034 Kijev
Tel: (044) 212 0310
Fax: (044) 212 3271
UK
25 Kensington Palace Gardens
London W8 4QY
Tel: (020) 7243 0803,
Fax: (020) 7727 5824
USA
2201 Wisconsin Avenue, N.W.
Suite 250
Washington D.C. 20007
Tel: (202) 965 5160-5/4453804,
E-mail: svkemb@ concentric.net
Yugoslavia
Bulevar umetnosti 18
111 50 Beograd
Tel: (011) 310 6000/310 6001–3

Getting Around

Domestic Flights

From and to Prague Airport: Brno, Bratislava, Karlovy Vary, Košice, Ostrava, Sliač, Piešt'any and Poprad. For information regarding flights not mentioned here contact a representative at one of the ČSA offices *(see Useful Addresses, page 326)*.
From and to Bratislava Airport: There are flights offered daily to Prague, Košice and Poprad.

Note that flights operating between Slovakia and the Czech Republic are not considered domestic, but international.

By Rail

Both the Czech Republic and Slovakia maintain a well-developed railway network. Travelling either first or second class is quite comfortable as well as relatively inexpensive. Information regarding current prices is available at railway stations. Train timetable information can be obtained around the clock in Prague by dialling (02) 264 930, or between 7am–3pm Mon–Fri on (02) 235.

By Boat

During the summer tourist season (1 May–15 October) sightseeing cruises are offered along the Vltava (Moldau) departing from Prague. For further information call EVD, tel: 231 0208/231 1915 or see their website: www.evd.cz. Daytime cruises last for one or two hours, or there is a 3-hour evening trip departing 7pm. Boats leave from Na Františku by Čechův Most. During summer there are also steamers which depart from Bratislava and travel in the directions of Vienna and Budapest along the Danube during the summer season. If you're really in a hurry, you can cruise these stretches in just a few hours on board a raketa (rocket) boat. Because ticket prices and schedules change constantly, it's best to enquire directly at one of the local travel agencies or actually at the quayside.

Public Transport

Tickets for the various means of public transport are available at kiosks, automatic ticket machines and newsagents. One-, 3-, 7- and 15-day passes are available. In Prague, for single-use tickets on the bus and tram (15-minutes travel time) or the metro (four stops), buy an 8 crown ticket. For one hour's worth of travel on all forms of public transport purchase a 12-crown ticket. Similar rules apply in Bratislava. Be sure to have the right ticket. Plain clothes inspectors abound and they will fine you if you do not have a valid ticket. Protestations that you are a foreigner and did not understand how to purchase a ticket have been heard thousands of times before and will be met with a shrug of the shoulders. Prague is the only city in the Czech and Slovak Republics with an underground system. Other cities rely on buses, trams and trolley buses, which although slow and antiquated do provide the visitor with the opportunity of getting to know a city.

Prague
The various means of public transport are cheap and well synchronised. The network includes trams and buses, the metro and the funicular up the Petřín Hill. Tickets can be purchased in shops, at the kiosks of the Prague Public Transport Executive, and at hotel receptions, as well as from the automatic ticket machines at the stops and stations. Remember that bus and tram drivers do not sell

tickets. For ticket sales and further information contact the information office of the Public Transport Executive at Palackého nám. 2, tel: 264 682, or in the Můstek metro station exit area on Jungmannovo nám. 1 (daily 7am–9pm), tel: 2422 5135.

METRO

The modern underground system links the centre with the suburbs and provides for convenient changes inside the city. It is a remarkably clean and fast means of public transport. The three lines have been developed with an eye towards expediency and by transferring it is possible to reach just about all the important tourist attractions in the city. Because of the frequency of the trains (3–12 minutes), you don't need to allow more than about 30 minutes even for journeys into the suburbs. The metro operates from 5am–midnight.

Metro signs outside the stations are small and square and decidedly inconspicuous, with a white M on a green, yellow or red background, depending which line the station is on. Network plans are prominently located at all entrances and above the platforms; the station you are at is highlighted; the stations you can change at are marked with the colour of the intersecting line.

VLTAVA CRUISES

The frequency of cruises on the River Vltava depends on the weather, but there are plenty to choose from during the summer. Some ticket prices include a meal on board. An evening cruise under the Charles Bridge is a wonderful experience. Information can be obtained from the quayside on the Rašín bank at the Palacký Bridge (Palackého most) or from:
Martin Tour, Štěpánská 61, Praha 1, tel: 2421 2473 (and at kiosks in the city centre).
E-mail: info@martintour.cz
www.martintour.cz

Pragotur, Obecního domu, Praha 1, tel: 232 5128.
Thomas Cook, Václavské nám. 47, tel: 2422 8658.

Trams and Buses

Among the many tram and bus routes within Prague, line 22 is probably the most interesting for visitors because it takes you on an almost complete tour of the city for the price of a single ride.

TAXIS

After midnight, with the exception of night buses, taxis constitute the sole form of public transport available (especially in Prague). You'll find a number of taxi stops in the Czech capital's city centre as well as in front of larger hotels. Even if the taxi driver seems reticent, insist that the taximeter is running before starting out. Official taxis can be recognised by their taxi signs and by the licence number posted inside the vehicle. They can be easily ordered by telephone. **Prague** tel: (02) 6677 6677.
Brno tel: (05) 4221 4221
Bratislava tel: (02) 16302

Drivers sometimes turn out to be very friendly individuals with an intimate knowledge of their city. Many have other professions, but can earn more by driving taxis. They may be engaged for a half or entire day to drive passengers into and around the surrounding countryside. Having first established that the car is in relatively good order and that the driver seems to know his way around and can perhaps even speak a bit of English, it pays to do a little bargaining until a mutually acceptable price is reached.

Private Transport

DRIVING

There are some 73,793 km (46,120 miles) of road in the Czech and Slovak Republics. Of these, only 403 km (252 miles) are

motorways running between Prague, Brno, Bratislava and Trnava. Main trunk roads are designated with the numbers 1–99.

In both republics, the use of double brake lights is prohibited and there is a mandatory seatbelt law. Traffic regulations are essentially similar to those in operation in other western European countries. Pay attention to no-parking signs as the traffic police will not hesitate to fine you should you ignore them.

CAR HIRE

You can hire a car from, amongst others (see below), the agencies Herz, Avis and Europcar, located in Prague. Credit cards are accepted. It goes without saying that prospective drivers must be in possession of a valid driver's licence. Rental rates including mileage begin at around £30 per day. There are several Czech car rental firms operating in Prague which are cheaper and expect payment in crowns. Those wishing to go with Avis or Hertz can book from home as this generally works out a lot cheaper. To hire a car you normally have to be at least 21 years of age and in possession of a valid driver's licence. Credit cards are accepted.

Car Rental Agencies in Prague
A RENT CAR, s.r.o.
Washingtonova 9 110 00 Praha
Tel: (02) 2421 1587
Autoopat, s.r.o.
Legerova 22 120 00 Praha 2
Tel: (02) 2426 2867/2426 2875
Fax: (02) 2426 1423
E-mail: rentcar@autoopat.cz
Europcar
Pařížská 28, 110 15 Praha 1
Tel: (02) 2481 1290
Fax: (02) 248 100 39
www.europcar.cz
National Car Rental
Masarykovo nábřeží 4, 120 00 Praha 2
Tel: (02) 2492 3719
E-mail: info@national-prague.cz

Where to Stay

Booking a Room

Booking a hotel room in Prague during the peak tourist season can prove to be difficult but there has been a proliferation of new hotels in recent years both in Prague and Bratislava and throughout the two countries. Outside cities, you'll find a number of travellers' inns along the national routes. These offer relatively inexpensive accommodation.

Price Categories

Prices are for a double room, with breakfast, in high season.
$$$$: over US$200
$$$: $100–200
$$: $60–100
$: under $60

Prague

HOTELS

The choice of hotels in Prague ranges from expensive luxury to cheap and simple. The expensive hotels conform to international standards. The bill can usually be paid in Czech crowns or in Western currencies. Credit cards are also accepted. Our list covers only some of the hotels typical of each category. The phone code for Prague is 02

Luxury
The Four Seasons
Veleslavinova 2
Praha 1
Tel: 2142 7000
Fax: 2142 6000
In the heart of the Old Town, the Four Seasons brings luxury accommodation to a new level. Located on the river bank, with brilliant views of Prague Castle, this hotel promises service over and above the other five-stars in the city – and delivers. This is the residence of choice for visiting glitterati and the jet set.

Grand Hotel Bohemia
Králodvorská 4
Praha 1
Tel: 2232 7944
Fax: 2232 9545
Truly grand, this Art Nouveau gem under Austrian management rates as one of the most beautiful (as well as most expensive) luxury hotels in Prague, with sumptuous, spacious rooms decorated in soft tones. Around the corner from the Powder Tower and less than five minutes' walk from Old Town Square, the hotel is also a practical choice for business travellers, as each room comes with an answering machine, fax and trouser press.

Hotel Savoy
Keplerova 6
Praha 1
Tel: 2430 2430
Fax: 2430 2128
The luxury choice near Prague Castle, lovingly renovated and painted a cheerful yellow. The good-sized rooms all come with substantial bathrooms. The Savoy is small by luxury hotel standards (55 rooms), which makes its service all the more personal.

Inter-Continental
Náměstí Curieových 5
Praha 1
Tel: 2488 1111
Fax: 2488 1118
Affording gorgeous views of Prague Castle (ask for a front-facing room), the Inter-Continental, with 365 rooms, offers all important hotel amenities. Its fitness centre and pool also score highly. The hotel is only ten minutes' walk from Old Town Square, down elegant Pařížská, and only steps away from the Jewish Quarter.

Jalta
Václavské náměstí 45
Praha 1
Tel: 2422 9133
The Jalta is a large, boxy yet utterly professional hotel located near the bottom of Wenceslas Square. All rooms have the amenities expected for the price; there is also a Japanese restaurant and casino on site.

Palace
Panská 12
Praha 1
Tel: 2409 3120
Fax: 2422 1240
Dating from 1906, this classy Art Nouveau-style hotel one block from Wenceslas Square successfully uses muted shades of green in its spacious rooms. Bathrooms are luxurious, each even equipped with a telephone. Business travellers will also find a PC port for their computer. There is a non-smoking floor. Two rooms (out of 114) have barrier-free facilities for travellers with physical disabilities.

Expensive
Best Western Meteor Plaza
Hybernská 6
Praha 1
Tel: 2419 2111
Fax: 2421 3005
A modernised, efficient hotel near Obecní dům; ask for a room that faces the courtyard, where it is quieter. The on-site wine cellar dates from the 14th century.

Diplomat
Evropská 15
Praha 6
Tel: 2439 4111
Fax: 2439 4215
An excellent choice for business travellers and those on the go, since this sizeable hotel (369 rooms) is situated midway between the airport and the city centre. Facilities are clean and modern, but slightly lacking in local charm. There is a non-smoking floor.

Corinthian Towers Hotel
Kongresová 1
Praha 4
Tel: 6119 1111
Fax: 6119 1238
Comfortable facilities in a high-rise hotel; views from any side will not disappoint, but do request a room which faces the direction of Prague Castle. Rooms are not huge but have every facility. There is a popular fitness centre on the upper floors, as well as a small but pleasant bowling alley. Five rooms

Holiday villas beyond indulgence.

BALEARICS ~ CARIBBEAN ~ FRANCE ~ GREECE ~ ITALY ~ MAURITIUS
MOROCCO ~ PORTUGAL ~ SCOTLAND ~ SPAIN

If you enjoy the really good things in life, we offer the highest quality holiday villas with the utmost privacy, style and true luxury. You'll find each with maid service and most have swimming pools.

For 18 years, we've gone to great lengths to select the very best villas at all of our locations around the world.

Contact us for a brochure on the destination of your choice and experience what most only dream of.

INTERNATIONAL
CHAPTERS

Toll Free: 1 866 493 8340
International Chapters, 47-51 St. John's Wood High Street, London NW8 7NJ. Telephone: +44(0)20 7722 0722
email: info@villa-rentals.com www.villa-rentals.com

Live it up!

Ride through the **past** in a **trishaw** and be welcomed into the **future** by **lions.**

For the time of your life, live it up in Singapore!
Explore historic back lanes and shop in malls of the future. Take part in a traditional tea ceremony at a quaint Peranakan house, then tee off for a birdie at one of our challenging golf courses.

Spice things up with some hot Pepper Crab and unwind in a world-class spa. Join a Feng Shui Tour to harness positive energy and later channel it into a night on the town. Come to Singapore and catch the buzz and excitement of Asia's most vibrant city.

Singapore NEW ASIA

www.newasia-singapore.com

For more information, mail to: Singapore Tourism Board, Tourism Court, 1 Orchard Spring Lane, Singapore 247729 or Fax to (65) 736 9423.

Name: _____   Address: _____

_____   Email: _____

(out of 531) are specially equipped for the physically disabled. The hotel is two metro stops from Wenceslas Square, and about 10 minutes' walk from Vyšehrad and Prague's Cubist houses.

Dům U Cerveného lva
Nerudova 41
Praha 1
Tel: 5753 3833
Fax: 5753 3814
The Red Lion is a lovely, small hotel on a romantic though busy Nerudova, with rooms featuring dramatic beamed ceilings and parquet floors. There are only 11 rooms, so book ahead. Prague Castle is a five-minute uphill walk.

Hotel Hoffmeister
Pod Bruskou 7
Praha 1
Tel: 5731 0942
Fax: 5732 0906
Comfortable, stylish Old-European style hotel in Malá Strana, near the Vltava. Film director Miloš Forman stays here when in Prague.

Kampa
Všehrdova 16
Praha 1
Tel: 5732 0508/0404
Fax: 5732 0262
A romantic hotel located on a quiet lane in Malá Strana, not far from its namesake Kampa Park, but also within easy reach, via several tram lines, of Prague Castle and Wenceslas Square. The 85 rooms, simply furnished, have the usual hotel amenities.

Maximilian
Haštalská 14
Praha 1
Tel: 2180 6111
Fax: 2180 6110
A luxurious choice on a serene square in the Old Town, not far from the heavenly shopping on Pařížská. Each room has a fax machine; pleasant service.

Prague Hilton Atrium
Pobřežní 1
Praha 8
Tel: 2484 1111
Fax: 2484 2036
The Atrium has all the facilities and standards one would expect from a Hilton hotel: its atrium foyer is stupendous, although the 788

rooms could be a bit larger. It is the largest hotel in the Czech Republic. The location is a bit out of the centre, but only about 15 minutes' walk from Old Town Square. Fitness facilities (indoor tennis and squash courts, pool, work-out equipment) are among the best in Prague.

Renaissance Prague Hotel
V Celnici 7
Praha 1
Tel/fax: 2182 2100
A large, modern, well-equipped hotel near Obecní dům. All rooms are air-conditioned and have sealed windows, which is good because there is construction in constant progress in the neighbourhood.

Moderate

Axa
Na Poříčí 40
Praha 1
Tel: 2481 2580
Fax: 232 2172
A simple, well-kept hotel (with just over 100 rooms) near the centre, the Axa appeals to families and sports buffs due to its 50-metre (160-ft) swimming pool, sauna, and fitness centre. The rooms, refurbished in the late 1990s, are pleasant and functional; the foyer is a bit over-whelming, due to an abundance of chrome and mirrors.

Bílá Labuť
Biskupská 9
Praha 1
Tel: 2481 1382
The White Swan is on a quiet side street within easy walking distance of the Old Town. The 54 rooms feature minibars and satellite TV in addition to clean, simple furnishings. Children up to age 12 stay for free in their parents' room.

City Hotel Moraň
Na Moráni 15
Praha 2
Tel: 2491 5208
Fax: 297533
Only two blocks from leafy Charles Square, the City Hotel is a bit off the beaten track, but upper-storey rooms offer fine views of Prague Castle. The 57 rooms are clean and pleasant, but without much character. This is a good choice for travellers who like being close to

the centre (Wenceslas Square is less than 10 minutes away via tram or metro) without having to be in the thick of things.

Hotel U staré paní
Michalská 9
Praha 1
Tel: 2422 8090
Fax: 2422 6659
A small, comfortable hotel on a picturesque street in the Old Town, near Old Town Square. All 18 rooms

Private Lodgings

Private lodgings and private rooms offer a comparatively inexpensive alternative to hotel rooms. There are a number of agencies through which you can book an apartment in the centre of Prague.

Prague
Aaron agency
Tel: (02) 8387 2030
Ada agent
Tel: (02) 5721 5217
E-mail: adaagent@seznam.cz
Alfa Tourist Service
Tel: (02) 2481 8200
www.alfatourist.cz
AVE
Located at the airport and the two main international train stations. Tel: (02) 2422 3226
Čedok
Na Příkopě 18
Tel: (02) 2419 7111
Hello Travel
Senovaïné nám. 3, Praha 1
Tel: (02) 2421 4212
Mary's
Italská 31, 12000 Praha 2
Tel: (02) 2225 2215
Top Tour
Rybná 3, Praha 1
Tel: (02) 232 1077
Fax: 231 6640

UK
Czechbook Agency
Jopes Mill Trebrownbridge near Liskeard, Cornwall PL14 3PX
Tel: (01503) 240 629
Czechdays
89 Valence Road, Lewes, Sussex BN7 ISJ
Tel: (01273) 474 738

are decorated with Scandinavian-style furnishings. There is also a popular (and soundproofed) jazz club in the basement.

Opera
Těšnov 13
Praha 1
Tel: 2231 5609
Fax: 2231 1477
This pink-and-white *fin-de-siècle* hotel has a certain old-world appeal, partly thanks to its relative proximity to Old Town. The rooms are plain but perfectly functional; all were renovated in the late 1990s.

Budget
Apollo
Kubišova 23
Praha 8
Tel: 688 0628
Fax: 688 4570
Boxy hotel without much character. Still, the prices are decent, the service is fine, and public transport is ample, although the bus journey to the centre takes 25 minutes.

Astra
Mukuřovská 1740/18
Praha 10
Tel: 781 3595
Fax: 781 0765
Convenient for the metro station Strašnická, which is reasonably convenient to the centre (15 minutes maximum to the Old Town). With 50 clean, large rooms, this hotel is a good choice for those seeking an inexpensive hotel.

Balkán
Svornosti 28, Praha 5
Tel: 5732 7180
Fax: 5732 7268
Clean, simple, no frills hotel with easy access via public transport to the major sites of Prague.

Central
Rybná 8
Praha 1
Tel: 2481 2041
Fax: 232 8404
The slightly shabby Central still offers affordable rooms only 5 minutes' walk from Old Town Square. There are 62 rooms, which are quickly snapped up given the location; reserve well in advance.

Hotel Olšanka
Táboritská 23
Praha 3
Tel: 6709 2202
Fax: 273 386
A huge boxy complex that offers basic, clean rooms and numerous hotel services (sauna, pool, several restaurants) that befit an establishment in a higher price range. Three tram lines connect in front of the hotel; the main train station is 10 minutes away by tram.

Mepro
Viktora Huga 3
Praha 5
Tel: 5721 5263
Fax: 527 343
Clean, with 26 simply furnished rooms. The location, near Petřín Park with its mirror maze and little Eiffel Tower, should appeal to families travelling with children.

Petr
Drtinova 17
Praha 5
Tel: 5731 4068
Fax: 5731 4072
A basic but perfectly fine hotel not far from Malá Strana, on a quiet side street in the Smíchov residential neighbourhood. There is ample public transport close by, but there is no restaurant on site.

PENSIONS

If the choice is between a hotel and a *pension*, go with the *pension* every time. Usually privately owned and managed, the service is personal and their prices are reasonable. These are a few of the best:

Betlem Club Praha
Betlémské nám. 9
Praha 1
Tel: 2421 6872
Fax: 2421 8054
Prices in this *pension,* across from historic Bethlehem Chapel on a peaceful square in the Old Town, include breakfast in 12th-century Romanesque cellars. The 20 rooms are attractively furnished; each comes with toilet and shower or bathtub.

Penzion Digital
Na Petynce 143
Praha 6
Tel: 2431 3739
Full service *pension*; use of fax machine, as well as laundry services, babysitting, local tours – and they will even walk your dog!

Penzion Sprint
Cukrovárnická 62
Praha 6
Tel: 312 3338
Fax: 312 1797
Tiny bathrooms but pleasant management and 12 clean, simply furnished rooms make the Sprint a good place to stay. About midway between the airport and the centre; a tram line is two short blocks away.

Pension Unitas (The Prison)
Bartolomějská 9
Praha 1
Tel: 232 7700
Fax: 232 7709
Notorious as the former convent that was turned into a prison under Communism and even housed dissident Václav Havel. It is possible to stay in his former cell if you reserve ahead. No en-suite rooms.

MOTELS

Motels offer a cheap alternative to hotels, particularly if you are travelling through the country and are only looking for one or two day-trips into the city.

Club Hotel Praha
E14 motorway towards Brno, Průhonice.
Tel: 67 75 08 68
Fax: 67 75 00 64
This 4-star hotel opened in 1991, with major sports facilities including tennis and squash courts, bowling alleys, swimming pools, fitness centre and much more. It is also situated adjacent to the Botanical Gardens and the grounds of Průhonice Castle.

Hotel Golf
Plzeňská 215a, Praha 5
Tel: 523251, 5721 5185
Fax: 5721 5213
Located on the E15 highway, the Hotel Golf has 129 rooms (with

satellite TV) as well as excellent sports facilities.

YOUTH HOSTELS

For information about the many Prague youth hostels, most of which are open in summer only (except Travellers Hostel), contact:
Čedok
Na Příkopě 18, Praha 1.
Tel: 2419 7111.
Travellers Hostel
Dlouhá 33, Praha 1.
Tel: 2482 6664.

Price Categories

Prices are for a double room, with breakfast, in high season.
$$$$: over US$200
$$$: $100–200
$$: $60–100
$: under $60

Karlovy Vary

Booking a room in Karlovy Vary is difficult in the high season, so be sure to try well in advance. The Kurf-info tourist offices can provide information about accommodation. They can be contacted on: 322 46 67; fax: 322 46 67 or email: kurinfor@plz.pvtnet.cz. Kurf-info has a website at www.karlovyvary.cz. The dialling code for Karlovy Vary is 017.

HOTELS

Grandhotel Pupp
Mírové náměstí 2
Tel: 310 9111/310 9606
E-mail: sales@pupp.kpgroup.cz
www.pupp.cz/www.hotel.cz/pupp
The best and most expensive hotel in town. Opened in 1701, the hotel has had many famous guests to stay. Stunning interiors. **$$$**
Hotel Jean de Carro
stezka J.D. Carro
Tel: 323 9002/323 0702
E-mail: cervena@premium-hotel.com
www.hotel.cz/jean-de-carro
www.premium-hotel.com.

A new centrally located hotel with views of the spa colonnade. **$$**
Hotel Kavalerie
T.G. Masaryka 43
Tel: 358 8330/322 9613
E-mail: kavalerie@volny.cz
www.hotel.cz/kavalerie.
Good value for money but not ideally located for the spa. **$$**

PENSIONS

Pension Palatin
Lázeňská 10
Tel: (019) 7002 473
E-mail: palatin@zce.cz
www.hotel.cz/palatin www.zce.cz.
Clean and comfortable pension. **$$**

Plzeň

Both agencies are located in the town centre, very close to the market place.
Municipal Information Centre
Náměstí Republiky 41
Tel: 203 27 50
Email: infocenter@mmp.plzen-city.cz
CKM, Dominikánská 1
Tel: 723 63 93
Fax: 723 69 09
Email: ckm_plzen@volny.cz
The dialling code for Plzeň is 019.

HOTELS

Hotel Rosso
Pallova 12
Tel: 722 6473
E-mail: recepce@hotel-rosso.cz.
Modern hotel on the borders of the old town. Comfortable en-suite rooms. **$$**
Pension City
Sady 5. května 52
Tel: 226 069
Centrally located in the old town this small pension is good value for money and has tasteful rooms. **$**
Continental
Zbrojnická 8
Tel: 723 6479
Fax: 722 1746
Located in the historic centre of town this 100-year-old hotel has seen many famous visitors. **$$**

Škoda
Náměstí Českých bratří 10
Tel: 275 252
Fax: 276 322
Not very impressive rooms, price includes breakfast. **$**
Slovan
Smetanovy sady 1
Tel: 722 7256
E-mail: hotelslovan@iol.cz
Communist-style hotel with shabby but stylish interior. **$**

CAMPING

Intercamp Bílá Hora
Ul. 28. října
Tel: 756 2225.

Brno

Brno is a city of trade fairs, so hotels are often booked up. If this is the case when you arrive, then either the room agency (tel: 23166, 23178–9) or these agencies should be able to help.
KiC
Old Town Hall
Tel: (05) 422 11 090
Email: kic.brno@brn.pvtnet.cz
Čedok
Nádražní 10
Tel: (05) 422 11 561
CKM
Česká 11
Tel: (05) 236 413
The dialling code for Brno is 05.

HOTELS

Grandhotel Brno
Benešova 18/20
Tel: 4251 8111
E-mail: grandhotel-brno@austria-hotels.telecom.cz.
Probably the best hotel in town although the interior does not measure up to the exterior with its Art Nouveau mural. **$$$**
Hotel Boby
Sportovní 2a
Tel: 727 2133
E-mail: hotel@boby.cz.
Outside of the centre and part of a huge entertainment complex. **$$$**

Price Categories

Prices are for a double room, with breakfast, in high season.
$$$$: over US$200
$$$: $100–200
$$: $60–100
$: under $60

Continental
Kounicova
Tel: 4151 9111
Four-star, impersonal and over-priced. **$$$**
International
Husova 16
Tel: 4212 2111
Four-star, in the city centre; modern and too expensive. **$$$**
Slavia
Solniční 15/17
Tel: 4232 1249
Four-star, recently renovated art nouveau hotel in the centre, beneath the castle. **$$**
Slovan
Lidická 23
Tel/Fax: 4132 1207
Located in the centre of Brno, near the old town quarter. **$$**

CAMPING

Camping Radka
Brněnská Přehrada
Tel: 4621 5821

Bratislava

For general information about the city and for help with finding accommodation contact the
Bratislava Information Service:
Klobučnícka 2
Tel: (02) 5443 3715
Email: bis@bratislava.sk.
Another source of information on accommodation can be found at www.travelguide.sk
The dialling code for Bratislava is 02. The following travel agencies will be able to help you find accommodation.
Tatratour
Mickiewiczova 2
Tel: 5292 7965/5293 2811–13
E-mail: bratisl@tatratour.sk

Satur
Jesenského 5–9
Tel: 5441 2904, 5441 0133
jesenskeho@satur.sk
Seneca Tours
Obchodná 22
Royko Passage
Tel: 5292 2622
www.senecatours.sk
Koala Tours
811 07 Mickiewiczova 16
Tel: 5296 5224/5296 5227
www.koala.sk
Limba
Medená 13
Tel/Fax 5441 8601
E-mail: limba@limba.sk
www.limba.sk

HOTELS

Hotel West
Koliba - Kamzik, PO Box 29
Tel: 5478 8692/5478 8693
E-mail: hotel@hotel-west.sk
www.hotel-west.sk.
Located about five minutes by car from the centre of town. **$$$**
Hotel Danube
Rybné nám. 1
Tel: 5934 0000/5934 0394
E-mail: danube@internet.sk.
Good views of the castle and the river from this luxurious French-run establishment. **$$$**
Hotel Devín
Riečna 4
Tel: 5443 0851/5443 3640
E-mail: devin@computel.sk.
This hotel is in the centre of the historical city of Bratislava on the Danube Embankment. Built by Slovak architect Emil Belus, it is one of the oldest hotels in Bratislava and a protected monument. **$$**
Hotel Forum
Hodžovo nám. 2
Tel: 5934 8133
E-mail: hotel@forumba.sk.
Built in 1989 this hotel is in the heart of town, near the business, shopping and cultural centres. Caters mostly to business travellers. **$$$**
Hotel Perugia
Zelená 5
Tel: 5443 1818
E-mail: info@perugia.sk.

In the pedestrianised zone of the historical centre, this quiet, top-class hotel has a terrace and facilities for business travellers. **$$$**
Hotel Tatra
Nám. 1. mája 5
Tel: 5927 2111/5927 2123
E-mail: recepcia@hoteltatra.sk.
Popular with businesspeople, this hotel is situated just north of the old town. **$$**
Hotel No. 16
Partizánska ul.16a
Tel: 5441 1672/5441 3398
Atmospheric, wood-panelled villa is about 10 minutes on foot to the old town. **$**

CAMPING

Areál zdravia – Zlaté Piesky
Senecká cesta 2
Tel: 4425 7373/4445 0592
E-mail: kempi@netax.sk
Open: (May–October)

Hostels

Youth Hostel Bernolák
Bernolákova 1
Tel: 5249 7723/5249 7721–2
$
Študentský domov Družba
Botanická 25
Tel: 6542 9808/6542 1968
E-mail: sr@sdjdr.uniba.sk. **$**

Where to Eat

What to Eat

The cultural differences between the Czech Republic and Slovakia were largely created by the outside influences that historically dominated the respective regions – the primarily Habsburg-Germanic influence on the Czechs and Moravians as opposed to the Magyar-Hungarian influence on the Slovaks. The division is reflected in the food, although the Bohemian, Moravian and Slovakian cuisines can all be characterised by the word "hearty".

The national Czech dish is roast pork served with cabbage and dumplings. Main meals customarily begin with a bowl of soup, followed by a hefty main course including meat and is finished off with pudding, fruit or a soufflé-like concoction accompanied by a sweet sauce. A variety of duck and fish dishes number among the national culinary specialities. In Slovakia goulash features prominently, alongside other typically Hungarian specialities. While the Bohemians tend to drink beer *(pivo)* with their meals, the people of Slovakia and Moravia prefer wine produced within their particular regions. The finishing touch to an enjoyable meal is frequently a good swig of Becherovka or Slivovitz.

As eating and drinking are significant activities for native Czechs and Slovaks, the portions served in restaurants are correspondingly large – and relatively inexpensive.

Since the beginning of 1991 many restaurants have fallen into private hands. In conjunction with this development and in contrast to nationally owned dining establishments, prices have become competitive. A higher bill is offset by more attentive service. Despite the fact that tips are generally included in the price of a meal, it is customary to round up the total when you settle the bill. If in doubt leave 10 percent. Because prices are comparatively low, overly enthusiastic tourists have a tendency to leave more than a 100 percent tip! This gesture, though generous, is inappropriate and locals will not be pleased.

No matter where you want to dine, it's wise to call in advance and reserve a table.

Prague

RESTAURANTS

There's no question about it: in Prague you can eat a lot and sometimes even quite well. Fans of plain old homecooking frequently consume roast pork and beef, goulash and duck served with either dumplings or cabbage twice a day. A main dish ordered in a beer pub or in one of the relatively inexpensive wine bars/*vinárna* (serving more than just wine) will seldom cost more than about £3. The meal is naturally washed down with a glass or more of beer on tap. Apart from ready-meals *(hotová jídla)*, the menu also includes "meals to order" *(jídla na objednávku)* such as freshly prepared steaks and roasts. These tend to be a bit more expensive.

Apart from the pubs and wine bars (listed in separate sections), the city has many excellent restaurants. The following is a list of establishments in the different districts of the city offering particularly good food and value for money.

THE LESSER QUARTER (MALÁ STRANA)

Bohemia Bagel
Újezd 16, Praha 1
Tel: 5731 0831

Its bagels will not be confused with the New York variety, but Bohemia Bagel makes an impressive attempt to jazz up its wide assortment (including tomato, basil and poppyseed) with tasty cream-cheese, all served in an informal cafeteria style. Unlimited refills on designer coffee; weekend brunches are always popular. **$**

Circle Line Brasserie
Malostranské nám. 12, Praha 1
Tel: 5753 0021

An elegant yet cosy restaurant that offers world-class cuisine in the *nouvelle*-style. The exquisite chocolate plate is almost too pretty to eat. Unfailingly terrific, discreet service. **$$$**

Price Categories

Prices are per person including a glass of wine or beer
$$$:   750 Kc and above
$$:   300–750Kc
$:   up to 300 Kc

Kampa Park
Na Kampě 8b, Praha 1
Tel: 5731 3493

Nouvelle-style cuisine served up on the banks of the Vltava. In fair weather, diners can enjoy a great view of Charles Bridge. **$$$**

Malý Buddha
Úvoz 46, Praha 1 (near Prague Castle)
Tel: 2051 3894

A serene tea-house atmosphere is the setting for fresh and delicious Asian cuisine, such as spring rolls and glass noodles with vegetables, along with an impressive selection of exotic juices. **$**

Nebozízek (The Little Auger)
Petřinské sady 411, Praha 1
Tel: 5731 5329

The menu is less spectacular than the restaurant's location halfway up Petřín hill (take the funicular), with a gorgeous view over the city and the castle. Czech staples, including potato and garlic soups and meat dishes, are good. **$$**

Palffy palác
Valdštejnská 14, Praha 1
Tel: 5732 0570

An intimate space tucked away on the second floor of a Malá Strana palace; offers excellent Continental cuisine and a charming, faded elegance. **$$**

U Černého orla
Malostranské nám. 14, Praha 1
Tel: 5731 6830
Traditional Czech dishes, cheerfully served. **$$**

U Malířů (The Painters)
Maltézské nám. 11, Praha 1
Tel: 5753 0000
Well established French restaurant with an impressive *haute cuisine* menu; probably the most expensive restaurant in Prague. Its setting, in one of the city's quietest and most romantic squares, is superb. **$$$**

U Maltézských rytířů (The Maltese Knights)
Prokopská 10, Praha 1
Tel: 5753 1324
A tiny cellar specialising in Czech cuisine and atmosphere. The homemade apple strudel alone is worth the visit. **$$$**

U Modré kachničky (The Blue Duck)
Nebovidská 6, Praha 1
Tel: 5732 0308
Delicious food, with game dishes a speciality. Elaborately decorated surroundings. **$$$**

U Patrona
Dražického nám. 4, Praha 1
Tel: 5753 0725
A charming pocket-size restaurant near Charles Bridge which offers a small, high-quality menu of French-inspired cuisine. **$$$**

U Tří houslíček (The Three Violins)
Nerudova 12, Praha 1
Tel: 5753 2062
Elegant setting in which to enjoy classic Czech food. **$$$**

U Vladaře
Maltézské nám. 10, Praha 1
Tel: 5753 4121
An ideal location for well-prepared Czech food. **$$$**

THE OLD TOWN

Amadé
U Milosrdných 10, Praha 1
Tel: 231 8867, 232 0101

Pleasant wine cellar near St Agnes' Convent serves Czech specialities and maintains a small but smart selection of fine wines. **$–$$**

Barock Bar & Café
Pařížská 24, Praha 1
Tel: 232 9221
Sushi and Thai food on one of the Old Town's most elegant streets. A place where the beautiful people go to see and be seen. **$$$**

Bellevue
Smetanovo nábř. 18, Praha 1 (near Charles Bridge)
Tel: 2222 1438
Fax: 2222 0453
Old World elegance with Continental cuisine and respectful presentation of Czech specialities (such as roast duck, brought to new heights with a delectable honey-lavender sauce). The name is fitting, since window tables afford views across the river to Prague Castle. **$$$**

Price Categories

Prices are per person including a glass of wine or beer
$$$:   750 Kc and above
$$:   300–750Kc
$:   up to 300 Kc

Chez Marcel
Haštalská 12, Praha 1
Tel: 231 5676
The bustling, informal charm of a French brasserie has been transplanted onto this quiet side street in the Old Town. Delicious fresh salads and hand-cut chips; daily specials such as *moules frites* or ratatouille. The crème brûlée is consistently flawless. **$$**

Jewel of India
Pařížská 20, Praha 1
Tel: 2481 1010
An elaborately appointed cellar space offers genuine Indian cuisine such as Boti kabob (lamb) and Murgh maghani (chicken in a tomato-based sauce). **$$$**

Kožička Pivnice-Cafe Restaurant
Kozí 1, Praha 1
Tel: 231 0852
The Little Goat is a hip Czech pub-restaurant for the younger generation; can get crowded. **$**

Obecní dům French Restaurant
Náměstí Republiky 5, Praha 1
Tel: 2200 2777
An unsurpassably sumptuous Art Nouveau setting for decent food at reasonable prices. **$$**

Red Hot and Blues
Jakubská 12, Praha 1
Tel: 231 46 39
Reasonably authentic New Orleans and Cajun-style cooking, with live jazz, blues or rockabilly most evenings. Full, hearty breakfasts served daily; the weekend brunches (with specialities such as Creole omelettes and spicy fried potatoes) are very popular. In pleasant weather the outdoor courtyard is a calming place to while away a couple of hours. **$$**

U Velryby
Jilská 24, Praha 1
Tel: 2491 2391
A Czech restaurant that appeals to the young and trendy. **$$**

U Zlaté hrušky
Nový Svět 3, Praha 1
Tel: 2051 5356/4778
The Golden Pear is an elegant setting for traditional food. Some have described the service as a bit frosty, though. **$$$**

V Zátiší
Liliová 1, Praha 1
Tel: 2222 1155
Fax: 2423 1187
Delectable main courses of the *nouvelle* variety, glorious desserts and a warm, sophisticated atmosphere. Highly recommended, whether for a business-related dinner or a romantic *dîner à deux*. **$$$**

Zlatá ulička (Golden Lane)
Masná 9, Praha 1
Tel: 232 0884
Yugoslav specialities on offer in a tiny, friendly cafe. Try anything with veal in it. **$$**

THE NEW TOWN

Buffalo Bill's
Vodičkova 9, Praha 1
Tel: 2494 8624
A wide variety of Tex-Mex favourites such as spicy burritos, tostadas and tortillas. **$$$**

Ceská restaurace
Krakovská 63, Praha 1
Tel: 2221 0204
Excellent, hearty Czech food and beer in a friendly atmosphere, just off Wenceslas Square. **$**

Dynamo
Pštrossova 221/29, Praha 1
Tel: 2493 2020
A few steps behind the National Theatre, Dynamo offers an imaginatively modern space and a menu filled with delicious options. Excellent pastas and big, fresh salads. The lunch specials are usually a great bargain. Pleasant service. **$$**

Marco Polo
Masarykovo nábřeží 26, Praha 1
Tel: 2491 2900/3853
A wonderfully eclectic menu offers everything from meatballs to salmon, delicate homemade pastas and creative salads. Situated on the river (no views, however, as Marco Polo is several steps below street level) behind the National Theatre; an ideal locale for an after-dinner stroll. **$**

Pivovarský dům
Lípová 15, Praha 2
Tel: 9621 6666
Independent-minded microbrewery

Vegetarian Places

Radost FX Café
Bělehradská 120, Prague 2
Tel: 2425 4776
This tiny restaurant is packed with eclectic style, and the menu is packed with imaginative dishes covering an international range – and all vegetarian. It's attached to a dance club of the same name (see page 350). The weekend brunch omelettes are enormous, and enormously good. **$**

Country Life
Melantrichova 15 (enter the courtyard), Prague 1
Tel: 2421 3366
Tasty all-vegetarian fare, served café style. The salad bar is extraordinarily bountiful by any standard. Table service begins at 6pm, at which point prices go up slightly. **$$**

serves up delicious Czech food in a clean, and for Prague, relatively smoke-free environment. Try the wheat or champagne beers with an appetiser of *pivní sýr* (garlicky and salty "beer cheese" to spread on the accompanying rye bread). **$**

U Kalicha (The Chalice)
Na Bojišti 14, Praha 2
Tel: 2491 2557
The great beer hall celebrated in Jaroslav Hašek's classic of Czech literature, *The Good Soldier Schweik*, frequented nowadays only by tourists. The Czech cuisine served is simple and hearty, but unfortunately not of tremendous quality. **$$$**

Universal
V Jirchářích 6, Praha 1 (off Národní třída).
Tel: 2491 8182
One of the best bargains in town. Tasty main courses with a French flair, dinner-sized salads, and desserts (such as the English Cream Dessert) as good as you'll find anywhere, at an unbelievably reasonable price. Reservations several days in advance are mandatory at peak hours. **$**

U Piráta
Vojtěšská 9, Praha 1
Tel: 2493 7625
Good honest Czech food, but with some rather quirky additions to the menu, such as crocodile. **$**

U Zlatého soudku
Ostrovní 28, Praha 1
Tel: 2491 2202
Veritable meat feasts. Recommended are the potato pancake stuffed with pork, beef and cabbage, or the Old Bohemian Dinner: a platter of pork, chicken and beef, potato and bread dumplings and cabbage. **$$**

Zlatý kohout
Karlovo nám. 24, Praha 1
Tel: 2223 2382
A terrific Continental selection, a warm, elegant ambience and attentive service make this a gem worth seeking out, just across from the New Town Hall. Soothing jazz is the usual background music. **$$$**

OTHER

Dolly Bell
Neklanova 20, Praha 2
Tel: 5793 6419
Yugoslav dishes in an imaginatively decorated restaurant. Veal ragout is a stand-out. **$$$**

Hanavský pavilon
Letenské sady 173, Praha 7
Tel: 3332 3641
Traditional Czech cuisine in one of Praha's main diplomatic quarters. **$$$**

Orso Bruno (Bruno the Bear)
Za Poříčskou bránou 16
Prague 8
Tel: 231 0178
Unpretentious Italian cuisine. Try the *scaloppini* with Gorgonzola cheese, chicken *cacciatore*, or *penne melanzane*. **$$**

Restaurace Ullmann
Letenský zámeček, Letenské sady 341, Praha 7
Tel: 5319 6674
Friendly restaurant in a very small château situated in Letná park, not far from Prague Castle. The beer garden is very popular with the locals in warm weather. **$**

U Bílé krávy (The White Cow)
Rubešova 10 (behind the National Museum), Praha 2
Tel: 2423 9570/9571
Connoisseur-quality steak with French variations: marinated in Cognac and served with garlic-herb sauce, for instance. **$$**

U Cedru
Na Hutích 13, Praha 6
Tel: 312 29 74
Authentic, delicious Lebanese food in a diplomatic district. **$$$**

U Počtů
Milady Horákové 47, Praha 7
Tel: 3337 1419
Off the beaten track, but the neighbourhood charm and old-fashioned decor make it worth a visit to sample traditional meals. **$$**

Velehradská vinárna
Velehradská 18, Praha 3
Tel: 627 6748
Unpretentious hideaway for well-prepared Czech food. The beefsteak with a dot of herb butter is tender and good. **$$**

Bratislava

The local cuisine has been refined by a host of influences from other cultural regions. While farming provides a variety of meat, vegetables and fruit, the forests and the lakes provide copious quantities of game and fish. Typical Slovakian dishes include more down-to-earth dishes such as the butcher's platter, roast goose with *Lokše* (unleavened bread), cabbage soup *(Kapustnica)*, potato dumplings with sheep cheese *(Bryndzové halušky)* and salted mashed potato with marjoram. Hungarian dishes can also be found: goulash in a variety of guises, seasoned with plenty of paprika, garlic and onions. *Lečo,* a vegetable and egg dish, was a great favourite with the Turks. The proximity of Vienna makes itself apparent through flour-based dishes: noodles, dumplings and pancakes, followed up by cake and espresso (known in Bratislava as "presso") or Turkish coffee.

RESTAURANTS

Restaurants are sometimes closed on Sundays. Booking a table is recommended. Some places might have a band playing; make sure that the amplifier isn't turned up so loud that you can't hear yourself speak.
Bakchus vila
Pod lipami 1
Tel: (02) 4371 1474
Live music every Tuesday with a wide variety of cuisine and wines. **$**
Butterfly
Panská
Just up the street from the British Embassy, this restaurant has the best steaks in the city. Good service. **$$**
Café restaurant Arkádia
Zámocké schody
Tel: (02) 5443 5650
A classy restaurant on the steps leading up to the castle. **$$$**
Červený Rak
Michalská 26
Tel: (02) 5443 1375

One of the oldest restaurants in the city located in the historic centre. Serves Slovak and international specialities. **$$$**
Jadran Grill
Rybárska brána
Tel: (02) 5443 1283
Yugoslav restaurant with a terrace which is usually full in the summer. One of the best-value restaurants in the city centre. **$**

Price Categories

Prices are per person including a glass of wine or beer
$$$:   750 Kc and above
$$:   300–750Kc
$:   up to 300 Kc

Leberfinger
Viedenská cesta 257
Tel: (02) 6231 7590
Expensive but high quality local and foreign meals. **$$$**
Le Monde
Ventúrska 1
Tel: (02) 5922 7518
French food to a high quality. **$$$**
Hotel Perugia
Zelená 5
Tel: (02) 5443 1818
Located on a narrow street leading into the main, historic square, the hotel restaurant offers efficient service and a good range of local and foreign food. **$$**
Hysteria
Odbojárov 9
Tel: (02) 4445 4495
One of the liveliest venues in Bratislava offering Mexican

Czech Beer

Czech beer is probably the finest in the world. Its quality is largely due to the famous Bohemian hops, which have been cultivated in Northern Bohemia ever since the Middle Ages. The hop centre is Žatec (Saaz). Both light *(světlé)* and dark *(tmavé* or *černé)* beer is available. The degrees (°) do not refer to the alcohol content but to the percentage of malt in the wort, which is boiled with hops to make

specialities at reasonable prices. The music can be deafening. **$**
Prašná bašta
Zámočnícka ulica
Tel: (02) 5443 4957
One of the friendliest restaurants in the city in the heart of the Old Town. **$**
Reštaurácia Rybársky Cech
Žižkova 1
Tel: (07) 5441 3049
Well known for its fish and steaks. Situated by the River Danube. **$**
Slovenská Reštaurácia
Hviezdoslavovo nám
One of the classic restaurants with waiters dressed in traditional garb. All the best Slovak specialities. **$$**

Drinking Notes

PRAGUE

Beer Halls
Domáci pivnice V Celnici
Na Poříči 6, Praha 1
Tel: (02) 24233246
A traditional-style beer house.
The James Joyce
Liliová 10, Praha 1
Tel: (02) 2422 1983
Irish pub. Yes, they do serve Guinness and it's pricey.
Kozička
Kozí 5, Praha 1
Tel: (02) 2481 8308
Serves Pilsner and late night goulash. Relaxed atmosphere.
Lobkovická pivnice
Vinohradská 10, Praha 2
Tel: (02) 2421 9032
Set in the fashionable area above

the brew. Light draught beer (10°) has an alcohol content of between 3 and 4 percent, lager (12°) five percent. The stronger, dark varieties (13° and more) are comparable with strong German beers. The most famous beers are *Pilsener Urquell* from Plzeň (Pilsen) and *Budvar* from České Budějovice (Budweis). *Slivovice,* plum brandy, is also widely available and should be treated with respect.

the National Museum, a pleasant
beer house with friendly service.
Martins Irish pub
Lublanská 57, Praha 2
Tel: (02) 2251 3411
Irish pub with lively atmosphere.
Pivnice Radegast
Templova 2, Praha 1
Tel: (02) 232 8237
An impressive beer house in the
German style, right in the heart of
the Old Town.
Pivnice u Švejků
Újezd 22, Praha 1
Tel: (02) 5731 3244
Situated across the river, this
establishment is the ideal place to
pack in some fuel before you climb
Petřin Hill.
U dvou koček
Uhelný trh 10, Praha 1
Tel: (02) 2422 9982
Popular pub serving Pilsner Urquell.
U Fleků
Křemencova 11, Praha 1
Tel: (02) 2491 5118
Locals avoid it like the plague but
some tourists have a good time.
The malthouse and brewery date
from 1459. Dark beer (13°) brewed
on the premises, accompanied by
traditional Praha cabaret.
U Kalicha
Na Bojišti 14, Praha 2
Tel: (02) 290 701
The beer hall made famous by

Jaroslav Hašek in *The Good Soldier
Schweik.*
U Pinkasu
Jungmannovo nám. 15, Praha 1
Tel: (02) 2423 0828
A popular pub that has been pulling
Pilsener Urquell since 1843.
U kocoura
Nerudova 2, Praha 1
Tel: (02) 57530107
One of the classic Mala Strana
beer halls. Set in stone with low
arching ceilings, a perfect place
to soak up the atmosphere of
the city.
U sv. Tomáse
Letenská 12, Praha 1
Tel: (02) 531 632
Serves strong Branik beer.
U zlaté podkovy
Nerudova 34, Praha 1
Cheap Pilsener, attentive service.
Affordable pub in what is now the
tourist belt.
U zlatého tygra
Husova 17, Praha 1
Tel: (02) 2422 9020
Pilsener Urquell 12°. The Czech
writer Bohumil Hrabal used to drink
here as have a host of dignitaries
including former US president Bill
Clinton, whose photo hangs on
the wall.
U zlaté trumpety
Týnská 2, Praha 1
Tel: (02) 2489 5787

The location could hardly be
better, which probably explains
the quantity of tourists to be
found here.
U vejvodů
Jílská 4, Praha 1
Tel: (02) 242, 10591
This is one the best places in town
to sample good Pilsner.

Wine Bars
The best wine comes from
Žernoseky in the Elbe Valley, where
the Melník wines are also
cultivated. Good vintages are also
produced in Southern Moravia, in
places like Mikulov, Hodonin,
Znojmo or Valtice. Some wine bars
also serve wine from their own
cooperatives.
Blatnice
Michalská 8, Praha 1
Tel: (02) 263 812
Moravian wines from the area
around Blatnice.
Česká vinotéka
Anežská 3, Praha 1
Tel: (02) 2231 1293
Offers a wide variety of Czech
wines, especially from South
Moravia, the country's premier
wine-growing area.
Klášterní vinárna
Národní 8, Praha 1
Tel: (02) 2493 0070
This large wine bar is built in the

Coffee Shops in Prague

Archa
Letohradská 34, Praha 7
A popular café near the theatre of
the same name
Blatouch-Café Bar
Vězeňská 4, Praha 1
One of the busiest and trendiest
cafés in town. Can be hard to get a
seat but worth the effort.
Café Milena
Staroměstské nám. 22, Praha 1
Reasonable prices for Old Town
Square: coffees, pastries and ice
cream.
Evropa
Václavské nám. 29, Praha 1
Bask in an art nouveau jewel;
sometimes there's a cover charge
for live music.

Globe Coffeehouse and Bookstore
Janovského 14, Praha 1
The coffee house for Prague's
European and American expats, the
Globe offers a light selection of
acceptable food. Coffees and
desserts are best. Settle in for the
afternoon and read the newspapers
that are provided.
Gulu Gulu
Betlémské náměstí 8, Praha 1
Centrally located, lively bar. Popular
with locals and visitors alike.
Hogo Fogo kavárna
Salvátorská 4, Praha 1
A trendy and popular coffee bar with
a pleasant, relaxed atmosphere.
Kavárna Obecní dům
Obecní dům, Nám.

Republiky 5, Praha 1
Prague's flagship art nouveau
building plays host to a classic
central European coffee house.
Recently restored interior.
Kavárna Praha-Roma
V jámě 5, Praha 1
Elegant, old-style Italian café,
appetising and unusual pastries.
Kavárna Slavia
Národní Třída 1, Praha 1
The king of Prague coffee bars, the
Slavia was once a favourite of the
dissidents and has recently been
restored to its former glory.
Plha Café
Klimentská 2, Praha 1
Fair selection of coffees and,
amazingly, no smoking allowed.

walls of the former Ursuline convent, and serves wines from Moravia and Slovakia.

Lobkovická vinárna
Vlašská 17, Praha 1
Tel: (02) 530 185
An historic wine bar in the Lesser Quarter, dating from the 19th century; serving wines from Mělník.

Makarská
Malostranské nám. 2, Praha 1
Tel: (02) 531 573
Balkan specialities and wines. High-quality restaurant.

Slovácká vícha
Michalská 6, Praha 1
Tel: (02) 263 815
Bzenec wine served.

U mecenáše
Malostranské nám. 10, Praha 1
Tel: (02) 533 881
There was an inn here as long ago as 1604; today this wine bar is among the nicest in the city.

U červeného lva
Nerudova 41, Praha 1
Tel: (02) 5753 3832–3
A fine Malá Strana bar with professional service and the standard selection of Czech wines.

U labutí
Hradčanské nám. 11, Praha 1
Tel: (02) 2051 1191–2
Exclusive wine bar near the castle, serving South Moravian wines.

U patrona
Dražického nám. 4, Praha 1
Tel: (02) 5314 97–9
Cosy atmosphere, South Moravian wine. Very high quality and pricey.

U pavouka
Celetná 17, Praha 1
Tel: (02) 2481 1436
Historic wine bar with Gothic and Renaissance halls; serves wines from South Moravia.

U sudu
Vodičkova 10. Praha 1
Tel: (02) 2223 2207
One of the most popular wine bars in central Prague. Set on three levels it is popular with all age groups but especially students.

U zelené žáby
U radnice 8, Praha 1
Tel: (02) 2423 4474
Beautifully appointed, this establishment has poured wine from Velké Žernoseky since the 15th century.

BRATISLAVA

Wine Bars

In this city of wine, the fruit of the vine and not beer is the most popular drink. Viticulture here has a long tradition stretching back to the Middle Ages, and even connoisseurs will find something to delight their palette. Most of the wine sold in Bratislava is dry white; it can be found in the traditional streetside pubs, the so-called *Viechas*, which are not only found in the small wine villages in the country, but also in the centre of Bratislava itself, for example on the Vysoká and the Obchodná ul. In

October, after the harvest, there are large quantities of new wine to be found everywhere. The wine bars *(vináreň)* also have extensive menus. Wine bars are open until 11pm, though some stay open longer. They are sometimes closed on Sunday.

Karloveská Viecha u Kadnára
Líščie údolie 108
Tel: (02) 6542 4160
Cosy and friendly.

Kláštorá vináreň
Františkánska 2
Tel: (02) 5443 0430
Pleasant wine bar, good service set in the heart of the old town.

Vináreň pri Kaplnke
Roľnícka 31
Tel: (02) 4371 1161
Friendly service with a decent selection.

Vináreň Veľkí Františkáni,
Františkánske nám. 10
Tel: (02) 5443 3073
Beautiful wine cellar, professional service, a fine selection (especially the Tokaj) and good food.

Vináreň Vysoká 44
Vysoká 44
Tel: (02) 5296 1167
Pleasant surroundings. Frequented by students.

Vinotéka San Francesco
Sedlárska 5
Tel: (02) 5441 4357–62
Perhaps the biggest selection of foreign and domestic wines in the country. Pricey but very high quality. Non smoking.

Pubs and Bars in Bratislava

The selection of pubs in the city has grown enormously in recent years making Bratislava one of the best bets in the region for a good time. The relative dearth of tourists means that the locals tend to be very welcoming to foreigners. In contrast with Prague, the waiter will usually ask for payment as soon as your drinks arrive.

Aligátor, Laurinská ul. 7
Every Thursday live (and loud) blues music. This cellar bar has a wide selection of beers.

Ante portas, Michalská ulica 26

Trendy and young, one of the city's growing list of good-time venues.

El Diablo, Sedlárska ulica
Right next to the Irish pub, this bar has a Mexican theme.

Harley Davidson Saloon,
Rebarborová 1
Hang-out for bikers and almost everyone else. Grilled food is prepared in front of you in the garden in summer.

Kelt, Hviezdoslavovo nám. 26
Busy, often crowded and full of people looking for fun. This is one of the city's trendiest bars.

Koník pub, Mlynské Nivy
Close to the main bus station this bar has a Wild West feel. Serves Czech Budvar amongst others.

Montana's Grizly Bar, Michalská 19
The owner hails from Montana, hence the name. Great selection of beer and superb summer terrace.

Reštaurácia a piváreň Stará sladovňa – Mamut, Cintorínska 32
One of the biggest pubs you'll have ever been to. Service can be slow.

17's Bar, Hviezdoslavovo nám. 17
Small, friendly bar serving some of the best Czech beer in town.

Attractions

Cultural Centres

The cultural centre of the Czech
Republic is undoubtedly Prague.
Artists from other towns and cities
wanting to establish themselves
generally head for the capital,
although a lively small theatre
scene has developed over the past
few years in Brno. Bratislava is the
cultural centre of Slovakia; excellent
opera and ballet are performed at
the Slovakian National Theatre.

The exact times of concert,
opera and theatre performances
can be found in the local calendar
of events available from the tourist
board. They are also advertised on
billboards. Tickets for concerts and
operas in the main internationally
acclaimed venues can be booked in
licensed travel agencies abroad.

Tickets for other events can be
bought in advance at booking
offices, agencies, hotels and
information offices.

Museums

For details of museums in the
Czech and Slovak Republics please
refer to the relevant pages in the
Places section of this guide.

Prague
Antonín Dvořák Museum
(Muzeum Antonína Dvořáka), Villa
Amerika, Ke Karlovu 20, Praha 2
Tel: (02) 298 214
In a beautiful little building, designed
by Kilian Ignaz Dientzenhofer.
Arts and Crafts Museum
(Uměleckoprůmyslové muzeum),
Ulice 17. listopadu 2 (opposite the
Rudolfinum), Praha
The glass collection is probably the
largest in the world.

Bedřch Smetana Museum
(Muzeum Bedřicha Smetany),
Novotného lávka 1, Praha 1
Tel: (02) 2422 9075
Housed in the former waterworks
on the banks of the River Vltava.
Ceremonial Hall, Ulice U starého
hřbitova. Children's art from the
Terezín ghetto.
Crypt Museum of St Francis
Crusaders Square, Křižovnické
náměstí, Praha 1
An interesting exhibition of the
treasures of the medieval order of
the Knights of the Cross.
High Synagogue
Červená Street
Display of sacred textiles.
Historical Military Museum
(Vojenské historické muzeum),
Schwarzenberský palác,
Hradčanské nám., Praha 1
The collection is one of the largest
of its kind in Europe.
Judaic Museum
Different departments of the
National Judaic Museum can be
found in the synagogues of the old
Prague Ghetto.
Klaus Synagogue
Ulice U starého hřbitova
Exhibition of art of Jewish traditions
and customs.
Maisel Synagogue
Maiselova Street
Silver from Czech synagogues.
Museum of Czech Glass
Staroměstské náměstí 27, Praha 1
Display of glassware and view of
working forge.
Museum of the City of Prague
(Muzeum hlavního města Prahy),
Nové sady J. Švermy, Praha 8
The main attraction is the famous
model of the city constructed in
1826–34.
Museum of Czech Music/Bertramka
Mozartova 15, Praha 5
Mozart lived in the Villa Bertramka
when he was in the city.
Náprstek Museum
(Náprstkovo muzeum), Betlémské
nám. 1, Praha 1
Ethnographic exhibits and technical
gadgets are displayed in the
Museum of Asiatic, African and
American Cultures.
National Literature Museum
Památník národního písemnictví,

Strahovské nadvoří 1, Praha 1
Museum of Czech Literature, plus
the Strahov Gospels.
**National Memorial to the Victims
of the Heydrich Terror**
(Orthodox Cathedral of SS Cyril and
Methodius), Resslova 9, Praha 2
View the crypt where paratroopers
of the Czechoslovak army held out
against the SS after assassinating
the detested Nazi governor of
Bohemia and Moravia.
National Museum
Národní Muzeum, Václavské nám.,
Praha 1
Tel: (02) 2423 0485
Predominantly a natural science
museum.
National Technical Museum
(Národní technické muzeum),
Kostelní 42, Praha 7
There are automobile and
locomotive exhibits as well as a
photographic exhibition; the
Astronomy Department contains
sextants from the 16th century.
Old Jewish Cemetery
Ulice U starého hřbitova
Old-New Synagogue
Červená street
Pinkas Synagogue
Široká 23
Monument to victims of the
Holocaust.
State Jewish Museum
Jáchymova 3, Praha 1

Bratislava
Slovakian National Museum
Vajanského nábr. 2
Municipal Museum
Old Town Hall, Primaciálne nám. 2;
Apponyipalais, Radničná 1; St
Michael's Gate, Michalská
Johann Nepomuk Museum
Klobúčnická 2
Treasury of the Franciscan Church
Dibrovo nám

Galleries

Prague
The collections of the **Národní galerie**
(National Gallery) are housed in
several different buildings.
House of the Black Madonna
Celetná 34, Praha 1
Tel: 2421 1732
Permanent exhibition of Czech

cubist art (1911–1919). The building is a modernist masterpiece by Josef Gočár dating from 1911–12. The exhibition includes paintings, sculptures, furniture and ceramics by Gutfreund. Exhibitions of leading exponents of Cubism.

Městská knihovna (City Library)
Mariánské nám. 1, Praha 1
Modern art collection.

Palais Kinsky
Staroměstské nám. 12, Praha 1
The magnificent rococo facade of Palais Kinsky overlooking Old Town Square now houses the National Gallery's rich collection of graphic art, regarded as one of the finest in Europe. Among the prints, drawings, engravings and miniatures are works by Hollar, Rembrandt, Rubens, Picasso, Kokoschka and Mucha.

The Rudolfinian Collection
Hradčany (Second Courtyard), Praha 1
In the 16th century, the collection of Rudolf II was one of the most important in Europe. Partially restored after many losses, it can be seen in the castle gallery.

St Agnes Covent
U milosrdných 17, Praha 1
Czech 19th-century art. Romantic landscapes and portraits form the core of the exhibition which also reveals the influence of the national revival on artists as diverse as Mikoláš Aleš and František Ženíšek. The most gifted artist of this period was Josef Mánes, but visitors may prefer Jakob Schikaneder's evocative scenes of old Prague.

St George's Monastery
Hradčany; Jiřský klášter, Praha 1

Old Czechoslovakian art. The collection of medieval religious painting and sculpture is magnificent and includes many works dating back to the 14th century, widely regarded as a 'golden age'. The portraits of the saints by the Master of the Vyšší Brod Altar and Master Theodoric (two artists active in the reign of Charles IV) once adorned the royal chapel in Karlštejn Castle.

The Sternberg Palace
Hradčanské nám. 15, Praha 1
Houses the National Gallery's impressive collection of European Old Masters. Durer's *Feast of the Rose Garlands* (1506) is possibly the most famous painting in the exhibition, but there are also some fine works by Cranach, Bruegel, El Greco, Goya, Canaletto, Rembrandt and Rubens, two of whose paintings, *Martyrdom of St Thomas* and *St Augustine* were commissioned by the Church of St Thomas in Prague's Lesser Quarter.

Veletržní Palace
Dukelských hrdinů 47, Praha 7
Tel: 2430 1111
This enormous glass-fronted building is a Constructivist masterpiece, designed by Oldřich Tyl and Josef Fuchs for the Prague Trade Fair of 1928. Vincent Kramář, a formidable champion of cubist art, donated the works by Picasso, Braque and Derain, while the paintings by leading Impressionist and post-Impressionist artists were acquired by the state in the 1920s and 1930s with the active

encouragement of the Czech president, Tomáš Masaryk. The priceless collection includes works by Renoir, Monet, Degas, Seurat, Van Gogh, Gauguin and Cézanne. The Veletržní also has outstanding canvases by other leading members of the 20th-century avant-garde: Chagall, Vlaminck, Dufy and Leger, among others.

Zbraslav Castle, outside Prague (April–November only). Czech 19th- and 20th-century sculpture.

Bratislava
Art Gallery of the Fine Arts Foundation
Michalská 7
Art gallery with various exhibitions.
Galleries of the City of Bratislava
Archbishop's Palace, Františkánske nám. 11, Mirbach Palais, Pálffy Palais.
Slovakian National Gallery
Rázusovo nábr. 2

Theatre & Opera

Prague
Archa Theatre (Divadlo Archa)
Na Poříčí 26, Praha 1
Tel: (02) 2171 6111
New, progressive theatre with emphasis on the avant-garde. Visiting foreign performers.
Divadlo na Vinohradech
Nám. Míru 7, Praha 2
Tel: (02) 9655 0111
Divadlo v Celetné
Celetná 17, Praha 1
Tel: (02) 2481 2762
Mime theatre in the Czech tradition.

Buying Tickets in Prague

Prague has a very rich and varied cultural palette. To get tickets, it is recommended to go directly to the box office in order to get the best price. At the box office you may be dismayed to see the sign *Vyprodáno* – Sold out. But don't let you that put you off. If you are polite and point out that you came all the way just to see it then there's a good chance you'll be successful. It is also possible to get tickets through tourist

agencies, but expect to pay a hefty commission.
Ticket agencies in Prague:
Bohemia Ticket International
Malé Náměstí 13, Praha 1
Tel: (02) 2422 7832
Na Příkopě 16, Praha 1
Tel: (02) 2421 5031.
PIS
Pražská informační služba (Prague Information Service),
Staroměstské nám. 28, Praha 1
Tel: (02) 2448 2018

Tiketpro
Štěpánská 61, Praha 1 (located in the Lucerna Passage)
Tel: (02) 2481 4020
Ticketpro
Salvátorská 10, Praha 1
Tel: (02) 2481 4020
Top Theatre Tickets
Celetná 13, Praha 1
Tel: (02) 232 2536
Box offices for the National Theatre and Laterna Magika are in the glass buildings of Národní třída.

Laterna Magika
Národní třída 4, Praha 1
Tel: (02) 2491 4129
Laterna Magika performances.
National Marionette Theatre
(Národní divadlo marionet)
Žatecká 1, Praha 1
Tel: (02) 232 3429
Puppet theatre for all ages.
National Theatre (Národní divadlo),
Národní třída 2, Praha 1
Tel: (02) 2491 3437
Opera, ballet and theatre.
Ta Fantastika Theatre Prague,
Karlova 8, Praha 1
Tel: (02) 2422 9078
Theatre on the Balustrades
(Divadlo na Zábradlí),
Anenské nám. 5, Praha 1
Tel: (02) 2222 2026
Famous as the theatre where
President Havel worked; his plays
are still performed here. Theatre
and mime.

Cinema in Prague

Interesting English-language
movies and classics are shown
at Dlabačov, Bělohorská 24,
Praha 6 (beside the hotel), tel:
(02) 311 5328, and Ponrepo
Film Club, Národní 4, Praha 1,
tel: (02) 2422 7137. The latter
sometimes offers silent-film
classics with live piano
accompaniment.

Bratislava
Divadlo Astorka "Korzo 90"
Suché Mýto 17, 814 99 Bratislava
Tel: (02) 533 2350
Malá scéna (Little Stage),
Dostojevského rad 7, Bratislava
Nová scéna Bratislava
Živnostenská 1, 812 14 Bratislava
Tel: (02) 5292 1139
Radošinské naivné divadlo
Istropolis, umelecké a kongresové
centrum, Trnavské mýto, 832 21
Bratislava
Tel: (02) 526 3169/526 4291
Slovakian National Theatre
Gorkého 4, Bratislava
Tel: (02) 533 3083
Opera and ballet stage: Gorkého 2,
Bratislava, tel: (02) 533 5085
Theatre stage: Divadlo P. O.

Hviezdoslava, Gorkého 17,
Bratislava, tel: (02) 364 011
Štúdio "S"
Nám. 1. mája 5, 811 06 Bratislava
Tel: (02) 321 130/321 584

Concert Halls

Prague
Bertramka
Mozartova 169, Praha 5
Tel: (02) 5731 7465/5731 8461
Beware: this is one of the most
expensive chamber concert
venues in the city, but it is the
main venue for the Mozart
festival.
Municipal House
Smetana Hall (Obecní dům), nám.
Republiky 5, Praha 1
Tel: (02) 2200 2100
The home of the Prague
Symphony.
Palace of Culture (Palác kultury)
Květná 65, Praha 4, 5
Tel: (02) 6117 2736
Prague Chamber Opera
(Komorní opera Praha)
Novotného lávka 1, Praha 1
Tel: (02) 2451 1026
Light opera fantasies based on
works of Mozart.
Rudolfinum
Nám Jana Palacha, Praha 1
Tel: (02) 2489 3352/3111
The permanent home of the Czech
Philharmonic.
St Agnes Monastery
(Anežský klášter)
U milosrdných, 17, Praha 1
State Opera (Státní opera)
Wilsonova 8, Praha 1
Tel: (02) 2422 7683/7693
    See Nightlife, page 350
section for contemporary music
venues.

Bratislava
Nová scéna (New Stage),
Kollárovo nám.
Slovenská filharmónia
Medená 3, 816 01 Bratislava
Tel: 544 333 51–3
Štúdio Novej scény
(Studio of the New Stage).
Suché Mýto 17
Štúdio S
Nám. 1 mája 5
Tel: (02) 321 130/321 584

Music Festivals

Prague
The international and internationally
famous **Prague Spring Festival**
takes place every May/June.
Concerts are held in historical
rooms and churches, including St
Vitus's Cathedral and the exquisite
Spanish Hall. While certain key
concerts are sold out as soon as
tickets become available, a
surprising number of tickets can be
bought at the last minute. The
Prague Spring box office is located
at Hellichova 18, Praha 1, tel: (02)
5732 0468. **Mozart's Prague** is
another late-June/early-July festival
that attracts international
performers. Most concerts are held
in Bertramka and the Lichtenstein
Palace. The **Agharta Jazz Festival**,
usually held in June, has brought
jazz greats such as Michel
Petrucciani and Pat Metheny to
Prague. Agharta Jazz Centrum,
Krakovská 5, Praha 1, tel: (02)
2421 2914/2221 1275.

Bratislava
The monthy magazine *Kam v
Bratislave* outlines cultural events
in the city. The most important
perennial events are the Spring
Music Festival, the International Art
Festival in September and the Jazz
Festival in October. Performances
of opera and ballet take place in the
National Theatre, orchestral
concerts in the Redoute building of
the Slovakian Philharmonic.

Czech Sightseeing
PRAGUE

It is not difficult to find your
bearings in Prague, especially as
the most important sights can be
reached on foot. The city's small
centre (Praha 1) is divided into the
historic quarters of Malá Strana
(Lesser Quarter), Staré Město (Old
Town), and Nové Město (New Town).
The latter is centred around
Wenceslas Square and extends to
the road Na příkopě. Adjacent and
to the north is the Staré Město,
which extends across the Old Town

Square (Staroměstské náměstí) and the right bank of the Vltava and the Charles Bridge. The picturesque Malá Strana lies on the left of the river. Two other self-contained districts are the Josefov (Jewish Quarter) and Hradčany, the Castle Quarter.

It's a good idea to allow yourself at least three days for a visit to Prague. Many agencies, including the state travel agency Čedok, not only organise tours of the city but cultural events as well. The 3-hour city tour "Historic Prague" is run throughout the year. Departure points are the âedok bus park in the Bílkova 6 (opposite the Intercontinental Hotel) and the hotels Panorama, Forum and Atrium.

Private tours of the city are organised by the Prague Information service (PIS), as well as travel agencies (see Useful Addresses, page 326), and tours of Hradčany are organised by Informační středisko pražského hradu, Praha 1 (Hradčany), Vikářská 37 (on the northern side of St Vitus's cathedral), tel: 2101/3368.

The following daily tour programme is designed to aid visitors who are only in Prague for a short stay but who prefer to make their own way around rather than join an organised tour.

Day 1

It is suggested that your first day's sightseeing is spent strolling through the winding streets and alleyways of the Old Town to the Jewish Cemetery and the Old Town Square. The day can be concluded not far from the Powder Tower with a classy dinner at the Hotel Paříž.

The tour commences at Wenceslas Square and leads via the Na můstku right into the Old Town, and the main sights to be seen here are as follows: the Flea Market – Old Town Hall – Old Town Square with the Jan Hus Monument – Karlova ulice – Clam-Gallas Palais – Husova ulice – Bethlehem Chapel – Náprstkova ulice – Bank of the Vltava with the Smetana Museum – Old Town Bridge Tower and the Crusaders' Church – Clementinum

and the Church of St Saviour – Platnéřská ulice – Maiselova ulice – Jewish quarter with the old Jewish Cemetery, Klaus Synagogue, Old-New Synagogue and the Jewish Town Hall.

The visitor can now pause for lunch and has the choice between the Kosher restaurant in the former lower council chamber of the Town Hall, the wine bar U Golema (Maiselova 8) or the restaurant U Barona (Pařížská 19). After lunch go back along the Pařížská to the Old Town Square with the Church of St Nicholas, Palais Kinsky and the Týn Church. Then into Štupartská ulice – Church of St James – Celetná ulice – Powder Tower – Municipal House. Reward yourself at the end of a long day of sightseeing with a sumptuous dinner in the Paříž restaurant next door.

Day 2

The second day of sightseeing might lead you over the Charles Bridge to the Lesser Quarter and up to Hradčany. This day's tour could end in a typical Lesser Quarter pub serving both beer and meals.

The starting point is at the Old Town Bridge Tower. Having walked across the Charles Bridge, you'll be greeted by the Lesser Quarter Bridge Towers. The tour continues into the Lázeňská ulice – the Church of St Mary in Chains – Velokopřevorské náměstí – Island of Kampa – the Maltese Square with the Nostiz Palais (housing the Ministry of Education and the Arts), and into Karmelitská ulice with the Vrbovský palác (No. 25). Along Mostecká ulice (Bridge Street) and to the Lesser Quarter Square with the Church of St Nicholas. Here it's time for a break, before the walk up to the castle. There are the two pubs, the U Glaubiců and the U Schnellů, or the café in the middle of the square.

Then into the Neruda Alley and up to the Hradčanské náměstí and on: Loretánská ulice – Loreto Shrine – Nový Svět – back to Schwarzenberg Palais – Archbishops' Palace – Prague Castle with St Vitus's Cathedral and

the Royal Palace – St George's Basilica – Mihulka Tower – Golden Alley – Lobkovic Palais – Black Tower – Old Castle Steps – Valdštejnská ulice. And there we reach the Valdštejnská Hospoda (Tomášská 16, tel: (02) 5753 1759), our tip for a hearty Bohemian meal. If you don't get a place there, we suggest you go down the Tomášská to the Lesser Quarter Square, turn left at the corner to arrive at the venerable pub U Svatého Tomáše in Latenská 12, (tel: 02-2451 0016).

Day 3

The third day's excursion could take you across Wenceslas Square and the New Town, with the National Theatre, the Vltava Quay and Charles Square. Dinner is a choice of either good, solid Bohemian food in U Fleků, or refined Russian dining in the Volha.

The tour begins at the equestrian statue of St Wenceslas in front of the National Museum and continues down Wenceslas Square past the classic art nouveau hotels – Evropa, Zlatá Husa, and Ambassador – the Alfa Palais (No. 28) and the Peterka House (No. 12) to the Koruna Palace at the end. Do an about-face and amble back along the other side of the square until you've reached about the halfway

Guides & Interpreters

Čedok agencies and the various tourist information centres located in individual cities (for example PIS in Prague and BIS in Bratislava) all offer foreign language-speaking tour guides to travel groups as well as to independent travellers for day excursions or longer trips. They can also furnish you with an interpreter or translator upon request. It is not unusual in Prague to "rent" a tour guide who then accompanies you on foot through the city. The price for an hour of this particular kind of service is about 70 crowns per person.

point, and then left into the Jindřišská ulice with the Hotel Palace; then along the Panská ulice – Na příkopě – Powder Tower and back to Wenceslas Square. Then continue into the Jungmannovo náměstí with the Church of St Mary of the Snows – Národní třída with the Maj department store – Kanka House (No. 16) and the Church of St Ursula (No. 8). For lunch, the monastery wine cellar offers a selection of tasty wines and dishes, or failing that there is the pub U Medvídků just around the corner (Na Perštýně 7, opposite the Máj department store).

The end of the Národní třída is completely dominated by the National Theatre. The Café Slávia stands opposite. Now walk upstream along the bank of the Vltava. Your route: Slavic Island – Mánes House – Jiráskův Bridge where the Vltava cruisers pull in and where there is a small pub with terrace called "Vltava" – Resslova ulice – the Church of St Wenceslas – the Church of Sts Cyril and Methodius Church – Charles Square with the "Faust House"; the Church of St John on the Rocks is located to the south, opposite the Emmaus Monastery; back via the Church of St Ignatius and the New Town Hall which provides a counterpoint to the Faust House.

Especially in the late afternoon the U Fleků is the perfect place to sit back and take the weight off your feet (turn left by the Town Hall into the Myslíkova and take the second right into the Křemencova). But for those who don't like the noise here, perhaps a better choice is U Medvídků, Na Perštýně 7. Praha 1, tel: (02) 2422 0930.

AROUND PRAGUE

Čedok organises a number of day-long excursions into the environs of Prague. The tours include: Castles in Bohemia, Southern Bohemia, Gothic Architectural Jewels in Bohemia, Attractive Central Bohemia, Vineyards of Bohemia and Cruises on the Vltava. The buses depart from the Panorama Hotel at 8am, the Forum Hotel at 8.10am, the Atrium Hotel at 8.20am and from Čedok, Bílkova 6, at 8.40am. Tickets may be purchased from the hotel receptions as well as from Čedok, a.s. Prague Na Příkopě 18 111 35 Praha 1, tel: (02) 2419 7111; www.cedok.cz; Prague Ruzyně Airport, tel: (02) 2011 4421.

For those with their own car there is a host of attractions in the vicinity of the Czech capital, all of which are easy to reach. Here is a selection:

Průhonice: Renaissance palace with botanical garden, reached via the motorway to Brno. The palace contains one of the largest herbarium collections in the world.

Konopiště: Palace with rose garden, bathing pool and English-style park. The original 14th-century castle was converted in the 18th century and served as a hunting lodge for the Austrian archduke Franz Ferdinand until his assassination in Sarajevo. There is a weapons collection with over 5,000 pieces.

Slapy Dam: A popular summer excursion for the people of Prague, located in the Vltava valley to the south of the city.

Karlštejn: Built by Charles IV in 1348 as the representative residence of the king and the depository of the crown jewels. Situated to the southwest of Prague, it is considered to be one of the most beautiful castles in Europe. It can be reached from the motorway in the direction of Plzeň as far as Beroun.

Koněprusy: Caverns near Karlštejn castle, discovered in 1950. Remains of prehistoric man as well as a coin-forging workshop dating from the 15th century.

Křivoklát: 15th-century castle set in an extensive area of forest which has been adopted by UNESCO in the programme "Man and the Biosphere". In the summer there are performances of music and theatre.

Rakovník: One of the oldest towns in Central Bohemia in the middle of

The Natural World

Apart from historical sights, there are plenty of interesting things to see in Prague. Here are some ideas:

Prague Zoo is situated in Praha 7, Troja, and can be reached by metro line C, getting out at Nádraží Holešovice station and continuing on the 112 bus. A visit to the zoo can also take in nearby Troja Castle. Founded in 1931, today the zoo is home to 2,000 animals of 600 species. The breeding of the Przewalski horse is of international importance: Pražská zoologická zahrada, Praha 7 Troja, U Trojského zámku 3. Opening hours: October–March 7am–4pm; April 7am–5pm; May 7am–6pm; June–September 7am–7pm.

The Botanical Gardens are part of the university and are to be found in the Nové Město not far from the Church of St Nepomuk on the Rocks: Botanická zahrada, Praha 1, Na slupi. Open 7am–7pm.

Prague Observatory, Praha 1, Petřín 205, next to the the the cable car station on Petřín Hill. Open daily except Monday: January, February, October, November, December 6–8pm; March, September 7–9pm; April, August 8–10pm; May, June, July 9–11pm.

the hop growing area. Its historic centre contains a number of important monuments.

Kladno: Historic mining town to the northwest of Prague (past Ruzyně Airport). There is a baroque palace with a museum of mining.

Lidice: A memorial to the Nazi massacre of 1942 in which all menfolk were shot and women rounded up and taken away to Ravensbrück concentration camp. The surviving children were dispersed throughout Germany to be renamed and raised as Germans. In an action that formed part of the Germans' brutal reprisals for the assassination of the deputy leader of the SS,

Reinhard "The Hangman" Heydrich, by the Resistance, the village was burned to the ground. Situated between Prague and Ladno.

Veltrusy: Baroque palace with original interior, the Veltrusy contains a collection of Asian porcelain, crystal and tapestries. It can be reached by following the E55 in the direction of Teplice. Nearby is the village of **Nelahzeves** with the house in which Antonín Dvořák was born.

Mělník: A wine-producing town at the confluence of the Vltava and the Labe (Elbe), whose origins go back to the 9th century.

Mladá Boleslav: Home of Škoda cars. Přemysl castle dates from the 10th century. Ancient centre containing interesting examples of avant-garde blocks of flats from the 1930s. It is situated to the northeast of Prague along the E65.

Přerov nad Labem: Open-air museum of vernacular architecture located to the east of Prague on the E67 towards Poděbrady.

Kutná hora (Kuttenberg): In the 13th and 14th century this town became the economic centre of Bohemia on account of its silver mines, and was the site of the royal mint. The Brass Music Festival "Kmochs Kolín" takes place here in June. The imposing Church of St Barbara was designed by Peter Parler. It is situated some 16 km (10 miles) to the southeast of Kolín.

Český Šternberk: One of the best-preserved castles in the country, dating from the 13th century. Its location on a clifftop above the River Sázava made it impregnable for centuries. Musical performances are held here in the summer. It lies to the southeast of Prague along the E50.

Terezín (Theresienstadt): The fortress town of Terezín, which never withstood a war, became notorious under the Nazis as a ghetto and concentration camp for Czechoslovak Jews and other so-called undesirables. It was not a "killing factory" as such, like Auschwitz, but for the most part was used as a holding prison until the inmates could be sent in cattle cars to Auschwitz and other concentration camps. Of the 140,000 inmates who passed through Terezín, 120,000 died. The old prison now houses a well-maintained museum documenting the atrocities.

Slovakian Sights

BRATISLAVA

Bounded by the Danube to the south, the historical city centre is easy to get around. The urban motorway, which connects the city to Vienna in the west, Brno and Prague in the north and Central Slovakia in the east, divides the Old Town from the Castle. But it can be crossed by bridges and subways and so both parts of the city can easily be explored on foot. For trips out to the suburbs there are trams and trolley buses. One should allow at least two days to see the sights of Bratislava. Following are suggestions for two round tours of the Old Town, and a stroll through the New Town.

Brno

Visitors based in the Moravian capital of Brno have a number of interesting sights in the vicinity, which include:

Slavkov (Austerlitz): It was here, in 1805, that Napoleon defeated the Austrians under Franz I and the Russians under Alexander I at the so-called "Battle of the Three Emperors".

Pernštejn Castle: This fairy-tale castle is one of the largest and best-preserved in the entire Czech Republic.

Moravian Karst: An extensive system of caves, grottoes and underground streams, most impressive around Blansko in the north and including the spectacular Macocha Abyss.

Day 1

From St Michael's Gate to the cathedral and up to the castle. From the gate, walk up the Michalská, past the university library to arrive in the Jiráskova with the Palais Leopold de Pauli and the Palais of Marshal Pálffy, as well as the Academia Istropolitana. At the rococo palace of Count Erdödy turn right as far as St Martin's Cathedral. The castle is reached via its impressive staircase. Return via the north side of the cathedral through the Kapitulská with the Provost's Palais (No. 19), the Collegium Emmericanum and the Canon's House. There is a good fish restaurant in the Prepoštská, the U zlatého kapra (the Golden Carp). Pass the Convent of St Clare and turn right through the narrow Baštová to arrive at St Michael's Gate once again.

Day 2

From St Michael's Gate via the town hall and the Bishop's Palace to the Danube Promenade. Opposite the Baštová, the narrow Zámočnická leads to the eastern part of the Old Town. You will come to the Dibrovo námestie with the Franciscan Church and the Palais Mirbach. From there the route continues to the Hlavné námestie, with the Jesuit Church, the Town Hall and the Fountain of Roland. The Kostolná ulica leads to the Bishop's Palace. Further towards the Danube is the Slovakian National Theatre and a block further is the Danube Promenade with the Slovakian National Gallery and the Slovakian National Museum.

Day 3

A stroll through the New Town. In the northeast of the Old Town is the Square of the Slovakian National Uprising, the actual city centre. It is bounded in the south by Kamenné Square and in the north by the Poštová pedestrian precinct, which is crossed by the Obchodná shopping street. From the Hotel Forum one can visit the elegant villa district of Bratislava, with fine late-19th century houses and the Slavín Monument.

AROUND BRATISLAVA

The environs of Bratislava offer a number of attractions, of which the following are only a selection:

Devín Castle: Situated 10 km (6 miles) to the west of the city at the confluence of the Morava and the Danube, this famous ruin can also be reached by riverboat. There has been a castle on the site ever since the days of the kingdom of Great Moravia. The present building dates from the 13th century, and the hill on which it stands offers magnificent views of the surrounding countryside. It is the site of an annual folklore festival held in July.

Senec: Lying 24 km (15 miles) to the east of Bratislava on main road No. 61, this is a popular resort with its own artificial lake. On the way is the excellently preserved baroque palace at Bernolákovo.

Železná studnička: A centuries-old mineral spa situated 5 km (3 miles) to the north of Bratislava.

Stupava: 18 km (11 miles) to the north of the city, Stupava boasts a Renaissance palace as well as a fascinating pottery museum and the remains of a Roman camp.

Malé Karpaty (Little Carpathians): These hills are famous for the cultivation of wine. Wine villages are strung out along road No. 502, the most famous of which are Jur pri Bratislave with its Gothic church of St George, Pezinok with its Gothic parish church and Renaissance palace, and Modra with its vintners' school and research institute.

Komárno: Situated at the confluence of the Váh and the Danube, 104 km (65 miles) to the southeast of Bratislava, this old port is well worth a visit on account of its beautiful old town and impressive fortifications, which are best viewed from the river.

Festivals

Czech Republic

A visit to Prague could be combined with a visit to one of the countless festivals or sporting events that take place in the country throughout the year. Here is a selection (approximate dates only):

December/January
Prague: Prague Winter – a theatre and music festival.

March
Karlovy Vary: jazz festival.

May/June
Prague: Prague Spring Music Festival.

May/July
Mariánské Lázně: International music festival.

May/August
Luhačovice: Concertino Praga – debut performances from a variety of talented young musicians.

June
Kolín – Central Bohemia: International Brass Music Festival "Kmochs Kolín".
Poděbrady: International Brass Band festival.
Teplice: Shostakovich festival.
Strakonitz/Bohemian Forest: Folklore Festival.
Mozart's Prague – international orchestras perform Mozart's works (June to early July)

June/July
Strážice – Southern Moravia: International meeting of different folk groups in ethnic costume, with traditional dancing performances and music.
Luhačovice: Janáček festival.

June/September
Teplice: Castle music.

July
Karlovy Vary: International Film Festival – alternate years.

Chrudim – Eastern Bohemia: Puppet Festival.
Znojmo – Southern Moravia: Royal Festival – medieval tournaments and events.
Železný Brod – Eastern Bohemia: Folklore Festival.

August
Domažlice – Western Bohemia: Chode Festival, a festival of the culturally independent border people with dancing, music and bagpipes.
Mariánské Lázně: Chopin Music Festival.

September
Žatec – Northern Bohemia: Žatec Hops Festival (middle of September).
Karlovy Vary: Dvořák autumn festival.

September/October
Teplice: Harvest Festival.

October
Pardubice, Eastern Bohemia: Big international steeplechase – one of the most gruelling and notorious steeplechases in the world.

Slovakia

Gay film festival Bratislava/ different times of the year each year.

June
Rožňava – Eastern Slovakia: Hungarian Folklore Festival (second half of June).
Trenčianske Teplice – Central Slovakia: Art Film, international film festival.
Svidník – Eastern Slovakia: Ukrainian Festival (end of June).
Terchová – Malá Fatra: Jánošík Festival in commemoration of the man referred to as the Slovakian Robin Hood (last weekend).

July/August
Východná – Central Slovakia: The most colourful and lively festival of ethnic costumes and folklore to be found in Slovakia.

October
Bratislava: International Jazz Festival (end of October).

Nightlife

General

More than a decade after the Velvet Revolution, the nightlife in Prague has been transformed beyond all recognition and is now at least as exciting as in any similar-sized city in the West. Bratislava is still some way behind but big changes are underway there as well. Apart from the dozens and dozens of nightclubs and late-night bars Prague offers a fine selection of jazz clubs. The Reduta Jazz Club and the Rock Café (both in Prague) are international meeting places for music enthusiasts. Prices vary but generally a night out on the town in either Prague or Bratislava will come to a mere fraction of what you are used to paying back home.

Prague

Nightclubs and Discos

If you like hanging out with German tourists, prostitutes and black marketeers, the discos on Wenceslas Square are clearly the places for you. You will see old-style strobe lights in the first or second floors of the buildings as you walk up and down the bottom half of the square. Take your pick – they are much of a muchness. For those who like the more mainstream clubs a selection of the best in the city follows. Prague is rapidly gaining a reputation as the good-time capital of central Europe. Don't miss out. Facilities are usually up to Western standards and most clubs have bouncers. It is common, and sometimes obligatory, to leave your coat and bags in the cloakroom. You will be charged a token fee for the pleasure. Admission prices vary but most fall within a range of 50–200 crowns and some are free.

Jo's Garáž
Malostranské nám. 7
Praha 1
Tel: 5753 4976
Jo's "garage" is the consistently packed dance space of the expat institution Jo's Bar upstairs. A DJ spins pop hits until the wee hours.

Klub Lávka
Novotného lávka 1
Praha 1
Tel: 2421 4797
Open 24 hours a day, seven days a week, this raucous entertainment complex near Charles Bridge attracts all kinds for dancing, drinking, and food (Italian and American). The disco (house, pop, Latin American) is on the lower level.

La Habana Club
Míšeňská 12
Praha 1
Tel: 5731 5104
Almost like a visit to Cuba, with hot salsa on the soundtrack and inventive rum concoctions to drink.

Radost FX
Bělehradská 120
Praha 2
Tel: 2425 4776
Still the king of dance clubs, with animal-print furniture, Prague's most attractive waiting staff, and top local and international DJs. Gay night "hot house" parties are held one night a week; call for details.

Roxy
Dlouhá třída 33
Praha 1
Tel: 2481 0951
The best DJs in Prague play in this old converted theatre, with occasional live music and films.

XT3
Pod Plynojemem 5
Praha 8–Karlín
Tel: 9614 8871
A small, not-so-well-kept secret catering to aficionados of electronic dance music, leaning towards drum'n'bass, break beat, cool jazz and trance.

Jazz

Agha RTA Jazz Centrum
Krakovská 5
Praha 1
Tel: 2221 1275

There are now at least a dozen clubs in Prague where you can gamble your money in the company of a special breed of *nouveau riche* locals, many of whom have earned their money on the black market and need to launder it. They take the matter very seriously indeed. Only foreigners give tips to the croupiers. Bets are placed in US dollars. The casinos are open from 9pm–4am. The two listed below are a safe bet.

Blue Diamond Casino, Hilton Hotel, Pobřežní 1, Praha 8.
Casino Admiral Bohemia, Prague Congress Centre, Praha 4. Open daily 5pm–5am.

This intimate (some say cramped) cellar space off Wenceslas Square offers some of the top local jazz acts, beginning at 9pm each evening. The acoustics are excellent; be sure to arrive early, as the best seats go fast. The on-site CD shop is Prague's best for jazz recordings.

Golem Club
Na Perštýně 18
Praha 1
Tel: 2222 0677
A businessmen's club known colloquially as the "Millionaires' Club", this comfortable and relatively smoke-free venue hosts occasional jazz of a high standard.

Jazz club U Staré paní
Michalská 9
Praha 1
Tel: 2422 8090
Popular jazz and supper club; musicians sometimes from abroad.

Jazz Club Železná
Železná 16
Praha 1
Tel: 2423 9697
This performance space off Old Town Square presents a variety of adventurous musical acts, but focuses mainly on jazz and world music. The Sunday afternoon jamming sessions to accompany poetry readings in English and Czech are popular.

Malostranská beseda
Malostranské nám. 21
Praha 1
Tel: 5753 2092
A popular venue for some of the best in local blues, jazz and folk.
Metropolitan Jazz Club
Jungmannova 14
Praha 1
Tel: 2494 7777
Reliable locale for swing and Dixieland jazz.
Reduta
Národní třída 20
Praha 1
Tel: 2491 2246
Dark, increasingly shabby perennial favourite with the tourist crowd. The same jazz groups may be enjoyed at better clubs elsewhere in Prague.
U Malého Glena
Karmelitská 23
Praha 1
Tel: 5753 1717
Intimate basement club and a hip bar with good acoustics.

Rock and Other Music Clubs
Klub Delta
Vlastina 887
Praha 6
Tel: 3331 1398
Hard, gloomy rock; worth the trek to this distant Prague neighbourhood only for those who like their music loud and live.
Klub Hrob
Sokolovská 144
Praha 8-Karlín

Tel: 684 0263
"The Grave" offers live rock nightly, and throws in a popular once-a-week film screening along the lines of *Mad Max* or *A Clockwork Orange*.
Lucerna Music Bar
Štěpánská 61
Praha 1
Tel: 2421 7108
Big, shabby space off Wenceslas Square pulls in locals and tourists for a varied programme of rock, pop, jazz and/or blues. Occasional concerts by major performers on European tours are a draw throughout the year.
Palác Akropolis
Kubelíkova 27
Praha 3-Žižkov
Tel: 2271 2287
This converted theatre in a working-class neighbourhood is a relaxed venue for high-quality music of all kinds, especially Gypsy tunes and world-music acts. It is also the venue for major foreign bands who'd like to do a "small club date" while in Prague.
Rock Café
Národní třída 20
Praha 1
Tel: 2491 4414
Rock, rock and more rock; its location on National Avenue means, however, that the clientèle tends to be touristy and generally undiscriminating.

Gay Prague
"A" Klub
Milíčova 32
Praha 3
Tel: 9000 1748
Mostly women; women only on Fridays. Otherwise, men are welcome provided they have a female escort. Comfortable, relaxed club for dancing, talking, flirting. The decor is by local female artists.
Piano Bar
Milešovská 10
Praha 3-Vinohrady
Tel: 627 5467
Gay and lesbian. Open only until 10pm. Eclectic clientèle enjoys drinks, snacks, good talk. Gay and lesbian reading material is also available for browsing through.
Pinocchio
Seifertova 3, Praha 3
Tel: 2271 0773
A newly remodelled, trendy club catering to men of all ages. Pinocchio is well known to foreign visitors, and features a lounge, full bar and dance club. Open all night.
U Střelce
Karolíny Světlé 12
Praha 1
Mixed. Midnight "Travesty" (transvestite) cabaret every Friday and Saturday. Popular and most recent incarnation of the Střelec series of Prague gay clubs. Dancing and carousing.

Nightlife in Bratislava

There is not as much nightlife in the Slovak capital as there is in the Bohemian metropolis, but things are changing fast. New clubs and bars are springing up all over the place. If you're not sure where to go your best bet is probably the Irish Pub just off the Old Square. It is a great place to meet people who will recommend the best current venues in town and may even take you along with them. Buy them a Slivovica and see what happens!
A selection of the best clubs currently open follows:

Charlie's Pub
Špitálska 4. Bratislava. Tel: (02) 5292 5139. For years this was the only place to go out dancing for most people. Still offers a great atmosphere but gets very crowded and it's noisy.
Cirkus Barok
Pri Dunaji. Bratislava. Partying goes on well into the night on this club right on the Danube river. Highly rated by locals and foreigners alike.
Harley-Davidson Pub
Rebarborová 1. Bratislava. A 10-minute taxi ride from the centre but well worth it. Has strippers – male

and female – on some nights and plenty of music. Raucous.
Jalta,
Gorkého 15. Bratislava. A blast from the past right in the centre of town just past the National Theatre. If you want to see what nightclubs were like under communism, drop in.
Kráter
Vysoká ul. Bratislava. Well-run, Western-style club with good live music and a restaurant upstairs.
Raiders Café and Extreme Club,
Bajkalská ul. Bratislava. 10 minutes from the centre by taxi. If you like dancing this is the place for you.

Shopping

Prague

Shopping in Prague is rapidly becoming indistinguishable from shopping in any western European capital. There is still some catching up to do but advances have been such that you can more or less rely on being able to find anything you want. The main supermarket in the city centre is Tesco, located right next to the Národní Třída metro station. Other supermarkets and hypermarkets are to be found on the outskirts of the city.

Many Western visitors come looking for bargains in the antiques shops. But beware. The days of the wordly wise Westerner taking advantage of local ignorance about the true value of their antiques are long gone. You should also be aware that the export of items of domestic historical significance is subject to strict controls. Most antique dealers will be used to the problem and should be able to advise you on how to get a permit.

Bohemian glass is also a big favourite and there are dozens of outlets in the city centre. Shop around because there are bargains to be found.

If you are looking for souvenirs, the vendors on Charles Bridge or the market on Old Town Square are good bets. Since Prague is nothing if not picturesque, hand drawn sketchings or paintings of the main sights may make for good and inexpensive options. Marionettes and costume jewellery are also on sale in the boutiques leading to and from the Old Town Square as well as elsewhere. Classical music buffs can also take advantage of decent quality and low price CDs.

As far as local produce is concerned, a Prague ham or a stick of salami may be a nice idea. In terms of drinks, a bottle of Czech Becherovka or Moravian Slivovice represent distinctively local and cheap options.

If you are footsore after days of trekking through Prague's cobbled streets, relatively cheap and good-quality shoes are on offer at the Bat'a store at the bottom of Wenceslas Square.

Most shops are open between 10am and 6pm but there are plenty which stay open later, especially the big department stores. A selection of some of the special retail shops in and around the city centre follows.

International and Second Hand Bookshops
Anagram Bookshop
Týn 4, Praha 1.
Tel: (02) 2489 5737.
E-mail: anagram@terminal.cz
Nearest metro, Náměstí Republiky.
Mon–Sat 9.30am–7.30pm; Sun 10am–6pm. A wide range of English-language books from philosophy to fitness.
Big Ben Bookshop
Malá Stupartská 5, Praha 1.
Tel: (02) 2482 6565.
E-mail: books@ bigbenbookshop.com.
Located round the corner from Náměstí Republiky metro station.
Mon–Fri 9am–7pm; Sat, Sun 10am–6pm. Sells English-language books and newspapers.
The Globe
Janovského 14, Praha 7.
Tel: (02) 2491 7230.
E-mail: globe@login.cz
10am–midnight daily. Near the Vltavská metro station. A wide selection of English-language fiction and non-fiction, new and second-hand. Has a café next door. A favourite of expatriates, the Globe also sells newspapers and has a community noticeboard.

Arts & Crafts, Puppets and Toys
Look through the markets dotted around the centre of the city, especially the one on Old Town Square. Otherwise try: **Obchod u Šaška**, Jílská 7, Praha 1, or **Dřevěné Hračky** Karlova 26, Praha 1.

Crystal and Glass
Shops selling crystal and glass are all over the city. A few of the best are listed:
Cristallino
Celetná 12, Praha 1.
Tel: 2422 3027.
Jan–Mar open 9am–noon; Apr–Dec open 9am–8pm.
Bohemia Moser
Na Příkopě 12, Praha 1.
Tel: (02) 2421 1293.
Bohemia Crystal
Široká 7 Praha 1.
Tel: (02) 2481 3154.
Krystal
Václavské nám. 30, Praha 1.

Antique Shops

Alma
Valentinská 7, Praha 1, Staré Město.
Tel: (02) 232 5865.
Radnické schody 9, Praha 1, Hradčany.
Tel: (02) 2051 3869.
Tynská 7, Praha 1, Staré Město.
Tel: (02) 231 0723.
E-mail: shop@almamahler
Antikvariát U Karlova Mostu
Karlova 2, Praha 1.
Tel/fax: (02) 2422 9205.
Sells antique prints and books.
Jan Hunek Starožitnost
Pařížská 1, Praha 1.
Tel/fax: (02) 232 3604.
Offers a fine selection of antique glass and crystal.

Music
Agharta Jazz Centrum
Krakovska 5, Praha 1.
Tel: (02) 2221 1275.
Jazz CDs.
Bonton Megastore
Palace Koruna, Václavské náměstí 1, Praha 1.
Popron
Jungmannova 30, Praha 1.
Tel: (02) 2421 1982.

Department Stores
Koruna Palác
Václavské náměstí.
Tel: (02) 2421 9526.
Right at the bottom of Wenceslas Square.

Kotva
Náměstí Republiky 8, Praha 1.
Tel: (02) 2480 1111.
The largest department store in the centre of town. Next to Náměstí Republiky metro station.
Krone/Julius Meinl
Václavské náměstí 21, Praha 1.
Tel: (02) 2423 0477.
Next to Můstek metro.
Pavilon
Vinohradská 50, Praha 2.
Tesco
Národní Třída 26, Praha 1.
Tel: (02) 2422 7971.
Right next to Národní Třída metro.
Most large department stores have a supermarket, often in the basement. A delicatessen to be particularly recommended is **Fruits de France** at Jindřišská 9, Praha 1.

Bratislava

Bratislava's range of shopping facilities is improving fast. You can find most of what you want in the Old Town and on the SNP Square. A bottle of Slivovica – Gazdovská is among the best – will make a good present as will Tokaj wine and porcelain or locally produced fabrics. There are new galleries springing up around the centre of town which also offer good buys.

Department Stores

Carrefour
Danubia Centre, Panónska cesta.
Tel: (02) 6829 2111.
Hypermarket and superstore complex.
Dunaj
Nám. SNP 30.
Tel: (02) 5443 0882.
Slovak department store.
Polus City Centre
Vajnorská.
Tel: (02) 4929 9111.
A massive new shopping centre which contains a Carrefour supermarket.
Tesco
Kamenné nám. 1.
Tel: (02) 5921 8111.
Right in the centre of town.

Bookshops
La Reduta
Palackého 2.
Slovak and English-language books.
Big Ben Bookshop
Michalská 1.

Antiques
Galeria Naráky
Panská 17.
Secession
Palackého 8.
Steiner
Ventúrska 20.
Starožitnosti
Michalská 22.
Starožinosti
Kozia 15.

Art Galleries
Artemiss
Hviezdoslavovo nám. 14.
Tel: (02) 5443 2677.
Gallery Donner
Klobúčnícka 4.
Tel: (02) 5443 3753.
Gallery Priestor
Somolického 1.
Tel: (02) 54418262.
Gallery X
Zámočnícka 5.
Tel: (02) 5443 1729.

CD Shops
Bontonland Megastore
Michalská 25.
Tel: (02) 5443 1986.
Victory Music
Michalská 3.
Tel: (02) 5443 4993

Sports and Leisure

Spectator Sports

ICE HOCKEY

While in terms of crowd sizes the world's quickest team sport comes second in the popularity stakes, during the winter it has no serious competition. The Czechs have come close to dominating the international ice hockey scene in the second half of the 1990s and have several stars playing top roles in the NHL. There are strong teams naturally from Prague (Sparta) and Bratislava (Slovan). In general games are played on Tuesdays and Fridays after 6pm.

FOOTBALL

By the middle of the 1990s Czech footballers were beginning to be noticed abroad and now play in all of the top European leagues. The domestic game, despite the loss of many top players, remains vibrant with Sparta and Slavia Prague featuring as regular participants in the UEFA Cup and the Champions League. For almost all domestic games it is possible to purchase tickets at the gate. For derby matches, especially between Sparta and Slavia, you may need to go to the grounds and buy a ticket in advance. Slovak football has not enjoyed the same level of success as Czech football but Slovan Bratislava, Inter Bratislava, Trnava and Košice are gradually establishing themselves. The Czech and Slovak leagues have two breaks: December to February and June to August. Tickets are extremely cheap compared with

Western countries and facilities at the top clubs are improving. Sausages with mustard and sometimes beer are offered for your refreshment at a very low cost.

Participant Sports

CAVING

The Karst regions of the Czech and Slovak Republics contain vast cave systems, which are partly open to the public. The most famous ones are the Koneprusy Caves between Karlštejn and Beroun in Central Bohemia, the cave complex of Demänovské jaskyne in Central Slovakia and the Dobšinská ľadová jaskyňa ice caves, also in Slovakia. The focal point of the Moravian Karst (Moravský kras) is the Punkva Cave, which is accessible by boat.

GOLF

There is an 18-hole golf course half an hour from the centre of Prague at the Golf and Country Club Karlštejn, Bělec 280, 26727 Liteň. Tel: (0311) 684 716–17. The course is set in beautiful surroundings. You could also try the D Club Lišnice, Lišnice 0382, 252 03 Řitka, Praha-Západ. Tel: (305) 592 651.

HIKING

For both Czechs and Slovaks, hiking has been a popular activity for generations. The combined republics have a total 50,000 km (30,000 miles) of marked trails, from the gentle hills of the Bohemian Forest to the alpine summits of the High Tatras.

All paths are colour marked and often say how long a certain stretch is expected to take. The majority of routes are tailored to the average walker, so that normal equipment is sufficient except in the high mountains, where one has to expect rapid changes in the weather. If it gets cloudy in the mountains do not continue as snow

storms are possible even in summer. The hiking maps (turistická mapa) are very detailed and there are different sets for winter and summer.

The winter maps (zimní mapa) show the pistes and ski-lifts and the summer maps (letní mapa) show the campsites.

ICE SKATING

Slavia Praha IPS Stadium
Vršovice, Praha 10.
Prague Exhibition Grounds
(Výstaviště), Winter Stadium (Zimní stadion), Praha 7.

MOUNTAINEERING

The hardest routes are to be found in the High Tatras and in the Lesser Fatra (Malá Fatra). Excellent training for rock-climbing can be found on the sandstone crags of the "Bohemian Switzerland" (České Švýcarsko) around the Labe (Elbe) Valley in Northern Bohemia. Again, you are advised to bring along all your own gear as quality equipment is difficult to get hold of.

Mountain Rescue

Slovak Mountain Rescue
Okruzna 25
058 01 Poprad
Tel: 421 52 227 81
Mountain Rescue Service
Avalanche Rescue Centre Jasna
032 51 Demanoská Dolina
Tel: 421 44 916 95

SWIMMING

People do swim in the rivers but this is not recommended. All the top hotels have swimming pools which are not expensive by Western standards. Cheaper options are:
Bazín Slavia
Vladivostocká 10.
Tel: (02) 6731 0924.
Cardiofitness Axa
Na Poříčí 40.
Tel: (02) 232 9359.

Hotel Olšanka
Táboritská 23.
Tel: (02) 6709 2111.
Podolí
Podolská 74, Praha 4.
Tel: (02) 6121 434.
Also has heated open-air pools for winter swimming.
Sportcentrum YMCA
Na Poříčí 12.
Tel: (02) 2487 5811.

TENNIS

Tennis is a big game in the Czech Republic and the general standard is high. The Prague Tennis Arena on the island of Štvanice is an international-class stadium and is used for major tournaments. Tourists can get a game at the following clubs.
Club Hotel Praha
Průhonice 400.
(On the outskirts of Prague just off the Prague-Brno motorway)
Tel: 677 50868.
Has six indoor and four outdoor tennis courts.
Hotel Hilton
Pobřežní 1, Praha 1.
Tel: (02) 2484 1111.
Two indoor courts.

WATERSPORTS

There are extensive river and stream systems as well as countless lakes and reservoirs, most of which have been constructed in the past 40 years for energy purposes. Most of the artificial lakes have now blended in with the natural environment to become a watersport paradise. Slovakia has the best stretches for canoeists. In the spring, when the snow has melted, streams and rivers offer fantastic possibilities for white-water canoeing. Things are more leisurely on the dam lakes or on the Danube, whose islands and meadows supporting unique flora and fauna make it an important European biosphere. The most popular stretches for boating in the Bohemian part of the country are the upper reaches of the Vltava and its tributaries the Sázava, Otava and Lužnice. The lower reaches of the Vltava and Labe are less suitable on account of pollution.

WINTER SPORTS

The best conditions for alpine skiing are provided by the Low Tatras in Slovakia; fans of cross-country skiing find ideal conditions in the Iser Mountains, the Krkonoše, the Beskids and the Bohemian Forest.

In comparison to the Alps, the prices for ski-lifts are very low. Queueing is the rule, especially during public holidays and at weekends. You should preferably bring all your own gear as rented skis and boots don't generally meet the standards to which Westerners are accustomed.

Further information can be obtained from Čedok and other travel agencies.

Skiing in Slovakia

www.ski.sk – List of ski-centres, snow reports, accommodation
www.tatry.sk – Official website of High Tatras mountain range
www.skijasna.sk – Activities and accommodation in Demanovska Dolina ski centre
www.enelux.sk/jased – Jasenska dolina ski centre
www.skidonovaly.sk – Donovaly ski centre

Spas

The Bohemian spas have been famous as far back as the Middle Ages. In the Czech and Slovak Republics today there are a total of 57 recognised health spas, 36 of which are in Bohemia and Moravia and 21 in Slovakia. Listed below are the major spas (together with the conditions they treat).

CZECH REPUBLIC

Western Bohemia
Františkovy Lázně
Gynaecological diseases.
Jáchymov
Diseases of the spine and locomotor system, neuropathy, metabolic disease (gout).
Karlovy Vary
Stomach and intestinal ailments, gall-bladder trouble, diabetes.
Mariánské Lázně
Kidney and urinary disorders, metabolic disease (gout and diabetes), disorders of the digestion system, general problems with the respiratory tract, diseases of the spine.

Spas Elsewhere
Luhaãovice (Moravia)
General problems with the respiratory tract, disorders of the digestion system, diabetes.
Poděbrady (Central Bohemia)
Heart problems and circulatory disturbance (especially for children).
Teplice (Northern Bohemia)
Problems with the locomotor system, vascular disease.
Třebová (Southern Bohemia)
Problems with the locomotor system.

SLOVAKIA

Bardejovské Kúpele
Disorders of the digestion system, general problems with the respiratory tract, metabolic diseases.
Nový Smokovec
Problems with the respiratory tract.
Piešt'any
Chronic rheumatism, neuropathy.
Sliač
Heart problems and circulatory disturbance.
Štrbské Pleso (in the High Tatras)
Asthma and other allergies.
Trenčianské Teplice
Problems with the locomotor system.

Further information about individual spas can be obtained at Čedok offices or from Balnea, Pařížská 1, Praha 1, tel: (02) 232 3767/292 868. Slovakoterma, Radlinského 13, Bratislava.

Language

General

Czech and Slovak are Western Slavic languages with a common linguistic background and are closely related. Czechs and Slovaks have no trouble at all communicating with one another and the differences on restaurant menus, or maps, for example, are too slight to be apparent to most tourists.

Pronunciation

Vowels
Accents above the letters indicate long vowels: á, é ,í, ó, ú, ů
ý   long "e".
ou   pronounced like the vowel sound in "show"
ě   pronounced ye

Consonants
č   pronounced "ch"
ř   pronounced with a silibant. Very difficult for non-Czechs. Just say "r".
š   pronounced sh
ž   pronounced with a "j" as in "journey"
The Czech letters ě, ř and ů do not exist in Slovak; Slovak also contains its own letters such as ľ (soft l), í (long l), ô (wo) and ä (pronounced ey).

Vocabulary

Useful Words and Phrases
yes *ano*
no *ne*
thank you *děkuji*
please *prosím*
good morning *dobré ráno* (or *dobré jitro*)
hello *dobrý den*
good evening *dobrý večer*
goodbye *na shledanou*

sorry *promiňte*
How much is that? *co to stojí?*
Could you give me *dejte mi*
I would like to *chtěl bych*
how far/long? *jak dlouho/daleko?*
good *dobrý*
bad *špatný*
cheap *levný*
expensive *drahý*
hot *horký*
cold *studený*
vacant *volný*
occupied *obsazeno*
open *otevřeno*
closed *zavřeno*
I don't understand *nerozumím*
lunch *oběd*
supper *večere*
I would like to pay *budu platit*
coffee house *kavárna*
restaurant *restaurace*
pub *hostinec*
beer hall *pivnice*
wine bar *vinárna*
breakfast *snídaně*
lunch *oběd*
supper *večeře*
free *volno*
table *stůl*
chair *židle*
knife *nůž*
fork *vidlička*
spoon *lžíce*
plate *talíř*
glass *sklenice*
waiter *číšník*
head waiter *vrchní*
waitress *servírka*
napkin *ubrousek*
menu *jídelní lístek*
speciality *specialita*

Time of the Day
morning *ráno*
noon *poledne*
afternoon *odpoledne*
evening *večer*
hour *hodina*
day *den*
night *noc*

Days of the Week
Monday *pondělí*
Tuesday *úterý*
Wednesday *středa*
Thursday *čtvrtek*
Friday *pátek*
Saturday *sobota*
Sunday *neděle*

Drinks
herbal liqueur *Becherovka*
tea *čaj*
black tea *černý čaj*
coffee *káva*
Turkish coffee *černá káva*
white coffee *káva s mlékem*
coffee with whipped cream *vídeňská káva*
lemonade *limonáda*
beer *pivo*
small beer *malé pivo*
dark beer *černé pivo*
lager *světlé pivo*
draught beer *točené pivo*
slivovitz *slivovice*
white wine *bílé víno*
red wine *červené víno*
water *voda*

Food
bažant pheasant
biftek steak
bramborák potato fritter
brambory potatoes
buchty Bohemian sweet dumplings
chléb bread
bílý chléb white bread
černý chléb brown bread
cukr sugar
drůbež poultry
fazole beans
guláš goulash
houby mushrooms
hovězí beef
hovězí pečené roast beef
hovězí vařené boiled beef
hruška pear
husa goose
houska roll
kachna duck
kančí wild boar
kapr pečený fried carp
kapr smažený garnished carp
kapr vařený boiled carp
kapusta savoy cabbage
kaše bramborová mashed potatoes
knedlíky bramborové potato dumplings
knedlíky houskové white bread dumplings
knedlíky ovocné fruit dumpling
králík rabbit
krocan turkey
kuře chicken
kuře smažené roast chicken
kyselé zelí sauerkraut
ledvinky kidneys

máslo butter
jablka apple
meruňky apricots
mrkev carrots
ořechy nuts
ovoce fruit
palačinky thin pancakes
párky sausages
pečené roast meat
pečivo biscuits
polévka soup
polévka držťková tripe soup
pstruh trout
rajčata tomato
roštěnka roast meat
ryba fish
rýže rice
salám sausage, salami
salát salad
sardinky sardines
sekaná meat loaf
sladký sweet
slaný salty
srnčí roast venison
štika pike
šunka ham
telecí veal
třešně cherries
uzenina smoked meat
vejce na měkko soft-boiled egg
vejce na tvrdo hard-boiled egg
vepřové roast pork
zajíc hare
zelenina vegetables
zmrzlina ice cream
zvěřina game

Numbers

1	*jeden*
2	*dva*
3	*tři*
4	*čtyři*
5	*pět*
6	*šest*
7	*sedm*
8	*osm*
9	*devět*
10	*deset*
11	*jedenáct*
12	*dvanáct*
20	*dvacet*
100	*sto*
200	*dvěstě*
300	*třista*
400	*štyřista*
500	*pětset*
1,000	*tisíc*

FOLESHILL

Further Reading

Franz Kafka

Amerika by Franz Kafka (translated by W. and E. Muir), Penguin Modern Classics. Kafka's tale of a young boy exiled from his European home and his misadventures on his own in the New World.

The Trial by Franz Kafka (translated by W. and E. Muir), Penguin Modern Classics. Probably the best-known of Kafka's works (along with the novella *The Metamorphosis*), *The Trial* tells the story of Josef K. who is arrested, accused and tried – but no one will tell him the charge.

The Castle by Franz Kafka (translated by W. and E. Muir), Penguin Modern Classics. In Kafka's great unfinished, final novel the protagonist, simply called K., arrives in a strange town on page one, and spends the rest of the book attempting to gain entry into an impenetrable castle. Some interpret this tale as an allegory for man's search for enlightenment; but there isn't too much that is uplifting in this relentlessly frustrating story that ends, literally, in mid-sentence.

Description of a Struggle and other stories by Franz Kafka (translated by W. and E. Muir), Penguin Modern Classics. Kafka's early short stories show the flashes of genius that would be given its full measure in his novels. Of special interest are the descriptions of Prague, local references of a kind that do not appear in his later works.

Diaries by Franz Kafka (translated by W. and E. Muir), Penguin Modern Classics. This collection of Kafka's private musings, ideas for stories and recordings of daily events provides a rich insight into the author's life. A good companion piece is *Letters to Friends, Family and Editors*, which shows the author as witty, ironic and charming.

Other Classic Literature

The Engineer of Human Souls by Josef Škvorecký (translated by Paul Wilson), Picador. Powerful fictional tirade against the Communist regime; it also explores expatriate life in Toronto, the destination of many Czech émigrés after the 1968 Warsaw Pact Invasion.

The Good Soldier Schweik by Jaroslav Hašek (translated by Sir C. Parrot), Heinemann. This irreverent and very funny classic of Czech literature relates the misadventures of Josef Schweik – an unwilling conscript into the Austrian army – and his efforts to avoid being sent to the front through servile sabotage.

Too Loud a Solitude by Bohumil Hrabal (translated by Michael Henry Heins), Harcourt Brace Jovanovich. The melancholy story of a paper-shredder who tries to save the books he loves but which he should be destroying in his job.

Selected Poetry by Jaroslav Seifert (translated by E. Osers), André Deutsch. Poems by a winner of the Nobel Prize for Literature.

Tales of the Little Quarter by Jan Neruda (translated by Michael Henry Heim), Central European University Press. Stories of people and places in Malá Strana.

Laughable Loves, The Farewell Party, The Book of Laughter and Forgetting, The Unbearable Lightness of Being, Life is Elsewhere, The Joke by Milan Kundra (Faber/Penguin). Kundra is the most famous and well-loved of Czech novelists outside of the country. His novels are set at various times during his life and reflect the political upheaval of the Velvet Revolution and beyond. The Book of Laughter and Forgetting is perhaps the most critical of his works set in the communist era.

General Reading

Czechoslovakia: The Velvet Revolution and Beyond, by Robin Shepherd (Macmillan). Acclaimed account of the division of Czechoslovakia and the first ten years of post-communist reform.

Prague: A Guide to Twentieth Century Architecture by Ivan Margolius (Ellipsis London). Handy pocket-sized guide to the landmarks of Prague with black-and-white photographs.

Prague in Black and Gold by Peter Demetz (Penguin). Demetz's first-hand account of the history of the city ends at the end of World War II.

Czech, Moravian and Slovak Fairytales by Fillmore (Hippocrene Books). Fifteen traditional tales from the Czech and Slovak Republics. A good read for both adults and children.

The Shores of Bohemia by Derek Sayer. An account of the cultural history of Prague and Bohemia with the emphasis on visual art.

We the People: the Revolutions of 1989 by Timothy Garton Ash (Penguin). On-the-spot, readable account of the Velvet Revolution.

Disturbing the Peace by Václav Havel (Vintage Books). Accessible collection of personal thoughts on Czech history in the form of essays.

Other Insight Guides

Three distinctive series from Apa Publications are designed to meet your travel needs.

The 200-strong Insight Guides series includes the following titles covering Czech and Slovak destinations: Prague and Hungary.

There are also over 120 *Insight Pocket Guides*, with an itinerary-based approach designed to assist the traveller with a limited amount of time to spend in a destination. Titles in this series include Prague, Kracow and Budapest.

Insight Compact Guides offer a highly portable encyclopaedic travel guide packed with carefully cross-referenced text, photographs and maps. Titles include Poland and the Czech Republic.

Insight Fleximaps combine clear detailed cartography with essential travel information. The laminated finish makes the maps durable, waterproof and easy to fold. Titles in the region include: Prague and Budapest.

ART & PHOTO CREDITS

INSIGHT GUIDE
Czech & Slovak Republics

Cartographic Editor **Zoë Goodwin**
Production **Sylvia George**
Cover Design
Klaus Geisler, Tanvir Virdee
Picture Research
Hilary Genin, Natasha Babaian

Index

Numbers in italics refer to photographs

a

accommodation 332–336
Adršpašskoteplické skály (CZ) 225
agriculture 39, 69–70, 246
collectivisation 45, 70
architecture
art nouveau 115–7
baroque 64, 197
Drevené kostoly (wooden churches) 306
in Prague (CZ) 144, 166–7
rural 60, 70–71, 201, 231–2, 249, *266*, *291*
art and crafts 195, 257, 301
see also museums and galleries
glass *36*, 185, *188*, *222*, 224, 229, 230
lace-making 230
arts and entertainment 89–93, 103–7, 109–12, 343–346
see also folklore, music
Czech Philharmonic Orchestra 139, 152
film 109–12
fringe theatre 105–6
Lanterna Magika 106, 107, *107*
National String Quartet 139
National Theatre (Prague) 56, 103–4, 106
puppet theatre *106*
Slovenské Národné divadlo (Slovakian National Theatre) (Bratislava, SK) 56, 104, 280
Slovakian Philharmonic Orchestra 280
Austerlitz *see* Bojiště u Vlavkova

b

Banská Bystrica (SK) 297–8
Banská Štiavnica (Schemnitz) (SK) 299
Bardejov (SK) 305, *306*
Bardejovské Kúpele (SK) 306
Barrandov Film Studios 41, 111
Bat'a, Tomáš 258
Bathory, Countess Elisabeth 287
Bechyně (CZ) 185
Becquerel, Antoine 209
Bedřichov (CZ) 224
Bela IV 185
Beneš, Eduard 36, 39–40, 41, 44, 55

Bielovodská dolina (valley) (SK) 318
Blansko (CZ) 240
Blatnice (CZ) 238
Blatnický Hrad (castle) (SK) 300
Bohemia (CZ) 15, 21, 22, 23, 59, 71, 133, 183–233
see also individual place names
spa towns 133
Bohemian Forest *see* Šumava
Bojiště u Vlavkova (Battlefield of Austerlitz) (CZ) 240
Bojnický Zámok (castle) (SK) 300
Boleslav I 22
Boleslav II 22–3
Boubín Forest (CZ) 60
Bratislava (SK) 43, 267, 271–81
Akadémia umenia (Academy of Fine Arts) 275
Apponyi Palais 279
Carlton Hotel 280
Collegium Emmericianum 278
Dóm sv. Martina (St Martin's Cathedral) 273
Farmaceutické múzeum (Museum of Pharmacy) 275
Františkánsky kostol (Franciscan Church) 278
Ganymedova fontána (Ganymede Fountain) 280
Hlavné námestie (Main Square) 278
Horský Park 280–81
Hrad (castle) 277–8
Hradné schody (castle steps) 277
Hviezdoslavovo nám (square) 280
Kamenné námestie (square) 280
Kanovnov Dom (Canon's House) 278
Kaplnka sv. Kataríny (St Catherine's Chapel) 275
Kapitulská (Priests' Alley) 278
Klarisky (Convent of St Clare) 278
Kostol Jezuitov (Jesuit Church) 278–9
Stĺp sv. Márie (St Mary's Column) 278
Kráľovská maďarská komora (Royal Hungarian Chamber) 275
Michalská brána (St Michael's Gate) 274, *275*
Mirbachov palác (Mirbach Palace) 278
Municipal Art Gallery 278, 279
Municipal Museum 279
Múzeum historických zbraní (Museum of Historic Weapons) 275
Múzeum hodín (Clock Museum) 277

Nový most (bridge) 276–7
Pálffyho Palác (Palace of Marshal Pálffy) 275
Palác Leopolda de Pauli (Palace of Lepold de Pauli) 275
Prepoštsky Palác (Provost's Palace) 278
Primaciálny palác in Primaciálne námestie (Bishop's Palace) 279
Hall of Mirrors 279
Rokokový palác grófa Erdodyho (Rococo Palace of Count Erdody) 276
Reduta Hall 280
Slavín monument 280
Slovenské Národné divadlo (Slovakian National Theatre) 56, 104, 280
Slovenské národné galéria (Slovakian National Gallery) 280
Slovenské národné múzeum (Slovakian National Museum) 280
Slovenská národná rada (Slovakian National Committee) 278
Spanish Room 280
Staromestská radnica (Old Town Hall) 279
Univerzita Komenského (Komenský University) 280
Brecht, Berthold 98
Schweik 98
Břeclav (Lundenburg) (CZ) 245
Břetislav 23
Brno (CZ) 92, 133, *235*, 236–7, 239–40
autumn music festival 92, 240
Brněnský drak (Dragon of Brno) 237
College of Music 92
Dominikánslý kostel (Dominican Church) 237, 239
Dům umělců (Artists House) 239
Há Divadlo (Ha Theatre) 106
Horni trh (Herb Market) 236–7
Hrad Špilberk (Spilberk Castle) 239
Hudební fakulta (College of Music) 240
Janáčkova opera a baletní divadlo (Janacek Opera House and Ballet Theatre) 239
Katedrála sv. Petra (St Peter's Cathedral) 236, *237*
Kostel sv. Jakuba (Church of St James) 239

A
B
D
E
F
G
H
I
J
a
b
d
e
f
g
h
i
j
k
l

INSIGHT GUIDES

The world's largest collection of visual travel guides

A range of guides and maps to meet every travel need

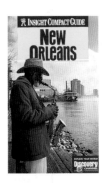

Insight Guides

This classic series gives you the complete picture of a destination through expert, well written and informative text and stunning photography. Each book is an ideal background information and travel planner, serves as an on-the-spot companion – and is a superb visual souvenir of a trip. Nearly 200 titles.

Insight Pocket Guides

focus on the best choices for places to see and things to do, picked by our local correspondents. They are ideal for visitors new to a destination. To help readers follow the routes easily, the books contain full-size pull-out maps. 120 titles.

Insight Maps

are designed to complement the guides. They provide full mapping of major cities, regions and countries, and their laminated finish makes them easy to fold and gives them durability. 60 titles.

Insight Compact Guides

are convenient, comprehensive reference books, modestly priced. The text, photographs and maps are all carefully cross-referenced, making the books ideal for on-the-spot use when in a destination. 120 titles.

Different travellers have different needs. Since 1970, Insight Guides has been meeting these needs with a range of practical and stimulating guidebooks and maps

"I was first drawn to the Insight Guides by the excellent "Nepal" volume. I can think of no book which so effectively captures the essence of a country. Out of these pages leaped the Nepal I know – the captivating charm of a people and their culture. I've since discovered and enjoyed the entire Insight Guide series. Each volume deals with a country in the same sensitive depth, which is nowhere more evident than in the superb photography."

Sir Edmund Hillary

✕ INSIGHT GUIDES

The world's largest collection of visual travel guides

Insight Guides – the Classic Series
that puts you in the picture

Alaska	China	Hungary	Munich	South Africa
Alsace	Cologne			South America
Amazon Wildlife	Continental Europe	Iceland	Namibia	South Tyrol
American Southwest	Corsica	India	Native America	Southeast Asia
Amsterdam	Costa Rica	India's Western	Nepal	Wildlife
Argentina	Crete	Himalaya	Netherlands	Spain
Asia, East	Cuba	India, South	New England	Spain, Northern
Asia, South	Cyprus	Indian Wildlife	New Orleans	Spain, Southern
Asia, Southeast	Czech & Slovak	Indonesia	New York City	Sri Lanka
Athens	Republics	Ireland	New York State	Sweden
Atlanta		Israel	New Zealand	Switzerland
Australia	Delhi, Jaipur & Agra	Istanbul	Nile	Sydney
Austria	Denmark	Italy	Normandy	Syria & Lebanon
	Dominican Republic	Italy, Northern	Norway	
Bahamas	Dresden	Italy, Southern		Taiwan
Bali	Dublin		Old South	Tenerife
Baltic States	Düsseldorf	Jamaica	Oman & The UAE	Texas
Bangkok		Japan	Oxford	Thailand
Barbados	East African Wildlife	Java		Tokyo
Barcelona	Eastern Europe	Jerusalem	Pacific Northwest	Trinidad & Tobago
Bay of Naples	Ecuador	Jordan	Pakistan	Tunisia
Beijing	Edinburgh		Paris	Turkey
Belgium	Egypt	Kathmandu	Peru	Turkish Coast
Belize	England	Kenya	Philadelphia	Tuscany
Berlin		Korea	Philippines	
Bermuda	Finland		Poland	Umbria
Boston	Florence	Laos & Cambodia	Portugal	USA: On The Road
Brazil	Florida	Lisbon	Prague	USA: Western States
Brittany	France	Loire Valley	Provence	US National Parks: East
Brussels	France, Southwest	London	Puerto Rico	US National Parks: West
Budapest	Frankfurt	Los Angeles		
Buenos Aires	French Riviera		Rajasthan	Vancouver
Burgundy		Madeira	Rhine	Venezuela
Burma (Myanmar)	Gambia & Senegal	Madrid	Rio de Janeiro	Venice
	Germany	Malaysia	Rockies	Vienna
Cairo	Glasgow	Mallorca & Ibiza	Rome	Vietnam
Calcutta	Gran Canaria	Malta	Russia	
California	Great Britain	Mauritius, Réunion		Wales
California, Northern	Greece	& Seychelles	St Petersburg	Washington DC
California, Southern	Greek Islands	Melbourne	San Francisco	Waterways of Europe
Canada	Guatemala, Belize &	Mexico City	Sardinia	Wild West
Caribbean	Yucatán	Mexico	Scandinavia	
Catalonia		Miami	Scotland	Yemen
Channel Islands	Hamburg	Montreal	Seattle	
Chicago	Hawaii	Morocco	Sicily	
Chile	Hong Kong	Moscow	Singapore	

Complementing the above titles are 120 easy-to-carry Insight Compact Guides, 120 Insight Pocket Guides with full-size pull-out maps and more than 100 laminated easy-fold Insight Maps